INSTITUTIONS, POLICIES
AND
ECONOMIC PERFORMANCE

CARNEGIE - ROCHESTER CONFERENCE SERIES ON PUBLIC POLICY

A supplementary series to the Journal of Monetary Economics

Editors

KARL BRUNNER
ALLAN H. MELTZER

Production Editors

ANGELA L. BARNES
GAIL McGUIRE

VOLUME 4

NORTH-HOLLAND PUBLISHING COMPANY
AMSTERDAM . NEW YORK . OXFORD

INSTITUTIONS, POLICIES
AND
ECONOMIC PERFORMANCE

Editors

KARL BRUNNER

Graduate School of Management
The University of Rochester

ALLAN H. MELTZER

Carnegie-Mellon University

1977

NORTH-HOLLAND PUBLISHING COMPANY
AMSTERDAM . NEW YORK . OXFORD

ISBN North-Holland for this volume: 0 7204 0564 5

First edition : 1976
Second printing : 1977

Publishers:

NORTH-HOLLAND PUBLISHING COMPANY
AMSTERDAM . NEW YORK . OXFORD

Sole distributors for the U.S.A. and Canada:

ELSEVIER/NORTH HOLLAND, INC.
52 VANDERBILT AVENUE
NEW YORK, N.Y. 10017

Library of Congress Cataloging in Publication Data

Main entry under title:

Institutions, policies and economic performance.

(Carnegie-Rochester conference series on public
policy ; v. 4)
Papers presented at Carnegie-Rochester Conference
on Public Policy held Nov. 1974 and April 1975.
1. United States--Economic policy--1971-   --Con-
gresses. 2. Organization for Economic Cooperation and
Development--Congresses. 3. United States. Federal
Home Loan Bank Board--Congresses. 4. Inflation (Finance)
--Congresses. I. Brunner, Karl, 1916-   II. Meltzer,
Allan H. III. Series: Carnegie-Rochester conference
series ; v. 4.
HC106.7.I57   330.9'73'0925   76-44242
ISBN 0-7204-0564-5

Aug'84.

PRINTED IN THE NETHERLANDS

INTRODUCTION TO THE SERIES

The Carnegie-Rochester Conference on Public Policy was initiated several years ago through the efforts of the Center for Research in Government Policy and Business at the University of Rochester and the Center for the Study of Public Policy at Carnegie-Mellon University. This book is the fourth volume in a new series which presents the papers prepared for the conferences, plus the comments of discussants and participants.

Policies depend not only on theories and evidence, but on the structure of policymaking bodies and the procedures by which policies are made, implemented and changed. The conferences direct the attention of economists to major problems of economic policy and institutional arrangements. We hope that the papers and the conferences will encourage further research on policy and on the effects of national agencies and international institutions on the choice of policies.

The Carnegie-Rochester Conference is an open forum. Participants are united by their interest in the issues discussed and by their belief that analysis, evidence and informed discussion have lasting effects on the public and its institutions.

This fourth volume of the series, offered as a supplement to the Journal of Monetary Economics, contains papers presented at the November 1974 and April 1975 conferences. Additional volumes will be mailed to subscribers as a supplement to the journal. The editor of the journal will consider for publication comments on the papers published in the supplement.

K. BRUNNER
A.H. MELTZER
Editors

CONTENTS

INSTITUTIONS, POLICIES AND ECONOMIC PERFORMANCE

Karl Brunner
University of Rochester

and

Allan H. Meltzer
Carnegie-Mellon University

The tradition of economic theory usually disregards governmental institutions and the constraints they impose on policy making. But "governments" use and allocate resources. These activities supplement or displace the private sector. In addition, governments redistribute income and remove (or create) external diseconomies (or economies).

A prevalent view of the government and its operations attributes to the persons making and executing "government decisions" a dominant concern for the public interest. According to this view, governmental institutions function to improve general welfare. They create external economies or benefits and lower external costs and diseconomies. "Market failures" are recognized and markets appropriately supplemented or replaced by well-operating government institutions.

The public interest view of government should be contrasted with an alternative hypothesis about the behavior of the governmental sector. We may refer to this alternative view as the private interest view. According to this view, "governmental" behavior emerges from the self-seeking responses of politicians and administrators to their respective incentives and opportunities. The making and execution of policies differ consequently from the patterns to be expected by attention to a benevolent public interest.

Studies of government decisions, recommendations, and actions form part of the raw material which offers potential evidence bearing on the conflicting views about "government": the public interest and the private interest view or possibly some other alternatives. The papers in this volume provide material at those levels.

The papers by Christ and by Fratianni and Pattison discuss the policies recommended by the Joint Economic Committee (JEC) of the U.S. Congress and by the Organisation for Economic Co-operation and Development (OECD). Both papers analyze the recommendations and discuss the relation between policies recommended by these advisory groups and received economic theory. Jaffee and Swan analyze the purposes served and the policies chosen by one of the principal agencies concerned with thrift institutions, the Federal Home Loan

Bank Board (FHLBB). Laidler and Hamburger and Reisch test some alternative theories of inflation and compare policies and the outcomes of policies in several countries.

I. ADVISING THE POLICY MAKERS

The Joint Economic Committee of the U.S. Congress is an advisory body, organized to review the policies of the Administration and to make recommendations to the Congress. The Committee's principal concerns are domestic and international economic policy, but the Committee interprets its mandate broadly. In recent years, hearings have also been held and reports issued on energy, income maintenance, tax reform, transportation, and other topics of interest to the members or the staff. The Committee's distinguished membership, its reputation for responsible consideration of alternative proposals, and the quality of its reports has enhanced the Committee's influence within Congress and with the Administration, the press, and the concerned public.

Carl Christ discusses the main work of the Committee during the four years, 1971-74. He finds much merit in the reports and recommendations on budget reform and income maintenance. The Committee was among the first to recommend reform to control total spending and appropriations and has done careful work on the problem of income maintenance. The JEC has also advocated the use of markets in place of direct controls, regulations, and fixed prices in international trade, pollution control, and transportation, to cite a few of many examples.

Christ concludes, however, that the Committee's support for market solutions is often qualified. "In dealing with microeconomics - - international trade, agriculture, energy, and credit availability - - the Committee is too ready . . . to assume that, when a problem arises, the Federal government has the capacity and the responsibility to solve it; and too ready to accept the claims of every group in the economy that, when there are changes in tastes, or technology, or the availability of resources, or population, every group should be protected from the effects of such changes. Government should provide basic freedom and opportunity, but should not try to solve every problem (especially insoluble ones); nor should it suppress competition to create or perpetuate the economic position of any group."

Recommendations about macroeconomic policy have tended to favor short-term over long-term solutions. Christ criticizes the Committee for its acceptance of the belief that there is an attainable trade-off between inflation and unemployment, and for the frequent recommendation that the long-term target for the unemployment rate be set at 3 percent (or below 4 percent), unemployment rates that have rarely been achieved and cannot be maintained without ever-increasing inflation. "Inflation illusion" is the name Christ gives to the belief that policy makers can bring about a permanent reduction in the unemployment rate by accepting a rise in the maintained rate of inflation. It is worth noting in this regard that, on average, unemployment in the years 1948-1975 is slightly higher (4.93 percent) than for the years 1900-1929 (4.65 percent). Given the errors in the data, the difference is probably not significant. There is, however, no evidence that discretionary policy reduced the average unemployment rate in the postwar period below the average rate achieved under the gold standard, although the variance of the rate has been reduced. The postwar average is lower than the prewar average only if the years 1929-1940 are included in the prewar sample.

Can macroeconomic policy lower the average unemployment rate to 3 percent or 4 percent, as the Committee reports suggest? Christ is doubtful and suggests that attempts to do so can only succeed for a time and at a cost of accelerating inflation. Christ concludes, "It would be better to choose fiscal and monetary policies to obtain a stable price level, rather than to force ourselves to endure inflation for the sake of ineffectual attempts to lower unemployment." He suggests that more effective ways to reduce average unemployment include reform of the income maintenance and welfare systems to remove disincentives to work and elimination of the minimum wage law. However, he does not expect the average unemployment rate to fall substantially below 5 percent or to reach the 4 percent goal recommended by the Committee if inflation is avoided.

Christ recommends price stability as a main goal of policy. He urges that monetary policy be kept within the 2-6 percent range once recommended by the Committee's majority. A further suggestion is that evidence be accumulated to show that discretionary fiscal and monetary policy adds more to stability than to instability.

Jerry Jasinowski of the JEC staff and Robert Weintraub discussed Christ's paper at the Conference. Additional comments were reviewed from participants and from several JEC staff members who wished to respond to Christ's paper. The responses make a number of points and one provides a rare insight into some of the workings of the Committee and the power of the Chairman.

Christ criticized the recommendation, repeated in the 1971, 1972, and 1973 JEC report, that called on the Federal Reserve to lower the long-term rate of interest, and pointed to the inconsistency of demands for lower market rates and higher money growth. Two members of the staff - - Jasinowski and John Karlik - - agree with Christ. Karlik notes that the "...emphasis on low interest rates reflects the views of our former Chairman from Texas." If the recommendation reflects only the power of Congressman Patman, we can expect this particular recommendation to lose its sponsor and to disappear. But, how many other recommendations that have no rational bases remain solely because a powerful member persuades the majority to yield to his whim?

The critics take issue with Christ on a number of issues, and particularly on his criticisms of the Committee's recommendations about inflation and unemployment. The statements make clear that the Committee and its staff are more inclined to believe there is a reliable short-term trade-off than Christ and much recent research suggest. Courtenay Slater goes further and agrees that frequently policy has contributed to instability, but adds that there is no reason to conclude that, ". . .discretionary policy is inevitably, or even typically, destabilizing. Rather, I would presume that policy makers can learn from the mistakes of the past and do better next time."

Keynes warned that today's advisors and policy makers are the slaves of dead economists and philosophers in that the policies they recommend are based on the theory they learned at an earlier time. Michele Fratianni and John Pattison consider the extent to which Keynes' warning is true of the OECD.

Each year, the OECD advises the governments of the 24 member countries on stabilization policies. Fratianni and Pattison attempt to develop the theoretical framework used by the OECD's Department of Economics and Statistics as the basis for its analyses and recommendations. They recognize that some would deny that such a framework exists. In a formal sense, the denial is most likely correct, but the authors believe that the absence of a formal model is not the relevant criterion.

"The theoretical basis of analysis of the OECD is the Keynesian income-expenditure model. Although the model is not formally spelled out, it can be easily reconstructed. . . ." Fratianni and Pattison present, as the OECD "model," a set of equations determining nominal income in which money has no role. Neither money nor interest rates affects income or expenditure, and prices are not determined by the model. However, interest rates are used as the indicator of monetary policy; high market rates of interest are evidence of restrictive monetary policy.

Countries in the OECD are mainly open economies in which trade and payments cannot be ignored. The OECD used the absorption approach to the balance of payments. Policy recommendations made extensive use of "assignments" under which monetary and fiscal instruments were given specific tasks. Monetary policy was expected to control interest rates while fiscal policy controlled nominal income. Exchange rate adjustments were ruled out in the 60s. In the early 70s, changes in exchange rates were recognized as a means of correcting "fundamental" disequilibrium in the balance of payments.

Once floating rates become the principal means of balance of payments adjustment, the OECD accepted the change. The discipline of fixed rates operating on the balance of payments account was replaced by the discipline of floating rates operating on relative rates of inflation.

The OECD's analysis of the causes of inflation changed as inflation rose. Fratianni and Pattison trace the development of the analysis and the mixture of ideas that emerged. The OECD does not carefully distinguish inflation from changes in relative prices. There are a number of "pushes" and "pulls" including "tax-push" in countries with value added taxes.

Analysis of inflation does not appear to have altered the basic Keynesian framework but to have served as a supplement. Conflicts among the differing views of the member governments and the views of the Secretariat were not reconciled, and it is not apparent that conflicts were clearly perceived. Fratianni and Pattison make clear, however, that the reliance on the expectations augmented Phillips curve increased in the 70s.

One view, not often found in government documents, is that fiscal expansion is a main cause of excess demand. Fratianni and Pattison quote a 1970 report by the Secretary General assigning importance to ". . .the inflationary consequences of rising demands for public expenditure which are not matched by a willingness to pay. . .claims for higher incomes put forward in real terms, including a compensation for increased direct and indirect taxation, and social security contributions." The argument is repeated in later reports, but the mechanism by which these claims generate inflation is not made explicit. The financing of the budget is not mentioned and the implication is that financing does not matter. Apparently, workers and taxpayers demand higher nominal incomes, and this raises prices independently of the way in which the budget is financed. As in most discussions of this kind, there are no distinctions between high and rising prices or between relative and absolute prices.

One recent theory of inflation that has attracted attention attributes inflation to the effects of cost-push in an economy with two sectors. Real wages increase in the more productive sector of the economy, usually the export sector which faces foreign competition. The wage increases in the more productive sector are matched by the employers in the less productive sector, so costs increase and push up prices.

The two-sector model would complement the fiscal theory of inflation proposed by the OECD if the public sector is treated as the less productive sector. The financing of the budget to pay money wages to government employers or employees of the nationalized industries could then serve as an explanation of increases in the domestic component of the monetary base. The

OECD did not make this connection, and rejected the two-sector theory as an inadequate explanation of world inflation. The inadequacy was correctly recognized by the OECD as the failure to explain the origin of inflation. In the two-sector, cost-push model, all inflation is imported, but there is no explanation of why inflation starts or ends.

Explanations of inflation based on cost-push, societal wants and needs, frustration, and alienation are generally uni-directional explanations. Now that inflation has fallen in many countries, several popular explanations of inflation must either be rejected or augmented.

The OECD's eclectic view of the causes of inflation carries over to policy. Fratianni and Pattison argue that the approach to policy, called multi-policy, reflects the divergent views of the member governments. They write, ". . . [the] organization has 24 paying customers . . .[E]ach . . . must be given some satisfaction in terms of the analytical approach to anti-inflationary policy. A large number of countries are strict believers in the Nordic two-sector model. Others, particularly the United States and Canada, are on record as accepting an expectations augmented Phillips curve approach. Others believe that inflation has more to do with sociology than economics . . .[T]he published OECD views on inflation are a curious mixture of the views of a group of delegates from 24 countries and a small group of OECD economists." (Emphasis in the original.)

Fratianni and Pattison show the evolution of the OECD's analyses of monetary and fiscal policy. Consultants appear to have had an important role in restructuring the discussion of the transmission mechanism. Policy recommendations appear to have remained with the Secretariat. Acceptance of the usefulness of assigning policies to specific tasks probably contributed to the complete separation of monetary and fiscal policy and to the complete disregard of the problem of financing budget deficits or surpluses.

Bent Hansen, a long-term consultant to the OECD on fiscal policy, and Donald Hodgman discussed the Fratianni and Pattison paper at the Conference. Officials of the OECD did not respond to several requests for comments on the papers and did not accept our invitation to reply.

Hansen notes the difficulties in inferring beliefs from published documents, the absence of a uniform OECD view, and the evolution of ideas as research and experience accumulate. Nevertheless, he writes of the Department of Economics and Statistics at OECD that, ". . .it is undoubtedly true that it was entirely dominated in its thinking by British Keynesianism - - that is, Keynesian theory with a British institutional background. It was always firmly anchored in British institutions and tended to think that a policy that is good in Britain must be good for any other country." (Emphasis in the original.)

6

Hansen offers a simple explanation for the reliance on the textbook Keynesian model and the very slow acceptance of the Phillips curve. The directors, Milton Gilbert and J.C.R. Dow, held these views. They chose Hansen as a consultant with the intention of making ". . .an impact on certain unenlightened governments. A number of countries did in fact adopt the methodology, at least for internal work in ministries of finance, and there is no doubt that vague expressions in country reports . . . followed from evaluations based on this methodology."

Hansen accepts the criticism that his work neglected the financing of fiscal policy. In long discussions, he had not persuaded Dow that "liquidity effects" or real balance effects should be included. Dow acknowledged the theoretical point but argued against making it for the theoretical, empirical, and institutional reasons that Hansen reports. Moreover, Hansen argues, some of the arguments are valid and not open to criticism if the central bank controls interest rates.

Hodgman also believes that the Fratianni and Pattison paper is ". . . a fair characterization of the views held in the past, at least by some of the top-level personnel. . .and reflected in their published pronouncements on stabilization policy." However, Hodgman believes that OECD officials have a more diversified range of opinions and less influence on public policy than the paper suggests.

Fratianni and Pattison conclude their paper with a discussion of the OECD as an organization. The OECD has, in their view, a predilection for incomes policy; neglects monetary policy; relies on the simple Keynesian model; and holds a shifting, eclectic view of the causes of inflation. These and other actions, the authors argue, reflect two dominant goals: prestige and self-preservation. It is difficult to quantify the extent to which the OECD has acquired "prestige" but there is no doubt about survival. In the crowded field of international economic organizations, the OECD has managed to survive the Marshall Plan that provided its original reason for being; and has grown to maturity with a large staff, a large budget, and, according to Hansen, a sense of missionary zeal ". . . as an overseas missionary post for British Keynesianism trying to form continental European budgetary policies."

II. HOUSING AND MORTGAGE POLICIES

Economists devote considerable attention to monetary policy and central banks, and the effect of monetary policy on housing is a perennial theme in the discussion. Housing is a long-lived durable asset, and housing purchases are postponable, so it is not surprising that there is evidence of an interest elastic demand for housing. In addition, a number of writers argue that some form of "credit rationing" increases the effect of monetary policy on housing in the short run.

Most countries have responded to the combination of analysis and the political power of the housing industry by providing specialized financial institutions. In the U.S., the Federal Home Loan Bank Board is one such institution. Dwight Jaffee and Craig Swan were asked to discuss the policies pursued by the FHLBB and to consider both the rationale and the effects. Harris Friedman of the FHLBB and Edward Kane discussed the papers at the Conference.

Several issues are treated in these papers. Jaffee and Swan argue that the principal policy instruments available to the Federal Home Loan Bank System (FHLBS) have negligible effects on the housing stock in the long run. The amount of housing is demand determined, and there is no evidence that FHLBS or other operations in the mortgage market affect tastes, opportunities, or the size and rate of growth of population.

Some believe there is an effect on productivity. The effect is said to occur because smaller fluctuations encourage greater capital intensity in the building industry and thus lower costs of production. Both authors agree that there is little evidence to support this conjecture. In fact, the relative growth of the prefabricated and on-site segments of the building industry provides information about demand for the two types of housing. But, there too, firm conclusions are difficult to draw because the rate of growth of capital in on-site home-building may be higher than casual observation suggests. Substantial fabrication occurs away from the construction site, so the capital at the construction site is a poor indicator of capital.

If there are no long-run effects of mortgage market policy on housing, the principal short-run effects are on the timing of building activity. As Jaffee notes, a majority of the House Banking and Currency Committee wanted the FHLBB to ". . .regulate the supply of mortgage credit in a way that will discourage building booms and support normal construction year in and year out." Congress has not been that explicit in setting goals for the mortgage market agencies, but it has legislated a national housing goal and required the Department of Housing and Urban Development (HUD) to report on the extent to which there is progress toward the goal. Of course, operations that shift the timing of building activity do not help to achieve long-term goals. Today's increase is tomorrow's decrease.

The papers raised several issues concerning the short-run effects of FHLBS policies on housing. One is the extent to which the FHLBS is the captive of the Savings and Loan Association (SLA) industry. A second is the quantitative magnitude and duration of the effects of mortgage policies on housing. Third, Jaffee appraises some recent changes in policy and some proposed changes. A fourth topic not discussed at the Conference is raised here. Are there better alternatives that have not been explored?

Jaffee rank orders the three goals of the FHLBB. "When a trade-off occurs, FHLBB policy seems to reflect a clear ordering of priorities: savings flows first; then, mortgage market activity; finally, housing investment." Kane argues that, ". . .FHLBB policy is keyed primarily to SLA savings inflows and profit rates and that, except as a matter of public (and especially Congressional) relations, the Board cares about families' housing needs and the welfare of the construction industry only insofar as they impinge on these SLA variables." (Emphasis in the original.)

Jaffee and Swan consider the effects on housing of short-run disequilibrium in the mortgage market. Both argue that any effect of mortgage market policy on housing occurs by supplying mortgages, to eliminate some of the excess demand for mortgages without changing the mortgage rate. The main point is that non-price terms are changed to clear the mortgage market by reducing availability, so the increase in supply of mortgages by the FHLBS and others increases availability at a given mortgage rate.

Swan accepts the disequilibrium as a fact and notes some evidence which suggests that others have cited disequilibrium in the mortgage market as a reason for mortgage operations and as a rationale for the equations in their models.[1] Jaffee recognizes that there is a problem of explaining why lenders prefer to ration credit rather than allow the mortgage rate to clear the mortgage market. Slow adjustment of mortgage rates has long been noted, but a satisfactory explanation of the adjustment is lacking. Jaffee offers some suggestions, including usury laws, slow adjustment by governments of regulated rates on FHA and VA mortgages, and the use of forward commitments. He concludes, "[I]n such a disequilibrium situation, support may be effective in providing a short-run stimulus to housing investment. However, it is unlikely that there is more housing investment under this regime than would develop out of an equilibrium system. It is a classic case in which one form of government intervention - - ceilings - - invites further intervention - - mortgage support - - in a lengthening chain of inefficiency."

Swan cites the evidence from simulations to show that several researchers have found mortgage policy an effective means of increasing housing and mortgages. Kane, in his comments, offers some reasons for not accepting the evidence as conclusive. To his list should be added any effect on open market rates induced by the sale of open market securities to finance FHLBB operations, since these effects are often neglected in the simulations.

---

[1] One of the studies cited by Swan, however, can be cited on the opposite side. P. Dhrymes and P. Taubman conclude, ". . .that the mortgage rate is the only term of the mortgage important in determining the demand for mortgages" (Dhrymes and Taubman in Friend, 1969, p. 115).

The size and reliability of the effects of mortgage market operations on housing remains an open issue. The rationale for the operations is an open issue also. Almost everyone who has written on mortgage and housing policy has recognized that fluctuations in homebuilding may minimize the social cost of adjustment of variable monetary and fiscal policies. Quite apart from the issue of whether mortgage policy is effective in reducing variability of homebuilding is the issue of desirable social policy. Are fluctuations in the production of housing and durables a least cost solution? Would the social cost of fluctuations be lower if stabilization policy were more gradual? These questions were not addressed at the Conference.

Optimal solutions to the housing problem are neglected in the discussion of the role of the FHLBS and other mortgage agencies. If the principal arguments in the loss function of the FHLBS are protection of the SLA clients, as Kane alleges and Jaffee accepts, mortgage policy is unlikely to be optimal. There are almost certainly less costly ways than Regulation Q, usury ceilings, portfolio restrictions, borrowing and relending operations, and the like, to protect thrift institutions.

An obvious alternative to government operations in the mortgage market is to separate housing subsidies from mortgage operations and to allow SLAs to borrow in the open market. The intermediation function performed by the Federal Home Loan Banks (FHL Banks) must occur either because the clients are subsidized or because many of them are too small to borrow on the open market.

If size is an important reason for intermediation by a government agency or agencies, why do SLAs remain small? Why do not mergers or growth eliminate small associations and increase the average size of those that remain? Can it be that the FHLBB discourages mergers so as to maintain a large number of clients distributed throughout congressional districts? Have most SLAs paid for their protection by being kept at less than minimum efficient size by rules on merger, by requirements that restrict the radius within which SLAs lend, and by rules that prevent competition?

We do not have answers to these questions. Progress has been made in understanding the aims, functions, and goals of the mortgage market institutions, and the papers at the Conference showed that some careful and creative work is underway. But, as Jaffee remarks, "A disturbing and continuing theme in U.S. housing and mortgage policy is that policy is always indirectly aimed at the target, while. . .efficient direct measures are left unutilized." (Emphasis in the original.)

To these puzzles, we must add another. Suppose we accept that there is a net social benefit from maintaining a lender of last resort. Currently, some functions of the lender of last resort are provided by the deposit insurance agencies, the Federal Deposit Insurance Corporation (FDIC) and the Federal Savings and Loan Insurance Corporation (FSLIC); by the insurance of customer accounts held by stock exchange brokers, the Securities Investor Protection Corporation (SIPC); by the FHL Banks; and by the Federal Reserve Banks. Should a single lender of last resort - - a monopolist - - be given responsibility for lending to the financial system? Or does the agency-client relationship increase social benefits more than it increases costs?

III. <u>POLICIES TO REDUCE INFLATION</u>

Rates of inflation differed across countries in the 50s and 60s, and exchange rates were adjusted at infrequent intervals. Under fluctuating rates, in the 70s, countries have more opportunity to pursue independent policies, so rates of inflation were expected to diverge more than in the past. David Laidler and Michael Hamburger and Rutbert Reisch test some alternative theories of inflation using data for several countries, and compare some effects of anti-inflationary policies. Michele Fratianni and Pieter Korteweg discussed the papers at the Conference, and Robert Rasche submitted a critical comment on Laidler's paper.

Both papers test some hypotheses about inflation by estimating the same equation for the same time period in different countries and by comparing estimations of alternative equations. The comparisons are of interest for the information they provide about our knowledge of the process generating inflation and for their policy implications.

If inflation results from a variety of "causes" and is dependent on particular structures - - the extent of unionization, monopoly power of corporations, and similar factors that differ over time and across countries - - then there is little hope of finding a systematic explanation of inflation. That an inflation hypothesis is supported by data from several countries lends support to the conclusion that systematic responses become manifest despite differences in institutional arrangements.

Laidler attempts to formulate a "sociological" explanation of inflation and to compare this theory to the hypothesis known as the "inflation augmented Phillips curve." His task is made difficult by the carelessness with which the sociological explanation is formulated, or perhaps by the care taken to avoid testable implications. Suggestions about the importance of labor unions and strikes as measures of social unrest are formulated as a testable proposition and compared to a particular form of the inflation augmented Phillips curve developed earlier by Laidler and others formerly at the University of Manchester. The version used includes a measure of expected world inflation and implies that, in a steady state, world inflation is constant.

The data on inflation which Laidler uses for his tests are loosely related. Frequent references in theoretical literature on inflation to the "law of one price," as if it were a universal truth, may mislead some economists into a belief that rates of price change were highly correlated under the dollar standard. Laidler's data for the U.S., Italy, Japan, U.K., Germany, and Switzerland during the years 1954-1970 show the following distribution of simple correlation co-efficients.

Correlation	Frequency
Zero or less	1
.01 - .20	2
.21 - .40	3
.41 - .60	5
.61 - .80	4

The highest correlation, 0.75, means that, at most, slightly more than half of the variance is explained. The average R^2 is approximately 0.25.

Laidler sees the opportunity presented by differences in rates of inflation in the various countries. Any explanation based on institutional, structural, or social processes in a particular country lacks generality. Explanations based on aggregate demand, "monetarist" explanations in Laidler's terminology, imply that the inflation transmission mechanism is the same in each country. "It is the differences among national inflation rates that a monetarist must explain, while the sociologist must explain the similarities."

One problem with Laidler's sociological explanation is that the distinction between one-time changes in monopoly power and steady increases in monopoly power is not drawn. A union may strike to increase its power or to maintain its power. Alternatively, the duration of strikes may contain more information about the divergent anticipations of inflation held by workers and managers than about "power." The problem, as Laidler recognizes, lies with the inchoate form of the sociological explanation.

Several tests of the alternative theories are attempted, including comparison of predicted and actual inflation for several years following the estimation period. Laidler concludes that there is strong evidence of the importance of excess demand and substantially better evidence to support the expectations augmented Phillips curve than the sociological explanation of inflation. He emphasizes the comparative ability of the alternative hypothesis to explain the sample data and to predict beyond the sample period.

Policy implications differ for the two explanations. Proponents of the sociological explanation generally propose wage and price controls as the principal anti-inflation policy. Monetarists generally favor control of aggregate demand and particularly reduction in the rate of growth of domestic and international money. Laidler concludes that his analysis and the evidence provide little support for the belief that wage and price controls have had sustained effects. However, fixed exchange rates also reduced the ability of individual countries to control inflation independently. Inflationary expectations dominate the trend rate of inflation in all countries, according to Laidler. The end of the fixed exchange rate system increased the opportunity for countries to control domestic inflation. Laidler concludes his paper with some conditional forecasts about the direction and timing of changes in the rates of inflation in the countries studied. Where the conditions held, the forecasts have proved to be reliable. The rate of inflation peaked in Germany and Switzerland earlier than in other countries, and has declined. Inflation rose in Italy for a time and, following a restrictive policy in late 1974, fell in the U.S.

Hamburger and Reisch ". . .seek to determine the extent to which existing theory can explain fluctuations in prices and output (employment). Within the limits of this knowledge, we then attempt to evaluate the role that traditional economic policy can play in moderating these fluctuations." The models chosen are the supply oriented theory of inflation developed by Robert Lucas, and the now traditional explanation, formalized by Jerome Stein, in which the rate of price change depends on aggregate excess demand. Neither the Lucas nor the Stein model assigns influence to foreign impulses, so Hamburger and Reisch adjust the equations along the lines suggested by the work of Korteweg.

The results for the Lucas model are comparable to the earlier results reported by Lucas and, where comparisons can be made, are slightly better than the results reported by Laidler. The results for the Stein model were less consistent. The estimates for Germany and the U.S. are consistent with the model, but estimates for the U.K. are much less so. Neither model forecast the 1974 rates of inflation with acceptable accuracy but, as Hamburger and Reisch note, the one-time change in the 1974 price level makes it ". . .difficult to assess the seriousness of this deficiency."

The authors note that, apart from the positive influence of money, the coefficients of the Stein model of inflation vary over time and across countries. The coefficients of the Lucas model are more stable. This leads the authors to suggest that macroeconomists may place too much emphasis on demand and too little emphasis on supply.

Hamburger and Reisch reach a conclusion about a main issue raised by Laidler. The differences among countries are much less impressive than the similarities. They write, "The qualitative similarity in results for the various countries examined is also an important finding, implying that the underlying structures of these economies may have more elements in common than not."

To explore this issue, the authors pool the data in a single equation relating five-year average rates of monetary expansion to five-year average rates of change of nominal income in four countries used in their study. Tests of differences among countries are unable to reject the proposition that, for the years 1951-1975, all countries are drawn from the same population.

The principal conclusion from the study is drawn by the authors. "Considering the differences in the money-supply processes in these economies and their evolution over time, the results are impressive. They suggest that, over five-year periods, variations in the growth of money have a significant and well-determined effect on the growth of [nominal] income, essentially independent of the process that determines the money stock." This conclusion contrasts with the eclectic theories offered by the OECD, the JEC, and similar agencies responsible for advising governments, and with the policies of some governments, e.g., Britain, that continue to deny the inflationary effects of excessive monetary expansion.

REFERENCE

1.   Dhrymes, P., and Taubman, P., "An Empirical Analysis of the Savings and Loan Industry," in Study of the Savings and Loan Industry,(directed by I. Friend), Washington, D.C.: U.S. Government Printing Office, 1969.

AN EVALUATION OF THE ECONOMIC POLICY PROPOSALS
OF THE JOINT ECONOMIC COMMITTEE OF THE
92ND AND 93RD CONGRESSES

Carl F. Christ*
The Johns Hopkins University

I. INTRODUCTION

An evaluation of the economic policy proposals of the Joint Economic Committee during two Congresses is a little like an evaluation of two translations of the Bible. There are many books and chapters, many authors, and many interpretations of the true meaning of what has been written. The dissenting and supplementary views may be likened to the Apocrypha, and the energy crisis to the Flood. Be that as it may, the task has given me a renewed appreciation of the demands we place upon our Senators and Representatives, and a renewed respect for democracy as a way of government. Imperfections it assuredly has, but I do not know of a better way.

This paper concentrates on the 21 reports (see Appendix) of the Committee and its Subcommittees, issued between January, 1971, and February, 1975. Hearings, staff studies, and papers prepared for the Committee are excluded.

The paper is organized as follows. First is a brief description of the Committee's origin and mandate. Second is information on the political composition of the Congress and of the Committee since 1971. Third is a sketch of important economic events since 1966. Fourth is a description of the way the Committee's reports are organized. Then the four main sections of the paper appear, describing and evaluating the proposals contained in the Committee's and the Subcommittees' reports: macroeconomic policy; redistribution of income and wealth; private vs. public decisions in resource allocation; and exchange rates and the international monetary system. A summary and conclusion will be found at the end.

The Origin and Mandate of the Joint Economic Committee

The Full Employment Act of 1946 called for "maximum employment, production, and purchasing power;" created the Council of Economic Advisers and directed that the President make an annual economic report;

* Helpful comments were made by the discussants and by Bela Balassa, Bruce Hamilton, Allan Meltzer and Jürg Niehans.

created the Joint Economic Committee of the House and Senate (until 1956 called the Joint Committee on the Economic Report), and directed it "... (1) to make a continuing study of matters relating to the Economic Report; (2) to study means of coordinating programs in order to further the policy of this Act; and (3) . . . each year . . . to file a report with the Senate and the House of Representatives containing its findings and recommendations with respect to each of the main recommendations made by the President in the Economic Report and . . . such other reports and recommendations to the Senate and House of Representatives as it deems advisable." Since 1967, the Committee has had 10 members from each house, six from the majority party and four from the minority party. The chairmanship belongs to one house and the vice-chairmanship to the other, a switch taking place with each new Congress.

Composition of the Congress and the Joint Economic Committee Since 1971

Table 1

Party Representation at the Opening of the 92nd, 93rd, and 94th Congresses

	92nd Congress 1971-1972		93rd Congress 1973-1974		94th Congress 1975-1976	
	Senate	House	Senate	House	Senate	House
Democrats	54	254	56	240	60	289
Republicans	44	179	42	192	37	144
Buckley	1	0	1	0	1	0
Independent	1	0	1	1	1	0
Vacant	0	2	0	2	1	2
Total	100	435	100	435	100	435

Table 1 shows the party composition of each house at the opening of each Congress since 1971. The Democrats have had the majority in both houses throughout, and, hence, have had both the chairmanship and the vice-chairmanship of the Joint Economic Committee. Table 2 lists the members of the Committee and some of the senior staff since 1971. Little turnover of membership occurred during the period under study, 1971-74: one change in the Senate (Schweiker for Miller), and one in the House (Carey for Boggs).

Table 2

The Joint Economic Committee in the 92nd, 93rd, and 94th Congresses

Committee Members and some Senior Staff	92nd Congress 1971-1972	93rd Congress 1973-1974	94th Congress 1975-1976
Senate Democrats	William Proxmire John Sparkman J.W. Fulbright Abraham Ribicoff Hubert H. Humphrey Lloyd M. Bentsen	Same as 92nd Congress	Hubert H. Humphrey John Sparkman William Proxmire Abraham Ribicoff Lloyd M. Bentsen Edward Kennedy
Senate Republicans	Jacob K. Javits Jack Miller Charles H. Percy James B. Pearson	Jacob K. Javits Charles H. Percy James B. Pearson Richard S. Schweiker	Jacob K. Javits Charles H. Percy Robert Taft, Jr. Paul J. Fannin
House Democrats	Wright Patman Richard Bolling Hale Boggs Henry S. Reuss Martha W. Griffiths William S. Moorhead	Wright Patman Richard Bolling Henry S. Reuss Martha W. Griffiths William S. Moorhead Hugh L. Carey	Wright Patman Richard Bolling Henry S. Reuss William S. Moorhead Lee H. Hamilton Gillis W. Long
House Republicans	William B. Widnall Barber B. Conable, Jr. Clarence J. Brown Ben B. Blackburn	Same as 92nd Congress	Clarence J. Brown Garry Brown Margaret M. Heckler John H. Rousselot
Chairman Vice-Chmn.	William Proxmire Wright Patman	Wright Patman William Proxmire	Hubert H. Humphrey Wright Patman
Executive Director	John R. Stark	John R. Stark	John R. Stark
Director of Research	James W. Knowles	(none)	(none)
Senior Economist	Loughlin F. McHugh*	Loughlin F. McHugh John R. Karlik** Courtenay M. Slater**	Same as 93rd Congress

    *   Beginning in mid-1972
** Beginning in mid-1974

Some Important Economic Events of 1966-1974

Remember that, in 1966-68, Federal fiscal and monetary policy were expansive: deficits were larger than usual, and the money stock was growing faster than previously. Inflation, as measured by the CPI, reached the alarming rate of 4.8 percent for the 12 months ending January, 1969, and the unemployment rate for 1968 was 3.6 percent. The Republican administration which took office in 1969 set out to stop inflation, without increasing unemployment and without wage and price controls, by applying the traditional methods of mild fiscal and monetary restriction. Inflation of the CPI (at seasonally adjusted annual rates) reached 8.4 percent for one month, March, 1969, but gradually declined, reaching 4.4 percent for the 12 months ending July, 1971, and 2.4 percent in February, March, and July of 1971. Unemployment climbed to 6.6 percent by January and February, 1971, and declined to 6.2 percent by July. The balance of payments had a large deficit. In August, 1971, the administration abruptly imposed a wage-price freeze (known as Phase I of a five-phase controls program), suspended the convertibility of the dollar into gold, imposed a 10 percent surcharge on imports, and began to shift monetary and fiscal policy to an expansive stance again. (I cannot resist the conjecture that if there had not been an election only 15 months from August, 1971, controls would not have been imposed, and the fiscal-monetary policy stance would not have been shifted to expansion.) These expansive policies were maintained until early 1973 (fiscal) and 1973-1974 (monetary), when inflation became so rapid that restrictive policies were again adopted. Most controls were removed in the spring of 1974. Inflation of the CPI reached an annual rate of over 12 percent in 1974 before beginning to decline. Unemployment reached a low of 4.6 percent in October, 1973, and rose through May of 1975. In 1975, monetary and fiscal policy were being turned around to a strongly expansive stance again.

Reports of the Joint Economic Committee and Its Subcommittees

The Committee's procedure for the annual Joint Economic Report is for the majority to write the main body of the report (typically about 80 pages); for the minority to write a shorter report which appears as "Minority Views;" for the whole Committee to write a "Statement of Committee Agreement" (which varied in 1971-74 from one-third of a page to 13 pages in length); and for any member to have the right to add footnotes and/or separate supplementary views. Other reports of the Committee and its Subcommittees are similarly done, except that it is not uncommon to find a report that has no minority views, or even one that is unanimous.

Apart from the Joint Economic Reports, the longest reports in 1971-74 are Income Security for Americans: Recommendations of the Public Wel-

fare Study, and Achieving Price Stability Through Economic Growth (abbreviat-
ed by its acronym, APSTEG). These reports are numbers 660 and 663 in the
Committee's list (see Appendix), both released in December, 1974. APSTEG is
devoted to the simultaneous problems of inflation and unemployment, which
became acute in 1974. Another important recent report is A Reappraisal of U.S.
Energy Policy (number 636), released in March, 1974.

II. MACROECONOMIC POLICY

Unemployment and Inflation

The most important economic policy problem, in the Committee's
view, is to maintain high employment and lick inflation at the same time. This
is repeated in report after report, and in the minority views as well. Much attention is given to what levels of unemployment and inflation are possible and
acceptable, and what policies should be chosen in pursuit of these aims. Nevertheless, this matter is not even mentioned in the statements of joint views of the
majority and minority that appear at the beginning of each of the Joint Economic Reports for the years 1971, 1972, 1973, and 1974. Perhaps the Democratic and Republican members differed so sharply on this subject that they
were unable to define any joint views.

The reports of the Committee reflect the views of the majority party,
which was Democratic during the period surveyed. In the 1971 Joint Economic
Report, the Committee advocates,". . .as a long-term objective the twin goals of
an unemployment rate no higher than 3 percent and an annual increase in the
GNP deflator of no more than 2 percent." (p. 35). In the 45 years since 1929,
this has been achieved in only one year - - 1953.In the 1972 version, the Committee's view is, "If the necessary structural and institutional reforms are undertaken, a combination of a rate of unemployment below 3 percent and an inflation rate (as measured by the GNP deflator) no higher than 2 percent can be
achieved and sustained." (p. 15). The 1973 report says, "A reduction in unemployment to no more than 4 percent . . . can and should be achieved within the
next 12 months. [It was 5.1 percent in February, 1973.] . . . An unemployment
rate no higher than 3 percent should continue to be our longer run objective."
(pp. 18-19). In the 1974 report, we read, "Our longer term employment goal
should continue to be an economy in which an unemployment rate no higher
than 3 percent can be combined with a reasonable degree of price stability."
(p. 34). In APSTEG, the Committee's most recent report as of this writing,
there is a further retreat from these aims. "There appears to be no fundamental
reason why, if proper policies are followed, the United States cannot in the

future combine rates of price increase of 3 percent or less with rates of unemployment of 4 percent or less." (p. 25). In only three of the last 45 years has this occurred: 1952, 1953, and 1966. (The GNP deflator was chosen as the price index, as above.)

The minority views appended to the Joint Economic Reports for 1971-74 are less ambitious regarding unemployment and inflation. It must be remembered that the majority were attacking the policies of the Republican Administration, whereas the minority were defending them. In the 1971 Joint Economic Report, the minority views make no significant mention of this matter. In 1972, they echo the President in advocating the reduction of unemployment below the 6 percent level prevailing in 1971 (p. 95); they do not state a target for inflation, but note without comment the forecasts of 3 to 4 percent inflation for 1972 (p. 91). In 1973, they express satisfaction with the reduction in the unemployment rate to 5.1 percent, but assert that this is too high as a long-run goal (p. 102). They note with satisfaction that the GNP deflator ". . . rose only 3 percent in 1972 . . ." (p. 105). In 1974, they " . . . agree with the Council of Economic Advisers that the goal of 'maximum employment' . . . was approximately met in 1973." (p. 97); the average unemployment rate in 1973 was 4.9 percent. They add that inflation was unsatisfactorily high in 1973 (p. 99); the CPI increased 8.8 percent from December 1972 to December 1973.

In my view the Committee has made an extremely serious mistake in selecting as its twin long-term goals an unemployment rate of 3 or 4 percent or less at all times, coupled with a fixed stated upper limit on the inflation rate.The two are incompatible in the United States economy given current policies with respect to the minimum wage, unemployment compensation, and welfare. The Committee did not originate this mistake and is not alone in making it. Others making the same mistake in the last decade are Presidents and their defeated opponents; Councils of Economic Advisers (except for the 1975 Council, see pp. 94-97 of their 1975 Report); and many members of both houses of Congress. This mistake renders successful macroeconomic policy almost impossible.

Inflation can be kept at any constant average annual rate over long periods--negative, zero, or positive--by means of monetary and fiscal policy. The average inflation rate was negative 3 percent a year in the United States between 1864 and 1896, a period of rapid economic growth. It was approximately zero between 1826 and 1860, and in the 1920s. Some South American countries have experienced inflation rates of the order of 50 percent a year, or more, for many years. We can set a zero average inflation rate as our goal, and achieve it, if we are prepared to bear the adjustment costs.

Unemployment is not subject to such arbitrary control. Monetary and fiscal policy can affect the unemployment rate, but cannot hold it continuously at or below an arbitrariliy low rate such as 4 percent, in the United States, without continuously accelerating inflation.

In the 45 years since 1929 (when good unemployment statistics began to be available), there have been only three episodes when the average unemployment rate for the year was at or below 4 percent for two consecutive years or longer. These were the six years,1943-48; the three years,1951-53; and the four years, 1966-69. With that exception, after 1929, there has been no year when the average unemployment rate was at or below 4 percent. For the post-war period, 1946-74, the unemployment rate averaged 4.9 percent. For 1955-74, it averaged 5.0 percent.

Consider the three episodes when the unemployment rate remained at or below 4 percent. In each case, fiscal and monetary policy had shifted toward expansion - Federal deficits became larger than usual, and the stock of money was growing more rapidly than immediately before. We know that such macroeconomic policy changes strengthen aggregate nominal demand, as compared with what was previously expected. We also know that the first response of the private economy to these changes is an increase in real output and employment. If the new expansionary policy stance is maintained, output begins to push against the limits of capacity. Then prices and wages begin to move upward from their previous path, as buyers and sellers realize that capacity utilization has become unusually high; the rate of inflation cannot remain as low as the original rate (be that negative, zero, or positive) without the appearance of shortages, in the face of the increased rate of growth of nominal aggregate demand.

Then, with unusually high employment, what happens next depends upon what macroeconomic policy is followed. If the increased rate of growth of aggregate nominal demand is maintained, the rate of inflation settles at a higher rate than before. Buyers and sellers come to expect the higher rate of inflation to continue, and sellers of goods and labor no longer regard price increases of that magnitude as evidence of abnormally high real demand. Hence, the levels of capacity utilization and employment decline toward more normal levels. That is approximately what occurred in 1966-73 when, after four years of high employment in 1966-69, fiscal and monetary policy in 1972-73 was expansionary. Inflation continued, buyers and sellers began to expect continued inflation, and the unemployment rate again rose above 4 percent.

Suppose, however, that the increased rate of growth of nominal aggregate demand is not maintained, after having caused output to rise and press against capacity, but instead macroeconomic policies are returned to their former stance. Then nominal aggregate demand cannot support the continuation of price increases that began when output began to press against capacity; inflation slows toward its former rate. If the adjustment of prices is much delayed, there is likely to be a period of abnormally high unemployment. (The Committee is aware of this. See APSTEG, p. 75.) That is what happened in 1949, after the growth of nominal aggregate demand slowed following World War II; in 1954, after the 1950-53 boom; and (though the Committee may not recognize it yet) in 1974-75, after the growth of nominal aggregate demand slowed following the inflation of 1966-73.

Is it possible to maintain the level of unemployment below 4 percent indefinitely? Probably not. It could be done for a while. What would be required, each time buyers and sellers start to adjust to the prevailing rate of inflation, would be a further increase in the rate of growth of nominal aggregate demand, so that sellers would believe that real demand was remaining abnormally high. This process would require a continuously accelerating rate of inflation. Other countries' experiences with hyperinflations suggest that societies will not tolerate continuously accelerating inflations indefinitely.

Inflation Illusion

Economic policy regarding unemployment and inflation in the U.S. today is severely hampered by an illusion. It is the illusion, shared by the Committee and others, that it is possible to obtain a permanent reduction in the level of unemployment by accepting a higher constant rate of inflation. I call it "inflation illusion." The recognition of this illusion is not new. It has a cousin, called money illusion.

Money illusion is the view that whenever the nominal price of a good or service is greater in one situation than in another, its real value is higher in the first situation than in the second. If it prevails, sellers whose supply curves are rising will offer larger quantities in the first situation than in the second. A worker with money illusion continues to offer the same amount of labor so long as his nominal wage is fixed, even if consumer prices are rising; he does not respond to a change in his real wage if it occurs through price changes rather than through nominal wage changes.

Similarly, inflation illusion is the view that whenever the rate of inflation is positive, real aggregate demand for output and labor is high relative to capacity, and vice versa. It is based partly on the correct view that upward pressure on the price level increases when real aggregate demand increases in the vicinity of full employment, and decreases when real aggregate demand decreases. But it is based partly on the incorrect view that the normal or average level of unemployment, approximately 5 percent, is always associated with an inflation rate of zero, never with positive inflation.

22

In a situation where prices have been stable for some time and are expected to remain so, the normal or average rate of unemployment is associated with a stable price level. Then if real aggregate demand becomes high relative to capacity, prices soon rise and we see a positive rate of inflation. Or, similarly, if real aggregate demand becomes low relative to capacity, prices begin to fall after a brief delay, and we see a negative rate of inflation.

However, suppose that the economy has become adjusted to an inflation rate of 10 percent, and buyers and sellers of labor and output expect that inflation rate to continue. Then, there is no reason to expect the normal or average level of unemployment to differ from what it was under stable price expectations. It will be determined by workers' labor supply and employers' labor demand, as functions of tastes, real wage rates, the quality of labor, technology, and capital stocks. These are real factors, not significantly affected by constant inflation, once the economy has adjusted to the rate of inflation and comes to expect it to continue. In this situation, when real aggregate demand becomes high relative to capacity, prices start to rise faster than 10 percent. On the other hand, when a 10 percent inflation is expected to continue, and when real aggregate demand becomes low relative to capacity, prices begin to rise more slowly than 10 percent, e.g., 5 percent. This is approximately what happened in 1974 and early 1975.

The proper statement of the relation between unemployment and inflation is that high unemployment is associated with rates of inflation below what was previously expected, and low unemployment is associated with rates of inflation above what was previously expected. Either expectation can prevail when the actual rate of inflation is positive.

Events of the last 30 years have made it clear that when money illusion exists, it is shattered if the price level deviates from constancy. Events of the last eight years have shattered inflation illusion as well. We cannot, by adopting a higher constant inflation rate, mislead ourselves that aggregate real demand is permanently higher than normal, and, consequently produce at higher levels of capacity utilization and employment than normal. If we try, we will repeat the experience of 1966-73, when we had the higher rate of inflation, but not the reduction in unemployment. It would be better to choose fiscal and monetary policies to obtain a stable price level, rather than to force ourselves to endure inflation for the sake of ineffectual attempts to lower unemployment.

Unemployment

Are there any effectual means to reduce unemployment? The Committee writes of the possibility of structural and institutional reforms (mainly directed at price rigidities), for the purpose of reducing unemployment and inflation (see, for example, the 1972 Joint Economic Report, pp. 15 and 26). As argued above, any desired rate of inflation can be maintained; and the level of unemployment, in the long run, is largely unaffected by what constant rate of inflation is chosen. Let us consider whether there are reforms that might reduce the unemployment rate.

If the minimum wage were abolished, and also the welfare system (with its implicit 100 percent marginal tax rate on earnings for anyone who has the opportunity to earn less, or only slightly more, than the welfare program provides), and if instead a negative income tax were established, I believe that unemployment rates would be reduced. The minimum wage prohibits employment of members of the labor force who are ready, willing, and able to work at wages that employers are ready, willing, and able to pay. The welfare program has the effect, too often, of making it more profitable to be unemployed than to accept available employment. I will return to the negative income tax below. Improved training and labor market information could be helpful also.

It is possible to choose fiscal and monetary policies to make business recessions less severe than they were, on the average, from 1949 through 1975. More about this below. It would then be possible to reduce the peak and average levels of unemployment below those of the last 27 years. This might not lead to a corresponding increase in aggregate output, however; it is known, for example, that some unemployed workers use their time to travel, do home repairs, and other pleasurable or useful things. If periods of unemployment no longer occurred every four years or so, some of those workers could be expected to take longer vacations, or spend more time on strike, or take advantage of accumulated sick leave, or be absent more often; their total working time during a typical business cycle would not increase by as much as the decline in their unemployment.

Price and Wage Controls

The Committee has issued two reports (573 and 588) on price and wage controls in the last four years, and has given attention to them in the Joint Economic Reports from 1972 onward, and in APSTEG. The Committee's defense of controls consists chiefly in deploring inflation and asserting that it must be checked.

Recall that the authority for controls was passed by a Democratic Congress over the objections of the Republican Administration, and that controls were imposed in August, 1971, by the same Republican Administration. It is not surprising, therefore, that the views of the majority and minority members of the Committee exhibit some rather fancy footwork on controls. The majority attacks the Administration for doing a poor job of designing and administering Phases I, II, III, IIIA, and IV; the minority defends the measures taken by the Administration, while saying that, in principle, controls are bad and should be removed as soon as possible.

In discussing the effectiveness of controls, the Committee's reports concentrate on the behavior of prices and wages during the period of controls, with little attention to what happens after controls are removed. Although controls keep prices and wages temporarily lower than they would otherwise be, both the majority and the minority agree that controls should be temporary only. Therefore, in assessing the effect of controls on prices and wages, it is proper to ask what the effect of their imposition and subsequent removal would be. If prices and wages are not lower, after controls are imposed and then removed, than they would have been in the absence of controls, then it cannot be said that the controls prevented wage and price increases; they merely caused the increases to occur at a slightly later time.

The difficulty with price and wage controls is that when there is a need for them they do not work, and when they work there is not a need for them. To state this more completely, when monetary and fiscal policy causes or allows nominal aggregate demand to grow faster than real aggregate supply, then there is upward pressure on prices. The imposition of controls, in this situation, creates shortages; misallocation of resources; frustration of both would-be buyers and beleaguered sellers; evasion of the rules; and, finally, the scrapping of controls. They cannot do the job their advocates expect them to do, because the public will not tolerate the waste and frustration they cause, except during a recognized national emergency. On the other hand, when monetary and fiscal policy causes or allows nominal aggregate demand to grow no faster than real aggregate supply, then controls cause little waste and frustration (except in industries where demand is growing especially rapidly, or where resources are becoming exhausted, or where technology is improving especially slowly). But then they would not be necessary, because there would be no upward pressure on the price level.

I know of no U.S. instance of the imposition of price and wage controls when the monetary and fiscal policy stance was not expansionary, and when there was not upward pressure on the price level. In fact, the imposition of controls is usually accompanied by increased monetary and fiscal expansion, as if the controls provided assurance that there was no longer any need to worry about the inflationary consequences of monetary and fiscal stimulation. This was the case with controls in World War II, and in 1971-74. I believe that the CPI inflation rate would not have gone as high as 12 percent in 1974, and the price level would be substantially lower than it is today, if we had not had the price control program of 1971-74, for then we would not have pursued such expansionary fiscal and monetary policies from 1971 to 1974.

There is one situation in which a short-term (about six-month) price-and-wage control program might be useful, but the situation is so improbable that it can almost be dismissed. In 1969-70, for example, inflation had proceeded long enough, and under sufficiently persuasive conditions, that people had come to expect it to continue. A brief wage and price freeze imposed at such a time, coupled with an abrupt reduction in the rate of growth of nominal aggregate demand by a shift in monetary and fiscal policy (and this latter part is essential), could overturn such inflationary expectations. The economy could make the transition from inflation to price stability, without the overshooting of prices that occurs when firms and unions do not believe that inflation is going to slow down and end. But it is so unlikely that the government would impose both a price-wage freeze and restrictive fiscal and monetary policy at the same time, that I fear to recommend this strategy.

I conclude that price and wage controls are unlikely to be of any use in preventing inflation in the United States, and should be rejected.

In the 1974 Joint Economic Report, the majority and minority members agreed that the existing system of price and wage controls should be abolished (pp. 38 and 102). Still, the majority continues to advocate a permanent mechanism to administer price-wage policies, largely voluntary, but with some enforcement power; and standby authority for the President to reimpose controls on particular sectors of the economy (pp. 38-42). Similar proposals are advocated in APSTEG (pp. 79-83), which also calls for "a tough voluntary incomes policy." I believe that such proposals are ill-advised, first, because, insofar as they approximate the effects of price and wage controls, they do more harm than good; and second, because they make firms and unions less willing to cut prices and wages when their markets are soft, for fear that controls might be re-established and prevent increases later, if warranted by firmer demand.

Monetary and Fiscal Policy and Causes of Inflation

The Committee's view appears to be that inflation is caused, sometimes, by increases in particular prices, such as those of food or oil; sometimes, by devaluation of the dollar; sometimes, by the actions of large domestic firms or unions that have market power; sometimes, by the removal of price and wage controls; sometimes, by a too-rapid increase of real output in the vicinity of full employment; sometimes, by recession because productivity falls in recession; sometimes, by the rapid growth of exports; and sometimes, by expansionary fiscal and monetary policy (see especially APSTEG, pp. 20-36 and 78-80). The minority say they agree,(APSTEG, p. 131).

The Committee members do not seem to appreciate that, although many factors can be involved in the increase of a particular price or wage, inflation is an increase in the average level of prices, and that it <u>cannot</u> continue <u>unless</u> aggregate nominal demand is permitted to grow faster than real aggregate supply. This is true no matter what caused the initial price increases.

There have been many inflations in the world. Some have occurred under a gold standard, as in Spain when the gold stock grew rapidly following the discovery of gold in the New World. Most inflations have occurred under a managed paper standard. Then, the typical pattern of inflation is a rapid rate of growth of the stock of money, that is, paper currency plus bank deposits, created by the monetary authority, in the process of financing a continuing government deficit, or lending to (or buying promissory notes from) the private sector, or both.

In inflation, nominal aggregate demand grows faster than real total output. In a managed paper standard (such as most countries have today), this <u>cannot</u> continue <u>unless</u> monetary-fiscal policy provides for continued growth in nominal aggregate demand. No paper-standard inflation has ever persisted without such expansionary monetary-fiscal policy. Furthermore, no paper-standard inflation has ever been stopped in the continued presence of such expansionary monetary-fiscal policy.

The lesson of inflation for the United States is that we will stop the process of continuous inflation if, and only if, we manage our monetary-fiscal policy in such a way that nominal aggregate demand does not on the average grow faster than real total output.

What kind of monetary-fiscal policy does this imply? Consider some relevant magnitudes. The growth rate of potential real output in the United States has been 3 to 4 percent a year in this century, closer to 4 percent since World War II. Since 1900, the GNP velocity of M_1 (i.e., of demand deposits plus currency) declined more or less steadily until 1946, when nominal interest rates reached their lows, and rose steadily since, with nominal interest rates; velocity has not changed more rapidly than about 3 percent a year during any part of this period. Therefore, in order to have had a stable price level on the average since 1946, we would have needed a growth rate of M_1 somewhere between 1 and 4 percent a year; closer to 1 percent to offset the 3 percent growth rate of velocity, if velocity growth could be taken as given; but closer to 4 percent if the achievement of stable prices would have slowed the rise of nominal interest rates and, hence, reduced the growth of velocity.

During the eight years from 1966 to 1974, the average rates of growth were 6.2 percent for M_1, 1.8 percent for velocity, 2.8 percent for real

GNP, and 5.1 percent for the GNP deflator. (M_1 times velocity equals real GNP times the deflator.)

For the future, until we find that the rate of change of velocity moves outside the range of zero to 3 percent, an average growth rate of M_1 in the range of 1 to 4 percent a year would be required for a zero average rate of change of the price level. Fiscal policy will affect the required growth rate of M_1, by affecting the growth rate of potential output, and by the influence of Federal borrowing from the private sector upon interest rates and velocity.

The statement that a significant cause of the current inflation[1] is the recession, because productivity falls in recession, and the decline in productivity causes inflation (APSTEG, p. 80), is extraordinary. Productivity has fallen in recession for decades, but we have not had inflation coinciding with recession until 1974, when recession was superimposed upon expectations of continued inflation. As this recession has developed further, we see a decline in the rate of growth of prices, as we usually do in recession.

The Committee gives this erroneous idea repeated emphasis, especially in APSTEG. The very title of APSTEG (Achieving Price Stability Through Economic Growth) appears to be inspired by this fallacy.

Interest Rates

No account of the Committee's proposals would be complete without a discussion of interest rates. Every student of introductory economics knows that easy-money policies lead to lower nominal interest rates, and tight-money policies lead to higher nominal interest rates. But not enough people know that if easy-money policies are maintained to produce inflation, borrowers and lenders will come to expect inflation, and they will then make loan bargains at higher nominal interest rates, in order that the expected real rate of return on the loans, after adjusting for expected inflation, will be positive. This explains why nominal interest rates on many kinds of loans and securities have risen sharply since 1967, while the real rate of return on investment has not increased significantly.

In its Joint Economic Reports, the Committee repeatedly calls upon monetary policy to reduce interest rates. "Monetary policy should support the further decline of long-term interest rates. . . ." (1971, p. 21). "The Federal Reserve should develop appropriate policy tools to achieve lower long-term interest rates. . . ." (1972, p. 18). "It is the firm view of this Committee that the monetary authority should not permit interest rates to rise above present levels.

---

[1] The original draft mistakenly read, "the 1973-74 inflation." I am glad to acknowledge correction by both Courtenay Slater and John Karlik of the JEC staff.

If possible, interest rates should be reduced." (1973, p. 27). "Interest rates rose during most of the year. . . . Monetary policy in 1973 was basically restrictive. . . . For the year as a whole, the money supply grew at a rate of 5.7 percent. . . . A continuation of such growth would exert a drag on the economy in 1974." (1974, p. 32, with Senator Proxmire dissenting from the second sentence on the ground that a 5.7 percent annual increase in the money supply is not restrictive). The minority views do not agree with the Committee's reports concerning interest rates; in 1974, the minority views properly criticize the report, saying, "The end result of such an 'easy money' policy would have been just the high interest rates which such a misguided policy would have been aimed at avoiding in the short run." (p. 95). Representative Reuss understands this relationship (see the 1972 report, p. 12).

In calling for the money stock to grow at 6 to 7 percent a year, or more, and at the same time for low interest rates, the Committee is calling for effects that are incompatible in the long run. Rapid growth of the money stock can lower nominal interest rates in the short run, but will (unless continuously accelerated) lead to higher nominal interest rates as borrowers and lenders adjust to the continued presence of inflation. This is one of the difficulties in using changes in interest rates as an indicator of monetary policy. It is sometimes uncertain whether high nominal interest rates are the result of a tight money policy currently, or of an easy money policy in the preceding several years.

A great advantage of stabilizing the price level would be that real and nominal interest rates would be the same. This would simplify decision procedures leading to more efficient capital markets, and also would relieve savings banks and savings and loan associations of many severe difficulties resulting from high nominal interest rates.

The Budgetary Process

The Committee had agreed on the importance of Congressional procedures for reviewing the Federal budget long before the controversy over Presidential impounding of Congressionally authorized funds erupted in 1973. The statement of Committee agreement in 1971 (p. 3) says, "The Congress should adopt procedures for reviewing aggregate expenditures and receipts in order to make a determination as to the level of revenues and expenditures most consistent with the needs of the economy." Further, the Committee says, "Congress should adopt procedures for annual review of aggregate expenditures and receipts and for setting an appropriate expenditure ceiling in light of the needs of the economy." (p. 27). The minority views express similar ideas (pp. 129-36). The 1972 and 1973 reports give this matter less attention, but the

29

1974 report emphasizes it again. The statement of Committee agreement (p. 4) reads, "Congress should each year determine an expenditure total and the accompanying tax policy . . . Expenditure totals should be subdivided so that funds for various activities will be allocated according to congressionally determined priorities. . . . The tax expenditure budget . . . should be printed in the annual budget document."

The establishment of the new Senate and House Budget Committees, inspired in part by the recommendations of the Joint Economic Committee, gives the Congress the mechanism it needs to deal with budget totals, rather than dealing with particular programs and tax sources piecemeal.

Monetary and Fiscal Policy and Business Cycles

So far the discussion of monetary and fiscal policy has been in terms of its effects on the average growth rate of nominal aggregate demand, and the effect of that, in turn, upon the average rate of inflation. What of the short-term effects of monetary and fiscal policy, and the possibility of using it to moderate the severity of business cycles?

The Committee's reports of 1971-74 have not advocated frequent changes in monetary policy. They have favored a steadier rate of growth of the money stock than has actually occurred. However, in the attempt to bring unemployment down to 4 or even 3 percent, they have advocated rates of growth of the money stock that can only perpetuate inflation. In the 1972 Joint Economic Report (p. 18), we read, ". . . the money supply growth target should be at the upper limit of the 2-6 percent range recommended by this Committee for more normal circumstances." The minority says, ". . . we cannot presume to recommend a specific rate or range of monetary expansion. . . " but adds that the expanding economy ". . . will require substantial growth in the money supply." (p. 94). In APSTEG (p. 76), we read, "The immediate task of monetary policy must be to help halt the drop in real output. . . . money supply growth in the range of 6 to 7 percent may be adequate. However, should the economy be subjected to new external price shocks comparable to the food or oil price increases of 1973, monetary policy must be adjusted accordingly." The minority views (p. 132) are in general agreement.

The Committee is aware of pitfalls in attempting frequent changes in monetary policy as a way of correcting short-term fluctuations in the economy. APSTEG (pp. 74-5) states, "The economic effects of monetary policy changes appear only with a time lag of at least several months. Current policy must be formulated not only in terms of current conditions but of conditions as they are expected to be six to 12 months and even longer into the future." This means that if policymakers cannot foresee the cyclical stage of the economy six to 12 months or more ahead, they run a serious risk that monetary policy actions, taken in an attempt to moderate today's recession (or boom), may be too late, and may only exacerbate the opposite problem six or more months from now. The Committee gives insufficient attention to this risk.

The Committee believes that fiscal policy is an effective tool for reducing cyclical fluctuations in the economy. This may be deduced from statements like: "Because of the strong possibility that proposed policies will not produce the vigorous recovery projected by the Administration, both the Administration and the Congress should stand ready to enact an appropriate combination of expenditure programs and tax reductions to further strengthen the economy." (1971 Joint Economic Report, p. 21); "The Administration's budget policy recommendations should be rejected . . . [because] . . . The switch from a full employment deficit in 1972 to balance in 1973 will not achieve sustainable high employment." (1972 Joint Economic Report, p. 21); "Federal tax and expenditure policy in fiscal 1974 should be designed to produce an approximate balance between full employment receipts and full employment expenditures." (1973 Joint Economic Report, p. 21); "It is of the utmost importance that measures be taken immediately to counter the recession which is already emerging . . . Congress should enact a tax cut of approximately $10 billion . . . The net effect of the tax and spending changes proposed by the Committee should be to maintain an unchanged full employment surplus from Fiscal 1974 [$6.9 billion] to Fiscal 1975. . . ." (1974 Joint Economic Report, pp. 27 and 30); "Tax relief of $10 to $12 billion for low and moderate income persons should be enacted immediately. . . . In addition, improved unemployment compensation and an adequate program of emergency public service employment are essential . . . When the economic situation is changing as rapidly as at present, however, policy must be prepared to respond in a flexible way. We shall not hesitate to present additional or revised recommendations in the months ahead if the economic situation deteriorates beyond what is presently foreseen." (APS-TEG, pp. 5 and 68). Though the last quotation is not about fiscal policy, the Committee's discussions, summarized above, suggest that it refers chiefly to fiscal policy.

The delays involved in the enactment of fiscal policy legislation, and in its effects, are of the same order of magnitude as the lags in the effects of monetary policy. Hence, fiscal policy is subject to the same risk as mentioned above for monetary policy. This is the risk that, in the absence of good forecasts six months or more ahead, fiscal policy effects may come too late to correct the problem that engendered them, and may only serve to destabilize the economy, by reinforcing the next disturbance.

It is not clear whether our business cycle forecasts are sufficiently accurate for monetary and fiscal policy to have a net stabilizing effect on business cycles. Even if the forecasting problem were solved, it is not clear that the Congress can act with sufficient dispatch to produce a net stabilizing effect. I believe it _is_ clear that discretionary monetary and fiscal policies have had a net destabilizing effect on output and the price level, in the period since World War II; and that we can enjoy a modest improvement by the expedient of conducting monetary and fiscal policy in a steady manner, with no attempt to counteract specific cyclical disturbances.

Recommendations

My initial recommendation would be to move to a long-term growth rate of M_1 between 2 and 6 percent a year, [2] and to maintain the Federal full-employment budget such that the budget is balanced at 4 percent unemployment. Then at an average unemployment rate of 5 percent, the average deficit will be enough to permit both the money stock and the privately held Federal debt to grow at 2 to 6 percent a year.

My interim recommendation would be that the Joint Economic Committee obtain economic forecasts, and specify quarterly, by majority vote, what discretionary changes in monetary and fiscal policy (if any) they would enact to make the economy more stable than would the initial recommendation. These discretionary changes should not be enacted, but instead should be communicated to economists for an ex post study of whether they would have been stabilizing or destabilizing. The results should be published.

My long-term recommendation would be that, after two consecutive business cycles for which the Committee's proposed discretionary policies have been judged ex post to be stabilizing rather than destabilizing, the Congress then employ, in small doses, discretionary policies like those used by the Committee.

This may seem a stringent procedure, but where prosperity and depression are concerned, citizens should demand no less.

III. REDISTRIBUTION OF INCOME AND WEALTH

Public Welfare Reform

The Committee has had a good deal to say concerning redistribution of income and wealth in the United States, especially by the public welfare system. The committee has commissioned and published 18 studies of the

---

[2] Unfortunately, not enough is known about the time-path of the economy's response to permit calculation of the optimum path of monetary expansion to this long-term goal.

public welfare program, and has held numerous hearings on the matter. In December, 1974, the Subcommittee on Fiscal Policy, under the chairmanship of Representative Martha Griffiths of Michigan, published a report on its findings.

This report, entitled Income Security for Americans: Recommendations of the Public Welfare Study (number 660), is of major importance, and offers constructive proposals for dealing with one of the most vexing economic problems in America today. I hope it will be widely read and discussed, and that something like it will be adopted.

The Subcommittee proposes to scrap the programs for food stamps and Aid to Families with Dependent Children, and also the low-income allowance under the income tax, and replace them with a form of the negative income tax. Housing subsidies and the Basic Educational Opportunity Grants would be integrated into the new program in the sense that 80 percent of a family's housing subsidy, and all of its Basic Educational Opportunity Grant would count in the family's income for determining taxes and benefits.The unemployment compensation system would be revamped and partly replaced by the new program. Administration would be integrated with the income tax, and handled by the Internal Revenue Service.

A family of two adults and two children with no income would have a negative tax liability of $3,600 a year; that is, it would receive $3,600 a year from the Treasury. The marginal tax rate would start at 50 percent of wages, net of social security tax, and would fall to about 20 percent by the time such a family's wages, net of social security tax, reached $9,000 a year. If such a family had one wage-earner, with wages of $4,000 a year, net of social security tax, its tax liability would be negative $1,717; that is, it would receive $1,717 from the Treasury, and have a disposable income of $5,717. The break-even point for such a family, that is, the level of wages, net of social security tax, at which the family's net tax liability would be zero, would be about $7,000 a year. Families of more than four persons would receive more, or pay less, as would families with children without an adult at home to care for them. The marginal tax rate on property income, and on certain Federal benefits would start at 67 percent.

The net budget cost of this new program in fiscal 1976 is estimated at $15 billion a year ($17 billion if every eligible family participates). Approximately 16 million families and individuals would be eligible for payments from the Treasury in fiscal 1976. This is in contrast to the 18 million households eligible for food stamps under present policies.

No change in the social security system is proposed for the present, but it would be reviewed and altered so as to make it less a welfare system. The

33

Supplemental Security System for needy aged, blind, and disabled adults would be retained for the present, but eventually merged into the new system.

An income maintenance program such as this would provide a minimum level of income at low administrative cost, because a staff of welfare agents would no longer be necessary to check on eligibility; would not penalize marriage and family responsibility as the present system does; and would provide incentive to work for most people who can and would like to work. I believe it would be a significant improvement over the present wasteful, unproductive, and undignified system.

Tax Reform

Tax reform has received much attention from the Committee in the Joint Economic Reports of 1972, 1973, and 1974, and in the interim report (number 654) that preceded APSTEG by three months. For example, the 1973 report (p. 54) advocates, " . . . tax reform by eliminating or revising the following provisions in the individual and corporate income tax systems: corporate and individual capital gains, Asset Depreciation Range, investment tax credit, mineral depletion allowance, expensing of exploration and development costs, excess depreciation on buildings, and foreign tax preferences. . . . the minimum income tax should be made more effective . . . The Federal estate and gift taxes should also be consolidated and capital gains should be fully taxed at death. A Federally supported alternative to the tax exempt bond as a means of State and local finance should be established." (Senator Bentsen reserves judgment on these items.) In the 1974 report (p. 49) we find, "Special tax benefits granted to oil companies and to American firms investing abroad should be eliminated or sharply reduced. Specifically (a) the percentage depletion and current expensing of intangible drilling costs should be eliminated on both domestic and foreign operations; (b) payments to foreign governments for mineral extraction rights should be classified as royalties and not as taxes; (c) the practice of crediting taxes paid one foreign government against U.S. taxes due on income earned in another foreign country should be disallowed; (d) the deferral until repatriation of income taxes on earnings generated abroad by foreign subsidiaries of U.S. corporations should be abolished." (Senator Bentsen reserves judgment on tax changes regarding income from oil, gas, and foreign sources.) The report (page 50) continues, "The Administration's minimum income tax proposal (MTI), which would tax at least half of certain tax preferences at a graduated rate, should be enacted." (Again Senator Bentsen reserves judgment.) The Committee objects to the regressive nature of the payroll taxes that finance social security (but does not note that the retirement benefits are also regressive, being based on earnings up to the taxable upper limit).

34

The minority views in 1971-1974 are virtually silent on the subject of reducing special tax privileges, as are the statements of committee agreement.

The Congress in past years has been vulnerable to strong pressures from special interests for preferred tax treatment. One reason for the strength of these pressures is the steep progression in the schedule of personal income tax rates, up to a maximum marginal rate of 70 percent--wealthy people seek the creation of loopholes when rates are so high.

I can see no justification for many of the preferential provisions in the tax law, under which interest income from tax-exempt bonds is not taxed (and is not even reported); and under which the 111 taxpayers reporting adjusted gross incomes of over $200,000 in 1970 paid no Federal income tax in spite of the enactment, in 1969, of a minimum tax on tax preferences. (See the 1973 report, p. 51.)

If the tax system is to command respect, it must be fair, in the sense that it taxes people in the same income and wealth class at the same rate. The present Federal tax system does not approach this. The closing of all loopholes could be accomplished with no loss of revenue by a reduction in the top-bracket rates of the personal income tax. We would have a fairer tax system, and use fewer resources devising tax preference eligibilities. Phasing in such reforms over several years would facilitate orderly adjustment to them.

Federal Aid to State and Local Governments

The majority and the minority favored Federal aid to state and local governments, though they have not always agreed on the allocation formula or on what strings (if any) should be attached. In the 1972 Joint Economic Report and in APSTEG, the Committee suggests a counter-cyclical form of Federal aid, to protect state and local governments against the declining revenues during recessions. As noted earlier, the 1973 report suggested closing the tax-exempt bond loophole, and providing another way for state and local governments to borrow without having to pay the market interest rate.

The rationale for Federal aid is that some localities have lower per capita incomes (or higher per capita costs) than average, and hence their people cannot tax themselves sufficiently to provide an adequate level of public services. Federal financial aid to such localities is the alternative to direct Federal assumption of the responsibility for providing those services.

Foreign Aid

U.S. foreign aid has not been a very controversial subject within the Committee; more about it appeared in the statements of committee agreement than in the majority or minority views. There were proposals in 1971 for cutting U.S. military expenditures abroad, and in 1973 for obtaining cash compensation from the governments of countries so aided. In 1971, 1972, and 1974, the issuance of Special Drawing Rights (SDRs) to aid less-developed countries was suggested. In 1974, the emphasis shifted to encouraging oil-exporting countries to participate in aid to developing countries.

IV. PRIVATE VS. GOVERNMENT DECISIONS IN RESOURCE ALLOCATION

Optimal Allocation of Resources

The Committee emphasizes the need to strengthen competitive forces in the economy. However, in many areas of resource allocation, it favors a large role for the Federal government, as opposed to private choice. In reviewing the Committee's proposals on these matters, I shall focus on the concept of optimality of resource allocation.

An improvement in the allocation of resources is defined as any change in how resources are used, or how outputs are distributed, that benefits someone (or everyone), without harming anyone. An optimal resource allocation is a situation in which no improvements are possible--any change that benefits one must be at the expense of another. Note that _an_ optimal allocation has been defined, not _the_ optimal allocation. There is no unique optimum. A move from one optimum to another involves benefitting someone at the expense of someone else. Hence, a change from a non-optimal resource allocation to an optimal allocation can be an improvement, or it can be the sum of an improvement plus a change from one optimum to another.

The virtue of private enterprise, from a social point of view, is that, under suitable conditions, those who voluntarily trade with each other gain in the process; thus, voluntary transactions improve the allocation of resources. This is formalized in an important proposition of theoretical economics, thus: if an economic system is perfectly competitive, it will generate an optimal allocation of resources.

"Perfectly competitive" is a technical term, whose definition embodies the "suitable conditions" just mentioned. The main requirements for perfect competition are the following.

(1) Absence of market power. For every good or service there are many buyers and sellers, each small relative to the total, so that no one of them can influence the market price by his decisions to buy, sell, or stay out. Anyone is free to enter or not to enter any market.

(2) Perfect knowledge. Everyone knows the technology, the tastes of buyers, the properties of all goods and services (inputs as well as outputs), and the prices bid and asked by everyone else in every market.

(3) Absence of external effects. In every private contract, all costs and benefits accrue to the parties to the contract; there are no benefits conferred nor costs imposed upon others.

There are several reasons why the foregoing argument does not justify a completely laissez-faire economic policy on the part of government.

Efficiency vs. Equity

Optimal resource allocation or "economic efficiency" is not the only object of economic policy. Some degree of economic equality is another. The concept of optimal resource allocation does not address the question of equal ownership of resources.

One of the problems of economic policy is to increase economic equality without decreasing economic efficiency. Many measures that are intended to increase equality have a high cost in terms of allocative optimality. The minimum wage law is a good example; it forces unemployment upon some people who would prefer to work, perpetuating a non-optimal allocation, and often fails to increase equality besides. Farm price supports are another example, as is any price floor or ceiling. Among the best policies for redistributing income and wealth, causing the least losses of economic efficiency, are public education, public health measures for children, and the progressive death and income taxes, including the negative income tax advocated by the Subcommittee on Fiscal Policy (above).

Competition vs. Monopoly and Special Interests

No laissez-faire economy is perfectly competitive. Some markets exhibit monopoly power or monopsony power. Some participants conceal information from others. Many private contracts impose costs (e.g., pollution), or confer benefits (e.g., discovery and application of copyable technology) upon persons not party to those contracts.

Communities can, through their governments, sometimes compel their members to behave in a way that makes the economy more competitive, and hence more likely to approach optimal resource allocation. The antitrust laws, which the Committee seeks to strengthen, are of this type (see the 1973 report, p. 49, and APSTEG, pp. 5, 92, and 131-33). So are the disclosure rules for security markets, administered by the SEC. So are the proposals in the 1971 statement of committee agreement (p. 3) for environmental user charges, to insure that costs of pollution are borne by the parties to contracts that produce pollution, so as to induce them to find ways of avoiding it. So are the proposals in the 1973 report (p. 4), and the 1974 report (p. 10), and Report 600 to abolish all tariffs in 20 years, and to reduce or abolish non-tariff barriers to trade. So is the call in the 1971 report (pp. 3 and 106), and in the 1972 minority views (pp. 108-9) for a revamping of the regulation of transportation, with a view to giving more play to competitive forces. These are all laudable. Unfortunately, they do not command ardent lobbying support, for no one favors them except the ordinary citizen, who is not well organized.

Individuals and groups seek protection against competition, with the aid of constituted authorities. I believe Stigler was correct in saying,". . .as a rule, regulation is acquired by the industry and is designed and operated primarily for its benefit." [3] The Committee is less hospitable to special pleading than most public authorities, but their reports betray a tendency to yield.

Free Trade

The Joint Economic Reports, 1971-74, advocate liberalized foreign trade; those of 1973 and 1974 urge the elimination of all statutory tariffs within 20 years, and the reduction or elimination of non-tariff barriers as well. Both the majority and the minority take this view. (See the reports for 1971, p. 6; 1972, pp. vii and 133-35; 1973, p. 4; 1974, p. 10.) Subcommittee report 600 concurs. But this support wavers.

The 1971 statement of committee agreement notes the injury some domestic producers suffer from import competition, as we move toward free trade, and advocates financial assistance to them. The report also says (p. 7), "Occasionally, however, temporary restriction of imports will seem desirable..." and recommends that ". . .the degree to which imports are to be temporarily curtailed should be determined by the Tariff Commission." In APSTEG, the Committee prefers tariffs or income payments to quotas, which I applaud, because they permit more consumer and producer response to changed conditions than do quotas. On page 104 we find, "Import quotas on beef or any other agricultural commodity deprive consumers of the opportunity to purchase food at the lowest possible levels. . . . Either the enforcement of the countervailing duty statute against foreign subsidies or Federal payments to farmers according to the difference between market and target prices are preferable ways to assist agriculture." Senator Proxmire states, "I disagree with the assumption inherent

---

[3] Stigler (1971), p. 3.

38

in this paragraph that we should be a dumping ground for the world's produce.
... The dairy industry is an early warning signal."

Agriculture

The 1971 statement of Committee agreement (p. 3) says, "More assistance should be provided to rural America by the Federal government." The minority views (p. 128) say, "The Department of Agriculture should administer farm programs to maximize the net return to agriculture." Optimal resource allocation appears to be forgotten.

By 1974, when population and income growth put upward pressure on food prices worldwide, the Committee felt the show was on the other foot. In the 1974 report (pp. 58-59), we read, "... Congress should pass legislation establishing a system for managing exports of critical food and feedstuffs when projected market supplies are inadequate to meet domestic needs without drastically increasing prices. The Secretary of Agriculture should be authorized to (a) set up an export licensing system for agricultural commodities determined to be in critically short supply; and (b) require prior approval of such exports when necessary." The 1974 minority report (p. 121) says, "We believe that the transition of our farm economy from one of government support and subsidization to an independent sector relying on the market mechanism and independent planning is a great step in the direction of assuring the American people of adequate supplies of food at fair prices, and also assuring the American farmer of the income he deserves." But, two paragraphs later, it advocates legislation limiting food exports in order to hold down domestic food prices. This would deprive us of the improvement in resource allocation offered us by foreigners, in the form of large amounts of imports in return for food, and deprive foreigners of the improvement in resource allocation sought through trade with us.

Energy

The energy problem is not mentioned in any of the statements of committee agreement for 1971 through 1974, except for reference, in 1974, to foreign aid by oil-exporting countries. It is not discussed by the majority until 1974, when 20 recommendations on energy policy are reproduced (pp. 15-18) from a report of three Subcommittees, dated March 8, 1974 (number 636). APSTEG, (pp. 104-119 and 133-134) and the interim report that preceded it (number 654, pp. 38-40) also deal with energy policy.

In 1972 (p. 106), the minority advocates research to remove sulfur oxides from coal and oil; development of new energy processes--the fast breeder reactor, thermonuclear fusion, solar energy, coal liquefaction, and magnetohydrodynamic power cycles; the use of energy resources on Federal lands, including the outer continental shelf, in an environmentally acceptable way; provision of imports from such secure areas as Canada; provision of nuclear fuels; and energy conservation.

The 20 energy recommendations from number 636 are the following.

(1)   Oil prices should be rolled back, and controlled flexibly.

(2)   Congress should authorize a transferable-coupon gasoline rationing system or a rebatable tax.

(3)   The Federal Energy Office should adjust mandatory oil allocations as circumstances change.

(4)   The Government should provide public service employment to offset unemployment aggravated by fuel shortages.

(5)   Carpooling should be promoted, and the CAB should judiciously permit airline flight reductions.

(6)   Congress should reform transport regulation to eliminate wasteful restrictions on cargoes, backhauls, and routing.

(7)   Congress should fund mass transit systems, tapping the Highway Trust Fund forthwith.

(8)   Congress should authorize thermal efficiency standards for Federally-insured or subsidized new buildings.

(9)   Utility rate schedules should phase out quantity discounts and employ peak-load pricing.

(10) Royalty bidding should be used for Federal oil leases, rather than one-time bonus bids as at present. (The 1974 minority views (p. 105) propose this, too.)

(11) The following oil tax benefits should be removed or reduced: percentage depletion; current expensing of intangible drilling costs; the treatment as taxes (not as royalties) of payments to foreign governments for mineral extraction; and the crediting of taxes paid one foreign country against U.S. taxes on income earned in another foreign country.

(12) The Government should require submission of data on energy prices, sales, costs, profits, inventories, shipments, imports, and exports.

(13) Data on the location, extent, and value of energy resources on Federal lands and the outer continental shelf should be gathered and analyzed by a government agency.

(14) Though the present crisis may require extraordinary industry collaboration, no blanket antitrust or conflict-of-interest exemption should be given.

(15) Enforcement of antitrust laws must be stiffened. Congress should (a) require major petroleum producers to divest pipeline facilities, (b)

limit ownership of multiple energy sources, and (c) create a government energy corporation as a yardstick.

(16) The U.S. should ask the U.N. to direct Arab oil producers to comply with U.N. Resolution 2625 limiting the use of economic and political pressure.

(17) The U.S. should participate in international programs regarding energy exploration, development, and conservation.

(18) The U.S. should join in agreeing with other oil-consuming nations to share oil supplies in case of emergency.

(19) The U.S. should induce Arab oil producers to supply oil to the world; and to invest their surplus funds in the U.S., in other industrial countries, in World Bank bonds, and in energy-intensive export-manufacturing facilities in their own countries.

(20) The U.S. should encourage oil-producing nations to participate more in the international development banks.

APSTEG offers additional recommendations concerning energy, including for example the following. Increases in ceiling prices on new natural gas are proposed to encourage gas exploration and relieve the excess-demand pressure on gas, which is now cheap compared with oil (pp. 108-110 and, in the minority views, p. 133). A rollback in the price ceiling for new coal is proposed (pp. 106, 110). "The [coal price] controls, of course, would not apply to exported coal, and it would therefore be necessary to impose some regulation of exports. . ." (p. 110). The Committee sees ". . .no need. . .to guarantee a high minimum price for all energy resources through tariffs, import quotas, or other measures to assure the profitability of energy production." (p. 111). "The United States should not support international guarantees or an effort to set a price floor under the world petroleum market." (p. 118). "Congress should consider enacting a fuel conservation tax to obtain a sizable immediate cut in energy consumption." (p. 113).

The Committee frequently cites the recent oil price increase as an important cause of inflation, and argues for energy price ceilings to stop inflation. The Committee appears not to appreciate the distinction between a change in the average price level and a change in relative prices. To prevent inflation, it is necessary to prevent the price level from rising, but it is not necessary (or desirable) to prevent every price from rising.

The relative price of energy has risen substantially in world markets, but this need not cause inflation in the United States. Inflation depends on whether we follow monetary and fiscal policies that increase nominal aggregate demand faster than real capacity, or not. If we do not, sellers will be prepared to move their prices up or down frequently to avoid shortage or surplus, as

41

conditions change. If, on the other hand, whenever the price of some important product rises, monetary and fiscal policies increase nominal aggregate demand so that the average of other prices need not fall, then we will surely have continuous inflation.

My comments on several of the Committee's energy recommendations follow.

On recommendation 1: Price ceilings on energy are unwise. They are not necessary to combat inflation. They promote waste first by encouraging lavish use of a scarce product by those fortunate enough to get it; second, by consuming valuable resources in the attempt to get it; and, third, by encouraging sellers to sell in markets where the marginal value to users is less than in the controlled market.

On recommendations 3 and 14: Mandatory oil allocation by the Federal government is unwise for a similar reason. It allocates too much to some users and too little to others, in the sense that it prevents exchanges that would benefit both parties. The premise in no. 14 is incorrect: the crisis required no extraordinary industry collaboration.

On recommendation 2: If there is consensus that, during a sudden cutback of supply, the use of the price system to allocate gasoline results in intolerable redistribution of real income away from those who have the least satisfactory substitutes for gasoline (note that they are not necessarily the poorest), then either a rationing system with freely marketable coupons, or a tax rebate on a specified number of gallons, is more satisfactory than a rationing system with non-transferable coupons. But neither is needed now.

On recommendation 7, Federal funding of mass transit systems: The following would be preferable. Levy urban road-user charges, higher at peak traffic periods, to cover costs of capital in the road, and congestion. Levy mass transit-user charges on a comparable basis. Then let individuals choose what form of transport they prefer. I recently saw an estimate that the Washington, D.C. transit fare would have to be $2.50 per trip to cover the interest cost alone, allowing nothing for depreciation or operating cost. [4] This suggests that in some situations, mass transit may be too expensive to be worthwhile.

On recommendation 9: Peak-load pricing would improve resource allocation in public utilities, by reducing the capital requirements to generate a given amount of energy, and by apportioning burdens among customers according to the cost imposed by each customer's use. Quantity discounts

---

[4] This is based on a capital cost of $6 billion, which at 8 percent interest implies a $500 million interest cost per year. The Washington SMSA has about 800,000 employed. If 35 percent of these ride the subway twice daily on the average (a ridership approximately equalled by Chicago, exceeded by New York, and approached by no other U.S. city), the number of riders per year will be 35 percent x 2 x 800,000 x 365, namely 200 million. Thus the interest cost per trip would be $500 million ÷ 200 million = $2.50.

should be replaced by a two-part price, one for energy use and one for servicing the account.

On recommendation 11: Oil and mineral firms should be taxed the same way as other firms. The tax preferences the Committee opposes in this item should be abolished, with the exception of the last.

On recommendations 12 and 13: I favor obtaining information about the energy industry and making it publicly available, except for information that private parties legally spent their own funds to amass.

On recommendation 15: Antitrust enforcement is important. Divestiture of pipelines by major producers would make the petroleum industry more like a purely competitive one. But, it should be noted that a large share of the monopoly power of the industry could not be maintained without the assistance of government. The Federal oil import quota and the cartel-like output limitation, imposed through the Texas Railroad Commission, stifled competition and kept prices up. Even so, no firm has more than 10 percent of the U.S. market, and the major firms have had little success in preventing the emergence and growth of cut-rate competitors. I see no objection to establishing a government energy corporation to serve as a yardstick, <u>provided</u> that it is of modest size, and is given no cost advantages over private firms. However, there is not much to be gained from it. It may, like the Post Office or Amtrak, cost a fortune.

On the remaining recommendations: Without further comment, I regard numbers 6, 10, 19, and 20 as desirable; 4 as undesirable; and 5, 8, 15(b), 16, 17, and 18 as of uncertain merit.

The proper policy approach to energy firms (except public utilities) is to deprive them of special tax preferences, deprive them of government-sponsored protection against competition from each other or from abroad, apply the antitrust laws, and require them to be responsible for environmental damage (preferably by user charges). Then let them make as much profit as possible, taxing them and their stockholders under the ordinary progressive tax system.

Credit Allocation

In the 1973 Joint Economic Report, the Committee calls for a stand-by credit allocation system to assure that, in the event of tight money, credit will be available to builders, home-buyers, local governments, and small business (p. 27). "This Committee recommends that the Congress create a National Development Bank to provide adequate funds at reasonable rates of interest for all priority areas of the economy which cannot obtain funds through usual lending channels." (p. 28). Representative Reuss dissents, saying that such a bank " . . . could readily become the vehicle for large-scale bail-outs of mismanaged enterprises." (p. 28). Credit allocation proposals appear in the 1974 report (p. 33), and in APSTEG (pp. 75-76). The minority in 1973 says, ". . . Congress ought to consider what further credit allocation mechanisms could be developed to ease fluctuations in housing finance while causing minimum distortions in the money markets." (p. 110).

Government allocations of credit are like government allocations of oil or anything else--a favor to those who receive them, and an invitation to non-optimal resource allocation. They should be avoided.

An inspiration for these proposals was the difficulty home-buyers faced in borrowing funds. This difficulty arose, in part, because many states have legal ceilings for mortgage interest rates; when market-clearing rates rise above the ceiling, lenders channel their funds elsewhere. It arose, in part, because savings and loan associations and savings banks, which lend long and borrow short, had little money to lend; their portfolios of low-yielding mortgages prevented high yields to savers when market rates rose, and caused savers' withdrawals. One way to avoid this difficulty would be to remove mortgage interest-rate ceilings, and permit rates on mortgages to rise and fall as market rates change. Another way would be to conduct monetary and fiscal policy to keep the average inflation rate at zero, thus keeping nominal interest rates from going so high.

V. EXCHANGE RATES AND THE INTERNATIONAL MONETARY SYSTEM

The Subcommittee on International Exchange and Payments (later called the Subcommittee on International Economics) issued four reports on exchange rates, gold, and Special Drawing Rights (SDRs) in 1971-74 (numbers 517, 583, 606, and 629). In addition, each of the four Joint Economic Reports in 1971-74 addresses this topic. In most cases the proposals made by the Subcommittee appear in the Joint Economic Reports; I will concentrate on the latter, with the following exception.

Report 517 (p. 13) says, "The exchange rates of industrial nations should be realigned to eliminate the existing structural payments deficit of the United States." If the IMF does not do this, ". . . the United States may have no choice but to take unilateral action to go off gold and establish new dollar parities." This report was transmitted August 6, 1971, days before the President suspended convertibility of the dollar into gold. It was a good move, which could have been made years earlier, before we had sold so much gold so cheaply, in real terms.

Report 583, dated November 18, 1972, recommends that SDRs be made acceptable in lieu of gold in all international transactions with the IMF, and that, thereafter, American citizens be permitted to hold gold (pp. 4-5).

There is consensus in the Committee about exchange rates and the international payments system. One of the four Joint Economic Reports (1972) makes separate majority and minority recommendations but these do not clash. In 1971 and 1974, the statements of committee agreement about it are unusually long (12 and 6 pages, respectively). Of the four Subcommittee reports, only one (1971) is not unanimous; the others contain two brief "supplementary views," each a page long.

The view of the Committee is that exchange rate adjustments should be small and frequent (more recently, that the dollar should float, cleanly in the long run); that SDRs should replace gold and the dollar as the main international reserve asset (though the Committee realizes that some countries will want to hold some gold); and (in 1974) that the official gold price should be abolished.

These are wise recommendations (with one reservation, noted below). The issue of fixed vs. flexible exchange rates is not black and white. It is clear that, unless all other countries stabilize their price levels successfully, U.S. exchange rates ought not to be fixed forever. Fixed rates would force us to adjust to major payments disturbances (such as inflation or depression abroad) in ways that are inferior to exchange-rate adjustments, namely, undergoing imported monetary expansion and contraction, or imposing restrictions on international trade and capital movements, or both. Once it is decided that exchange rates are not to be fixed forever, then the question becomes-is it better to have exchange-rate uncertainty in small frequent doses under flexible rates, or to have it concentrated, under fixed rates, in large doses, at times when countries have severe deficits or surpluses, and must decide either to change the exchange rate or to defend it (by controls and/or a change in domestic macroeconomic policy)? On the whole, I prefer flexible rates; but, except during unsettled times such as the present, when flexible rates are imperative, either system is workable.

The reservation is that, in taking another step to divorce the world's monetary systems from gold, we are permitting more scope for monetary policy decisions that create inflation. The IMF is a new addition to the list of issuers of paper money (SDRs), and it is possible that the IMF might issue SDRs so fast as to add to world inflation. If this should happen, it would be important for the United States to reserve, and use, the right to appreciate the dollar against SDRs.

VI. SUMMARY AND CONCLUSION

The Committee shows sophisticated understanding of many aspects of fiscal and monetary policy, and concern for the objectives of price-level stability and a high average level of employment. It is seriously handicapped (as national economic policy has been since the early 1960s) by the illusion that it is possible to obtain a permanent reduction in unemployment, to about 4 percent, by accepting a modest inflation at a constant rate. Actually, if we accept any constant average rate of inflation, unemployment will, after a lag average about 5 percent, a little less if the right measures are taken. But, if we insist on monetary and fiscal policies aimed at keeping unemployment at 4 percent continuously, we will generate ever-accelerating inflation. Zero inflation would be preferable.

The Fiscal Policy Subcommittee's proposal to substitute a form of the negative income tax for the present welfare system, and the Committee's proposals for taxing people having the same income equally would, in my opinion, represent major steps forward.

In dealing with microeconomics - - international trade, agriculture, energy, and credit availability - - the Committee is too ready, in my opinion (along with the Congress) to assume that, when a problem arises, the Federal government has the capacity and the responsibility to solve it; and too ready to accept the claims of every group in the economy that, when there are changes in tastes, or technology, or the availability of resources, or population, every group should be protected from the effects of such changes. Government should provide basic freedom and opportunity, but should not try to solve every problem (especially insoluble ones); nor should it suppress competition to create or perpetuate the economic position of any group.

The Committee's proposals for small and frequent exchange rate adjustments are to be applauded. The proposals to substitute SDRs for gold as an international currency could free gold for other uses, but there is the possibility of more inflation if SDRs are issued too rapidly.

The work of the Joint Economic Committee has raised the level of economic literacy inside and outside the Federal government. As a study, rather than a legislative, committee, it has examined economic issues in comparative isolation from the parochial views of individual citizens and interest groups. It has assisted in the establishment of the new House and Senate Budget Committees. It has helped to bring attention to the influence that monetary policy has upon the economy. I believe it is a valuable institution, and should be maintained.

APPENDIX

List of Reports Published by the Joint Economic Committee
and Its Subcommittees
of the 92nd, 93rd, and 94th Congresses,
January, 1971 to February, 1975

(Excludes Hearings, Staff Studies, and Other Studies)

Note: Numbers in the left margin are for use when requesting single copies from the Committee.

507   Joint Economic Report on the 1971 Economic Report of the President. March 30, 1971. 152 p. (S. Report 92-49.)

517   Action Now to Strengthen the U.S. Dollar. Report on the Subcommittee on International Exchange and Payments, August 1971. 19 p. Y4.EC7:D69.

519   The 1971 Midyear Review of the Economy. Report, August 16, 1971. 31 p.

527   Report on Crude Oil and Gasoline Price Increases of November 1970: A Background Study. November 3, 1971, 102 p.

540   The Joint Economic Report on the 1972 Economic Report of the President. March 23, 1972. 159 p. (S. Report 92-708).

571   American Productivity: Key to Economic Strength and National Survival. Report of the Subcommittee on Priorities and Economy in Government. July 3, 1972.

573   Price and Wage Control: An Interim Report. Report of the Joint Economic Committee. May 22, 1972. 32 p. Y4.EC7:P93/12.

581   The 1972 Midyear Review of the Economy. Report. August 28, 1972. 40 p. Y4.EC7:EC7/28/972.

583   Gold, SDR's and Central Bank Swaps. Report of the Subcommittee on International Exchange and Payments. November 18, 1972, 16 p. Y4.EC7:G56/3.

588   Price and Wage Control: Evaluation of a Year's Experience. Report. December 14, 1972. 28 p. Y4.EC7:P93/13.

591   Housing Subsidies and Housing Policy. Report of the Subcommittee on Priorities and Economy in Government. March 5, 1973. 36 p. Y4.EC7:H81/2.

594   Federal Transportation Policy: The SST Again. Report of the Subcommittee on Priorities and Economy in Government. March 16, 1973. 24 p. Y4.EC7:T68/2.

595   The 1973 Joint Economic Report. Report on the President's Economic Report. March 26, 1973. 140 p. (H. Report 93-90).

600   A New Initiative to Liberalize International Trade. Report of the Subcommittee on International Economics. March 8, 1973. 32 p. Y4.EC7:IN8/18.

606   How Well Are Fluctuating Exchange Rates Working? Report of the Subcommittee on International Economics. August 14, 1973. 16 p. 5270-01938.

629   Making Floating Part of a Reformed Monetary System. Report of the Subcommittee on International Economics. January 9, 1974. 20 p. 5270-02138.

636   A Reappraisal of U.S. Energy Policy. Report of the Subcommittees on Consumer Economics, International Economics, and Priorities and Economy in Government. March 8, 1974. 56 p. 5270-02243.

640   The 1974 Joint Economic Report. Report of the Joint Economic Committee on the February 1974 Economic Report of the President. March 25, 1974. 152 p. (H. Report 93-927).

654   An Action Program to Reduce Inflation and Restore Economic Growth. Interim Report of the Joint Economic Committee. September 21, 1974. 56 p. Cat. No. Y4.EC7:IN3/4. Stock No. 5270-02536.

660   Income Security for Americans: Recommendations of the Public Welfare Study. Report of the Subcommittee on Fiscal Policy. December 20, 1974. 272 p. Stock No. 5270-02636.

663 Achieving Price Stability Through Economic Growth. A Report of the Joint Economic Committee. Pursuant to S. Con. Res. 93. House Report No. 93-1653. December 23, 1974. 152 p. Stock No. 5271-00430.

REFERENCE

1. Stigler, G.J., "The Theory of Economic Regulation," The Bell Journal of Economics and Management Science, Vol. 2, No. 1, (Spring 1971), 3-21.

AN EVALUATION OF
THE ECONOMIC POLICY PROPOSALS OF THE
JOINT ECONOMIC COMMITTEE OF THE
92ND AND 93RD CONGRESSES: A COMMENT

Jerry J. Jasinowski,* Senior Research Economist
Joint Economic Committee
Congress of the United States

Continuing the biblical analogy, I would say that Christ's paper, evaluating the Joint Economic Committee, is like the trials of Job, requiring patience, wisdom, and a not insignificant amount of faith. It certainly took enormous patience to read all the Committee's reports, wisdom to sift the good from the bad, and faith in economics as a science to use it so boldly in the political arena. I applaud Christ's effort as both stimulating and useful.

Having said that, I would be quick to add that Christ's paper is not, in my opinion, the Book of Job on the Joint Economic Committee. There are sins of both omission and commission that make the paper unsuitable for judging whether the JEC should be granted salvation, or banished to purgatory.

I see no point in commenting on those subject areas where Christ gave the Committee high marks, such as the budgetary process, welfare reform, tax reform, exchange rates, and so forth. Nor do I choose to discuss areas where he was somewhat critical of the Committee - - such as interest rates - - but where I find myself in substantial agreement with his critique. Rather, I will focus on four areas where I do not find Christ's criticism of the Committee acceptable: (1) The optimal allocation of resources; (2) monetary and fiscal policy and the business cycle; (3) wage-price policies; (4) unemployment and inflation.

I. OPTIMAL ALLOCATION OF RESOURCES ·

Christ's discussion of the optimal allocation of resources, i.e., policy recommendations to increase efficiency in both the public and private sectors, does not give the JEC its just due. Having noted some of the recommendations for increased efficiency the JEC has made, and lauded them, Christ minimizes the importance of these recommendations by saying, "Unfortunately, they do

---

* The views expressed herein are those of the author and are not necessarily shared by the staff or members of the Joint Economic Committee.

not command ardent lobbying support . . . . " So what? The degree of lobbying that emerges for the Committee's recommendations is irrelevant in evaluating the recommendations themselves. The Committee's role is to bring economic information to the attention of Congress and the public.

In a similar vein, Christ makes too much of the few cases where the JEC gave only qualified support to the principles of free trade and efficiency. The fact that the Committee recommended limited adjustment assistance in conjunction with a move toward free trade could mean more efficiency, rather than less, as implied by Christ. It might mean more free trade and fewer bankrupt firms, for example.

Christ takes a rather simple view of how one achieves efficiency, in areas such as agriculture, with the implication that efficiency is maximized by a completely free market. I do not share this view, in part because the supply/demand factors in U.S. agriculture are likely to lead to wasteful swings in prices and output, and in part because world agriculture trade does not occur in a free market when there are market economies trading with command economies. For these reasons, as outlined in recent JEC reports, there is a substantial role for government in agriculture, stabilizing farm prices, managing a grain reserve, and managing our exports in periods of short supplies in such a way as to avoid export controls.

Christ's evaluation of the JEC recommendations on efficiency misses the mark because it downplays the strong recommendations the Committee has made, and overplays, or oversimplifies, the JEC's recommendations that deviate from a simple efficiency criterion. In my opinion, the JEC, particularly under the leadership of Senator Proxmire, has been an extraordinary voice for efficiency in the deliberations of the Congress.

II. MONETARY AND FISCAL POLICY AND BUSINESS CYCLES

Christ's evaluation of the discretionary use of monetary and fiscal policy to moderate the business cycle is so negative that he believes the Committee should suspend such recommendations. I suggest that this is an unjustified conclusion, arising out of Christ's tendency to confuse what the JEC has recommended with what the government as a whole has yielded. While I do not shirk from putting a large part of economic policy responsibility upon the JEC, it seems an extreme position to make the Committee responsible for the rest of Congress, the Federal Reserve, and the President.

Let us look at what the JEC has recently recommended in the way of counter-cyclical monetary and fiscal policy.

With respect to monetary policy, the Committee has supported a steady monetary policy rather than frequent changes aimed at correcting short-term fluctuations in the economy. When the Committee has deviated from this position, because the Federal Reserve's monetary policies have been deficient -- which has been all too frequent -- it has made recommendations to get the Fed back on a sensible track. Criticisms of monetary policy belong primarily at the doorstep of the Federal Reserve, not that of the Joint Economic Committee.

The constructive role played by the JEC in monetary policy can be seen, for example, in the recommendations made in the second half of 1974. During this period, the Fed was conducting an extremely restrictive monetary policy, with the conventionally defined money supply growing at less than a 1 percent annual rate. On September 21, 1973, the Committee called for a "moderate shift toward less restrictive monetary policy. . . ." On December 23, 1974, in view of the continued tight monetary policy of the Fed, the Committee indicated that a rate of growth in the money supply of 6 to 7 percent was necessary.

That Christ criticizes these conservative recommendations, designed to get us back to normal monetary growth, is puzzling. In view of the Fed's retardation of the growth of the money supply in the second half of 1974, the JEC's recommendations would yield an annual rate of increase in the money supply of approximately 4 percent -- not extraordinary considering this was the worst economic slump since the Depression. What would Christ have us do instead? Ignore the near-zero growth of money supply in the second half of 1974? Stick to a 2 to 6 percent range for M_1 in the future, no matter what had been the rate in the past, or the state of the economy? To do so, in my view, would be to make monetary policy too mechanistic for public policy.

An equally constructive role can be documented in the recommendations of the Committee in the fiscal policy area. Without looking carefully at the timing of JEC fiscal policy recommendations, Christ criticizes fiscal policy as tending to occur too late in the cycle. The fact is that the JEC has been ahead of everyone in government circles, and of most private economists, in spotting the current recession and calling for prompt fiscal action. The fact that others, particularly the Executive, did not respond is not evidence that the JEC has not made sensible fiscal policy recommendations.

The Committee's fiscal policy recommendation submitted in March, 1974, was right on the mark:

> It is of the utmost importance that measures be taken immediately to counter the recession which is already emerging. . . . Congress should enact a tax cut of approximately $10 million. . . . The net effect of the tax and spending changes proposed by the Committee should be to maintain an unchanged full employment

budget surplus from 1974 to 1975 instead of increasing it as the Administration has proposed (Economic Report, p. 30).

The Committee was recommending a tax cut early in the downturn of the cycle - - about a year before the Administration did so. This tax cut was not prompt in coming because the Administration, and many members of the economics profession, did not support such a cut. But the shortsightedness of others is not our responsibility, and makes no case for the JEC's quitting the fiscal policy business.

III. WAGE-PRICE POLICY

"The Committee's defense of controls consists chiefly in deploring infla-tion and asserting that it must be checked," says Christ. This implies (a) that the JEC has been a staunch supporter of wage-price controls, and (b) that this support has been based on a simpleminded view of how to stop inflation. Here we have a sin of commission--Christ attributes a point of view to the JEC that the Committee itself has not taken.

The Committee has been quite restrained in its support of wage and price controls. Its position has been that controls are a limited policy instrument, useful only for short periods, and under special circumstances. In the 1974 annual report, for example, the Committee said:

> We have always believed that compulsory controls would be pri-marily effective as a short-run tool for dampening inflationary expectations and preventing the abuse of market power. Controls should not be maintained over a long period of time, absent a national emergency (p. 38).

Similar caveats run through the JEC reports along with considerable discussion of the circumstances under which controls would be appropriate and effective. The Committee argues that wage-price controls could only be effective in a period when there is no excess aggregate demand. In short, the Committee's position on the appropriate situation for controls is not unlike that supported by Christ.

While the Committee has not been an unqualified supporter of controls, it has tried to evaluate their effectiveness. In our recent APSTEG report, for example, the Committee examined the evidence evaluating controls for the periods for which studies were available, and, while acknowledging that there were substantial costs and inefficiencies to controls,concluded that the benefits were greater. The Committee also concluded the benefits would have been enhanced had the wage-price program been properly managed.

Christ concludes that the JEC evaluations of controls were inadequate because they examined only the controls period and not that following. This is a valid criticism. But, instead of providing any evidence on the deficiencies of controls, or on the effect on prices after controls were removed, Christ only speculates on their ineffectiveness.

It is my view that we are never going to satisfactorily answer the question: were controls effective? Exogenous food and energy shortages, currency devaluations, overstimulative monetary policy, and mismanagement of the controls system, occurring as they did in the controls period, blurred the impact of controls. In view of these uncertainties, and of the econometric studies that have been made, the Committee took a _modest_ position that controls had some favorable impact. On what appears to be less evidence, Christ _unequivocally_ concludes that controls did not and will not work. The Committee's position strikes me as far more judicious given the uncertainties in this area.

IV. INFLATION AND UNEMPLOYMENT

Christ charges that the inflation-unemployment debate in this country has been, and continues to be, handicapped by the pursuit of unrealistic goals for unemployment and inflation. I think he is right, but I cannot decide which is more unrealisitc: the JEC's 1971 long-term goals of 3 percent unemployment and 2 percent inflation; Christ's current goal of zero inflation; or the Administration's goal of 8 percent unemployment in 1976, and 6 percent unemployment in 1980.

If the Committee has been overly ambitious with respect to its long-term goals of unemployment and inflation, it has not, as Christ believes, ". . .made an extremely serious mistake in selecting as its twin long-term goals an unemployment rate of 3 or 4 percent or less at all times, coupled with a fixed stated upper limit on the inflation rate."

A close reading of the Committee's recent reports reveals a great deal of flexibility on short-term inflation and unemployment goals. The December 1974, APSTEG report, for example, indicated that 7 percent unemployment in 1976 was a realistic goal. Moreover, the Committee has never linked inflation and unemployment on the crude Phillips curve Christ describes. The Committee's record reflects a deeper understanding of inflation and its relation to unemployment, with the realization that inflation can occur, and persist, without strong aggregate demand to pull output and employment up.

Regardless of the JEC's views on the relation of inflation to unemployment, the fact remains that satisfactory levels of each have proved to be incompatible. The operative policy issue remains: why are they incompatible and what can be done about it?

Christ says low rates of unemployment and inflation are incompatible because economic policy suffers from inflation illusion, ". . .the view that whenever the rate of inflation is positive, real aggregate demand for output and labor is high relative to capacity, and vice versa." But this is not true, according to Christ, because output is not maintained at a high level in the face of a constant rate of inflation. Why? "Buyers and sellers come to expect the higher rate of inflation to continue, and sellers of goods and labor no longer regard price increases of that magnitude as evidence of abnormally high real demand. Hence, the levels of capacity utilization and employment decline toward more normal levels."

Perhaps Christ is right; we do not know enough about the inflationary process to dismiss this idea. Christ's paper raises more questions than it answers. Why shouldn't sellers adjust to this constant rate of inflation? What actions are buyers taking in this environment? Why should there be a general retrenchment in output unless we are dealing with an unanticipated inflation?

It is difficult to find support for Christ's inflation model in the 1966-1973 period he cites for illustration. He argues that unemployment began to increase after 1969 because buyers and sellers began to expect continued inflation. I submit other reasons why unemployment rose during this period. Aggregate demand was down because there was a recession in 1970 and well into 1971. There was also an extraordinary increase in the labor force for the period 1969-1973. It remains to be seen whether inflation had much to do with increasing unemployment during this period. (See Table 1.)

The JEC's view of the relationship between inflation and unemployment is more eclectic than Christ's. Aggregate demand inflation can drive output up and unemployment down. Large unanticipated inflation, on the other hand, as we had with the OPEC oil price increase, can lower consumer real income, lower output, and raise unemployment. Inflation and unemployment can move relatively independent of one another because of structural imperfections in product and factor markets. It is this last possibility that caused the Committee to advocate selective policy actions on both the price and unemployment side.

Table 1

Selected Economic Statistics

Year	Unemployment (percent)	CPI*	GNPD*[1]	GNP*	(1958 $) GNP*	M_1*	FES**[2]	CLF*[3]
1961	6.7	1.0	1.3	3.2	1.9	1.6	10.0	1.2
1962	5.5	1.1	1.1	7.7	6.7	2.3	5.7	0.2
1963	5.7	1.2	1.3	5.4	4.2	2.6	10.1	1.7
1964	5.2	1.3	1.6	7.1	5.7	4.2	2.8	1.8
1965	4.5	1.7	1.8	8.3	6.6	4.6	2.4	1.9
1966	3.8	2.8	2.8	9.5	6.4	3.5	-2.6	1.8
1967	3.8	2.8	3.2	5.9	2.3	4.5	-10.0	2.1
1968	3.6	4.2	4.0	8.9	4.8	7.3	-5.6	1.8
1969	3.5	5.3	4.8	7.6	2.8	5.6	8.8	2.5
1970	4.9	5.9	5.5	5.0	-0.5	4.8	4.0	2.5
1971	5.9	4.2	4.5	8.0	3.6	6.2	-1.5	1.7
1972	5.6	3.2	3.4	9.8	6.7	7.5	-10.3	2.9
1973	4.9	6.2	5.6	11.8	6.2	7.4	2.8	2.5
1974	5.6	10.9	10.2	7.9	-2.6	5.3	23.4	2.6

*   Percent change
** Billions of dollars
[1] Gross National Product Deflator
[2] Full Employment Surplus
[3] Civilian Labor Force

REFERENCES

1. _Achieving Price Stability Through Economic Growth_. A Report of the Joint Economic Committee. December 23, 1974. 152 p. (H. Rept. 93-1653).

2. _The 1974 Joint Economic Report_. Report of the Joint Economic Committee on the February 1974 Economic Report of the President. March 25, 1974. 152 p. (H. Rept. 93-927).

AN EVALUATION OF
THE ECONOMIC POLICY PROPOSALS OF THE
JOINT ECONOMIC COMMITTEE OF THE
92ND AND 93RD CONGRESSES: A COMMENT

Robert E. Weintraub,* Staff Director
U.S. House of Representatives
Subcommittee on Domestic Monetary Policy of
the Committee on Banking, Currency and Housing

Christ criticizes the JEC's 1971-74 analyses of and proposals to combat inflation and unemployment. He states, ". . .the Committee has made an extremely serious mistake in selecting as its twin long-term goals an unemployment rate of 3 or 4 percent or less at all times, coupled with a fixed stated upper limit on the inflation rate." This is not entirely fair to the JEC. The Committee is disturbed both when unemployment exceeds 4 percent and when inflation exceeds about 5 percent. But it does not follow that there is no consensus that an unemployment rate of 4 percent or less is "at all times" compatible with inflation less than some stated rate.

The Committee's policy recommendations are formulated in response to a particular pressing situation. Since it promulgated the 2-6 percent M_1 growth guidelines in the late 1960s (and it seems to have abandoned or ignored them recently), the Committee has not considered the question: does, as Christ contends, the attempt to achieve 4 percent or less unemployment generate accelerating inflation? I would like to see the Committee re-explore this crucial question. If it does, I hope that it again, as in the late 1960s, agrees with Christ's contention.

The Committee has not taken a position on the matter in recent years. Rather, disturbed by high rates of unemployment or inflation, or both, the Committee has followed its natural short-run orientation, concentrating on the most pressing problems. This approach can lead to trouble in the long run. Nevertheless, I think Jasinowski is right that, for the most part, the Committee's specific year-to-year M_1 growth proposals have been designed to correct Fed errors, though occasionally they have been error aggravating, as in 1972-73.

Christ pinpoints the long-run nature of the inflation-unemployment nexus as the crucial macro-policy question. In analyzing the causes of a particular wave of inflation, one can and should be a short-run eclectic and a long-run (3 years or more) monetarist. In my view, Christ has analyzed the inflation-unemployment connection correctly - - 4 percent or less unemployment is not always

* At the time of the Conference, Dr. Weintraub was on the Committee on Banking, Housing and Urban Affairs, U.S. Senate.

consistent with inflation below some stated limit. Attempting to achieve "at all times" 4 percent or less unemployment necessarily leads to accelerating inflation. Additionally, I believe that over a generation such a policy would result in higher average unemployment than if, as Christ suggests, we ". . .set a zero average inflation rate as our goal."

To understand Christ's awful truth, assume that a policy to accept higher inflation in order to lower unemployment were adopted. If the policy is successful, then, as expectations adjust to the new reality, the so-called Phillips curve shifts up - - the new higher rate of inflation becomes paired with a higher rate of unemployment than the rate previously achieved. In trying to reachieve the lower rate of unemployment, the rate of inflation accelerates, and higher and higher rates are paired with given unemployment rates. Trying to achieve a permanent, arbitrary unemployment rate lower than the prevailing rate results in accelerating inflation. Therefore, I can see no room for disagreement with Christ when he writes, "Economic policy regarding unemployment and inflation. . .is severely hampered by an illusion. It is the illusion. . .that it is possible to obtain a permanent reduction in the level of unemployment by accepting a higher constant rate of inflation." (Emphasis in the original.)

Given this awful truth, what should be done? The JEC suggests structural and institutional reforms to improve price and wage flexibility, and to increase price and wage elasticities. I believe that the major reform required is to end the economics of expediency. If it were understood that government would not respond more aggressively to recession than to inflation, then wages and prices might be more responsive to excess supply than currently.

I agree with Christ's belief that if the minimum wage were eliminated and the welfare system restructured, ". . .unemployment rates would be reduced." Further, I would recommend eliminating the tax on wage payments, in stages, as the easiest way to push the Phillips curves and line inward.

Christ opposes the Committee's recommendations of controls to check inflation. With Christ, I believe controls can flatten Phillips curves or pull them down for no more than a few months, time to get anti-inflationary macro-policies in place. Without such policies, controls are counter-productive within a year. This is a lesson of history.

A more important lesson is that controls are unnecessary. Prudent macro-policy can achieve maximum employment and stable prices, not "at all times" but in the long run. Given existing rigidities and elasticities, maximum employment means about 5 percent, and 4 percent if we eliminate expedient economics and make some structural reforms, and, above all, stop trying to move along short-run Phillips curves. Too often the policy adopted for moving along one curve is wrong for the curve as altered by policy. Christ comments correctly,

"The Committee gives insufficient attention to this risk."

It would be preferable if the budget deficit were a determined rather than a determining variable; this is not to say that tax reform, including indexing, is useless. It would be better still to set M_1 growth commensurate with the economy's long-run potential to increase production. Starting from 5 percent unemployment, this means 3 1/2 to 4 percent per year under prevailing labor force and productivity trends. (Note velocity trends and patterns are ignored, as they should be, especially if they are random.)

As a matter of arithmetic, not economics, starting from 9 percent unemployment, it could mean 16 percent M_1 growth the next year, or 10 percent per year the next two years, or 8 percent per year the next three, 7 the next four, 6 the next six, and so on, where the percents equal 4 percent for each year plus (using Okun's law as a first approximation) 12 percent to reduce unemployment to 5 percent, with the total divided by the number of years. I would recommend reaching 6 percent year-over-year by June and dropping gradually thereafter to 4; or alternatively, 8 percent next year, 7 the year after, 6 the third year, 5 1/2 the fourth, and so on, reaching 4 in the seventh year, and remaining at that rate - - allowing variance of ± 1 percent in any given year.

These simple measures can restore maximum employment without reigniting inflation. Short-run policies to maximize employment that tend to reignite inflation, as the stimulus confronts bottleneck sectors and markets, should be rejected. Reignited inflation impels speculative inventory build-ups at the same time it programs a fall in real spending by eroding the purchasing power of fixed incomes and assets. Inflation will, therefore, make average unemployment higher, not lower, over the long run. Christ understands this. Specifically, he states, "The lesson of inflation for the United States is that we will stop the process of continuous inflation if, and only if, we manage our monetary-fiscal policy in such a way that nominal aggregate demand does not on the average grow faster than real total output."

AN EVALUATION OF
THE ECONOMIC POLICY PROPOSALS OF THE
JOINT ECONOMIC COMMITTEE OF THE
92ND AND 93RD CONGRESSES: A COMMENT

William Cox
Joint Economic Committee
Congress of the United States

Christ's critique is striking for its blithe manner of overlooking the constraints of "political reality" that loom large in perceptions here. Moreover, he ignores the context of politics and events in which these recommendations were made. Though he is generally in accord with our energy recommendations, he quarrels with those on price controls. I try here to review some of the constraints on this issue.

New Oil Price Ceilings. It is understood that one does not attack inflation by approaching the price of each commodity individually. The Committee's recommendation of ceilings on oil prices was first made, however, in March 1974, when arbitrary oil price increases had just added an estimated 3 percent to the already appalling annual rate of inflation and were sapping rates of economic activity. At the time, it was felt that restraint on domestic oil prices could make a worthwhile contribution to stabilizing both production and price levels. The recommendation was repeated in December 1974 when some members of OPEC were discussing further increases in the world price.

The Committee also felt that a more gradual change in domestic oil prices would be more equitable, limiting the growth in windfall rents to domestic producers and factor suppliers, and cushioning the burden upon consumers. Theorists, like Christ, can say that we should deal with the problems of low-income consumers by redistributing income, but the fact remains that economic hardship exists in America and is likely to continue. Christ points out that unemployment has never been stabilized below 4 percent; I point out that income redistribution has never been very successful. The JEC did not believe that a restriction in the rate of oil price increases would exert significant deterrence to output expansion. Profits were very high. The industry would use its limited physical resources to exploit the ample lower-cost opportunities first, and it was felt by the Committee that pouring more money into the industry would bid up oil exploration and development costs without yielding more oil (as indeed has occurred). Christ is concerned about encouraging ". . . lavish use of a scarce product . . ." through price ceilings. What of the effect of pouring lavish sums of money into an industry with limited physical resources?

The Committee's recommendations concerning oil price ceilings also must be viewed in the context of political realities regarding natural gas prices. Increases in oil prices were likely to mitigate, politically, <u>against</u> increases in prices of natural gas. Does it not make sense, therefore, to work toward consolidating these two prices at some intermediate level (e.g., $7-8 per barrel of oil and the equivalent for gas), rather than permitting the present gross disparity to continue, or to increase? The latter policy permits oil producers to bid prices of drilling and pipeline equipment and manpower - - not to mention mineral rights - - to levels above those at which they can be employed for producing natural gas at interstate prices. This policy also discriminates against consumers of oil relative to users of gas.

Therefore, I do not believe that we can shrug off the need for fuel price controls and permit all prices to go to whatever level OPEC chooses to set. If we retain price controls, then the need for supply allocation follows. Congress is now addressing the issue of how long to retain controls, and under what conditions, if any, to terminate them.

<u>Federal Funding for Mass Transit</u>. Christ's suggestion of user charges for highways is well taken and accords with the general case for peak-load pricing of any service. If, however, the cost of auto trips in the inner city, including interest costs on the land value, construction expense, and maintenance, were calculated, I question whether the comparison with mass transit would favor the highway, particularly if the external economies from elimination of auto pollution, noise, and congestion are counted.

AN EVALUATION OF
THE ECONOMIC POLICY PROPOSALS OF THE
JOINT ECONOMIC COMMITTEE OF THE
92ND AND 93RD CONGRESSES: A COMMENT

Walter Dolde
Carnegie-Mellon University

Christ's analysis of the JEC and recent economic policy is an heroic accomplishment, both thoughtful and thought-provoking. Inferring the intent of policy, however, has always been fraught with danger and open to alternative interpretations. I want to suggest three points on which the issues are not as clear-cut as Christ's paper implies.

First, it is important to distinguish between attempts to use discretionary policy to drive employment and output above their normal levels from attempts to return employment and output to normal levels. The latter implies the use of restrictive policies when appropriate. Certainly many advocates of discretionary policy called for restrictive measures starting in 1965. In situations like the Vietnam buildup, where exogenous forces influence the economy primarily through the government sector, advocates of both rules and discretion agree that offsetting policy measures are required. When exogenous forces have their first impact on the private sectors of the economy, however, fixed rule advocates would not have policy variables respond, while discretion advocates would favor a response.

Christ characterizes those who would use discretionary policy to maintain employment permanently above its normal level as victims of inflation illusion - - the belief that non-accelerating price changes are also feasible. Some research-ers have raised the possibility, however, that the normal level of employment might itself be influenced by macroeconomic events. Accelerator effects on investment which change the path of the capital-labor ratio would change the real wage, the opportunity cost of job search, and the normal level of employment. Human capital built up through on-the-job training might also change the normal level of employment. As in economic growth theory, the transitions between steady states are less well-articulated and understood than are the steady states themselves.

Second, I want to distinguish between comparisons across steady states and comparisons among alternative steady states we might achieve, starting from the current initial conditions. Christ advocates, without qualification, the attainment of the steady state corresponding to zero inflation. He has not indicated how long employment must remain below its normal level nor how much output must be foregone to achieve a zero inflation rate. Neither has he suggested what rate of social time preference would justify his policy prescription. Like the golden rule, zero inflation may be the optimal steady state - - hardly a settled issue itself - - but it may not be worth achieving from arbitrary initial conditions.

Last, it is useful to ask whether discretionary policy has had a stabilizing effect or not. The critical issue here is the modeling of expectations. In common with many other researchers, Christ views expectations as rather sophomoric. Economic agents do well on price expectations, eventually distinguishing general inflation or deflation from relative price changes. With regard to output, however, agents are continually surprised by attempted counter-cyclical policy change. Christ concludes that these measures have been destabilizing, have come late, and have reinforced recovery tendencies in the economy. An alternative view is that agents expect and allow for certain policy behavior when output has been driven away from its normal level. With protracted, extreme periods of divergence from normal output ruled out by discretionary policy, those deviations which do occur are correctly expected to be mild and of short duration, thus generating smaller endogenous multiplier-accelerator responses.

This alternative provides one explanation for the precipitous decline in output and employment in late 1974. From 1973:IV to 1974:I the economy suffered an initial output decline of 15.2 billion 1958 dollars due to energy and related problems. Output demand by households and firms proceeded at a moderate pace in the expectation that policy would offset any protracted aggregate demand shortfall. By the third quarter of 1974 as monetary policy became increasingly restrictive and the administration discussed a tax increase rather than a tax cut, households and firms recognized that they had been fooled by policy which would not be used in the manner they had come to expect. Postponable commitments, particularly consumer ($-14.1 billion) and producer ($-5.6 billion) durable goods, were put off, and the recession set in rapidly.

AN EVALUATION OF
THE ECONOMIC POLICY PROPOSALS OF THE
JOINT ECONOMIC COMMITTEE OF THE
92ND AND 93RD CONGRESSES: A COMMENT

John R. Karlik, Senior Economist
Joint Economic Committee
Congress of the United States

Christ has presented a comprehensive and constructive evaluation of the policy recommendations offered by the Joint Economic Committee during the 92nd and 93rd Congresses. The staff and, I am sure, the Members of the Committee are grateful for this serious critique of our work. Criticism of this type is perhaps the most effective way of helping us both to adopt policies that make economic sense and to communicate the rationale underlying our policies to the general public. Throughout his commentary, Christ makes complimentary observations about the policy positions of the Joint Economic Committee; for these, too, we are grateful. While arguing with some of his criticisms, I hope that in accepting these compliments, I can avoid the impression of churlishness.

I shall focus my comments on two sets of JEC policy recommendations that Christ criticized: first, our joint unemployment and inflation objectives; and second, recommendations to lower interest rates. Perhaps his most serious criticism is directed at the joint inflation and unemployment targets:

> In my view, the Committee has made an extremely serious mistake in selecting as its twin long-term goals an unemployment rate of 3 or 4 percent or less at all times, coupled with a fixed stated upper limit on the inflation rate. The two are simply incompatible in the United States economy. . . .This mistake renders successful macroeconomic policy almost impossible.

He ascribes this apparent error to a phenomenon termed "inflation illusion," a concept I shall discuss presently.

Regarding feasible long-run equilibria, Christ apparently believes that the Phillips curve is vertical:

> . . .suppose that the economy has become adjusted to an inflation rate of 10 percent. . . .Then, there is no reason to expect the normal or average level of unemployment to differ from what it was under stable price expectations.

But, he continues:

> As argued above, any desired rate of inflation can be maintain-
> ed; and the level of unemployment, in the long run, is largely
> unaffected by what constant rate of inflation is chosen.

The latter statement implies that the Phillips curve is horizontal rather than vertical, if we assign the rate of inflation to the Y axis and the unemployment rate to the X. These two statements can be reconciled only at the single point in the quadrant that is Christ's long-run inevitable inflation-unemployment equilibrium.

Alternatively, the apparent contradiction can be reconciled by asserting that there is no functional relationship between unemployment and inflation rates. For example, the rate of inflation could be determined by the growth of the money supply, and unemployment could be determined by entirely different structural factors. But if there is no functional relationship - - and any plot only produces a random scatter - - then what is Christ complaining about? Changes in the rate of inflation will then alter nominal variables only, and the real world will proceed unaffected.

Christ contends, however, that there is an inflation-unemployment link:

> Monetary and fiscal policy can affect the unemployment rate,
> but cannot hold it continuously at or below an arbitrarily low
> rate such as 4 percent, in the United States, without continu-
> ously accelerating inflation.

He never outlines the workings of this link, nor does he explain the mechanism through which short-term deviations evolve toward his long-term equilibria.

Further, Christ states:

> Economic policy regarding unemployment and inflation . . . is
> severely hampered by an illusion. It is the illusion, shared by
> the Committee and others, that it is possible to obtain a per-
> manent reduction in the level of unemployment by accepting
> a higher constant rate of inflation. I call it "inflation illusion."
> (Emphasis in the original.)

It is difficult to understand why Christ charges the Joint Economic Committee with entertaining this illusion, since we have maintained that, through appro-priate structural changes, it should be possible over the long run to reduce both unemployment and inflation rates. For example, in the 1972 Annual Report, the Committee recommended that:

> An unemployment rate no higher than 3 percent remains an appropriate long-run target for the United States. If the necessary structural and institutional reforms are undertaken, a combination of a rate of unemployment below 3 percent and inflation rate . . . no higher than 2 percent can be achieved and sustained (p. 15).

Christ goes on to give two additional definitions of "inflation illusion" that jibe neither with one another nor with his earlier definition (above). He says that inflation illusion is the cousin of money illusion. While the latter reflects a lag in economic understanding on the part of businessmen and workers, the former, according to Christ, is a fantasy of economists.

While Christ discusses the possibility of structural reforms that would improve the unemployment-inflation mix, he fails to consider the likelihood or feasibility of such reforms; he dismisses them instead with the observation that the increase in output resulting from a reduction in the average level of unemployment might be less than one would expect because some unemployed workers indeed do productive things. This observation hardly meets the issue.

From 1971 to the onset of the recession, Administration economists argued that structural changes had occurred in the U.S. economy that made it impossible to return to previously conceived full employment goals without producing intolerably high rates of inflation - - not unlike what Professor Christ has maintained. The Joint Economic Committee saw its responsibility to resist this conclusion. Although it is difficult to demonstrate, we have believed that if the full costs were known - - in terms of higher rates of unemployment and inflation resulting from lack of competition, government regulations, and other rigidities - - politicians and the public would be willing to implement reforms far more painful than those that have been adopted to eliminate these market imperfections. Therefore, we have established joint unemployment-inflation goals as appropriate long-run objectives of structural reform.

Regarding the link between productivity and recession, Christ writes:

> The statement that a significant cause of the 1973-74 inflation is the recession, because productivity falls in recession, and the decline in productivity causes inflation (APSTEG, p. 80), is extraordinary . . . . This erroneous idea is worth special mention, because the Committee gives it repeated emphasis.*

---

*Editors' note: Karlik is quoting from the original draft of Christ's paper.

The statement Christ refers to actually said:

> Current and prospective inflation is not due to excess aggregate demand but primarily to the productivity decline associated with the recession, administered price increases in uncompetitive markets, and a variety of other cost-push factors (p. 80).

In December, 1974, there was no general excess demand. I think the Committee's statement is clear and entirely accurate. In APSTEG, we emphasized the counter-inflationary benefits to be derived from the productivity surge that will accompany a recovery.

Christ criticizes the Committee for advocating a more rapid growth of the money stock as a way to reduce interest rates. In my opinion, his observations are well founded. The emphasis on low interest rates reflects the views of our former Chairman from Texas. At the present time, however, when the Committee would like to see the economy expand at an annual real rate of 7 or 8 percent for 18 months to two years, the question arises whether the money supply should not grow for about a year at a rate significantly above the long-term trend.

The experiment Christ suggests, under which the Committee would plan counter-cyclical monetary and fiscal policies but would not recommend the implementation of such policies, is interesting but could hardly be carried out. The potential costs of adopting a passive stance are too large for such an undertaking to be feasible. At the same time, some check is essential on the magnitude of the discretionary policy mistakes that officials can inflict on the economy. The need for a check is the reason the Joint Economic Committee has proposed its 2 to 6 percent monetary growth rule. For the same reason, we have advocated the establishment of budgetary review procedures that will force the Congress to formulate spending priorities by considering alternatives within a fixed ceiling.

AN EVALUATION OF
THE ECONOMIC POLICY PROPOSALS OF THE
JOINT ECONOMIC COMMITTEE OF THE
92ND AND 93RD CONGRESSES: A COMMENT

Courtenay Slater, Senior Economist
Joint Economic Committee
Congress of the United States

Since I have had major responsibility for drafting and/or editing the domestic macroeconomic policy sections of all the Joint Economic Committee reports Christ has surveyed, I have naturally read his critique with great interest. I would like to join my colleagues on the Joint Economic Committee staff in commending him for undertaking this comprehensive review. I am pleased that Christ concludes by giving the Committee passing marks and wants to see it continue as an institution. However, on the way to reaching this reassuring conclusion, Christ makes clear his fundamental disagreement with the Committee's approach to macroeconomic policy.

Neither I nor any person on the Committee staff nor any individual member of the Committee agrees with every position taken by the Committee in the past five years. Nor do any of us, I hope, hold exactly the same views on every question that we did five years ago. Nonetheless, there is a consistent underlying point of view which runs through the Committee's recent statements on macroeconomic policy. It is a viewpoint which I, together with many other economists, share, although Christ, again together with many other economists, does not.

This brief comment cannot begin to fully explore this difference of viewpoint, much less to determine who is right and who is wrong. I think it would be helpful, however, simply to lay out the issues. To do so may at least reassure Christ, and others, of the Committee staff's awareness that they are issues, with persuasive arguments to be made on both sides of the case.

First, the Committee's reports clearly imply an underlying conviction that discretionary fiscal and monetary policy can contribute to improved macroeconomic performance. The Employment Act of 1946, which established the Committee, was predicated on this assumption. The Committee would be in an awkward position indeed if it felt its basic mandate was either impossible to achieve or counter-productive to attempt. (Incidentally, the Committee gives its major attention to the pursuit of high employment with reasonable price stability because this is what the Employment Act requires it to do, not necessarily because it is, as Christ states, ". . .the most important economic policy problem, in the Committee's view . . . .")

Christ's suggestion that the Committee retire from policy advice until it has "proved" during two business cycles that acceptance of the advice would have improved things, is not, of course, likely to be adopted. I am sure he does not expect it to be. However, he may be interested to know that the Committee is doing what is perhaps the next best thing. We currently have underway, and hope to publish soon, studies of what would have happened during the 1960s and early 1970s if (1) the actual budget had been balanced, (2) the full employment budget had been balanced, or (3) what appears in retrospect the "best" discretionary fiscal policy had been followed.

Second, the Committee's reports are based on the premise that it is possible to simultaneously pursue both high employment and reasonable price stability. I would argue that not only is it possible; it is a political imperative. In a democracy, the institutions of government must respond to the clearly expressed wishes of the citizenry on so fundamental an issue.

I strongly disagree with Christ's view that any specified rate of inflation can be achieved, but that the unemployment rate is not subject to similar control. We cannot guarantee control over either one. The necessity of pursuing two targets at once makes life even more difficult, but it does not render ". . . successful macroeconomic policy almost impossible."

Christ's point is well taken that we have no way of being sure that the specific numerical targets we have suggested are achievable and sustainable. I happen to believe the targets proposed in APSTEG - - 4 percent unemployment with less than 3 percent inflation - - are achievable within a 10 year time frame, and, I hope, sooner. I cannot prove this, however, and I reserve the right to change my mind if sufficiently persuasive evidence to the contrary is developed. For the Committee, the alternative to numerical targets is to present qualitative targets. This lays the Committee open to the charge that its objectives are vague and meaningless. A real quandary exists.

The fact that the numerical targets the Committee has recommended have seldom been achieved during the past 45 years does not mean much one way or the other. At least 30 of those 45 years have been dominated by the Great Depression and by three wars and their aftermaths. Only in the 12 year period from 1953-1965, and in the briefer period from 1970-1974 has there been a real opportunity to test modern techniques of macroeconomic management under peacetime conditions. I am not sure those doing the managing from 1953-1960 had their hearts in the effort. From 1961-1965, macroeconomic policy was, in my view, skillfully conducted and the results were impressive.

I would agree with Christ that from 1972-1974 discretionary policy has been destabilizing, and the Committee has so stated. It does not follow, however, that discretionary policy is inevitably, or even typically, destabilizing. Rather, I would presume that policy makers can learn from the mistakes of the past and do better next time.

Christ falls into his own trap with respect to numerical targets. How can he be so certain that 5 percent unemployment can be achieved without accelerating inflation, while 4 percent can not? Surely all such quantitative conclusions are subject to continuing re-evaluation in the light of new evidence. As part of its study program during the next two years, the Committee hopes to reassess in a serious way the quantitative import of ". . .maximum employment, production and purchasing power." If these studies should lead to the enunciation of new quantitative goals, I only hope the Committee will be attacked on the substance of its positions and not on the specious grounds of having changed its mind.

Another area in which Christ and the Committee part company has to do with the causes of inflation. Christ states the Committee's theory of inflation quite accurately. Inflation can and does have more than one cause and, therefore, may require a variety of cures. In a definitional sense, nominal demand must grow faster than real supply in order for inflation to occur. The really interesting question is: what causes this to take place? The same question can be stated in monetary terms by asking: what causes the growth of the money supply to exceed the rate necessary to accommodate the desired growth of real output?

The cause is not pure pig-headedness on the part of the monetary authorities. Nor is it incompetence. It certainly is not lack of concern about inflation. Whatever viewpoint one may have on monetary policy, it ought to be of interest to inquire into the political and economic factors, as well as the random events, which cause the Federal Reserve to behave as it does. I would not argue that the Joint Economic Committee has done as well as it might in investigating either inflation or monetary policy. However, I see the proper role of the Committee as going beyond the reiteration of some "rule" - - either of the money-supply or interest-rate variety.

I would like to make several other points on inflation, and I apologize if they sound like the pained cries of a sensitive author.

Controls. In general, contrary to the impression given by Christ, the Committee has not advocated controls and, therefore, has had no need to defend them by ". . .deploring inflation and asserting that it must be checked." The Committee did not call for price-wage controls prior to the imposition of the freeze in August, 1971, although some of its individual members did. Once the controls were imposed, the Committee felt its most constructive role was to monitor the control program and suggest improvements in its administration. The two reports on controls (publications 573 and 588) were part of this monitoring effort. They were not addressed to the more basic question of whether controls are or are not a good idea.

Incomes Policy. Since at least 1967, the Committee has supported an active voluntary price-incomes policy. The principal reason why such a policy is needed is the existence of a substantial degree of oligopoly power in important sectors of the U.S. economy. The theory behind a price-incomes policy and the ways in which such a policy might work have been spelled out in some detail in several Committee reports. The Committee viewpoint on this issue has many adherents within the economics profession, although Professor Christ is not one of them.

The Committee does not view price-incomes policy as a substitute for responsible fiscal and monetary policy. I hope the reports have made this clear.

Productivity. On page 80 of APSTEG, the Committee did not say, as Christ asserts, that ". . .a significant cause of the 1973-74 inflation is the recession, because productivity falls in recession. . . ."* The Committee said, "Current [i.e., late 1974] and prospective [i.e., 1975] inflation is not due to excess aggregate demand but primarily to the productivity decline associated with the recession. . . ." (Emphasis added.) This is an example of the Committee's eclectic theory of inflation, which Christ rejects. The history of past business cycles shows that prices have typically risen faster during the downturn than during the first two years of recovery. Cyclical swings in productivity are widely accepted as part of the reason for this pattern.

An aspect of the APSTEG report to which Christ does not refer is the charting of alternative growth paths for the remainder of this decade. The inexorable arithmetic of this exercise led to the conclusion that unemployment is extremely unlikely to fall even to 5 percent before 1979. Subsequent events have served only to reinforce this conclusion. Looking ahead to the problems of sustaining prosperity once it is regained is important, but so, too, are the day-by-day policy decisions which are required to keep the economy on a recovery path until that happy day is reached. I am glad Christ supports the continuation of the Joint Economic Committee as an institution. I hope the Committee can make the contributions to policy discussion which are needed if the remainder of the 1970s is to be a period of continued recovery and the 1980s one of stable prosperity.

---

* Editors' note: Slater is quoting from the original draft of Christ's paper.

THE ECONOMICS OF THE OECD

Michele Fratianni*

Catholic University of Louvain

and

John C. Pattison**

Ontario Economic Council

I. INTRODUCTION

Of the almost 200 governmentally sponsored or recognized international organizations only a few deal with macroeconomic policies, and these are generally constrained to particular aspects of policy making. Of this subset only the Bank for International Settlements (BIS) and the Organisation for Economic Cooperation and Development (OECD) deal exclusively with economic policy making in developed industrial nations. The BIS rarely commits itself to policy prescriptions in print but comments in a historical manner on the policies of the major nations. The OECD, on the other hand, with 1500 employees and its own printing facilities comments extensively on the state of and prospect for the world economy and its individual constituents through a voluminous output of publications.

The OECD consists of a large number of divisions of which perhaps three-quarters could be considered to deal largely with economic questions. These would include: (1) Economics and Statistics; (2) Fiscal Affairs (which includes competition policy, and some work on multinational firms); (3) Manpower and Industrial Relations; (4) Financial Affairs; (5) Environment; (6) Industry; (7) Education; (8) Development. Notwithstanding the above, when the economics of the OECD is considered, it is almost always with reference to the work of the Economics and Statistics Department, although some worthwhile studies have been produced by the other divisions. A significant proportion of the resources of each division is used to prepare internationally comparable statistics, or alternatively, to collect statistics which purport to measure the same variable in different nations.

If the economic analysis of the OECD, that is the analysis of the Department of Economics and Statistics, has any uniformity or consistency, it is because the head (an Assistant Secretary General) has always been appointed by the United Kingdom Treasury.[1]   In addition, many senior and a large number of

*On leave from Indiana University.

**The authors thank James Boughton, Bent Hansen, Donald Hodgman, and Niels Thygesen for helpful criticism.

[1] The Secretary General has in the past been selected from a small European country, the two Associate Secretaries General from the United States and France, and the three Assistant Secretaries General from Germany, Italy, and the United Kingdom.

intermediate and junior level appointments tend to come from the United Kingdom. [2] In the body of the paper, we will argue that this hereditary and nationalistic structure has produced an economic framework which is characteristically Keynesian in its general outline and Radcliffean in its specific application to monetary analysis.

The Economics and Statistics Department is subdivided into two directorates: the Country Studies Directorate and the General Directorate. The Country Studies Directorate makes forecasts twice a year of output, aggregate demand, the balance of payments, and prices on the assumption of given or unchanged policies. Each country "desk" also produces an annual economic review for each member country where recent developments as well as longer run structural aspects are analyzed. The General Directorate consists of a General Division which deals mainly with inflation, the Balance of Payments and Monetary Divisions, and a Growth and Allocation of Resources Division.

The work of the department is centered around two committees: the Economic Development Review Committee (EDRC) and the Economic Policy Committee (EPC).

The EPC is the more important committee and has three working parties (WPi, i = 2, 3, 4) and a group of short-term forecasters which meets regularly, as well as various ad hoc committees which meet irregularly for specific purposes. WP2 is serviced by reports from the Growth and Resource Allocation Division, WP3 from the Balance of Payments and Monetary Divisions, and WP4 (on inflation) from the General Economic Analysis Division. WP3 is essentially the Group of Ten.

Of all the working parties, WP3 is the most important and representation on the committee is usually at a senior level. Whereas most other OECD meetings can be attended by any member country, WP3 is restricted to the "Big Seven" (U.S., Canada, Japan, Germany, Italy, France, and the United Kingdom) plus Switzerland, Sweden, and representatives from the Benelux.

The EPC meets semi-annually, and is usually preceded by meetings of WP3, WP4, and the short-term forecasters. The papers prepared for the WPi are made available to the EPC as are Reports made by their Chairmen. The Country Studies Directorate prepares forecasts for each country; the Balance of Payments Division prepares forecasts of trade and current account balances, as well as terms of trade changes for individual countries. These are analyzed for accuracy and consistency at a meeting attended by short-term forecasters from each member country who meet in Paris four to six weeks before the EPC. The EPC itself is

---

[2] The hiring pattern is consistent with the salaries which are greater than the European level for economists but less than North American levels. If the need for economists capable of drafting fluently in the English language is added to the demand function, this would tend to increase the number of employees from the United Kingdom.

attended by high level officials, although the level varies from country to country. [3] The discussion is concerned with forecasts and likely policy responses. The larger countries begin the debate since their behavior is of concern to the smaller countries, whereas the reverse is not true. Often, policy responses will be solicited from the "smaller member countries" separately. After the meeting of the EPC, the OECD publishes its assessment of the international situation in the Economic Outlook. This can be substantially influenced by the major countries.

The output of the OECD can be subdivided into three major categories: publications which express the views of the Secretariat, Committees and consultants; mimeographed documents for the use of the governments of member countries which are, however, readily available to a larger audience; and secret documents (mainly the WP3 reports on balance of payments problems).

Given the high cost of bad policy making, we prepared this paper by reading those publications which have clear policy prescriptions. More precisely, we tried to cover the material over which the Department of Economics and Statistics has direct responsibility. The views of the Committees, on the other hand, usually represent a compromise of the viewpoints of the 24 member countries. Although consultants have produced a wide range of economic publications, it is not apparent that their reports have influenced the OECD's policy prescriptions. Indeed, we shall argue that the work of the consultants has had little, if any, impact on the "official" OECD framework of analysis.

We have had no access to the secret documents and our research might be substantially biased as a result. These documents, which are prepared primarily for WP3, contain a great deal of the thinking of the Group of Ten on questions of international monetary reform, capital flows and controls and, most recently, the oil crisis.

The major concern of this paper is to unveil the framework of analysis of the OECD with special emphasis on stabilization policies. This is done in sections II through V. We thought it important to add, however, a discussion on a subject which appears to be more related to the modus operandi and survivability characteristics of the institution than to the quality of its output, although in effect these two aspects are interdependent. In section VI we offer an explanation of the OECD as a bureaucratic entity, and appraise its actual and potential usefulness; in so doing, we suggest implicitly how the institution could be changed to better serve the objectives of the 24 client countries.

---

[3] The U.S. delegation has recently included the Chairman of the Council of Economic Advisers (CEA), a delegate from the Board of Governors of the Federal Reserve System, and assorted bureaucrats from the CEA, Federal Reserve, Treasury, and the State Department.

II. FRAMEWORK OF ANALYSIS

A framework for the analysis of the OECD must consist of three parts: the economic model that is used in the formulation of hypotheses for testing as well as for policy making; the structure and flow of information within the economics department; and the sources of inputs for the analysis. Although some would doubt that policy makers have a theoretical framework for analysis, it seems true that they must, mentally if not formally, use a set of relations describing the interaction of economic variables.[4]

The theoretical basis of analysis of the OECD is the Keynesian income-expenditure model. Although the model is not formally spelled out, it can be easily reconstructed from a careful reading of the <u>Economic Outlook</u> (and especially its "Technical Annex") and <u>Techniques of Economic Forecasting</u>.

Before detailing the features of this framework, it is important to note that not all economists in the Department of Economics and Statistics follow the same approach. Nor could a common framework be successfully enforced by the organization. A number of country experts follow and forecast the salient economic variables of OECD countries. Each is asked, at least twice a year, to project for a period of one year the basic components of aggregate demand, the supply of output, prices,and the current-account balance of the country he supervises. The actual forms used to make these forecasts are shown in Exhibit II of the Appendix.[5] A country expert can use, of course, a variety of methods to make this forecast. Only a few researchers use a complete econometric model; most rely initially on forecasts or projections made by economists working for the country's central bank, Treasury Department, Planning Bureau, or an equivalent institution. The projections are adjusted further by subjective criteria or by simple extrapolative techniques which have proved in the past to be fairly "reliable" in the forecasting sense. The forecasts are then transmitted to the "prospects" division which integrates them to make sure that they are consistent, especially with respect to output and prices. The Balance of Payments division forecasts terms of trade and OECD balance with the non-OECD world and prepares preliminary forecasts by country on the basis of a forecast of real GNP growth. It is then responsible for the consistency of balance of payments forecasts for all countries. Similarly, the general group which deals with inflation must look at the international consistency of inflation projections. The process reflects a preoccupation with balance sheet identities and the constraints involved in a closed system. Obviously, the initial forecasts made by such a large group

---

[4] See, for example, the remarks by a Swiss central banker described in Brunner (1972, pp. 3-12).

[5] We are grateful to the Economic Prospects Division for supplying these forms as well as discussing their procedures with Fratianni. Members of the Country Studies Directorate also helped provide useful information for this section.

will not all be compatible and adjustments are made on an iterative basis, assuming that announced government policies and exchange rates will not be altered. Often three or four iterations are required before all balance sheet identities are satisfied without violating the principles of the Keynesian system. Given the weights of the largest four or five countries, most of the adjustments must be made in terms of their forecasts. The forecasts are then sent to each capital, and national forecasters meet with the Secretariat. At this meeting, disagreements are aired and countries question each other as well as the Secretariat about the forecasts. Policy issues are excluded altogether. In light of the information received, the Secretariat must recalculate its forecasts. An obvious problem is presented at this stage, namely that countries may **try** to achieve objectives which are not compatible, particularly with respect to output or the balance of payments. In cases of a gross inconsistency for one of the large five or six countries, the problem is posed at the subsequent meeting of the EPC, or in some cases in WP3.

We want to make clear that we are not interested in the framework, or better frameworks, of analysis of each individual member of the Department of Economics and Statistics. We shall take it for granted that these frameworks are different. We are interested instead in the viewpoint of the Secretariat in interpreting these forecasts.

Let us begin with the determinants of aggregate demand. Our interpretation of the records suggests that the core of the framework, although not necessarily its details, is given by equations (1) - (4) below:

(1) $\qquad Y = N + C - Im ;$

(2) $\qquad C = c(Y_D) ;$

(3) $\qquad Im = m(Y_D) ;$

(4) $\qquad Y_D = g(Y),$

where

$\qquad N$ – exogenous component of aggregate demand
$\qquad C$ – consumption expenditures
$\qquad Im$ – imports
$\qquad Y_D$ – personal disposable income
$\qquad Y$ – national income.

With a knowledge of N, c, m, and g one can determine Y, Y_D, C, and Im. It is generally felt that reliable econometric knowledge is available concerning the marginal propensity to consume and import with respect to personal disposable income. A practical difficulty arises from the fact that a knowledge of Y_D is required to determine Y. [6]

The next step involves the determination of output which is obtained theoretically by the Walrasian system of equations of the real sector of the economy, but is forecast through an aggregate production function. An aggregate "potential" production function is used to estimate full employment ouput, where the "potential" production function differs from the actual production function by the use of "potential" values of the inputs rather than their actual values. [7]

The difference between actual and potential output is interpreted as an indicator of the utilization rate of resources in the economy. The frequency with which this statistic is used in the Economic Outlook seems to suggest that the quality of a stabilization program ought to be judged by how closely a member country keeps actual output to potential output. The gap is also used in discussion of inflation (see section III below). We find this emphasis on the potential output gap somewhat misplaced on two grounds. First, the quality of a stabilization policy should be measured in terms of a concept of output growth which is geared to the policy aims of each country. Different targets for output growth reflect different attitudes with respect to goals such as employment, inflation, exchange rate arrangements, etc. Second, the OECD full employment measure of output is not independent of the level of aggregate demand. [8] The gap does not close as fast as the "true" gap would during expansionary phases of the business cycle, while it is understated during the contractive phase of the cycle.

We have no significant or consistent evidence that the basic framework of analysis goes beyond the output market described above. [9] Although the Economic Outlook devotes a section to monetary developments, it appears that the interaction between the output (flow) and asset (stock) markets is rarely acknowledged nor are the long-run implications of the Keynesian model in the face of the

---

[6] This problem is solved by constructing an "Appropriations Account" (see Table 3 in Exhibit I of the Appendix) where wage, non-wage income, and direct taxes are autonomously projected. Several iterations are required in making the initial forecast of Y consistent with the projected value of C and Im. The iterative approach is described in detail in the U.S. chapter of Techniques of Economic Forecasting.

[7] See "The Measurement of Domestic Cyclical Fluctuations," Economic Outlook, Occasional Studies, July 1973. Alternatively, Okun's law equations are used as estimates of potential output.

[8] Economic Outlook, No. 13, July 1973, p. 11.

[9] It appears from recent issues of the Economic Outlook that more attention is being devoted to monetary developments. We have been advised that the interplay between country desks and the monetary division is increasing but this activity is "not as formal" as the role of other divisions.

two constraints given by the government budget and the balance of payments. Long-run considerations are obscured by the emphasis on a short-run planning horizon, a characteristic the OECD received as a mandate from its member. countries.

The Economic Outlook makes frequent reference to the terms "monetary and fiscal policy," but we have found their use vague because neither analytical content nor empirical import is assigned to them. Is fiscal policy measured as a change in government expenditures, tax rates, total tax revenues, or a weighted linear combination of these magnitudes? Is the size of the government budget deficit or surplus either at current levels of income or at full employment income a good indicator of the thrust of fiscal policy? These questions are taken up in two separate studies of the OECD (see section V below) but do not seem to be relevant for the framework of analysis of the Economic Outlook. Similarly, monetary policy means a constellation of policy events: changes in the discount rate; changes in reserve requirements; "moral" suasion; open market operations; etc. These instruments do not seem to affect a single indicator, or alternative indicators, of the thrust of policy in a systematic way. This shortcoming can be directly attributed to the failure of not having developed a theory of the money stock process.

The Keynesian mold within which the OECD operates has led to looking at interest rates as an indicator of the thrust of monetary policy. The way monetary policy discharges its effects on the real sector of the economy is similarly rarely discussed. Does monetary policy alter the position of the LM curve, while leaving the IS curve unchanged, or do both curves react to a monetary stimulus? If they do, what are the likely determinants of the magnitudes of the shifts? As in the case of fiscal policy, separate studies of the OECD (see section IV) have addressed themselves to these issues more or less successfully, but have left little imprint in the Economic Outlook which we have taken to be the principal medium through which the OECD makes its views known to the outside.

Moving to some issues of the open economy, we shall start with the way the OECD perceives the current-account adjustment process. The following quotation reveals that the process is explained along a Keynesian absorption approach.

> Whatever the method of adjustment, a deficit cannot be re-
> duced unless domestic demand rises less than output--so that a
> greater proportion of output is used for exports or to replace
> imports.... And the same is true, in reverse, of actions to re-

duce the current surpluses, . . . Domestic demand will have to rise by more than output, so that a greater proportion of demand is satisfied by imports or by diversion of goods from exports. [10]

The policy prescriptions which stem from this analysis are well known. When a country faces a positive potential-to-actual-output gap and a current-account surplus, the aim is to raise the level of aggregate demand through the appropriate use of monetary and fiscal policies. In dilemma cases such as a positive gap matched with a current-account deficit, the aim is to assign monetary policy to the external target and fiscal policy to the internal target.

Exchange rate adjustments are ruled out in the OECD reports of the 1960s. The balance of payments is viewed as a constraint on economic policy. External surpluses or deficits tell governments that corrective policy actions are in order. The complete elimination of a balance of payments disequilibrium is considered to be a very unlikely event "unless it is the result of co-ordinated action between the major industrialized countries." [11]

The position of the OECD on exchange rate arrangements has recently changed under the pressure of events. It is now conceded that exchange rate changes should be smaller and more frequent than in the past and that they should reflect changes in the countries underlying competitive positions. [12] Exchange rates should not be allowed to change in response to cyclical fluctuations in demand or as a result of capital movements. In essence, changes in exchange rates are now justified if a fundamental disequilibrium exists in the current account and in that portion of the capital account which is insensitive to interest rate differentials. Capital movements are assessed to be essentially destabilizing and thus cause unnecessary changes in exchange rates. [13]

The OECD warned in 1972, however, that competitive devaluations will generate inflation in the 70s just as they caused unemployment in the 30s. [14] The underlying argument in favor of more rigid exchange rates is that the latter provide a built-in discipline in the system in the sense that Mundell has been talking and writing about recently.

A different, and analytically more satisfactory, argument was advanced in 1973. The OECD recognizes that floating rates do away with the balance of pay-

[10] Economic Outlook, No. 4, December 1968, p. 6. (Some monetary aspects are discussed in terms ot the domestic liquidity of the banking system in the report on the adjustment mechanism by WP3, The Balance of Payments Adjustment Process, August 1966.)

[11] Economic Outlook, No. 4, December 1968, p. 6.

[12] Economic Outlook, No. 11, July 1972, p. 7.

[13] Economic Outlook, No.9, July 1971.

[14] Economic Outlook, No. 11, July 1972, p. 7.

ments constraint, a kernel in its framework of analysis. Countries are now free to choose their own inflation rates. They are no longer bound to accept the world inflation rate. On the other hand, the Organisation cautions that "floating does not, in fact, render countries fully independent of external economic constraints. For what used to be a 'deficit country,' the constraint created by a loss of reserves is replaced by the pressure exerted on prices by a depreciating exchange rate."[15] In other words, floating rates impose a discipline of their own to the extent that inflationary policies are reflected in devaluations and in an inflation rate which is above the world inflation rate. Only the nature of the indicator through which policies are assessed changes as we move from a fixed to a flexible exchange rate regime.

Although we have been critical of the framework of analysis, the advantages to the Organisation of its approach are obvious. The basic Keynesian model is well adapted to standardization and report writing (particularly for individual country studies), whereas the monetary approach is much more difficult to interpret and convey.

III. INFLATION

The problem of inflation and its solution has over the years become an increasingly important concern. A cursory look at the various issues of the Economic Outlook testifies to this concern. In addition, four separate reports have dealt specifically with this topic.[16]

Various aspects of inflation are handled by the Economic Policy Committee and in particular its WP4. The terms of reference of this working party are to exchange experience so as to assure overall stability of costs and prices.[17] Because of the way the terms of reference are spelled out, there is some concern with relative price movements as well as inflation; however, the distinction between the two is rarely made. A further qualification is that the group itself has declared that it is not the relevant body to discuss questions concerning monetary policy since this is the prerogative of other groups within the OECD (which however are not often concerned with inflation). This position is even more surprising given that central bankers are included in virtually all delegations to WP4 and dominate them in a number of cases.

---

[15] Economic Outlook, No. 13, July 1973, p. 11.

[16] Policies for Price Stability, A Report to the Economic Policy Committee by its Working Party on Costs of Production and Prices, 1962; Policies for Prices, Profits and Other Non-Wage Incomes, A Report Prepared for the Economic Policy Committee by its Working Party on Costs of Production and Prices, 1964; Inflation: the Present Problem, Report by the Secretary General, December 1970; Present Policies against Inflation, A Report by Working Party No. 4 of the Economic Policy Committee, June 1971.

[17] See the foreword (pp. 9-12) to Wages and Labor Mobility by the (original) chairman (1962-1974) of this committee, Pieter de Wolff.

As inflation has accelerated, so has the number of theories purporting to explain this phenomenon. The traditional explanation has involved the role of excess demand. A second major group of theories could probably be categorized as "cost-push." Within this category wage-push, tax-push inflation, income distribution problems and theories bordering on the sociological could be included. Some theories have tried to relate inflation to the oligopolistic power of large corporations either secularly or cyclically. Although the OECD has often recommended adopting policies to improve competition, it has correctly never pursued this line of argument as an approach to world inflation.

The outline of this section is as follows. Alternative theories of inflation will be considered in light of the views expressed in OECD publications. This will be followed by a discussion of policies towards inflation. In particular, we will examine the well-known OECD preference for prices and incomes policies.

A. Excess Demand

Every OECD paper on inflation has highlighted the necessary role of excess demand. For instance, the Report by the Secretary General of December 1970 noted that the ". . .evidence for a fairly close relationship between demand pressures and price increases has been presented . . . it is hard to see how this evidence can be ignored."[18] In the introduction to the same report, this view was strongly accented, ". . .excess demand should be eliminated and governments should be prepared . . . to accept a temporary reduction in the rate of activity until there are signs that better price stability has been achieved."[19] This view was reiterated in a report of WP4 six months later.[20] This is not to say very much. It is substantially more important to determine how excess demand and price pressures are interconnected and to decide upon the causes of excess demand.

In the analytic framework of section II, the existence of a condition of excess demand is indicated by a positive gap between the current level of real GNP and a measure of the economy's capacity. As this gap is diminished by the rising pressure of aggregate demand, output and prices increase, with output changes cominating price changes in the early stage of the disequilibrium process, and vice-versa in the later stage.

A variant of the excess demand model is the Phillips curve where excess demand is proxied by a labor market variable, usually the inverse of the rate of unemployment. As this approach failed to explain the acceleration of inflation

---

[18] Inflation: the Present Problem, p. 34.

[19] Inflation: the Present Problem, p. 10.

[20] Present Policies against Inflation, p. 27.

in the late 1960s, it became evident that since employees bargain for expected real rather than nominal wages, expectations of inflation must have distorted any simple relation between wage changes and excess demand. The fairly well-established empirical findings that wage changes are equal to the expected rate of inflation plus some relationship to the excess demand for labor means that with continuing excess demand inflation will continue to accelerate. Furthermore, the time required to restore price stability will tend to increase since inflationary expectations provide some momentum for further price changes, even after the growth of aggregate demand has been reduced.

As the rate of inflation rises, the extent of the necessary reduction in aggregate demand would have to be at a level which is politically unacceptable in order to have any short-run impact on prices.

It can be seen from most OECD publications on inflation that some form of a Phillips curve relationship was in the Secretariat's mind. Before 1972 or 1973, most references were to a simple Phillips curve relationship,[21] although in the 1971 report, Present Policies against Inflation, expectations were mentioned as being ". . .one school of thought, put most strongly by the representatives from Canada and the United States."[22]

Although, since at least December 1972, OECD publications echoed many of the sentiments of the expectations augmented Phillips curve school, it is far from obvious how much was intuition and how much was firmly reasoned analysis. For one thing, it appears that expectations were used to strengthen the case for a policy of prices and incomes, for instance, in the December 1972 Economic Outlook.

> To make an effective indentation on inflation by demand management alone would require draconian measures of restraint, which no country would wish to impose . . . The apparent success of the measures of price and income control adopted last year by the United States authorities lends support to the experience of several other countries that such measures may be useful, at least in dampening price expectations and giving a breathing space. [23]

---

[21] This can be seen in the discussions on demand pressures and the unemployment rate in various editions of the Economic Outlook.

[22] Present Policies against Inflation, pp. 27-28.

[23] Economic Outlook, No. 12, December 1972, p. 6.

In the issue of the <u>Economic Outlook</u> which followed, another implication of the expectations theory was outlined.

> There must be a serious risk that when . . . the rate of inflation advances toward double figures, a progressive acceleration will set in, because anticipatory action by various economic groups becomes too strong and too widespread for effective control.[24]

It should be noted that because of the role of price expectations, equal doses of restrictive demand policies accomplish less at higher than at lower rates of inflation. Consequently, a problem that the OECD has not squarely faced is that the relevant time horizon to check current inflation rates is much longer than the 12-18 month period on which the OECD puts so much emphasis.[25] With such a constraint the only possible policy measures which could work would have to influence expectations or operate directly on prices and incomes.

In considering the causes of inflation, reference should also be made to econometric analysis based upon modified versions of the Phillips curve approach. The following two-equation system was tested for Canada, France, Germany, Japan, the United Kingdom, and the United States (see Table 1).

$$\dot{w} = g(x_1, x_2, x_3, x_4, x_5),$$

$$\dot{p} = h(x_1, x_2, x_5, w),$$

where

x_1 - variable expressing an excess demand for labor
x_2 - expected price changes
x_3 - profits
x_4 - productivity
x_5 - dummy variables
w - wage rate
$\cdot$ - indicates percentage change.

Note that the $\dot{w}$ equation is a Phillips curve equation <u>cum</u> a variety of added factors. Both the $\dot{w}$ and $\dot{p}$ equations introduce the price expectations variable, but the system cannot test directly whether the long-run Phillips curve is vertical or not, because the equations are recursive rather than simultaneously interacting.

---

[24] <u>Economic Outlook</u>, No. 13, July 1973, p. 8.

[25] For some analytics on this point, see Duck, Parkin, Rose and Zis (1974).

If we were to treat the two equations tested in Table 1 as part of a simultaneous system, the coefficient of x_2 (the price expectations variable) in the reduced-form equation would be significantly below one, thus indicating that the long-run Phillips curve is steeper than the short-run but not quite vertical.

The observation that there is an inverse (short-run) relationship between inflation and unemployment is consistent with a variety of impulses which might generate an excess demand in the goods market. In the context of this paper, it is useful to identify fiscal, monetary, and Wicksellian origins of excess demand.[26] The OECD has had little to say in detail about the causes of excess demand, although it has regarded fiscal aspects as relatively more important than other forces. For example, the organization comments on ". . . the inflationary consequences of rising demands for public expenditure which are not matched by a willingness to pay for it, as evidenced by claims for higher incomes put forward in real terms, including a compensation for increased direct and indirect taxation, and social security contributions."[27]

It also notes the political difficulty of controlling public expenditures, ". . .perhaps most important has been the difficulty of reconciling the need for early and firm action to control demand with the political processes of democratic government."[28] Another variant is, ". . .the political problems of restraining procyclical public expenditure by junior governments remain important in many countries; and at all levels of government pressure for better public services limits flexibility on the expenditure side."[29]

Attempts to increase the government's share of total consumption at the expense of the private sector are inflationary. It is stated that in some countries with a large public sector the demand for public goods has been satiated with the growth of the public sector exercising a powerful brake on the real growth of private disposable household income.[30] The unanswered question is how this gets translated into generalized inflation, although it appears that higher nominal wage demands are made in compensation. Taken together, an increase in the size of the government sector financed by an increase in taxes that would keep total real expenditure constant would not change the price level in a standard Keynesian model, once equilibrium is reached. Within the context of the "crowding out" literature, public expenditures financed by taxes or borrowing from the

---

[26] For description and theoretical discussion with application to three countries, see Brunner, Fratianni, Jordan, Meltzer, and Neumann (1973).

[27] Present Policies against Inflation, p. 28.

[28] Inflation:the Present Problem, p. 33.

[29] Economic Outlook, No. 13, July 1973, p. 6.

[30] Van Lennep (1973, p. 16).

Table 1

Wage Equations (Ordinary Least Squares)

Dependent variable DW	Pressure variables — Labor markets $\frac{1}{u^2}$	VAC	U-VAC	$\frac{1}{U-V+4}$	Others INV*	Price variables DPy_{t-1}	DPc_{t-1}	Profits DPr_{t-1}	Productivity var. Dy	Other variables Dsv	Dummy 1968	Const.	R^2	STE*	DW**
Canada[e]	66.60[b] (5.30)						0.44 (4.17)					1.54 (3.83)	0.66	1.20	0.62
France[e]	0.30 (1.90)						0.36 (6.61)				9.28 (13.28)	4.92 (11.61)	0.84	1.20	0.33
Germany[c]			-0.99 (2.31)			1.02 (4.32)		0.07 (1.36)	0.71 (5.53)			-----	0.66	1.27	1.14
Japan	9.36 (3.54)						0.75 (3.16)		0.28 (3.18)			-----	0.60	2.60	1.06
U.K.[h]		3.68 (8.27)			0.003 (1.51)	0.52[d] (3.73)				5.41 (1.71)		-----	0.63	0.84	1.29
U.S.	42.24 (5.42)						0.44 (2.92)	0.02 (3.02)				1.84 (7.43)	0.75	0.68	1.15

*   Standard error of the equation in % of dependent variable.

**   Durbin Watson statistics

Note: Figures in brackets indicate the t-ratio.

Table 1 (continued)

Price Equations

Dependent variable DP	$\frac{1}{u^2}$	VAC	U - VAC	$\frac{1}{U-V+4}$	Others INV*	Lagged Prices	Pm	Wages	Dy	Dsv	Dummy 1968	Const.	R^2	STE*	DW**
Canada (DP*cnf)	19.52[a),f)] (2.52)					0.11 (1.54)		0.39[e)] (5.22)	-0.07 (1.71)			----	0.82	0.60	0.74
France (DF*c)	-5.09[f)] (4.21)					----	0.13 (5.30)	0.76[e)] (7.42)	-0.07 (1.08)			1.90 (1.99)	0.65	1.85	0.73
Germany[e)] (DPy)			1.50[a)] (2.58)			----		0.47 (10.73)	-0.32 (6.92)			----	0.90	0.37	2.63
Japan (DP c)	3.04 (2.01)					----		0.27 (3.73)				----	0.58	1.48	1.01
U.K.[d)] (DPy)		0.83[a)] (2.27)				0.22 (2.32)		0.24 (3.54)	-0.09 (1.56)	-2.08 (1.82)		----	0.60	0.48	1.24
U.S. (DP c)	20.10 (3.60)					0.38 (6.82)		0.44[g)] (5.07)	-0.13 (3.69)			-1.10 (4.69)	0.89	0.38	0.74

*   Standard error of the equation in % of dependent variable

** Durbin Watson statistics

Note Figures in brackets indicate the t-ratio.

89

Notes to Table I

All variables, except the pressure variables, are expressed
as overlapping four quarter percentage changes:

$$DX = \left[\frac{X_t}{X_{t-4}} \quad 100. \right] - 100$$

The pressure variables are four quarter averages.

W	hourly compensation per employee (in the case of Germany, total compensation divided by employment)
Py	GNP deflator
Pc	consumption deflator
P'c	consumer price
P'cnf	consumer price non-food
Pm	import unit value
U	unemployment rate
VAC	vacancy rate
DSV	change in vacancy ratio
y	gross national product (in the case of Canada and France, industrial production)
INV*	excess stocks
a)	t - 1
b)	t - 2
c)	half-yearly overlapping percentage changes
d)	two-quarter average
e)	hourly wages in manufacturing
f)	unemployment instead of 1/u
g)	$0.5 \, DW + 0.3 \, DW_{-1} + 0.2 \, DW_{-2}$
h)	The 1966-67 wage freeze has been partly allowed for by a 2 percent upward adjustment in the first quarter 1967 wage level used to estimate the wage equation.

[1] It must be kept in mind that the standard error is biased downwards when there is a high serial correlation in the residuals, as is shown here by the low Durbin-Watson statistic.

source: OECD, **Inflation: the Present Problem**, 1970, pp. 70-71.

public reduce private expenditures by a similar amount. But, to have inflation, such a model requires the explicit consideration of financial aspects.

If little detail is given on fiscal policy, even less is forthcoming on the relationship between monetary policy and inflation. Most of the internal OECD interest on the subject comes from WP3 which is concerned with the balance of payments and capital flows. The use of monetary policy has at times been recommended by default rather than on its own merit, "Monetary policy has represented an important part of the overall attack on inflation partly because of the continuing difficulties encountered by some countries in using fiscal policy effectively for this purpose." [31]

The type of exchange rate regime is of paramount importance in the OECD analysis. Under fixed rates of exchange and highly integrated capital markets, monetary policy is taken to have no long-run effect upon the level of income, whereas with a flexible exchange rate, monetary policy can have a sustained influence on income. [32] We thus should expect a shift of emphasis in the OECD's reports concerning the role of monetary policy as a stabilization tool before and after 1971, the year which marks the change from fixed to flexible rates.

We submit two citations as evidence that the OECD fully subscribed to the "offsetting capital flow" theory (see section IV). The first one is a convoluted statement from Present Policies against Inflation; the second one comes from the Report by the Secretary General in which there is the additional twist that monetary policy is further weakened by a cluster of highly substitutable financial assets.

> Since it is obvious that monetary policy has an important role to play in domestic demand management policies, it is inevitable that when conjunctural conditions differ . . . the resultant international capital movements will, to some extent, undermine the restrictive (or expansionary) policies being followed by respective countries. It is therefore important that monetary policy should not be pushed further-- in either an expansionary or restrictive direction-- than appears necessary to achieve domestic objectives. [33]

---

[31] Economic Outlook, No. 10, December 1970, p. 10.

[32] See Mundell (1968, Chapter 18).

[33] Present Policies against Inflation, p. 33.

With a large and diverse stock of outstanding financial assets, it takes a considerable time for the authorities to create a liquidity squeeze sufficiently severe to have an appreciable impact on spending decisions; the more so, the greater the degree to which domestic monetary policies are undermined by large scale capital inflows. [34]

Since the change to a flexible exchange rate system, comments on the efficacy of monetary policy have not been entirely consistent, partly, it would seem, because of uncertainty about the shape of a revised international monetary system. For instance, in July 1973 when currencies were afloat, the Economic Outlook contained the following passage, "The scope for moving towards greater monetary restraint has been somewhat enlarged by the present regime of more flexible exchange rates." [35] Six months earlier, in December 1972, the concern seemed to be that restrictive monetary policy to combat inflation would cause capital flows which could undermine a return to a fixed exchange rate system:

> . . . growth of money supply has been unusually rapid . . . it would be unwise to allow such abnormal rates of monetary expansion to continue for much longer, and monetary policy will everywhere have a contribution to make when restraint becomes desirable. In this respect, however, due attention has to be given to the possible impact on the international situation should monetary restraint be pushed too far in Europe. . . excessive reliance on monetary restraint could, through the effects of widening interest differentials on capital movements, impede the return of confidence in the international monetary system in its present transitional stage.[36]

Additional recognition of the changed role of monetary policy can be seen in the titles of the Economic Outlook. In July 1972, when the international monetary system was in great turmoil, the section title was "Exchange Rates, Capital Flows and Monetary Conditions." Six months later, as floating became more common, the titles were "Relative Monetary Conditions" and "Problems of Monetary Management." By July 1973, when floating was accepted, the title

---

[34] Inflation: the Present Problem, p. 33.

[35] Economic Outlook, No. 13, July 1973, p. 7.

[36] Economic Outlook, No. 12, December 1972, p. 7.

read "Domestic Monetary Conditions." In this connection it is interesting to see how a bureaucracy adapts to a changing economic environment.

The Wicksellian pathway to inflation is opened when the anticipated return from real capital investment is above the market interest rate. Given the high and rising rates of price increase which industrial countries have experienced, it is not obvious how nominal market interest rates have compared with the rising cost of capital equipment and anticipated future streams of returns. The OECD has, however, accented the importance of low or negative real financial market rates of interest often in conjunction with the positive returns from acquiring real assets. In this situation it pays to acquire real assets by borrowing. In this framework the inflationary mechanism is analogous to the Wicksellian one, with aggregate demand being fed by the discrepancy in returns. The OECD began to mention this mechanism in July 1973, ". . .adequate control of monetary expansion is unlikely to be achieved when real interest rates are very low." [37] Subsequently, the Wicksellian process was used to explain the demand for primary commodities where the expected future return from speculation was far greater than the negative real interest rate. In particular, it was noted that commodity prices did not begin to fall in 1974 until there was a rise in the Eurodollar rate. [38] The problem with the latter argument is that we are dealing with a relative price change or a change in the terms of trade and neither one necessarily involves inflation.

B. Cost-Push Theories

Various push theories have been recruited to explain inflation occurring simultaneously with substantial unutilized resources. According to the OECD, this view seems to fit the situation of France in 1968-69 and Italy in 1969. The institution gives no explanation why costs keep rising. The particular references to France and Italy suggest that the OECD has union activity in mind. In Present Policies against Inflation, "cost inflation" is given an empirically falsifiable content.

> 'Cost inflation' is an imprecise term. It can be used simply to describe the typical phase of the cycle when costs rise faster than prices; it can be extended to cover the lagged relation between demand pressure and prices resulting from the ebb and

---

[37] Economic Outlook, No. 13, July 1973, p. 7.

[38] Economic Outlook, No. 15, July 1974, pp. 25-37.

flow of inflationary expectations; or it may refer to forces pushing up costs and prices which are largely independent of present
or previous levels of demand (p. 2).

The evidence which refutes the second meaning of "cost inflation" comes
from the OECD itself, which has shown that price increases are not independent
of the deviation of actual from trend output. [39] It is clear that to the extent that
aggregate demand and price changes behave procyclically, inflation cannot be
independent of demand considerations.

International differences in unit labor costs are examined in every issue
of the Economic Outlook. The discussion emphasizes the effect of productivity
increases in lowering unit labor costs and ultimately direct "cost-push" forces.
Given that the components of unit labor costs interact in an economy in many
ways and that the inflationary interpretation and causation of unit labor costs
is far from unambiguous, we have found the simple comparison over time and
between countries of unit labor costs to be counterproductive in helping to
understand inflation.

Another popular view of "cost-push" inflation comes from the Nordic
two-sector model. In Present Policies against Inflation we read, ". . . there is a
fairly well established process whereby price developments in world markets have
a major influence on wage settlements in the export sector, which in turn largely
determine wage movements in the rest of the economy and hence the rise in the
domestic price level." [40] In the review of the possible channels of the international transmission of inflation published in the Economic Outlook of July
1973, a critique of this theory was given suggesting that although it has much
empirical support on an individual country basis, on a worldwide level it would
suffer from the "fallacy of composition." [41] That is, it explains how inflation
rates are transmitted but fails to explain the origin of world inflation.

Frustration theories of various kinds are widespread in spite of nonex-
istent empirical support within and outside the OECD. The argument that
income maldistribution plays a role was mentioned in the 1970 report, "It is
evident, however, that cyclical shifts between labour incomes and profits, and
between different categories of labour income, play a central role in the process
of wage /price inflation." [42] From the discussion it is not clear whether this

---

[39] See Inflation: the Present Problem.

[40] Present Policies against Inflation, p. 31.

[41] Economic Outlook, No. 13, July 1973, p. 84.

[42] Inflation: the Present Problem, p. 19.

is causal or just a spurious correlation with the business cycle. The report states, "The fact the discussion is in these terms should not be taken to imply that wages and salaries necessarily play a predominant causal role in the inflationary process." [43] It is likely that what the empirical work in this report shows is the result of correlation with the level of demand pressure which is in turn correlated with the rate of inflation.

In a more general context, this theory is not new and can be assimilated as a special form of the Keynesian inflationary-gap hypothesis. During inflation, desired investment exceeds desired saving. The inflationary process stops when everyone adapts to his financial situation or when desired investment of all groups is equal to desired saving. The important characteristic of models of this type is that inflation springs from the adjustment process towards an equilibrium distribution of income. [44] A stylized version of the income-share model divides the economy into workers and capital owners. Profits increase immediately after a price increase while wages adjust to price increases with a lag. The lag may reflect differences in information of the two groups about market processes. An excess demand for output will raise prices (the inflationary-gap) and profits but reduces real wage income because of the delayed adjustment of wages to prices. [45] The "clearing" of the goods market, or the elimination of the inflationary gap, occurs by redistributing real income against labor provided the marginal propensity to spend of profit earners is smaller than that of the workers.

There are three fundamental criticisms of this theory. First, since an inflationary gap must exist to begin with, the theory presupposes an explanation of how this gap was formed. Stated in slightly different terms, how was the initial equilibrium distribution of income disturbed? Second, inflation ends if one economic group loses at the expense of others. There is little reason to believe that any one significant group might want to pay the price of a lower real per capita income to see inflation terminated. Third, the empirical evidence does not confirm one of the major implications of the theory which predicts that inflation would produce a redistribution of income in favor of nonworkers. While wages are negotiated at regular intervals and in many cases are protected from inflation by escalator clauses, a large portion of financial wealth is denominated in fixed money terms and its real money value is at the complete mercy of inflation.

---

[43] Inflation: the Present Problem, p. 19.

[44] Harry G. Johnson (1963, pp. 42-47).

[45] Consult for example the model presented by Ackley (1961, pp. 434-436).

Where frustration plays a major role, in the OECD's view, is in the redistribution of wealth and income between the public and the private sector. "Inflation is, in part, a by-product of some of the most fundamental of society's unresolved problems - - for example, questions of income distribution, and incompatible claims by society for both public services and private consumption."[46] There are several channels whereby this occurs in OECD publications. First, tax changes result in higher prices either directly or via tax shifting. The OECD is usually careful in stipulating that this is one effect on prices independent of the aggregate demand effect, while the net effect over time will be a combination of the two. A concise statement of this view was given in the July 1973 Economic Outlook, "The use of the revenue weapon for dampening demand is constrained by the inflationary results of tax push: higher indirect taxes on consumer goods force up the cost of living and wage claims and in certain countries personal income tax increases may also be shifted to wages and prices." The phenomenon of net-of-tax bargaining is often mentioned in various reports on inflation. While it is a valid argument for altering relative wages or prices there is little firm empirical work to support such a contention. Even where tax variables perform well in wage and price equations the correlation between income tax yields and aggregate demand makes any conclusion tenuous and of dubious policy implications. Basically, this is only a partial equilibrium approach to inflation. The theory makes more sense at a macroeconomic level if government spending is considered, as well as marginal propensities to consume which differ between the public and private sectors.

A related mechanism mentioned by the Secretary General was that the insufficiency of public goods, in a country such as Italy, can drive wage earners to ask for higher nominal wage demands in compensation. [47] Note that this is just the reverse of the last point where inflation was caused by too large a public sector.

Finally, one alleged cause of inflation is pollution control expenditures.[48] This occurs because of supply constraints; the passing on of higher production costs; and, with higher consumer prices and tax increases (to finance some pollution expenditures), higher wage demands to compensate for the decline of real disposable income. It is difficult to see anything but a once-and-for-all change in a number of relative prices in pollution expenditures. Such a cause of inflation

---

[46] Economic Outlook, No. 11, July 1972, p. 10.

[47] Van Lennep (1973, p. 17).

[48] Economic Implications of Pollution Control, February 1974.

is invalid except for aggregate demand effects which, in turn, depend crucially on how expenditures are financed. [49]

C. World Inflation

The fact that inflation accelerated in virtually all industrialized countries at the same time and to the same degree is more than a coincidence. The 1970 Report by the Secretary General mentioned the possibility of common causation but did not explore this. In the follow-up by WP4, ". . . the conclusion was reached that for the seven larger countries the origin of present inflationary difficulties had generally been far more of a domestic than an external nature."[50] In a subsequent Economic Outlook it was stated that in, ". . .all but the very biggest countries . . . unless exchange rates are to be sufficiently flexible, it is difficult for a single open economy to do much better than the general trend." [51]

This is consistent with a simple Hume-Johnson-Mundell monetarist view of world inflation under fixed exchange rates. The importance of exchange rate changes in freeing a country from external inflation has been mentioned in most publications since the Report by the Secretary General in 1970 which stated that, "Where appropriate targets for different countries or groups of countries prove to be incompatible with balance of payments equilibrium, the authorities should be prepared to make timely adjustments in exchange rates." [52] Not unreasonably, all forecasts are made on the assumption of unchanged exchange rates.

Another theme in OECD papers is that price stability in earlier periods was associated with islands of stability[53] in the larger countries, and that the success of some of the larger countries in fighting inflation would ease the situation for the small countries. [54] This does not explain inflation, however.

Although the OECD's approach to world inflation presented above must appear fairly orthodox, it has been severely criticized by Harry Johnson as having ". . . a well known institutional bias . . . towards regarding each country as a special case." [55] This is not surprising since the 24 governments pay for this type

[49] See Victor (1972, p. 52).

[50] Present Policies against Inflation, p. 31.

[51] Economic Outlook, No. 13, July 1973, p. 9.

[52] Inflation:the Present Problem, p. 34.

[53] Inflation:the Present Problem, p. 7.

[54] Present Policies against Inflation, p. 24.

[55] Harry G. Johnson (1972, p. 16).

of analysis (see section VI below). It is true, however, that few resources appear to have been devoted to exploring inflation as a world phenomenon and that efforts by small countries within the OECD to develop concerted international action against inflation have not been successful.

The determinants of world inflation and its transmission have not received much attention aside from the 1971 "follow-up" report and the Economic Outlook, No. 13. In the latter, alternative theories of inflation were confronted with a set of data from a number of countries. The study appeared to refute the early monetarist view that world inflation resulted from U.S. balance of payments deficits; it suggested the role of traded goods prices and the change in international monetary arrangements as increasingly important causes of inflation. On the whole, the study should be assessed as inconclusive.

Since that time most economists working in this area have been much more careful in dealing with excess demand as an explanation of inflation. Stress has now been laid on the Vietnam War and its financing in the development of U.S. inflation. The theory that defensive money creation occurred in Europe in reaction to the U.S. deficits can also be omitted as a cause of the 1969 acceleration of world inflation. In fact, the growth of the non-U.S. OECD money supply did not accelerate until 1971 (for this work the OECD used IMF money supply data which leaves something to be desired with respect to coverage and comparability).

One aspect of the OECD's work that is not widely known is its discussion of possible coordinated international approaches to inflation. These arose via proposals made by Austria and Switzerland. The fact that very small nations were at the mercy of larger nations' policies was fully appreciated. Although exchange rate changes are a valid way to free a country from world inflation, continuous exchange rate appreciation was clearly not viewed as a second-best solution by the countries involved.

The international coordination of prices and incomes policies was also recommended (in the Economic Outlook, No. 13) on the ground that import prices cannot be controlled by one government. Not only would this plan provoke the opposition of pressure groups in all countries, but it would obscure the international adjustment mechanism. Almost universally export prices are excluded from price control policies.

D. Fighting Inflation: Price-Incomes Policies and the Shotgun Approach

One recommendation the OECD has been consistently making to control inflation since 1962 is the adoption of price-incomes policies. In Exhibit I of the Appendix, we offer a succinct set of programmatic statements made by the OECD on the subject. Before analyzing the reasons for such a recommendation it is important to note that many member countries have opposed price-incomes policy. In this respect it behooves us to differentiate reports which have been approved by all of the member countries, such as Present Policies against Inflation and reports written entirely by the Secretariat such as the Economic Outlook. In the former the influence of countries for and against the policy produces a much more balanced picture than in the latter.

First, let us consider the OECD Secretariat's view. The 1970 Report by the Secretary General states that, ". . . elements of price-incomes policy can make a valuable contribution to breaking a wage/price spiral as part of an overall stabilization program."[56]   The usual difficulties were mentioned as well as the fact that prices and incomes policies are not a substitute for proper demand management policies. This recommendation apparently was not mere intuition but a result of an analysis of the experience in particular countries where the OECD Secretariat found that the ". . . record seems to show fairly clearly that price-incomes policy of both the national bargain and guidelines variety has succeeded in restraining price rises for a period of up to one or two years."[57] Examples were given of particular successes such as in the United Kingdom and Finland, although the longer term results were deemed to be more doubtful and controversial. Considerable attention was devoted to the income distributional aspects and "harmony" among the social partners. One enigmatic statement refers to the belief that it is a ". . . mistake to base price-incomes policies too heavily on balance of payments considerations."[58]   It is also worth noting that price and incomes policies have been recommended for Japan during periods of substantial balance of payments surplus.[59]

A second justification for prices and incomes policies is that they enable expectations of future inflation to be reduced without the reduction in output that would otherwise be necessary to secure the same results. Since the expectations augmented Phillips curve seems fairly well grounded empirically, this approach might yield benefits, provided such policies are effective and the side effects are not too costly. This is the view of the OECD as reflected in many issues of the Economic Outlook. On the other hand, in 1969 the Economic Out-

---

[56] Inflation: the Present Problem, p. 40.

[57] Inflation: the Present Problem, p. 37.

[58] Inflation: the Present Problem, p. 40.

[59] See, for example, Economic Survey of Japan, July 1973, pp. 64-65. This is carefully hedged for the Japanese institutional case. It correctly recommended reducing import barriers as an appropriate prices policy.

look editorial stated that such policies could not be an emergency expedient but could serve as a useful adjunct to anti-inflationary policy in a longer perspective.[60] Clearly, there appears to be a contradiction involved, for a longer run anti-inflationary policy of this nature would not be able to exercise any dramatic influence on short-run inflationary expectations; at least this appears to have been the experience of countries with such longer run programs.

A third element in the OECD doctrine is that price-incomes policies cannot work when prices are rising exceptionally fast or when demand pressures are strong. Consequently, the time for action is when demand pressures are being abated.

The views of the members of WP4 are considerably different from those mentioned above. In Present Policies against Inflation, although the preferences of the "majority view" in finding these policies desirable are stated, the report is extremely guarded about the possible benefits. The minority view is stated clearly - - inflationary expectations will subside if governments can control price movements by aggregate demand management policies and that, thereafter, appropriate demand management policies alone should suffice. The report also notes that, ". . . to embark on what might have to be quite radical changes in an economic system which has served so well, for the sake of reducing the rate of inflation by one or two percentage points, would, as of now, be premature."[61]

What is the actual record of prices and incomes policies? The OECD produces no evidence, nor does it refer to any to corroborate its points concerning prices and incomes policies. At the present time, the widely perceived failure of such policies in the United States and the United Kingdom would bias a casual answer. The bulk of the rigorous testing has produced weak results on an individual basis. They generally tend to discredit any longer run success. The problems of determining when policies were enforced and the method of estimating coefficients of a simultaneous system are overshadowed by the greater need to have a proper specification of wage and price equations, as well as a knowledge of how prices and incomes policies would influence these equations. Nonetheless, the evidence, as it is, does not seem to support any significant success for such policies in reducing the rate of inflation.[62] Parkin has produced evidence that the effect of price guideposts on longer term price expectations appears to have been minimal, even though short-run expectations were altered. [63]

[60] Economic Outlook No. 6, December 1969, p. 6.

[61] Present Policies against Inflation, p. 35.

[62] See the articles in Parkin and Sumner (1972), in particular those by Parkin, Sumner, and Jones, "A Survey of the Econometric Evidence of the Effects of Incomes Policy on the Rate of Inflation," and Smith, "Incomes Policy."

[63] Parkin (1973, pp. 535-545).

Lipsey and Parkin found that guideposts tipped the Phillips curve in such a way as to lower the inflation rate with respect to the "controlled" market solution at low levels of unemployment, but actually raised it at relative high levels of unemployment. [64] In a study of the U.S. Phase II, Bosworth observes a lower inflation rate, but cannot conclude that the guideposts were responsible for it. [65] Robert J. Gordon instead finds that the wage-price control program moderated the rate of inflation during its first year by almost 2 percent. [66]

Feige and Pearce conclude that both Phases I and II left no traceable effect in calming inflation. [67] Finally, C. Jackson Grayson, Jr., the Chairman of the Price Commission during Phase II, has gone on record as saying that wage-price guideposts raise "false" expectations in the sense that the solution to inflation is believed to be easier than it actually is; and that under some circumstances it will prevent decreases in wages and prices which would occur under a market solution. [68]

The OECD appears to be aware that price-income guidelines have not worked in the past and are not likely to work in the long run. Nonetheless, it continues to recommend them on the basis of some evidence that they are able to restrain price rises for periods of one to two years. We would like to question the value of this evidence. Ulman and Flanagan, in reviewing the evidence of the effectiveness of incomes policy in restraining inflation for various countries, conclude that the guidelines on the whole failed to meet their objectives. [69] The same study advances the proposition that organizations such as the OECD and the IMF have recommended incomes policies as an instrument to correct balance of payments difficulties and to promote growth by restraining consumption. Our reading of the records does not confirm this proposition. Outside of the inflation argument, the OECD has looked at incomes policy as a social pacifier, the tool through which a government could achieve an income distribution which minimizes social strife. In Policies for Price Stability (1962) there is a heavy undertone of sociological reasoning which hints quite clearly at some notion of "social justice." This point is further discussed in Exhibit I of the Appendix.

[64] Lipsey and Parkin (1970, pp. 115-38).

[65] Bosworth (1972, pp. 343-83).

[66] Robert J. Gordon (1972, pp. 385-421).

[67] Feige and Pearce (1973, pp. 40-44).

[68] Grayson (1974).

[69] Ulman and Flanagan (1971).

It would be inaccurate on our part to conclude that wage-price guidelines are all the OECD has to offer as an anti-inflationary instrument. On the contrary, the Secretary General has warned that the solution to inflation may require a global or multi-purpose strategy or what Brunner has called the shotgun approach. This global strategy includes a long list starting from the appropriate use of fiscal and monetary policies (which were deemed in the same report not to be reliable in controlling the rate of inflation) and ending with an active program of trade liberalization.

We contend that a multi-policy approach is consistent with the objective function of the OECD (see section VI below). This organization has 24 paying customers each of whom has a say in the work program and must be given some satisfaction in terms of the analytical approach to anti-inflationary policy. A large number of countries are strict believers in the Nordic two-sector model. Others, particularly the United States and Canada, are on record as accepting an expectations augmented Phillips curve approach. Others believe that inflation has more to do with sociology than economics. Obviously, the smaller the country the smaller the importance attached to views which are not shared by those responsible for the drafting of OECD reports. Nonetheless, the published OECD views on inflation are a curious mixture of the views of a group of delegates from 24 countries and a small group of OECD economists.

Finally, we shall conclude our section on inflation by saying something about the OECD's views on indexation, a topic which has received a great deal of attention lately. There is no uniformity of views on indexation within the OECD. For instance, the recent report by the Financial Markets Division [70] is against the indexation of securities, whereas the Economics and Statistics Department apparently is generally in favor of indexation. [71] The latter department looks upon indexation as an instrument which prevents the redistribution of income either among groups in the private sector or between the private sector and the government. The 1971 inflation report gives the views of national delegations on this matter; however, as would be expected, the diversity of views leads to ineffectual conclusions.

---

[70] Indexation of Fixed Interest Securities, 1974.

[71] It is known that WP2 recommended that countries index their personal income tax brackets and exemptions. A WP2 document is referred to in Allan, et. al. (1974, pp. 355-365).

IV. MONETARY POLICY

The objective of this section is to analyze those passages of the Economic Outlook and other OECD publications which bear directly on the general topic of money and, in particular, on how money is generated in an economy and its impact on relevant financial and real variables.

A. Money in the Economic Outlook

As we have already indicated in section II, the measurement of the monetary impulse and its role in the general equilibrium of the system are not coherently developed in the Economic Outlook. We have, nonetheless, identified a number of issues raised by this publication to warrant an investigation on our part.

i) Monetary policy and interest rates. The first issue of the Economic Outlook states that:

> The experience of the past months has demonstrated that monetary policy can bring about a very rapid change in short-term rates by influencing the liquidity of the banking system. But the recent upward turn in long-term rates in some countries where monetary policy is still expansionary also shows that these rates do not necessarily follow the trend set by monetary policy in the short-term market. [72]

While an expansionary monetary policy (e.g., a purchase of securities by the central bank) is clearly recognized as having a depressing effect on short-term rates of interest, the positive association between monetary policy and rates of interest in the long run is not openly acknowledged. This latter aspect of the analysis may be ignored given the emphasis on short-run considerations by the OECD. We have no evidence to present in support of the thesis that the OECD feels that the effect of output changes and price expectations are not relevant in the formation of interest rates. However, we can state that if they are relevant they must be of secondary importance with respect to the thrust of monetary policy. This is a direct implication of the observation that interest rates have been used as a "good" indicator of the course of monetary policy.

---

[72] Economic Outlook, No. 1, July 1967, p. 15.

103

Evidence supporting the use of short-term interest rates as an indicator of policy can be found in the Economic Outlook. This finding is hardly surprising in view of the traditional preference of central banks to follow a similar approach. Nonetheless, references to money stock and bank credit figures have appeared in more recent issues of the Economic Outlook.

We recall that the interest rate is a good indicator of policy when, with reference to the IS-LM framework, changes in monetary policy cause the LM curve to move along an unchanging IS curve. Difficulties arise when shifts in the IS and LM curves are not independent of each other. Specifically, to the extent that the rate of interest and the policy-controlled monetary base (the instrument of monetary policy) behave procyclically - - which is the case for many countries - - and the rate of interest responds positively to output changes and negatively to changes in the monetary base, the rate of interest is a misleading indicator of the thrust of policy. This is so because a rise in the rate of interest may be interpreted to be tight even though money is expanding, although not fast enough to more than offset the "real" forces which push up the interest rate. [73] Essentially the quality of the rate of interest as an indicator of the thrust of policy deteriorates as the policy actions become marginally important with respect to non-policy actions. The choice of whether the money stock or the rate of interest is a better indicator of policy reduces to the following empirical proposition. If the dependence of the money stock on non-policy actions is small relative to the dependence of the rate of interest, the money stock is a better indicator of monetary policy. [74] The Economic Outlook presents no evidence to settle the argument.

ii) Monetary policy and asset substitutability. A major proposition of the Radcliffe Report was that the existence of a high degree of substitutability among various assets weakens the effectiveness of monetary policy. It also appears in OECD writing. [75] A corollary to this proposition was that money cannot be uniquely defined and that commercial banks have no unique role to play for they contribute to the creation of a quantity which is not unique. Thus,the money stock was relegated to a minor role, while the more general concept of liquidity moved to center stage.

In a world where (only) two assets are considered, money and bonds, it is true that the greater the substitution between money and bonds, the smaller the impact of money (and the greater the importance of fiscal policy) on economic

---

[73] Brunner and Meltzer (1969).

[74] Brunner and Meltzer (1969, pp. 15-16).

[75] Inflation:the Present Problem, p. 33.

activity. However, in a world where money interacts with bonds and capital, and money is not identified with bank credit, a high degree of substitution between money and bonds implies nothing by itself about the role of monetary policy. Indeed, as Brunner puts it, "A very high interest elasticity of money demand is consistent with a dominant role of monetary impulses, provided the interest elasticities in the credit market are even larger."[76]

iii) <u>Monetary policy as a deflationary force</u>. Monetary policy acts asymmetrically in the sense that it is more effective as a deflationary than as an expansionary force. The reason for the relatively poor performance of an easy monetary policy is justified by the assertion that, ". . .spending decisions depend importantly on factors other than the cost and availability of credit and may not respond very quickly to easier monetary conditions."[77]

iv) <u>The case for credit controls</u>. Credit controls, according to the OECD, have two advantages over "traditional" methods to bring about a tighter monetary policy.[78] First, they curtail credit without driving interest rates too high. Second, they reduce the lag between the initial policy impulse and its effect on bank credit.

The first reason seems to imply that high rates of interest are not important in dampening spending decisions or they have undesriable side effects, or both. It also implies that changes in bank credit and money shift the IS as well as the LM schedules. Referring to our earlier comments, it is difficult to reconcile the use of interest rates as indicators of the thrust of monetary policy with the recommendation of credit controls.

v) <u>The assignment problem</u>. Under a system of fixed exchange rates, monetary policy is believed to have a comparative advantage in influencing the external balance, while fiscal policy has a comparative advantage in influencing the internal balance. This is clear from a reading of the first issue of the <u>Economic Outlook</u>.

> . . .the events of 1966 show very clearly how much the direction and magnitude of international capital movements depend on the vigour with which monetary policy is used compared with other instruments of demand management.[79]

---

[76] Brunner (1971, p. 53).

[77] Economic Outlook, No. 1, July 1967, p. 16.

[78] Economic Outlook, No. 1, July 1967, p. 7. It has been suggested to us that our criticism on this point is dated. Prior to 1971, advocacy of credit controls was standard policy in the United Kingdom and (perhaps therefore) in the OECD, but credit controls are no longer held to be useful by either.

[79] Economic Outlook, No. 1, July 1967, p. 16.

B. Monetary Policy in the Monetary Study Series

Three country studies have so far been published by the OECD in its attempts to deepen its knowledge of the working of monetary policy. In order of publication, the countries are Japan, Italy, and Germany.[80] There are further studies in progress concerning the United States and France. The three published monographs provide useful information about the financial structure of these countries and the relevant institutional arrangements. To this extent they supplement works of a similar nature.[81]

The studies share a common research outline. The first part of the monographs deals with the general characteristics of the money and capital markets. Flow-of-funds data are used to illustrate the relative importance of various financial instruments, types of intermediaries, and markets. The second part is devoted to a description of the instruments of monetary policy and to how policy is formulated by the monetary authorities. A third section concerns itself with how policy instruments influence key financial variables. A final section discusses the transmission of monetary impulses to the real sector of the economy. Econometric evidence bearing on the various components of aggregate demand is presented in the Japanese and German studies. In the Italian study reference is made to the large econometric model of the Banca d'Italia. The emphasis placed on each of the four topics differs from study to study. The Japanese study stresses more the proposition that monetary policy has been the major driving force of business cycles in the 1960s and that it was assigned to satisfy simultaneously the internal as well as the external equilibrium.[82] The Italian study spends more time in discussing the bank credit market.

None of the studies develops a money market model of its own. All of them broadly reflect the "state of the arts" inside the home country's decision-making institutions. The German monograph relies heavily for the interpretation of monetary policy on the Bundesbank "free liquid reserves" approach. (Although the official definition of "free liquid reserves" has changed over time, it is equivalent to the sum of free reserves in the U.S. sense, "secondary liquidity" and

---

[80] Monetary Policy in Japan, Monetary Studies Series, December 1972; Monetary Policy in Italy, Monetary Study Series, May 1973; Monetary Policy in Germany, Monetary Study Series, December 1973.

[81] See Hodgman (1974); Holbik (1973); EEC (1972).

[82] Monetary Policy in Japan, pp. 9 and 58-65.

foreign reserve assets.) This approach has been severely criticized and has been abandoned recently by the Bundesbank. [83] The difficulty of explaining bank credit and the money stock on the basis of the Bundesbank conception of policy appears several times during the study; for example:

> To sum up the previous paragraphs, there is little evidence to suggest a stable impact of monetary policy on the main monetary aggregates, bank credit and the money stock (narrowly or broadly defined). The impact of bank liquidity management on bank credit has been influenced by, among other things, net inflows or outflows of capital and by the impact of M1 from variations in relative interest rates. [84]

It is not monetary policy which cannot exert a stable impact on the monetary aggregates, but the particular and restrictive conception of monetary policy as expressed by changes in "free liquid reserves" which exhibits this poor relationship. There are alternative and detailed explanations of the German bank credit and money supply processes which find a stable relationship between these magnitudes and the monetary base. [85] In other words, once we substitute the concept of central bank money for "free liquid reserves" as the relevant operating target in the system, we find a radical change in the interpretation of what monetary policy can or cannot do.

An issue which both the German and the Italian studies raise is the extent to which monetary policy is independent under fixed rates of exchange and highly integrated capital markets. [86] Both studies refer to the research of Kouri and Porter who test this hypothesis using a five-asset-market model. [87] A verbal description of the problem and of the relevant test implications goes as follows. Under fixed exchange rates the ability of the central bank to achieve target levels or growth rates of the total monetary base depends on the degree of integration of national capital markets. The central bank has direct control on the domestic component of the monetary base. Changes in the latter affect interest rates in such a way as to provoke an opposite movement in the foreign component of the

---

[83] Criticisms of "free liquid reserves" as an indicator have been raised over the years in the Konstanzer Seminars on Monetary Theory and Policy. See the paper by Neumann (1972). The motivation underlying the Bundesbank's decision to rid itself of "free liquid reserves" as an indicator of the thrust of policy is found in Bockelman (1974).

[84] Monetary Policy in Germany, p. 71.

[85] Neumann (1974).

[86] For Germany see Monetary Policy in Germany, pp. 57-66, and for Italy see Monetary Policy in Italy, pp. 49-50.

[87] Kouri and Porter (1974, pp. 443-67).

base. In other words, an expansionary monetary policy measured by an increase in the domestic component of the base is accompanied by a net outflow of capital and thus of the foreign component of the base. When a dollar increase in the domestic component of the monetary base is "offset" by a dollar decrease in the foreign component of the base, monetary policy is said by Kouri and Porter to be totally ineffective. This appears to be the case for Germany.

> We find that the offset coefficient approximates 100 percent for Germany and Australia and 50 percent for Italy and the Netherlands and conclude that under fixed exchange rates an independent monetary policy will only be effective in these latter countries. [88]

There is a fundamental difficulty with the Kouri-Porter analysis. Namely, that an "offset" coefficient equal to one is only one of the two conditions which must be satisfied to eliminate the usefulness of monetary policy under a regime of fixed exchange rates. The other condition is that, as capital flows in and out of the country, the foreign demand for domestic bonds is not affected. But if domestic bonds are traded, a capital outflow, "offsetting" an autonomous injection of base money, implies a reduction in the foreign holdings of domestic bonds and thus a change in the yield on bonds, although the total monetary base has remained unaltered. [89]

A particular useful feature of the Italian study is the description of the evolution of the Banca d'Italia in perceiving monetary processes. Like the Bundesbank, the Italian central bank until 1965 formulated monetary policy by using as an operational target a subset of bank reserves, namely excess reserves. This concept was abandoned in 1966 in favor of the monetary base concept which was used in a model of bank credit which followed (in principle but not in content) the research of Brunner and Meltzer. [90]

It was the intellectual foresight of Governor Carli who made this drastic switch possible. He perceived from an operational viewpoint the two great advantages of the new framework. First, the monetary base was potentially under the control of the authorities, whereas excess reserves were not. Second, the relationship between the monetary base and bank credit and the money stock

---

[88] Kouri and Porter (1974, pp. 443-467).

[89] Fratianni (1976).

[90] Fazio (1968).

was relatively stable, with stability improving the longer the period under consideration. [91]

C. Issues in the Transmission Mechanism

Interest in monetary economics exists because of the role of money in determining the level of economic activity. In the last ten years the relative importance of monetary and fiscal policy on the real sector of the economy has attracted the attention of many scholars and prompted a large amount of research, most of which was done in the United States. The work of Fisher and Sheppard reviews for the OECD much of this material with a view to sorting out evidence which bears directly on the long-standing debate between monetarists and Keynesians. [92] We shall summarize the main points raised by Fisher and Sheppard.

The two authors use the IS-LM framework as ". . . a representative device for interpreting the diverse positions of economists," [93] even though there are many economists who do not subscribe to the view that the IS-LM apparatus is capable of subsuming the different viewpoints. On this point we refer the reader to our discussion of the Radcliffe proposition that a high degree of substitution among financial assets weakens monetary policy (see section IV.A.ii). Be that as it may, Fisher and Sheppard assess the controversy according to five well-known propositions.

(a) Keynesians view the effect of monetary policy as occurring through the rate of interest.

(b) Monetarists instead stress the real balance effect which causes shifts in the IS curve.

(c) Monetarists and Keynesians alike recognize that changes in money affect the "real" sector and vice versa. However, monetarists state that the former transmission dominates the latter. Keynesians tend to take the opposite view.

(d) Keynesians assert that changes in money affect output and prices, but primarily output at less than full employment.

(e) Monetarists consider real income and output determined by the rest of the Walrasian system of equations. Monetary policy in the long run can alter only prices and nominal rates of interest.

---

[91] Fratianni (1971).

[92] Fisher and Sheppard (1972).

[93] Fisher and Sheppard(1972, p. 6).

Fisher and Sheppard review a selection of empirical material bearing on the above points. They settle dispute (c) in favor of the monetarists. There is substantial evidence to support both propositions (a) and (b). The impact of money on the household sector's expenditures in current prices is larger and more reliable than on expenditures in constant dollars. This is the major conclusion from empirical research on the household sector which points in favor of (e).

Although it is not specifically noted, the large econometric models in the United States have been cast in the Keynesian mold. The two authors review such models and offer the following criticisms.

(a) They lack the government budget constraint.

(b) Prices and wages are often ignored.

(c) There is no distinction between nominal and real rates of interest.

(d) They stress disaggregation without necessarily providing more information.

(e) Equations or blocks of equations are introduced on their own merit without much regard to the properties of the system as a whole.

Fisher and Sheppard finally take a look at the merit of the so-called "strong" monetarist position identified with the work done by the Federal Reserve Bank of St. Louis. They raise three types of criticism. First and foremost, causality can be inferred only from a tightly specified model. Neither the Anderson-Jordan one equation model nor the Anderson-Carlson model has a structure which is derived a priori. In the Anderson-Carlson model each equation stands out by itself, i.e., it is a reduced-form equation.

The second criticism is that the equation tested by Anderson and Jordan is not a reduced-form equation because it cannot be traced back to a model. In particular, the equation need not be consistent with any structure which economists would regard as acceptable. It is well known that reduced-form equations of over-identifiable systems yield coefficient estimates which are not able to shed information about the unique underlying structure. Anderson and Jordan complicate matters, according to Fisher and Sheppard, by not referring to a specific framework. Fisher and Sheppard heuristically develop a dynamic IS-LM model whose reduced-form equation for national income resembles the Anderson-Jordan equation with a major difference. Namely, the AJ equation ignores changes in income originating four quarters back which, in turn, could affect current changes in income through an accelerator-multiplier mechanism (this point was originally raised by the late Warren Smith).

Finally, Anderson and Jordan are accused of using the Almon lag structure technique inappropriately; in particular, (a) there is no a priori reason to constrain to zero the endpoints of the lag structures and (b) the "optimum" length of the lag structure should correspond to the minimum value of the standard error of the regression.

While we are in basic agreement with the methodological points raised by Fisher and Sheppard, we think that they miss an important merit of the Anderson-Jordan research. Namely, that their equation was meant to represent a "typical" (but possibly incomplete) reduced-form equation of competing models (with a structure) in which the money stock, or the monetary base, high-employment Federal expenditures and high-employment Federal tax receipts appear as the relevant policy impulses. There was no intention on the part of Anderson and Jordan to clearly identify the competing models, nor to provide one of their own. To a large extent we suspect that the study by Friedman and Meiselman for the Commission on Money and Credit and the ensuing controversy in the _American Economic Review_ of September 1965 provided a good reference point for the "approximate" structure underlying the tested equation. The objective instead was much more modest, and yet insightful: to estimate the relative size of the monetary and fiscal multipliers for those models in which the monetary base, autonomous government expenditures and tax revenues were treated as policy variables.

Money: Concluding Remarks

In the past 15 years great progress has been made in research on monetary economics. On many of the issues the OECD has taken positions clearly at variance with well established principles. On others, statements have been made without mentioning that they were open to debate. The Fisher-Sheppard study marked a clear improvement in that consultants were brought in to sort out the main points of an important debate. Other studies now in progress in the Department of Economics and Statistics appear to follow the good example set by the Fisher-Sheppard monograph. It is hard to say at this point whether we are just noticing a temporary phenomenon or the beginning of a permanent change in research strategy which aims at integrating the income-expenditure framework with asset-markets behavior.

V. FISCAL POLICY

This section is entirely dedicated to the work of Bent Hansen who in 1969 completed a study on the impact of fiscal policy for the "Big Seven" countries of the OECD.[94]   Three effects of fiscal policy are clearly differentiated.   The

---

[94] Hansen (1969).

total effect (E_T) is measured by the algebraic sum of the multipliers of national income with respect to government expenditures and total tax revenues. The discretionary effect (E_D) is given by the algebraic sum of the multipliers of national income with respect to government expenditures and the policy-controlled tax rates. Finally, the automatic effect (E_A) is obtained as a residual item by subtracting the discretionary from the total effect.

We can arrive at the above propositions in a more precise manner by using the basic Keynesian model of the OECD (see section II).

(5) $\qquad dY = dC + dN' + dG + dX - dIm,$

(6) $\qquad dC = c_1 (dY - dT) + dc_2,$

(7) $\qquad dIm = m_1 (dY - dT) + dm_2,$

(8a) $\qquad dT = tdY + Ydt,$

(8b) $\qquad dT = d\overline{T},$

where

$\qquad N' - N - G - X$
$\qquad G$ - government expenditures
$\qquad X$ - exports
$\qquad T$ - tax revenues.

Using (5) - (7) and (8a) we obtain the policy effect of fiscal policy.

(9) $\qquad E_D = \dfrac{dG - aYdt}{1 - a(1 - t)} \quad ,$

where

$\qquad a = c_1 + m_1.$

The total effect of fiscal policy is instead implied by (5) - (7) and (8b),

(10) $\qquad E_T = \dfrac{dG - ad\overline{T}}{1 - a}$

and

$$E_A = E_T - E_D .$$

There are two shortcomings with Hansen's approach. The first is that the fiscal impulses are being overstated when one or more asset markets are not explicitly included. This shortcoming applies to most of the literature dealing with the general subject matter of "fiscal performance." In the familiar IS-LM framework, the upward bias is proportional to the ratio of the interest sensitivity of the aggregate demand to the interest sensitivity of the money market. The proposition can be easily demonstrated by adding an investment function and a money market to the system (5) - (8),

$$(11) \qquad dN' = -b_1 dr + db_2 ,$$

$$(12) \qquad dM = e_1 dY - e_2 dr + de_3 ,$$

where r is the rate of interest and M the money stock which we shall assume to be under the control of the monetary authorities. In this enlarged system the corresponding discretionary and total fiscal effects are:

$$(13) \qquad E_D' = \frac{dG - aY dt}{1 - a(1 - t) + b_1 e_1/e_2} ,$$

and

$$(14) \qquad E_T' = \frac{dG - a\overline{dT}}{1 - a + b_1 e_1/e_2} .$$

E_D' and E_T' approach E_D and E_T, respectively, as $b_1 = 0$ or $e_1 = 0$ or $e_2 \to \infty$ or, in other words, as either the IS curve becomes perfectly inelastic or the LM curve becomes perfectly elastic at a given rate of interest.

In practice we have some fairly reliable knowledge that e_1 is not zero, that the income elasticity of the demand for money is close to unity and that the interest elasticity of the demand for money, far from being infinite, is numerically smaller than unity. We do recognize, however, that at the time Hansen made his study, few countries, outside the United States, had produced reliable estimates of b_1 and e_2. More information is now available as a result of the first crop of European econometric models.

If the money market is included in this framework for fiscal analysis, equations (9) and (10) or (13) and (14) represent instantaneous multipliers which hold at a given point in time, for given levels of the stock variables. If we ignore the capital stock in order to simplify the model, two financial stocks are held constant in the instantaneous run: the stocks of money and government securities, both of which are used to finance a government deficit. The stock of money is also affected by a surplus or deficit in the trade balance. The stock-flow equilibrium constraint underlying (5) - (7), (8a), (11) and (12) can be stated as

$$(15) \qquad X - Im + G - T + B = \frac{dM}{dt} + \frac{d(B/r)}{dt} \quad,$$

where B is the number of government perpetuities paying a $1 interest per period and where personal disposable income is now defined as $Y - T + B$ rather than $Y - T$. The constraint (15) is satisfied at a given point in time in a continuous model. The Hansen study, however, deals with discrete changes and (15) is no longer applicable. The relevant model, recast in first differences, can be reduced to

$$(16) \qquad \Delta Y[1 - a(1 - t)] + b_1 \Delta r = \Delta G + \Delta X + a[Y\Delta t + \Delta B] + \Delta b_2 + \Delta c_2,$$

$$(17) \qquad \Delta Y e_1 \qquad\qquad - e_2 \Delta r = \Delta M - \Delta e_3,$$

subject to the condition

$$(18) \quad \Delta G - t\Delta Y - Y\Delta t + \Delta X - m\Delta Y - mt\Delta Y - mY\Delta t + D + E + \Delta B = \Delta M + \frac{\Delta B}{r}.$$

Equation (18) says that the budget deficit at the beginning of the period (D), plus the change in government expenditures, plus the change in interest payments, minus the change in total tax revenues, plus the trade balance surplus at the beginning of the period (E), plus the change in exports, minus the change in imports must be equal to an increase in the stocks of money and government securities.

We are now ready to raise our second criticism; namely, that the fiscal multipliers considered by Hansen are independent of the financial aspect of the budget. This oversight may be particularly serious as Christ and as Hansen have noted.[95] The same point was raised by another OECD report.[96]

---

[95] Christ (1967, pp. 434-443); Hansen (1973, pp. 10-11).

[96] Lotz (1971, pp. 10-11).

Hansen was aware of the problem but avoided the solution by asserting that the financial effect of the budget is a subject of monetary policy.

> . . . it might be argued that since, at least on the aggregative level, changes in the liquidity of the private sector can be offset through appropriate measures of monetary policy, open market operations, etc., which affect the composition and value of assets and debts in the private sector, such effects can in this particular context be disregarded as belonging to the realm of monetary policy. [97]

But it is not clear that the financial aspect of the budget can be unambiguously classified as belonging to monetary policy alone. [98] Regardless of how one classifies this there are two important issues that must be raised. The first is that the basic notion that the impact of fiscal policy on economic activity is a direct relation of more (less) expenditures inducing more (less) income is substantially altered once the financial impact is properly incorporated. It is well recognized now that government expenditures financed by (base) money are more expansionary than expenditures financed by securities. There is some debate whether the latter might have a zero or even a negative effect on income as a result of "crowding out" private expenditures.

The second issue concerns the way the fiscal multipliers change as the set of policy instruments independently used by the authorities changes. With reference to (16) - (18), we notice that out of the four eligible policy variables (ΔG, $Y\Delta t$, ΔB and ΔM) one of them must be a linear combination of the other three. Which means that, once three instruments are independently maneuvered, the fourth one must acquire a value which is consistent with the solution of (16) - (18). Consider first the set of independently chosen instruments, G, $Y\Delta t$ and B. After replacing ΔM of the stock-flow constraint into the money market equation, the following becomes the discretionary effect of fiscal policy.

$$(19) \qquad E_D'' = \frac{(b_1 + e_1)\Delta G - [b_1(1 + m) + e_2 a]Y\Delta t + [e_2 a + b_1(\frac{r-1}{r})]\Delta B}{b_1 \delta + \beta e_2}$$

$$\beta = 1 - a(1 - t),$$

$$\delta = e_1 + t + m(1 + t),$$

---

[97] Hansen (1973, p. 17).

[98] See the term III of equations (10') and (10'a) as well as the relevant discussion on pp. 557 and 559 of Hansen (1973).

which differs markedly from (13) in both the weights attached to ΔG and $Y\Delta t$ and the presence of the new policy parameter ΔB.

If, instead, ΔG, $Y\Delta t$ and ΔM are the independently set policy instruments, the discretionary impulse is

$$(20) \qquad E_D''' = \frac{e_2\left[1 + a\,\frac{r}{1-r}\right]\Delta G - e_2 a[\,1 + \frac{r}{1-r}\,(1+m)]Y\Delta t}{b_1 e_1 + e_2 \beta'}$$

$$\beta' = \beta + a\frac{r}{1-r}[t + m(1+t)]\ .$$

A statistical application of multipliers (19) and (20) would have required, in addition to a knowledge of the slope properties of the investment and money demand functions, an understanding of the actual policy mix or policy mixes pursued by a given country over the sample period.

Hansen performed his statistical work on a model which has a close affinity to (5) - (8) but is more detailed in a variety of ways. The model is summarized in Table 5. To begin with, there is a distinction between changes in prices and changes in output. This distinction is only formal because the supply of output is assumed to be infinitely elastic at a given price level, according to the purest form of Keynesian economics. Supposedly, this assumption breaks down at high levels of resource utilization, but the model does not attempt to formalize the relationship. Hansen justifies this on the ground that appropriate data are not available to measure budget effects at full employment. A second difference in the empirical model is that direct and indirect taxes are explicitly introduced. Third, the government sector affects the output market by absorbing goods as well as labor services. Two alternatives are considered with respect to the treatment of the price government pays for goods and services. The first alternative, which is relevant for "market" economies, envisions the government to be a price taker. It follows that the prices the government pays for goods and services are not policy parameters. They are excluded from the measure E_D but are entered, of course, in E_T and therefore in E_A. In the second alternative, the government is capable of setting prices independently of conditions existing in the goods and labor markets of the private sector. Under this condition E_D incorporates the effect of such price changes.

Tables 2 and 3, which are taken directly from the Hansen study, show some of the most significant results. Table 2 requires no comment except that it is openly recognized that the assigned values to t_i, t_d, a and μ are rough approxi-

116

Table 2

Numerical Values of Coefficients used
in Multiplier Formulas

Country	t_i	t_d	a	μ
Belgium	0.15	0.10	0.75	0.50
France	0.21	0.08	0.75	0.15
Germany	0.16	0.17	0.70	0.20
Italy	0.13	0.08	0.70	0.17
Sweden	0.10	0.30	0.80	0.40
United Kingdom	0.09	0.20	0.68	0.28
United States	0.12	0.17	0.75	0.05

Table 3

Values of Multipliers

Country	Multipliers for Discretionary Changes				Multipliers for Total Changes		
	$dg^d + dl$	$(gdp_g + ldw)$	ydt^d	cdt_i	$dg^d + dl$	$(gdp_g + ldw)$ and $dT_d{}^*$	dT_i
	1	2	3	4	5	6	7
Belgium	+1.42	+0.42	-0.46	-0.62	+1.60	±0.60	-0.80
France	+1.94	+0.94	-1.02	-1.36	+2.76	±1.76	-2.34
Germany	+1.67	+0.67	-0.81	-1.15	+2.27	±1.27	-1.82
Italy	+1.89	+0.89	-0.96	-1.39	+2.38	±1.38	-1.98
Sweden	+1.44	+0.44	-0.63	-0.79	+1.92	±0.92	-1.15
United Kingdom	+1.56	+0.56	-0.70	-1.03	+1.96	±0.96	-1.41
United States	+2.12	+1.12	-1.35	-1.80	+3.48	±2.48	-3.30

* + to be used for $(gdp_g + ldw)$, - for dT_d.

mations of the true parameters. Table 3, which was compiled using the formulas of Table 5 and the data of Table 2, provides information about the average thrust of fiscal policy over the sample period for a unit increase in g^d, ℓ , t_i, t_d, p_g, w, T_i, and T_d. These results are tabulated below by excluding from the discretionary effect of the budget expenditure changes attributable to prices and wages paid by the government.

Table 4

Values of Multipliers

Country	Discretionary	Total
Belgium	0.34	0.80
France	-0.44	0.42
Germany	-0.29	0.45
Italy	-0.46	0.40
Sweden	0.02	0.77
U.K.	-0.17	0.55
U.S.	-1.03	0.18

source: Table 2

We notice that balanced budgets are expansionary, while the discretionary effect of fiscal policy is negative. The actual impact of fiscal policy will, of course, depend on the numerical changes of the various components of the government budget over the sample period.

Fiscal performance is assessed by Hansen both in terms of its long-run impact on output and on its ability to reduce cyclical fluctuations in output. The long-run impact on output is measured by the average budget effect, i.e., by

$$\bar{e}_T = \frac{1}{N} \sum_{i=1}^{N} \frac{E_{T,i}}{Y_{-1-i}} \, ,$$ where N is the number of observations (and similar formulas

for $\bar{e}_A$ and $\bar{e}_D$). The value of $\bar{e}_T$ was found to be positive for all countries except the United Kingdom. Substantial differences emerge depending on whether the central government or general government (which includes state and local governments as well as investments made by government-owned enterprises) is the relevant institutional unit. While, on the whole, $\bar{e}_T$ of the general government was positive, that of the central government was negative. The discretionary component $\bar{e}_D$ was found to be larger than $\bar{e}_T$ implying that $\bar{e}_A$ has acted as a built-in stabilizer.

The stabilization quality of fiscal policy was assessed essentially using the ratio of two standard deviations

$$\sqrt{\frac{\Sigma(g - \bar{g})^2}{\Sigma(g^* - \bar{g}^*)^2}}$$

where $g = dy/y_{-1}$, g^* stands for the percentage change in real income that would occur in the absence of fiscal intervention, $\bar{g}$ and $\bar{g}^*$ are the sample means of g and g^*, respectively. When the above ratio is equal to one, fiscal forces exert no stabilizing effect; if it is equal to zero, stabilization is perfect; if it is larger than one the budget injects destabilizing forces into the system.

Hansen is careful to point out that a stabilization objective is a commendable deed on the part of governments if the act of stabilizing has an intrinsic merit or if the trend around which a stabilization program is orchestrated is consistent with the goals of economic policy (see our discussion of potential output in section II). Using the ratio of the two standard deviations as the appropriate "loss" function, the United Kingdom seems to have achieved a perverse policy in the sense that the above ratio was larger than unity for the three concepts of budget measures. France and Italy, the two countries which spend all the tax revenues they collect, have destabilized the economy through discretionary measures but have relied on strong automatic effects to achieve a total stabilizing effect. Finally, for Belgium, Germany, Sweden and the United States both discretionary and automatic effects were stabilizing.

The finding that total budget effects were stabilizing prompts the question: what are the main determinants of economic fluctuations? The monetarist position asserts that the real sector of the economy is dynamically stable and that business cycles result primarily from the money stock cycles. The Hansen study, although it cannot answer this question directly because the model excludes asset markets, attempts to provide evidence about the alternative explanation that disturbances in the real sector of the economy spark the dominant impulses underlying economic fluctuations. Various graphs are shown in the book which indicate that exports or exports plus investment are closely correlated with the output cycle.

As a concluding note to this section, we must remind the reader that we have found little or no evidence that the <u>Economic Outlook</u> has used the term "fiscal policy" in a manner which is consistent with the model or the measurement procedures developed by Hansen, or as summarized more recently by Lotz. We have no evidence, of course, that these procedures were not used by individuals within the Organisation. In fact, it is almost impossible to pinpoint either the analytical substance or the empirical content of the term "fiscal policy" as used in the Economic Outlook. One explanation is that since the actual effects of fiscal policy depend upon the financial aspects, and since the 24 countries each have different monetary institutions and situations at each point in time, a proper analysis would have required a good deal more effort and have had the disadvantage of exposing the Secretariat to a specific interpretation of the economic system. Such an outcome, as we will argue in Section VI, is inconsistent with one of the objectives of a bureau.

Table 5

The Hansen Model

(1) $y = i + c + g + \ell + x - m$

(2) $P_y y = P_i i + P_c c + P_g g + w\ell + P_x x - P_m m$

(3) $c = a \dfrac{P_y y - T_i - T_d}{P_c} + \beta$

(4) $P_c = P(1 + t_i)$

(4a) $P_c = P + \dfrac{T_i}{c}$

(5) $T_i = Pct_i$

(5a) $T_i = \bar{T}_i$

(6) $T_d = (P_y y - T_i)t_d + \gamma$

(6a) $T_d = \bar{T}_d$

(7) $m = \mu(i + c + g + x)$

where y, c, i, g, ℓ, x and m refer to real national income, real private consumption, real investment, real government purchases of goods and servic.., labor employment in government, real exports and real imports. The P with the subscripts refer to the relevant price deflators while w is the government wage rate. The initial level of all prices, including the wage rate, is set equal to unity. T_i and T_d are revenues from indirect and direct taxation, respectively; while t_i and t_d are the corresponding marginal tax rates. Differentiating (1) - (7) totally and solving for the discretionary effect E_{DH} and differentiating (1) - (3), (4a), (5a), (6a), and (7) totally and solving for the total effect E_{TH} gives,

$$E_{DH} = \frac{1}{\Delta}[(1 + t_i)(dg^d + d\ell) - \frac{a}{a}(1 - \mu)\,cdt_i - a(1 - \mu)ydt_d],$$

and

$$E_{TH} = \frac{1}{\delta}[(1 + \left(1 - \frac{a}{a}\right)\frac{T_i}{c})(dg^d + d\ell) + a(1 - \mu)(gdp_g + \ell dw) - \frac{a}{a}(1 - \mu)dT_i$$

$$-a(1 - \mu)\,dT_d]$$

where $dg^d = dg(1 - \mu)$, a = average propensity to consume,

$$\Delta = 1 + t_i - a(1 - \mu)(1 - t_d), \text{ and } \delta = 1 + \left(1 - \frac{a}{a}\right)\frac{T_i}{c} - a(1 - \mu) .$$

VI. THE OECD AS A BUREAUCRACY

There are two useful functions for an international organization like the OECD. The first is to provide a medium through which the burden of international adjustment can be shared among nations. This is intended not only in the narrow sense of responses to balance of payments deficits and surpluses under a more or less fixed exchange rate system, [99] but to encompass policy making in general. The most obvious need is for countries to keep one another informed about the anticipated level of demand, particularly where there are few barriers to trade or capital flows; as well as to address questions of international tax jurisdictions, antitrust laws, and multinational firms' activity. The second area concerns simply the exchange of information between member countries, not only on the economic outlook but also on institutional and policy changes.

---

[99] For alternative schema see Mundell (1968, Chapter 13).

Foreign ministries, treasuries and central banks spend considerable resources inquiring about policy alternatives pursued by other countries, their relative merit, as well as various types of data. An intermediary such as the OECD enjoys, quite obviously, economies of scale in this field (if nothing else by communicating with 2 rather than the 14 languages of the OECD membership).

With respect to the first point, one can inquire if such cooperation is possible. At the simplest level of analysis it can be shown that no committee procedure exists to satisfy simultaneously a number of "relevant" criteria such as transitivity, pairwise comparisons, equal treatment for different motions, unanimity, one-man one-vote, etc. In practice some of these criteria are of doubtful relevance or they could lead to impossibility or intransitivity in only a small percentage of the cases. For example, one-country one-vote may be a valid democratic principle but with disparate economic sizes and minimal interaction between some pairs of countries, it could be costly if its implementation were not constrained by criteria of relevance. Institutions develop practical solutions to this problem. One remedy is the time-honored practice of compromise. For example, each year the OECD reviews the economic performance and policy decisions of various member countries. A clash of opinions often occurs between the EDRC, which is in charge of such reviews, and the representatives of the countries under study. The struggle systematically ends with the deletion of potentially embarrassing comments from the published document.

Another remedy comes from an implicit bargaining process between small and large countries. For example, although Iceland could in principle have an equal voice with the United States in matters of trade or economic policy, it would usually decide not to exercise this right. By contrast, Iceland would have at least equal status with the United States, Norway, Canada, the United Kingdom and a few other countries on the Fisheries Committee.

A. Objectives of the Bureau

There are a number of theories of bureaucracy, often having features peculiar to the bureaucracies being studied; however, the assumption of a stable preference function containing prestige and self-preservation seems a reasonable point of departure. Behavioral standards which could apply to operational bureaus do not apply in a straightforward manner to the OECD because the latter has no means to implement policy. If this organization were judged by the standard of improving international economic cooperation, the events of the last eight years or so would have led to its dissolution. But the demand for OECD services has grown, as evidenced by the fact that a number of new members have joined the club.

Beyond any doubt the tendency for self-preservation has been a dominant objective. The organization has survived the end of its initial mandate. The Organization for European Economic Cooperation (OEEC) was initially set up to administer the Marshall Plan aid. Since then the OECD has gradually expanded its output by producing research which would be acceptable to various, and often contradictory, viewpoints. Eclecticism was chosen over dominant-impulse hypotheses as a general methodological vehicle. Indeed it is eclecticism, and not the reliance on falsifiable hypotheses, which raises the chances of survival of an institution. As Brunner has pointed out, it is clearly rational and advantageous for a bureau to produce "vague, inchoate and malleably suggestive ideas" and to choose a wide set of instruments in order to protect against specific criticism and to avoid being tagged with a bad policy. [100] The reader can prove for himself, by referring to our earlier sections, that the OECD's output fits this strategy quite well. Recall that because many countries wanted to accent the role of international trade prices, the Nordic two-sector model was adopted by the OECD. Recently, international inflation has been in demand by the member countries since this takes some of the pressure off their domestic policy decisions. The use of sociological theories is an extension of this principle: it protects both the OECD and its member countries from criticism concerning the failure of traditional policies to generate immediate results.

The importance of self-preservation as an institutional goal can be further evidenced by the observation that central governments and central banks are almost never blamed for inflation in OECD reports. The reader will recall that the failure to control spending of lower-level governments is mentioned, but this strengthens the position of the dominant federal or central governments which pay the OECD's bills. The avoidance of conflict with groups that could influence the organization's status is a major tenet of bureaucratic theory. The application of this to the forecasts and country studies makes these documents of questionable value aside from background information on policies, institutions and past performance. Another example comes from our discussion of monetary policy which showed that in the monetary studies of individual countries, rather than resort to separate models, approaches developed by the central banks themselves were used even where they were well known to be of dubious quality.

Although self-preservation is a primary objective, prestige also plays an important role in the utility function. We use prestige to mean the ability to influence governments in taking policy actions other than those contemplated by the governments themselves, as well as the way outsiders assess the quality of the organization's output. Indeed, the motivation for this report reflects the concern

---

[100] Brunner (1972, p. 7).

123

and interest of the academic world about some of these aspects of the organization. An important question, which we cannot properly answer is: what is the marginal rate of substitution between self-preservation and prestige? We offer here only some observations. On the one hand, being too close to the official line of governments reduces autonomy and also the prestige of the institution. It does, however, raise the chances of self-preservation. Being too far away, on the other hand, raises the independence characteristic of the organization but lowers prestige and ultimately threatens survival. The OECD as an organization does oppose governments on selected issues and in selective ways. For instance, if unanimity were a criterion, prices and incomes policies should never be mentioned. Nonetheless, many views not shared by governments are published so as to generate prestige at the expense of self-preservation. This is made possible by the small weights in the budget and in the OECD GNP by individual countries (see Table 6). The budget weights are based upon GNP at factor cost adjusted for size of population (to help Turkey) with an upper limit of 25 percent for any one country. This reduces the U.S. share and increases the potential independence of the Secretariat from the views of the U.S. representatives.

One characteristic of bureaus raised by Meltzer [101] was the nature of the political process that forces such groups to promise more than they can deliver. This is partly to generate prestige. The OECD continually recommends policies to increase international economic cooperation even if it cannot produce the goods. In a dynamic sense this is probably a reaction to failures over time. For instance, the OECD has been a vendor of price and incomes policies but these have never been demonstrably successful. Consequently, it recommended international price and incomes policies to get around the logical inadequacies of their domestic counterparts, notwithstanding that such a proposal would produce even more problems. Even though it never has to implement policies, the OECD has accented the difficulties of macroeconomic management. This is not displeasing to its customers and is consistent with the observation made by Acheson and Chant that increasing the seeming complexity of policy-making helps to defend against criticism and increase self-preservation. [102] In this case the OECD is simply providing the service its government clientele desires.

B. Role of Employees

The nature of the OECD as a forum organization requires frequent contacts with the country customers. The employees of the organization play a

---

[101] Meltzer (1972, p. 2).

[102] Chant and Acheson (1973, pp. 362-379).

Table 6

GNP Weights and Budget Weights
of Countries within the OECD

	GNP Weights [1]	Budget Weights[2]
Canada	3.67	5.45
United States	47.75	25.00
Japan	9.53	14.80
Australia	1.71	2.42
Austria	0.69	0.96
Belgium	1.25	1.80
Luxembourg	0.05	0.10
Denmark	0.75	1.01
Finland	0.49	0.68
France	7.14	9.80
Germany	9.01	12.58
Greece	0.45	0.60
Iceland	0.02	0.10
Ireland	0.19	0.26
Italy	4.47	6.15
Netherlands	1.51	2.31
Norway	0.55	0.74
Portugal	0.30	0.37
Spain	1.55	2.16
Sweden	1.49	2.16
Switzerland	0.98	1.60
Turkey	0.61	0.62
United Kingdom	5.84	7.88

[1] 1970 GNP's and exchange rates

[2] 1974

crucial role. We submit that the production function of this organization is unnecessarily constrained and biased to produce outputs which are desired by countries which have been given monopoly powers in specific research areas. The United Kingdom treasury has had the right to select the Assistant Secretary General in the Economics and Statistics Department and the outcome has been an over-representation of U.K. economists with a definite Keynesian-Radcliffean disposition. The U.S. Associate Secretary-General has influence over much of the administration of the organization; the Italians, Germans and French have similar monopoly positions. In addition, OECD wages favor Europeans relative to non-Europeans. Mobility of the staff is discouraged because of perceived net high costs implicit in fast turnover.

Our conclusions are that the staff of the OECD is hired in a highly compartmentalized fashion and that the general climate of the organization does not encourage the free interaction of researchers with different viewpoints. There have been and are, of course, individuals in the Department of Economics and Statistics who have disagreed on both the framework of analysis and the policy prescriptions of the Secretariat. However, a priori reasoning suggests that independent judgment can be aired only if the individual is willing to accept the risk of a less rapid career advancement within the organization and the home government. One factor which tends to reduce independence of judgment is that many staff people have held jobs with their home governments or expect to take a government job in the future. Finally, we must note that, while an organization of the size of the OECD is capable of toning down "strong" views through the intermediation of its senior members, it cannot outright reject all alternatives suggested by the "young Turks." To do so would mean seriously endangering morale and would eventually generate a high staff turnover. We would expect a compromise between the acceptance of the official Secretariat's views and the tolerance of opposing views to be reached where the marginal cost to the Secretariat of the opposing views is offset by a lower staff turnover.

C. Club Membership

We shall conclude our analysis by briefly exploring the optimal structure of a set of international organizations and the criteria for belonging to particular clubs. Within the OECD, for instance, at what point does a new member impose congestion charges on existing members? Conflicts of interest can be translated into a cost. WP3 is restricted to the Group of Ten in principle. Various countries such as Spain and Australia, which have attempted to join, have apparently been rebuffed by the existing members (even though the Secretary-General encouraged at least the participation of Australia). It can be seen from the GNP weights that the marginal contribution of a new member, if weighted by GNP, must be small, whereas the costs imposed are likely to be increasing. According to the theory of clubs, optimality occurs where the net increase in benefits from joining a club equals the aggregate decrease in benefits for the existing members; however, the analysis assumes that the number of clubs for each collective good is one. The existing theory does not deal with clubs whose services are complementary as a set of international organizations would have to be. It has, instead, concentrated on clubs whose services are substitutable. Competition among clubs might reduce the costs to society of the few existing clubs. A significant qualification to unrestricted competition comes from the shape of the long-run average cost curve of these clubs. The more pronounced are economies of scale, the stronger the argument for an "efficient" regulation of international clubs. The question remains: who will be the regulators of this scheme of international organizations and who will bear the policing costs?

VII. CONCLUSIONS

We have analyzed, or better, interpreted, in this paper the economics of the OECD as it is practiced by its Department of Economics and Statistics. Our conclusions are that the general framework of analysis is Keynesian with a dominance of fiscal impulses over monetary impulses; that the financial sector of the economy is described along the lines of reasoning of the Radcliffe Report; that monetary policy is virtually powerless under fixed rates of exchange because of the operation of "offsetting capital flows;" that fixed rates of exchange were preferred over flexible rates so long as the OECD's member countries were not floating; that the institution's approach to the causes and cures of inflation has been eclectic with the very important exception of recommending prices and incomes policies.

We attributed two institutional objectives to the OECD: self-preservation and prestige (influence). We found that an eclectic approach to research which satisfies the various, and often opposing, views of the country clients is an optimal strategy in maximizing the first of the two objectives. One perplexing result is why direct intervention to control prices has been so fervently preached by the OECD in spite of contrary theoretical arguments, empirical evidence, and, most important of all from the optics of the institutional goals of the OECD, against the official position of many governments. We offered the tentative explanation that the right of a few, almost exclusively European, governments to appoint Secretaries-General biases decision making and thus threatens the achievement of an optimal degree of independence. The 24 countries, collectively involved, have a clear interest in improving the structure, although individually the governments, and particularly those with monopoly rights in appointing Secretary-General-level positions, would be expected to oppose any such reorganization.

Finally, the fact that the United Kingdom Treasury appoints the Assistant Secretary-General in charge of the Economics and Statistics Department can be seen to have (over time) influenced economic thinking in favor of the received Keynesian analysis with a Radcliffean view of monetary matters.

APPENDIX: EXHIBIT I

The OECD's Primer on Incomes Policy

Various documents of the OECD deal with the practical problem of what is an incomes policy and how it should be applied. Here we have selected those passages which we think are representative of the institution's thinking on this subject.

1. The Definition of a Price-Incomes Policy

What is meant by an incomes policy, as the term is used in most member countries, is that the authorities should have a view about the kind of evolution of incomes which is consistent with their economic objectives, and in particular with price stability; that they should seek to promote public agreement on the principles which should guide the growth of incomes; and that they should try to induce people voluntarily to follow this guidance. In this broad sense, it appears that many member countries are trying to evolve incomes policies. [103]

2. Inflation and the Wage-Push

. . . labour costs per unit of output rise if total payments to labour rise faster than total production, and that rising labour costs are almost certain, sooner or later, to lead to rising prices because they account for such a large part of total costs in the economy as a whole. [104]

Controlling inflation requires that wage increases should be kept within the boundaries of productivity increases. There is, however, one exception.

If a country's incomes policy has resulted in its becoming an island of low cost in a world of high and rising costs, the grant of wage increases in excess of the growth of productivity, i.e., acceptance of some cost inflation, may be the most expedient policy. The situation in the Netherlands in 1954-55 had some of these features. [105]

---

[103] Policies for Price Stability, p. 23 .

[104] Policies for Price Stability, p. 24.

[105] Policies for Price Stability, p. 27.

3. The Simple Average Productivity Criterion and "Social Justice"

Although the OECD recognizes that a uniform average productivity criterion creates sectoral imbalances in the sense that the rule protects declining industries relative to expanding industries, the organization makes its case for the simple rule because the application of more complicated rules would require a degree of sophistication on the part of the public which does not exist in today's societies. In addition, wage increase differences based on productivity differentials are potential threats to "social harmony" or "social justice."

> . . . if wages in fact rise in each industry at the same rate as labour productivity in that industry the result would in due course be an inefficient and inequitable pattern of wage relations between industries and occupations. (Emphasis added.)

And in addition,

> Rates of wage increases established in certain industries may spread by imitation to other parts of the economy. [106]

What "social justice" is we are not told. It is regrettable that the OECD makes use of a term which is so ambiguous; it means different things to different people. Theologians have struggled with the concept of "justice" for centuries. For those theologians of the middle ages the adjective "just" was finally construed to signify being absent of fraud, violence and privileges. [107] In the OECD writing "social justice" is instead a catch-all phrase entitling governments to reduce income differences produced by the market. But in order to do so, each individual must be treated differently. It implies a systematic discrimination against those individuals whose marginal revenue product "as the market assesses it" is relatively high and in favor of those whose marginal revenue product is relatively low. According to what criteria can then such a program be judged "social" and "just"? The problem is further complicated by the frequent use that governments make of their ultimate legal power in granting privileges and monopoly rights to specific sectors of the economy. Again, there is nothing "social" or "just" in treating different individuals or groups of individuals in different ways. The impression one gets is that those who scream the loudest about "social justice" do so often to protect existing positions of privilege.

---

[106] Policies for Price Stability, pp. 28-29.

[107] See v. Hayek (1966, pp. 601-17).

4. Enlarging the Guidelines to Cover Non-Wage Incomes

Since costs other than wages, according to the OECD, are also important determinants of inflation, it is recommended that strict guidelines be applied to non-wage incomes.

> First, it is held that the behavior of profits and other non-wage incomes is an important cause of rising prices, either in isolation or in supporting and reinforcing a rise in wages. [108]

There is, however, a supplementary reason to place a lid on non-wage incomes.

> Second, more general political and social considerations suggest the need to complement a wages policy with a parallel policy towards other incomes, aimed at correcting what are regarded as undesirable or unacceptable trends in the evolution of the different classes of income. [109]

At this point price-incomes policies become a program through which the prices of the output as well as of the inputs are simultaneously controlled.

5. Enforcing the Guidelines

It is openly recognized that a compulsory program of price and income controls can be effectively enforced only in the very short run. Over a longer period of time the policing costs become too high relative to the alleged benefits of such a program. Hence, the OECD recommends voluntary compliance. The better educated the public, the OECD reasons, the more likely that a scheme of "self restraint" is likely to succeed. Most economists would argue that just the opposite is true.

---

[108] Policies for Prices, Profits and Other Non-Wage Incomes, p. 15.

[109] Policies for Prices, Profits and Other Non-Wage Incomes, p. 15.

APPENDIX: EXHIBIT II

FORECASTING FORMS USED BY THE ECONOMICS AND STATISTICS DEPARTMENT

Table 1

Demand and Output Forecasts	1972 Current prices	per cent of G P	Percentage changes							Indices 1972 = 100, seasonally adjusted						
			1972/1971	1973/1972	1974/1973	1975I/1974I	1972	1973	1974	1972 II	1973 I	1973 II	1974 I	1974 II	1975 I	
A. Demand and Output (changes and indices in volume terms)																
Private consumption																
Government consumption																
Gross fixed capital formation																
Final domestic demand (b)										( )	( )	( )	( )	( )	( )	
(Stock building) (a)			( )	( )	( )	( )				( )	( )	( )	( )	( )	( )	
Total domestic demand																
Export of goods and services																
Imports of goods and services			( )	( )	( )	( )				( )	( )	( )	( )	( )	( )	
(Foreign balance) (a)			( )	( )	( )	( )				( )	( )	( )	( )	( )	( )	
G.P. at constant prices (b)	..	..								( )	( )	( )	( )	( )	( )	
G.P. price deflator																
G.P. at current prices		100.0														
B. Memorandum items																
Consumer prices (c)	..	..								( )	( )	( )	( )	( )	( )	
Industrial production (b)	..	..														
Breakdown of gross fixed capital formation																
Stock building at 19 prices			1971	1972	1973	1974				1972II	1973I	1973II	1974I	1974II	1975I	
Actual rates																

a) The yearly and half-yearly rates of change refer to changes in stock building and in the foreign balance expressed as a percentage of G.P. in the previous period. These two figures plus the rate of change of final domestic demand broadly equal the rate of change of G.P. In practice, however, divergences are possible because the rate of change of final domestic demand is not expressed as a percentage of G.P.
b) Rates of change at annual rates

c)

Table 2		Years			Half-years, seasonally adjusted					
Trade and Payments Forecasts					1972	1973		1974		1975
		1972	1973	1974	II	I	II	I	II	I
A. Current Balance (value SDR million) Exports (f.o.b.) Imports (f.o.b.) Trade balance Services and private transfers, net Official transfers, net Current balance Memorandum item: Current balance in U.S. $										
B. Memorandum items Foreign Trade (Customs basis) Exports in volume (f.o.b.) in local currency Imports in volume (c.i.f.) In local currency		(Percentage changes over previous years)				(Indices 1972 = 100, seasonally adjusted)				

Table 3 Appropriation account for House-holds	1972	Percent change over previous year			1972	percent change over previous year	
		1973	1974			1973	1974
Employment Compensation of employees Income from property and others Current transfers received Total Income				Less: direct taxes Disposable income Current transfers paid Consumers' expenditure Saving ratio			

Current Economic Indicators (1972 = 100 seasonally adjusted)	1972Q3	1972Q4	1973Q1	1973Q2	1973Q3	1973Q4	1974Q1		
Industrial production Exports (customs basis, loc. curr.) Imports (customs basis, loc. curr.) Wholesale prices (not sea. adj.) Consumer prices (not sea. adj.)									

| Table 4 Selected background Statistics | Aver. 1964 to 1972 | Actual | | | | | | | | | Estimates 1973 | Forecast | |
		1964	1965	1966	1967	1968	1969	1970	1971	1972		1974	1975 I
A. Percentage changes from previous years at constant (19) prices Private consumption Gross fixed capital formation of which:													
G. P. G. P. price deflator Industrial production Employment Compensation of empl. (cur. prices) Productivity (G. P. / Empl.) Unit labor costs (Comp. / G. P.)													

134

Table 4

| | Aver. 1964 to 1972 | Actual | | | | | | | | | Estimates | Forecast | |
		1964	1965	1966	1967	1968	1969	1970	1971	1972	1973	1974	1975
B. Percentage ratios													
Gross fixed capital formation as percent of G. P. at constant prices													
Stockbuilding as percent of G. P. at constant prices													
Foreign balance as percent of G. P. at constant prices													
Compensation of employees as percent of G. P. at current prices													
Direct taxes as percent of household income													
Household saving as percent of disposable income													
C. Other indicators													
G. P. gap (as percent of potential G. P.)													
Current balance (Million U.S. dollars)													

135

REFERENCES

1. Ackley, G. <u>Macroeconomic Theory</u>. New York: Macmillan, 1961.

2. Allan, J.R., <u>et</u>. <u>al</u>., "Indexing the Personal Income Tax: A Federal Perspective," <u>Canadian Tax Journal</u>, 22, (July-August 1974), 355-365.

3. Bockelman, H., "Problems of Monetary Policy in Germany," Fifth Konstanzer Seminar on Monetary Theory and Monetary Policy, June 1974.

4. Bosworth, B., "Phase II: The U.S. Experiment with an Incomes Policy," <u>Brookings Papers on Economic Activity</u>, Washington, D.C.: The Brookings Institution, (1972:2), 343-83.

5. Brunner, K., "A Survey of Selected Issues in Monetary Theory," <u>Schweizerische Zeitschrift für Volkswirtschaft und Statistik</u>, (May 1971), 1-146.

6. _____, "The Ambiguous Rationality of Economic Policy," <u>Journal of Money, Credit and Banking</u>, IV, No. 1, (February 1972), 3-12.

7. Brunner, K., Fratianni, M., Jordan, J., Meltzer, A.H., and Neumann, M., "Fiscal and Monetary Policies in Moderate Inflation," <u>Journal of Money, Credit and Banking</u>, V, No. 1, II, (February 1973), 313-353.

8. Brunner, K., and Meltzer, A.H., "The Nature of the Policy Problem," in <u>Targets and Indicators of Monetary Policy</u>, (ed. K. Brunner), San Francisco: Chandler Publishing Company, 1969.

9. Chant, J.F., and Acheson, K., "Mythology and Central Banking," <u>Kyklos</u>, 26, fasc. 2 (1973), 362-379.

10. Christ, C.F., "A Short-run Aggregate Demand Model of the Interdependence and Effects of Monetary and Fiscal Policies with Keynesian and Classical Interest Elasticities," <u>American Economic Review Proceedings</u>, (May 1967), 434-443.

11. de Wolff, P. <u>Wages and Labor Mobility</u>. Paris: OECD, 1965.

12. Duck, N., Parkin, M., Rose, D., and Zis, G., "The Determination of the Rate of Change of Wages and Prices in the Fixed Exchange Rate World Economy, 1956-1970," Manchester University, mimeo, 1974.

13. EEC, <u>La politica monetaria nei paesi della comunità europea</u>, 1972.

14. Fazio, A., "Base Monetaria, credito e depositi bancari," Quaderni di Ricerche, No. 2, Ente per gli studi monetari, bancari e finanziari "Luigi Einaudi," 1968.

15. Feige, E.L., and Pearce, D.K., "The Wage-Price Control Experiment - - Did It Work?" Challenge, (July-August 1973), 40-44.

16. Fisher, G., and Sheppard, D., "Effects of Monetary Policy on the United States Economy," OECD, Economic Outlook - Occasional Studies, December 1972.

17. Fratianni, M., "Bank Credit Formation, Money Supply Processes, and Monetary and Fiscal Policies in an Open Economy: The Italian Experience, 1958-69," Ph.D. thesis, Ohio State University, 1971.

18. _____, "Domestic Bank Credit, Money and the Open Economy," in Bank Credit, Money and Inflation in Open Economies, (eds. M. Fratianni and K. Tavernier), Supplement to Kredit und Kapital, forthcoming, 1976.

19. Gordon, R.J., "Wage-Price Controls and the Shifting Phillips Curve," Brookings Papers on Economic Activity, Washington, D.C.: The Brookings Institution, (1972:2), 385-421.

20. Grayson, C.J., Jr., "A Strong 'No' to Price Monitoring," Wall Street Journal, August 12, 1974.

21. Hansen, B., "On the Effects of Fiscal and Monetary Policy: A Taxonomic Discussion," American Economic Review, LXIII, No. 4, (September 1973), 546-571.

22. _____. Fiscal Policy in Seven Countries, 1955-1965 (Belgium, France, Germany, Italy, Sweden, United Kingdom, United States).Paris: OECD, 1969.

23. v. Hayek, F.A., "The Principles of a Liberal Social Order," Il Politico, (1966), 601-617.

24. Hodgman, D.R. National Monetary Policies and International Monetary Cooperation. Boston: Little Brown, 1974.

25. Holbik, K., (ed.) Monetary Policy in Twelve Industrial Countries, Federal Reserve Bank of Boston, 1973.

26. Johnson, Harry G., "A Survey of Theories of Inflation," Indian Economic Review, (August 1963), 29-66.

27. _____,."Inflation and World Trade: A Monetarist View," Journal of World Trade Law, (January-February 1972), 9-19.

28. Kouri, P., and Porter, M., "International Capital Flows and Portfolio Equilibrium," Journal of Political Economy, 82, No. 3, (May-June 1974), 443-467.

29. Lipsey, R.G., and Parkin, M., "Incomes Policy: A Reappraisal," Economica, (May 1970), 15-38.

30. Lotz, J., "Techniques of Measuring the Effects of Fiscal Policy," OECD, Economic Outlook - Occasional Studies, July 1971.

31. Meltzer, A.H., "The Political and Economic Aspects of Policy Making," Journal of Money, Credit and Banking, IV, No. 1, (February 1972), 1-2.

32. Mundell, R.A. International Economics. New York: Macmillan, 1968.

33. Neumann, M.J.M., "Bank Liquidity and the Extended Monetary Base as Indicators of German Monetary Policy," in Proceedings of the First Konstanzer Seminar on Monetary Theory and Monetary Policy, Kredit und Kapital, (ed. K. Brunner), 1972.

34. _____, "A Theoretical and Empirical Analysis of the German Money Supply Process, 1958-1972," draft, May 1974.

35. OECD, The Balance of Payments Adjustment Process, August, 1966.

36. OECD, Economic Implications of Pollution Control, February 1974.

37. OECD, Economic Outlook, No. 1, July 1967.

38. OECD, Economic Outlook, No. 4, December 1968.

39. OECD, Economic Outlook, No. 6, December 1969.

40. OECD, Economic Outlook, No. 9, July 1971.

41. OECD, Economic Outlook, No. 10, December 1970.

42. OECD, Economic Outlook, No. 11, July 1972.

43. OECD, Economic Outlook, No. 12, December 1972.

44. OECD, Economic Outlook, No. 13, July 1973.

45. OECD, Economic Outlook, No. 15, July 1974.

46. OECD, Economic Surveys: Japan, July 1973.

47. OECD, Indexation of Fixed Interest Securities, 1974.

48. OECD, Inflation: the Present Problem, Report by the Secretary General, December 1970.

49. OECD, "The Measurement of Domestic Cyclical Fluctuation," Economic Outlook - Occasional Studies, July 1973.

50. OECD, Monetary Policy in Germany, Monetary Study Series, December 1973.

51. OECD, Monetary Policy in Italy, Monetary Study Series, May 1973.

52. OECD, Monetary Policy in Japan, Monetary Study Series, December 1972.

53. OECD, Policies for Prices, Profits and Other Non-Wage Incomes, Report Prepared for the Economic Policy Committee by its Working Party on Costs of Production and Prices, 1964.

54. OECD, Policies for Price Stability, A Report to the Economic Policy Committee by its Working Party on Costs of Production and Prices, 1962.

55. OECD, Present Policies against Inflation, A Report by Working Party No. 4 of the Economic Policy Committee, June 1971.

56. OECD, Techniques for Economic Forecasting, 1965.

57. Parkin, M., "The 1973 Report of the President's Council of Economic Advisers: A Critique," American Economic Review, LXIII, No. 4, (September 1973), 535-545.

58. Parkin, M., and Sumner, M. (eds.) Incomes Policy and Inflation. Manchester: Manchester University Press, 1972.

59. Ulman, L., and Flanagan, R.J. <u>Wage Restraint: A Study of Incomes Policies in Western Europe</u>. Berkeley: University of California Press, 1971.

60. Van Lennep, E., <u>Politique Bugetaire et Inflation</u>, Societe Royale d'Economique Politique de Belgique, (April 1973), No. 369.

61. Victor, P.A. <u>Economic Implications of Pollution Control</u>. New York: Macmillan, 1972.

THE ECONOMICS OF THE OECD: A COMMENT

Bent Hansen
University of California, Berkeley

The question that the authors of this paper have tried to answer is both interesting and important. Analyzing past and present policies of member countries, forecasting future developments and giving advice on policies, serving as a kind of secretariat to the group of ten countries and engineering joint resolutions on international policy matters, the Organization of Economic Cooperation and Development has undoubtedly played a role in forming economic policy-making in the developed world. Those who feel that the only true progress in economic policy during the post-war period has been due to the increasing availability of primary and aggregated data would tend to emphasize that side of the activities of the OECD.

It is a difficult task, however, to infer the basic thinking, the paradigms of an international organization, from its current publications. This is what the authors attempt to do. Not only may publications have been formulated as compromises between opinions of member countries or between conflicting views within the organization itself, it must also be recalled that such publications more often than not have to be relatively non-technical and, hence, cannot operate on a high level of rigor. The authors have, in addition to publications for which the organization is directly responsible, had access to widely circulated, unpublished material and monographs by consultants in which compromise and simplicity have not blurred the picture; but such sources may not express the views of the organization or may apply theories and techniques that its mandarins do not favor. Or consultants' monographs may coincide with the views of the mandarins to such an extent that it becomes impossible to trace any changes in views of the organization after the appearance of a monograph. Consultants may be selected so as to support the views of the organization vis-à-vis member countries.

Be that as it may, any attempt to distill the OECD paradigm from its publications should acknowledge the fact that considerable progress has been made in academic theorizing - - monetarist as well as Keynesian - - about economic policy matters during the twenty-odd years the organization has been active in its present style. It is not only the OECD that has adjusted to a changing environment, and its views at any time should in all fairness be evaluated against the background of what was then considered advanced academic thinking. Moreover, a "revealed paradigm" will disclose only what the organization, rightly or wrongly, thought quantitatively important at any particular point of time and may not necessarily indicate differences in pure theory. Organizations are not supposed to write textbooks covering all possible cases. Macro-models, after all, are simplifications, and in the present state of the art of empirical economics it should give rise to no surprise if economists, starting out from exactly the same underlying abstract theory, come out with very different macro-models, simply because opinions differ about the quantitative importance of variables and relations. If, for instance, Klein's pioneering models did not distinguish between real and nominal rate of interest, it is surely not because Klein did not know about such theory or was against it, but probably because he at that time thought that the distinction was quantitatively unimportant. The "revealed paradigm" method cannot make such differences. As I shall argue below, the authors fail to come to grips with the fiscal versus monetary policy issue for precisely this reason.

The authors begin and end their paper with references to the Treasury Chambers in London and to the views of the Radcliffe committee and their allegedly predominant influence. Quite apart from the fact that until 1961 the Director of the Department of Economics and Statistics was an American, that the economics of the OECD are not all that different from those of the old OEEC, and that neither the Treasury Chambers nor the Radcliffe committee were thought very highly of at the top of the department, it is undoubtedly true that it was entirely dominated in its thinking by British Keynesianism - - that is, Keynesian theory with a British institutional background. It was always firmly anchored in British institutions and tended to think that a policy that is good in Britain must be good for any other country. This circumstance probably helps us more than any reading of the OECD's publications to understand the department's paradigm, but it would be entirely wrong to infer that the department was no more than an arm of the Treasury in London. Rather than emphasize the British Treasury so strongly, the authors might also have taken a look at the persons at the top, in particular Milton Gilbert (the American) and J.C.R. Dow (the Englishman). Both are well known from their scholarly writings - - Gilbert for his work on national accounting and related problems, and Dow for his studies (with Dicks-Mireaux) on wages and excess demand in Britain and for a rather critical book on British economic policy.[1] If, for instance, the question is raised why the OECD was slow to adopt the Phillips curve and preferred to analyze labor markets in terms of vacancies and unemployment, the answer is probably that both Dow and Dicks-Mireaux were in the Department of Economics and Statistics.

---

[1] Dow and Dicks-Mireaux (1958 and 1959) and Dow (1964).

142

In preparing this comment, I made no exegetic exercises in the scriptures of the OECD. I have based it mainly on my own experience with the OEEC and the OECD, among other assignments as a member of their Committee on Rising Prices from 1959 to 1961, and as a consultant-expert on fiscal policy at the disposal of the Heller Committee on Fiscal Policy from 1965 to (effectively) 1969. I shall concentrate on those matters about which I have had the opportunity of getting some inside knowledge of the thinking at the top of the Department of Economics and Statistics, partly through committee meetings, partly through discussions with directors of the department - - first Milton Gilbert and later J.C.R. Dow - - and with personnel in the department. The authors discuss mainly OECD publications and views relating to the period of exchange rate flexibility and high inflation after 1971. My experience with the OECD does not cover that period. To some extent my comments are therefore complementary to the authors' discussion.

I. FISCAL AND MONETARY POLICY EFFECTS

The authors have taken my monograph, Fiscal Policy in Seven Countries, 1955-1965, as a prototype of fiscal thinking in the OECD, although they find little impact of this study on the organization's views as expressed in the Economic Outlook.

Concerning the impact of this study, I shall emphasize that the analysis was much in line with prevailing OECD thinking, and that one of the reasons why I was asked to make this study was that I had been involved earlier in this kind of work in Sweden. The intention of the OECD was to make an impact on certain unenlightened governments. A number of countries did in fact adopt the methodology, at least for internal work in ministries of finance, and there is no doubt that vague expressions in country reports and in the Economic Outlook to the effect that fiscal policies in this or that country have been expansionary or the opposite at times followed from evaluations based on this methodology. Another thing is that in several of these countries (Italy, for example) model building on a larger scale soon replaced my rather primitive model.

Apart from the crudeness of the model applied (which was dictated mainly by the shortage of data for some of the countries, and by the time allocated for the study), Fratianni and Pattison's main criticism is directed toward the delimitation of fiscal and monetary policy, and they claim that ". . .fiscal impulses are being overstated when one or more asset markets are not explicitly included" because ". . .fiscal multipliers considered by Hansen are independent of the financial aspect of the budget." They quote me to the effect that financial aspects of the budget can be disregarded as belonging to the realm of monetary policy, and criticize this partly as being ambiguous, partly as erroneous in the sense that fiscal multipliers depend upon the incorporation of the financial sector. Generally, I have no difficulties in accepting this criticism, because it largely coincides with my own views. Yet I shall explain how the position in the OECD monograph was reached, partly to show that it can in fact be defended as being perfectly logical, partly to throw some light on the "economics of the OECD."

At the time when I accepted the assignment to write the monograph, and also later during the course of the work, I had long discussions with Dow about the delimitations between fiscal and monetary policy. Both of us were fully aware of the mechanism of the public budget constraint and the link thereby established between budget deficit (surplus) and private sector assets. There was no "oversight" here. [2] I suggested considering "liquidity effects" from the budget by assuming that - - at given interest rates - - real balances in the private sector change by the amount of the deficit, to let such real balance changes enter in the multiplicand (with a certain weight), and let the multiplier include coefficients of the real balances in the consumption function. Dow's arguments against this proposals were the following.

(a) The terms of reference strictly limited the study to fiscal policies, and even debt management operations could and should not be considered. (This is a point that throws some light on the bureaucracy of the OECD.)

(b) Econometric studies have so far (that is, in 1965) shown only negligible and statistically insignificant effects on private consumption and investments from real balances, at least in the short term. Thus we may as well forget about them, in particular because we are interested in short-term policies.

(c) Moreover, since the central bank operates on the rate of interest as its main policy instrument, any given change in the liquidity of the private sector can always, at the given interest rate, be neutralized through appropriate open-market operations; this is a matter that belongs to the realm of monetary policy and may thus legitimately be ignored in discussions of the effects of fiscal policy.

---

[2] To substantiate this statement, let me refer to Hansen (1958, Ch. III, Section 8) where the public budget constraint was applied several years before Christ introduced it in the American debate. I took it over from Ohlin, who had used it with great effect in criticizing Swedish government policies at the outbreak of World War II. See Ohlin (1941).

I found the argument about the terms of reference a bit phony, but there was no doubt that this was an overriding consideration. While I was unhappy about dropping the real balance effects, it had to be admitted that the then existing empirical evidence for real balance effects was weak, to put it mildly. Against my subjective beliefs, I therefore gave in at this point to what at that time were considered to be the facts. I was, on the other hand, entirely in agreement with Dow in considering the rate of interest as a policy control variable with the implication that money supply is endogenous to the model and, hence, cannot be ascribed specific policy effects. Dow obviously had the British banking system (as it was at that time) in mind, with the bank rate being of central importance for institutional interest rates; and for a number of European countries with small and negligible open capital markets and institutional rates more or less dictated by the central bank, the assumption of the rate of interest as the basic monetary policy instrument was, to the best of my understanding, a realistic description of then existing institutions and modes of policy operation. Recall also that with pegged exchange rates it made little sense to consider money supply as a policy instrument.

We therefore agreed to proceed on these assumptions. Dow, as the good British Keynesian he was, of course had no formal model behind his arguments. But it is easy to show that with (a) no financial asset effects on real flows, and (b) with the rate of interest as a controlled policy parameter, it is indeed possible to separate the effects of fiscal and monetary policy completely and unambiguously. To show this, I shall use the system set up by the authors. I assume with them that the rate of interest only appears in the investment function, and I consider only the simplest case with given tax revenues. We then have

(5) $dY = dC + dN' + dG + dX - dIm$,

(6) $dC = c_1 (dY - dT) + dc_2$,

(7) $dIm = m_1 (dY - dT) + dm_2$,

(8b) $dT = d\bar{T}$,

(11) $dN' = - b_1 dr + db_2$.

We have here five equations to determine dY, dC, dIm, dT, and dN'. The solution for dY is

$$dY = \frac{1}{1 - c_1 + m_1} [dX + dc_2 - dm_2 + db_2 + dG - (c_1 - m_1)d\bar{T} - b_1 dr]$$

$$\underbrace{}_{\substack{\text{impacts of} \\ \text{exogenous disturbances}}} \quad \underbrace{}_{\substack{\text{fiscal impact}}} \quad \underbrace{\phantom{-(c_1 - m_1)d\bar{T} - b_1 dr}}_{\substack{\text{monetary} \\ \text{impact}}}$$

Fiscal and monetary impacts are nicely additive and have the same multiplier in which no "financial" coefficients appear. Hence, the separation between fiscal and monetary policy effects is complete. The authors are unable to come out with this result because they assume that money is the control variable. It is at this point they go wrong in their interpretation of the methodology.

But what about the financial sector? If we just add the money equation suggested by the authors,

(12) $dM = e_1 dY - e_2 dr + de_3,$

things do not work out in a satisfactory manner.

With dr fixed by the authorities, and dY determined by (5), (6), (7), (8b), and (11), equation (12) obviously must determine dM. In other words, to keep r at its desired level, the central bank has to sell government securities "on tap" to such an amount that (12) is fulfilled. But since

(13*) $dM + dB = dW,$

where W is private financial net wealth and B is the value of government bonds held by the private sector, we have

(14*) $dB = dW - e_1 dY + e_2 dr - de_3,$

with the implication that

$$dM/dW = 0 \text{ and } dB/dW = 1;$$

that is, the wealth effect on money holdings is zero, but on bond holdings equal to one. This is hardly an acceptable portfolio theory, but we need only to mend (12) to

(12') $dM = e_1 dY - e_2 dr + e_3 dW + e_4, \qquad 1 > e_3 > 0,$

to arrive at a reasonable description of the financial system. For now we have

$$(14') \qquad dB = (1 - e_3)dW - e_1 dY + e_2 dr - e_4,$$

with

$$dM/dW = e_3, \qquad dB/dW = 1 - e_3, \qquad dM/dr = -e_2, \qquad dB/dr = e_2.$$

Hence with $dr = 0$, dY determined by (5), (6), (7), (8b), and (11), and a deficit in the budget so that private financial wealth is increasing period after period by $G - \bar{T} = dW$, what the central bank (treasury) has to do is to operate in the market to insure that dM and dB increase in the proportion $e_3/(1 - e_3)$.

II. MONETARY POLICY

I do not feel particularly competent to explain the details of the OECD views in monetary matters. These began to change at the end of the sixties when not only M_2 but even M_3 made its appearance in England, and M-ism became the fashion there as in the United States. Until then, however, it appears to me that any interpretation of the OECD views has to start out from the assumption that the monetary control variable par excellence is the rate of interest with auxiliary instruments such as reserve rations, credit ceilings, hire-purchase controls, and the like, but with money supply or liquidity as endogenous variables through which perhaps policy effects may work themselves out, but to which for purely conceptual reasons specific policy effects should not in any case be ascribed. And if a single indicator of monetary policy and its effects had to be selected, it would have to be a weighted sum of the monetary policy measures and not money supply. Assume, for the sake of the argument, that there is a ceiling, L, on durable consumer goods financing and that we simply represent this in the model above by adding a new term, say $c_4 L$, to the consumption function. $c_4 dL$ will then appear additively in the multiplicand of the expression for dY and the impact of monetary policy would be $c_4 dL - e_2 dr$.

There is nothing in this approach that a priori assumes that monetary policy is not important, and I do not think that it can be substantiated that the OECD should under all circumstances consider monetary policy thus defined as unimportant. It has always acknowledged the strong impact on construction in the United States of changes in interest rates, and of the British controls with hire-purchase of consumer durables, just to mention two examples. But it is true that if we insist upon a complete separation between fiscal and monetary policy effects in line with the model in Section 1, the underlying assumption must be that "money does not matter" in the special sense that there are no direct effects of financial stocks on real flows. The OECD never formalized its approach in regard to monetary policy, but I have always understood it to have had something like this in mind, at least until the end of the sixties. And I do not see that "Radcliffean" is the best word for characterizing the approach.

III. INCOMES POLICY

The commitment of the OECD to incomes policy actually dates back to the old OEEC, when the majority of its Committee on Rising Prices recommended wage policies combined with the abolition of government-sponsored price increases (in agriculture, for instance), the free play of foreign competition to cope with domestic monopolies, and, if needed, control with international cartels (oil was not specifically mentioned in the final report, but was one of the commodities the committee discussed in its meetings). The views of this committee dominated OECD thinking during the sixties.

The authors' discussion of this issue calls for the remark that incomes policy was never recommended by the Committee on Rising Prices as a substitute for what it calls "demand management" policies, an expression that is wide enough to cover both Keynesian and monetarist types of stabilization policies. Incomes (wages) policy was called for only if factor prices would tend to increase more than productivity in a situation with complete balance between demand and supply of commodities and factors (full utilization of resources), and without inflationary expectations, it should be added today. Nobody can deny that with imperfect factor and commodity markets this might, indeed, be the case. The OECD strongly believes that it is in fact the case in most countries. The OECD may be wrong, but that is an empirical matter that has nothing to do with the subsequent problem, whether incomes policy actually works or not. If we are in fact confronted with the situation described above, neither Keynesian nor monetarist policies can secure stable prices at full utilization of resources; something then has to be done about the factor markets - - and that is precisely what incomes policy is about. Hence, the stubborn insistence of the OECD on incomes policy. If I am not mistaken, leading monetarists agree in principle; although monetarists in that case would probably insist on going to the root of the matter, unionism and the like, and would not be satisfied with superficial price and wage controls. The authors themselves explain why the OECD more recently has tended to recommend price controls - - namely, to break expectations. The Committee on Rising Prices did not recommend price controls; it did not discuss inflationary expectations either, which at that time were not considered a quantitatively substantial problem.

IV. THE BALANCE OF PAYMENTS

The authors discuss at length the views of the OECD on exchange rate policies; its views differed little from those of the IMF and are not particularly interesting. The authors do little to illuminate its thinking on the balance of payments adjustment process. To tell the full story at this point, it would, of course, be necessary to have access to all documents written for Working Party III; they are not available. From the published sources it is very clear, however, that insofar as current account is concerned, the OECD attempted to merge the expenditure (absorption) approach with something that could be called the "competitiveness approach." This approach is akin to the purchasing power parity approach, but differs from the latter by not making comparisons between prices (retail, wholesale, implicit deflators, and so forth), but rather between unit wage costs in manufacturing industry. Almost any OECD publication concerned with balance of payments problems brings in comparative unit wage cost data if available.

The competitiveness approach can be combined with the expenditure approach in different ways. An apparently simple solution is to graft a variable, expressing relative unit wage costs directly, onto the conventional Keynesian export and import function. Let $UWC = uwc_\$ \times R/uwc_{dom}$ where uwc stands for unit wage costs, foreign ($) and domestic (dom), respectively, and R is the foreign exchange rate (domestic currency per US $). We may then write, say,

$$(7') \qquad Im = m_1(Y - T) - m_2 UWC + m_3 ,$$

$$(7'') \qquad X = x_1 Y_w + x_2 UWC$$

where Y_w is world income. Formulated like that, the "competitiveness approach" would have some affinity with both elasticity and the purchasing power parity approach.

The competitiveness approach, however, becomes a more independent method of analyzing balance of payments problems when modelled in the shape of a familiar, simple trade model. I discuss it geometrically. Assume that a small country produces and uses only one single commodity. Wages are the only variable cost factor. In Figure 1, MC is then the country's marginal cost curve. Without controls the price level, p_{dom}, in the country is determined by foreign

149

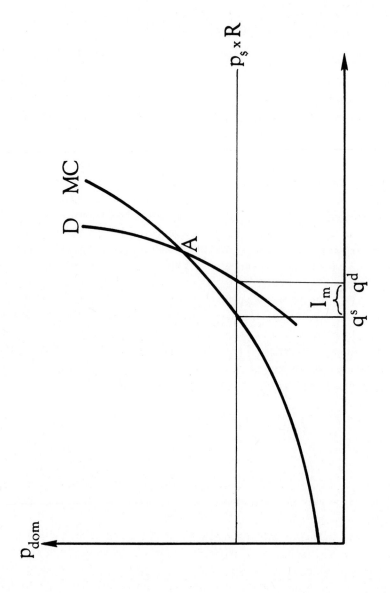

Figure 1

prices converted into domestic currency, $p_{dom} = p_S \times R$. Foreign prices may be determined by foreign unit wage costs. Production, q^S, is determined exclusively by MC, foreign prices and the exchange rate. Under certain regularity assumptions in regard to technical progress, it is clear that relative unit wage costs determine the level of production and its development.

Let total domestic effective demand, q^d, be determined by total real disposable wage-income and profits and real government demand. As I have drawn the figure, $q^d > q^S$ and $q^d - q^S = Im$, which here equals net imports or the trade deficit. At other prices, wage income and profits would be different, and a total effective demand curve, D, can be traced out as a function of p_{dom}, given MC. Its slope may be negative or positive. Unless public demand is very large, it will cut the MC curve at a point, A, with balance of trade equilibrium. However, the MC being an ex ante curve, this point may be to the right of full employment production. An attempt to create balance in foreign trade would lead to excess demand for labor and wage (demand!) inflation. Were point A to the left of full employment production, trade balance would coexist with unemployment. And a shift in the effective demand curve, for instance through a change in fiscal policy, would only affect the current account deficit but not production and employment.

The reader will easily recognize a close affinity between this model and the policy recommendations of the British "New Economics." Employment is determined independently of domestic effective demand. Changes in domestic demand will affect the balance of trade and leave employment unaffected. Hence the natural policy recommendation: use the exchange rate to keep employment full (more precisely, to keep the labor market in the desired state of tightness) and then use the budget for balancing foreign trade. And if exchange rates are pegged, only incomes policy can guarantee full employment.

While the OECD thinking (in agreement with old Keynesians such as Kahn) seems largely to have followed the model obtained by adding equations (7') and (7'') to the standard Keynesian setup, the views of the "New Economics" are so closely related to the conceptual apparatus of the OECD that it would not be surprising if similar views could be traced in the OECD publications.

V. THE BUREAUCRACY

Much of what the authors have to say about the OECD as a bureaucratic organism always seeking justification for its own existence, trying to be useful to the member countries and striking a balance between them, is certainly true. The committees I was involved in offer interesting examples of the policy games in which the OECD takes part. The Committee on Rising Prices was appointed in 1959 very much because the MacMillan government needed support for an incomes policy. The Committee on Fiscal Policy was originally the brainchild of the Council of Economic Advisers in the U.S. who needed leverage in their efforts to get the tax cut of 1964 through. For various reasons, however, the committee did not start working until the American tax cut was a fact - - and Heller lost interest in the committee. The committee was then dormant until the German economy in 1965 got in trouble for the first time since its great take-off after World War II, at the same time that both France and Italy were having problems. The German Federal Government had until then managed - - and managed very well, much to the annoyance of the Department of Economics and Statistics - - with Erhard's crude quantity theory; France had budgetary principles that were largely incomprehensible, and Italy had no principles at all. The time had therefore come to spread the Keynesian gospel to the pagans, and the committee was activated. The U.S., Britain, and Sweden were included in the study to show how fiscal policy should be pursued; Belgium, France, Germany, and Italy - - to learn. It would hardly be wrong in this instance to characterize the OECD as an overseas [3] missionary post for British Keynesianism trying to form continental European budgetary policies.

---

[3] I recall once having seen an internal OECD document where France and Germany were called "overseas countries"!

REFERENCES

1. Hansen, B. The Economic Theory of Fiscal Policy. London: Allen and Unwin, 1958.

2. _____. Fiscal Policy in Seven Countries, 1955-1965 (Belgium, France, Germany, Italy, Sweden, United Kingdom, United States). Paris: Organisation for Economic Co-operation and Development, 1969.

3. Dicks-Mireaux, L.A., and Dow, J.C.R., "The Determinants of Wage Inflation: United Kingdom, 1946-56," Journal of the Royal Statistical Society, A, 122, Part II, (1959), 7-174.

4. Dow, J.C.R. The Management of the British Economy, 1945-60. Cambridge: University Press, 1964.

5. Dow, J.C.R., and Dicks-Mireaux, L.A., "The Excess Demand for Labour: A Study of Conditions in Great Britain, 1946-56," Oxford Economic Papers, 10, No. 1, (February 1958), 1-33.

6. Ohlin, B.G. Kapitalmarknad och räntepolitik. Stockholm: Kooperativa förbundets bokförlag, 1941.

THE ECONOMICS OF THE OECD: A COMMENT

Donald R. Hodgman

University of Illinois

Fratianni and Pattison have undertaken to discover, report and criticize "the economics of the Organisation for Economic Co-operation and Development" with special emphasis on stabilization policies. This is an ambitious undertaking. Moreover, it presupposes that there is a framework for economic analysis which can be identified with the OECD and that there is a useful purpose to be served by describing and criticizing this framework. I shall return to these presuppositions later. But first, I shall consider the authors' procedures and findings.

Among the international organizations concerned with economic matters such as BIS, IMF, UNESCO, UNCTAD and IBRD, the OECD has been selected for attention because it deals ". . .exclusively with economic policy making in <u>developed</u> industrial nations." (Emphasis in the original.) It has a payroll of 1500 employees and its own printing facilities, and ". . .comments extensively on the state of and prospect for the world economy and its individual constituents. . . ."

A major problem faced by the authors was to limit the scope of their undertaking so as to make it manageable. The steps in this progressive narrowing are indicated by the following features of the authors' procedure.

(a) They had no access to unpublished working papers and minutes involved in the internal discussions of the various specialized committees and working parties.

(b) Among the voluminous economic materials published by OECD since its inception in December 1960, the authors have concentrated on the work of the Economics and Statistics Department which is only one, though the major one, of the Departments that are concerned with economic matters.

(c) Within the work of the Department special attention has been directed to the views of the so-called Secretariat to be understood as the group of higher-ranking permanent staff. These views are presumed to be discernible in the analysis and interpretations presented in the semi-annual publication entitled <u>OECD Economic Outlook</u>.

(d) Certain special studies prepared by Consultants to the Department such as Bent Hansen and Wayne Snyder, and Gordon Fisher and Daniel Sheppard have been carefully reviewed, but Fratianni and Pattison find little evidence that consultants' studies have had much influence on the analytical framework and perspective of the Secretariat.

(e) The final narrowing of focus occurs within the Secretariat when the authors state, "<u>If the economic analysis of the OECD</u>, that is the analysis of the Department of Economics and Statistics, <u>has any uniformity or consistency</u>, it is because the head (an assistant Secretary General) has always been appointed by the United Kingdom Treasury. In addition, many senior and a large number of intermediate and junior level appointments tend to come from the United Kingdom." (Emphasis added.)

This progressive narrowing of focus permits Fratianni and Pattison to identify a framework of analysis which they feel has played a key role in the published views of the OECD on stabilization policy. They describe this framework as ". . .characteristically Keynesian in its general outline and Radcliffean in its specific application to monetary analysis." I think this is a fair characterization of the views held in the past, at least by some of the top-level personnel in the Economics and Statistics Department and reflected in their published pronouncements on stabilization policy. But clearly much greater diversity of perspective and much wider choice of subject matter and approaches to economic research are found in the full range of publications of OECD departments, divisions, committees and consultants. Thus, it may be somewhat misleading to accept the authors' report as an adequate characterization of the role of the OECD in economic research and interpretation of economic developments. How adequate the characterization is depends upon the purpose to which one wishes to apply it. I shall return to this point later.

Fratianni and Pattison analyze a number of deficiencies in the Keynesian income-expenditure framework that they believe has guided top-level OECD officials in their comments on national and international economic developments. The principal deficiencies identified by the authors appear to be these:

(a) neglect of asset markets such as the money and credit markets and their interactions with the output market;

(b) omission of the central governments' budget constraint and of the balance of payments constraint in the analysis of feasible policy alternatives;

(c) no theory of the money supply process and thus no clear conception of monetary policy instruments and indicators;

(d) lack of a clear conception of fiscal policy instruments (excepting studies by consultants such as Bent Hansen);

(e) overstatement of the degree to which national monetary policy is rendered ineffective by international capital flows under fixed exchange rates.

These are the chief systematic shortcomings stressed by the authors. Is there an alternative, comprehensive, and articulated analytical framework which is free of these deficiencies? Yes, there is. It can be found in the writings of economists to whom the label of "monetarist" has become attached but most particularly in the analytical framework which Karl Brunner and Allan Meltzer have been developing in recent years. In effect the public pronouncements of the OECD on economic policy are being criticized for not being sufficiently "monetarist" in the more sophisticated sense of that term.

In addition to these criticisms of the income-expenditure approach, Fratianni and Pattison fault the OECD Secretariat on certain other analytical issues:

(a) their penchant for relying on controls rather than free markets, especially in the area of credit controls and control over prices and incomes;

(b) their choice of too short a planning horizon for policy recommendations;

(c) their understatement of the role of excess aggregate demand in a process of continuing inflation and in that of worldwide inflation; and,

(d) their tardiness in joining the intellectual and policy swing from fixed to flexible exchange rates.

This is a lengthy and rather comprehensive list of deficiencies in the analytical framework of the OECD's Secretariat. Is the Secretariat guilty as charged? If so, do Fratianni and Pattison in their paper correctly identify the cause of the problem in tracing it to ". . .the fact that the United Kingdom Treasury appoints the assistant Secretary-General in charge of the Economics and Statistics Department. . . ."? What are the implications of the authors' assessment for an evaluation of the performance of the OECD in promoting rational and appropriate economic policies?

In my opinion the Secretariat of the OECD probably is "guilty as charged" with respect to the allegiance of some high ranking officials to the Keynesian analytical framework for stabilization policy and their neglect of the newer perspectives incorporated in the monetarist approach. [1]

The imprint of their views on OECD research strategies and policy pronouncements has resulted in the OECD becoming something of an institutional bastion for a non-monetarist approach to stabilization policy. This fact makes the OECD fair game for a critical review by professional economists holding to a different intellectual persuasion. It is useful to point out OECD tastes and biases in economic analysis. Criticism should be tempered, however, by acknowledgement that many aspects of a "correct view of the world" still are open to further analytical refinement and empirical testing as discussion at this conference is likely to demonstrate. Moreover, it is unrealistic to expect an international, policy-oriented organization to be at the forefront in applying new developments in economic theory. Such an organization is more likely to lag than to lead in this process.

The author's characterization of "the economics of the OECD" is too monolithic to do justice to the diversity of concepts employed and research undertaken by that organization. In their effort to reduce this diversity to a

---

[1] On this point, see Hodgman (1971) especially pp. 769-70.

manageable core, the authors have surely overstated their case - - perhaps for emphasis. Senior officials may have put their interpretive imprint on important policy advice offered by the OECD. But the wealth of OECD publications covers a broader spectrum of views than those of the senior Secretariat. This is not to deny that, for example, monetary studies have suffered relative neglect by the Department of Economics and Statistics.

The authors also devote some discussion to the bureaucratic behavior of the OECD in terms of the goals of survival and prestige. By these criteria the OECD must surely be regarded as a very successful bureaucracy. But there is another aspect of the bureaucratic nature of the OECD which may be more relevant to the authors' concern with "the economics of the OECD." This is the intermeshing of the OECD bureaucracy with the bureaucracies of the various national delegations, some of which are very large and politically very powerful. The Secretariat must be careful not to appear to become the tool of any one country. Moreover, some of the policy advice offered by the OECD to national governments represents a repackaging with OECD imprimatur of policy views that originated within these same national governments. The OECD "impartial" endorsement may make the advice easier to adopt domestically. Both of these bureaucratic considerations tend to reduce the independent influence of the OECD Secretariat in setting a policy line.

Finally, there is the question of the basic function of the OECD in the realm of economic policy formation. Is it basically an economic advisory group with an important technical task to perform in communicating the "correct view of the world" to policy implementers in the governments of the member nations? Do responsible national officials accord much weight to policy recommendations from the OECD in setting national economic policies? I am inclined to think that the role of the OECD in promoting rational and constructive national economic policies is both more modest and more subtle. The OECD may make its most important contribution in facilitating international communication on issues of economic policy and by providing, through its many meetings and discussions, an educational seminar for policy makers from national delegations and government agencies, thus raising their economic sophistication. It can help also in the process of international standardization of statistics and in developing a common language and set of concepts to be used in discussing economic policy problems. In these ways the research and the policy views of the OECD do contribute to the general process of national and international policy formation in the economic sphere. For this reason they merit critical scrutiny. But the "economics of the OECD" is more diversified conceptually and in subject matter, as well as less influential in both intellectual and policy circles, than one would be led to believe from Fratianni's and Pattison's treatment.

REFERENCE

1. Hodgman, D.R., "British Techniques of Monetary Policy," <u>Journal of Money, Credit and Banking</u>, III, No. 4, (November 1971), pp. 760-779.

THE FEDERAL HOME LOAN BANK SYSTEM SINCE 1965

Dwight M. Jaffee

Princeton University

I. INTRODUCTION

The Federal Home Loan Bank System (FHLBS) was created by an Act of Congress in 1932 as an emergency measure to deal with the crisis of mortgage delinquency. Within several years, additional legislation allowed for Federal chartering of savings and loan associations (SLAs), and created the Federal Savings and Loan Insurance Corporation (FSLIC) and the Home Owners' Loan Corporation (HOLC). The HOLC almost single-handedly solved the delinquency problem, and must rate among the most successful U.S. government ventures, not the least because it disbanded on schedule. The rest of the structure remained, however, and is the foundation of the system today.

The FHLBS consists of three parts: (i) the Federal Home Loan Bank Board (FHLBB); (ii) the 12 regional Federal Home Loan Banks (FHL Banks); and (iii) the member institutions, primarily SLAs. Centered in Washington, D.C., the FHLBB operates under a Board of three members, and with a staff of approximately 400 employees.[1] For administrative purposes, the FHLBB is split into a series of "offices," such as the Office of Economic Research, Office of General Counsel, and Office of Examinations and Supervision. Since 1955, the Board has been an "independent" agency in the Executive Branch, but it reports to Congress, and is financially self-supporting under the supervision of Congress. The regional FHL Banks are corporations owned by the member institutions; they also are self-supporting and pay dividends to members under guidelines set by the FHLBB. The FHL Banks are the primary operational element in the administration of Board policies and operate independently, although subject to Board guidelines. Federally chartered member institutions now number over 2,000, while approximately the same number of state-chartered SLAs have FSLIC insurance, and thus come under many FHLBB regulations. FSLIC is a corporation, with no outstanding stock, under the direction of the FHLBB.[2]

---

[1] There is also a group of approximately 900 SLA examiners associated with the Board. The Board members are appointed by the President for four-year terms; not more than two Board members may be from the same political party (whatever that means). The current chairman is Thomas R. Bomar. A concise introduction to the FHLBS can be found in FHLBB (1971).

[2] Formally, the legal and regulatory structure is complicated by a hierarchy which includes the Congressional Acts as amended; FHLBB regulations, rulings, opinions, and guidelines; FSLIC regulations; and FHL Bank regulations. There is not a current and convenient compendium of these strictures.

The history of the FHLBS can be separated into three parts. The first period extends from 1932 through the aftermath of World War II. The policy issues facing the System during this period were related to the emergency conditions of the times - - first the Depression and then the War - - and are largely independent of later developments. The second period extends from the early 1950s through 1965. Some forerunners of recent debates on FHLBB policy can be found in the discussions of episodes in 1955, 1959, and the early 1960s (McKinley 1957, Grebler 1960, Bloch 1963, and Schwartz 1970).[3] Generally, however, the SLA industry prospered during this period, and FHLBB policy was not in the spotlight. Developments <u>within</u> the System were perhaps more interesting during this period, and include a running feud with the Banking Commissioners of Illinois over failing SLAs, and a real brawl with Mr. Thomas Gregory, president of a California SLA, which involved the shift of the FHL Bank of Los Angeles to San Francisco.[4]

Since 1965, the policy decisions of the FHLBB have become more important, and while the Board is still not a household word, its actions receive increasing analytic scrutiny by economists, and increasing attention by the Executive and the Congressional branches of the government. Though anticipated by developments in 1964 and 1965, the impulse for this new interest was the money crunch of 1966. Interest has remained keen through the periods of high interest rates and inflation, and of concurrent sharp fluctuations in mortgage market and housing investment activity since then (Grebler and Doyle 1969, and Schwartz 1970). Other relevant factors have included increased commercial bank competition for time deposits, the start of the Department of Housing and Urban Development (HUD) in 1968, and the possibilities for electronic funds transfer and related technological advances.

The object of this paper is to provide a survey and an evaluation of the major policy issues and decisions of the FHLBS since 1965. I intend to proceed on three levels. In section II, the "fundamental issues" are considered - - the role of the FHLBS as an instrument of housing policy, as an agent in the mortgage market, and as the regulator of the efficiency and viability of the member SLAs. In section III, the principal policy instruments of the FHLBB - - advances policy, liquidity regulations, and interest rate ceilings - - are discussed in more detail. In section IV, a variety of current issues is considered, some closely, and with at least mention of most areas of general interest.

---

[3] Histories and studies of the SLA industry for this period are also available, including Ewalt (1962), Kendall (1963), and a number of papers in the project directed by Irwin Friend (1969).

[4] See Marvell (1969) for the inside story on these and other developments. Actually, the FHLBB had a serious enforcement problem during this period since its only weapon against a violating SLA was to expel it from the System - - which was what the Board did not want. A legal change in 1966, however, gave the Board diverse enforcement powers, including the right to issue "cease and desist" orders (Marvell, 1969).

II. THE FUNDAMENTAL ISSUES

Two questions arise concerning FHLBS policy. What objectives should the System pursue? What objectives can the System feasibly meet? Within the System, relatively few answers are available to these questions. The Depression legislation was directed primarily at refinancing delinquent mortgages (through the HOLC); thus, there is little in the Acts or supporting testimony relevant to current issues. Also, over the years, the FHLBB has not issued many policy statements, so official material has only limited value.[5] On the other hand, renewed interest in the System has led to considerable outside discussion, and a summary is attempted here.

A. What Objectives Should The System Pursue?

Aggregate Versus Sectoral Stability

Perhaps the major and most persistent dilemma has been the apparent trade-off between macroeconomic stabilization policy and the stability of the housing sector. It is generally conceded that monetary policy has its main impact on the housing sector, and this is reflected in a predominantly counter-cyclical pattern for housing investment.[6] The FHLBB is thus caught between the national policy of aggregate stabilization (the Employment Act of 1946) and the national priorities toward housing (the Housing Act of 1949 and recent affirmations). The legislation for the FHLBS provides little reference on this point, although Grebler (1960, p. 62) has stressed the majority view of the House Banking and Currency Committee that the System would, ". . . regulate the supply of mortgage credit in a way that will discourage building booms and support normal construction year in and year out." Bloch (1963, p. 206) has noted, from the same report, that, "The homeowner should not be subject to the vicissitudes of the general money market. . . ." It is unclear, however, whether these statements reflect a major thrust of Congressional intent; also it is noteworthy that they were written in a period of infrequent macroeconomic stabilization policy intervention.

---

[5] The main publications of the FHLBB are now the monthly Journal, the Annual Report which appears in the April issue of the Journal, and the working papers of the Office of Economic Research. Prior to 1971, the Annual Report was published in a self-contained volume, and for some years did discuss policy objectives. The Journal has a statistical section, although the Fact Book of the U.S. Savings and Loan League is a more complete source for both data and other "facts" (such as FHLBB regulations). Offsetting these limitations, however, is the fully cooperative spirit of the Office of Economic Research and other departments. The Office of Economic Research has also published a study (FHLBB, 1975) on current proposals, discussed below.

[6] Grebler and Doyle (1969, p. 1306) point out that other major sectors of the economy, for example, the auto industry, have cyclical fluctuations comparable to those of housing. The housing sector does differ, however, in that monetary policy appears as the source of the fluctuations.

Is shifting resources in and out of the housing sector a socially desirable means for implementing macroeconomic policy? The high interest rate elasticity of housing would indicate that investors are easily induced to postpone housing expenditures; thus, the sector appears to be the right candidate for induced counter-cyclical fluctuations. Two objections arise, however. First, the high interest rate elasticity may be the result of the policy role assigned to housing. For example, the high interest rate elasticity may be due in part to the low capitalization of the construction industry, and the low capitalization may in turn be the result of the industry's highly cyclical experience. Second, the measured interest elasticity of housing demand may combine a true interest rate effect and an availability effect that tends to correlate with interest rate movements. If the availability effect is important, then there are grounds for arguing that tight money discriminates against housing, in the sense that the transmission mechanism for funding housing investment tends to break down in such periods. If that is so, then the "first-best" policy prescription would be to eliminate the availability effects; I shall return to this point.

If the housing sector is protected, then monetary policy would have to be even stronger to carry out a given macroeconomic goal. Moreover, a stronger monetary policy would lead to more claims for protection from the unprotected sectors, and leave us either without a monetary tool or right back where it started from. Countering this, however, is the proposition that without the constraint of the housing sector, the Federal Reserve could carry out monetary policy in a more flexible and effective manner (see Pierce and Graves, 1972).

This dilemma is unlikely to be resolved in a clear-cut way, although the FHLBB has been proceeding toward a policy of protecting the housing sector. For example, in 1955 and 1966, the FHLBB used restrictive policies to limit advances to members, whether of its own volition or due to Treasury restrictions.[7] In 1969 and 1974, in contrast, advances to members were encouraged, even to the extent of providing subsidized loans. This is indicated in Table 1, which shows that advances outstanding increased nearly 100 percent in 1973, and by the same percentage again over the 1972 base in 1974. This is also illustrated in the increasingly strong, though brief, policy statements from the Board:

> . . . the Board chose, in 1967, to maintain System liquidity so that the System could serve as a buffer for the mortgage market. This was in accord with the legislative history of the System and efforts of the Administration to reduce the unusually severe impact on housing of general credit restraint. (FHLBB, Annual Report, 1967, p. 51);

---

[7] Debt issues of the FHLBS must be approved by the Treasury, and it appears that either rejection or, at least, compromise has occurred. The power of the Treasury is a bit peculiar since, at the same time, the FHLBS has the emergency power to place its debt, currently in the amount of $4 billion, with the Treasury.

The primary goal of Federal Home Loan Bank System credit policy last year [1969], in keeping with its statutory responsibility, was to provide members with the maximum funds economically feasible to meet savings withdrawals and mortgage demands. (FHLBB, Annual Report, 1969, p. 37) ;

Number one, we need to work to stabilize funds flows to housing so that we can eliminate, to the degree that we have the capability of doing so, the destructive boom and bust cycles that we have in residential housing. . . . (Statement of Chairman Bomar, Journal of the Federal Home Loan Bank Board, July 1973, p. 2).

Long-run Stimulus to Housing

The promotion of a long-run stimulus to housing investment, in contrast to cyclical stabilization, appears to be a less complicated objective. Congressional intent is clear in view of recent programs for stimulating housing, starting with the HUD Act of 1968. However, there may be a dilemma for FHLBB policy if there is a trade-off between the use of available instruments for long-run and short-run purposes. For example, it has been suggested that if advances were extended to maximize the growth rate, then there would be nothing left for short-run stabilization. Whether or not this is a constraint depends on the System's own policies. Before 1965, the FHLBS was frequently a net supplier of funds to the government security market and was hesitant to place demands on an already tight market.[8] Recently, the System has moved to an unequivocal debtor position, and appears prepared to move further to meet short-run needs. Short-run stabilization and long-run stimulus, therefore, would not appear to be contradictory goals, although the feasibility of a long-run stimulus is an open question which I discuss below.

Mortgages and Savings Deposits as Separable Goals

Savings deposit flows, mortgage market activity, and housing investment frequently move together, so there may appear little need to distinguish them as policy objectives. However, the variables can move in different ways, and there are instruments that discriminate between them. For example, available evidence suggests that Regulation Q ceilings have protected the savings flows to the SLAs, but have had a neutral or even negative effect on housing investment (Fair and Jaffee, 1972). Similarly, there is the possibility, demonstrated below, that FHLBB advances may stimulate the mortgage market, but without an appreciable effect on housing investment.

---

[8] Bloch (1963, p. 212) points out that the System was a net supplier of funds in that holdings of government securities by the FHL Banks and by members frequently exceeded the debt issues of the FHL Banks. Also, the FHL Bank debt was short-term, and thus was not suitable for financing long-term investments.

Table 1

Various Time Series: 1955-1974

	Housing Starts[a] (Millions)	FHLBB Advances Outstanding[b] (End of Period, $ billion)	Interest Rate in % (Annual Average) on:			
			SLA Deposits[b]	SLA Mortgages[d]	FHLBB Advances[c]	FHLBB Debt Issue[d]
1955	1.62	1.42	2.94	5.12	2.56	2.47
1956	1.32	1.23	3.03	5.15	2.80	3.35
1957	1.17	1.27	3.26	5.25	3.69	4.07
1958	1.31	1.30	3.38	5.34	3.75	3.42
1959	1.52	2.13	3.53	5.46	4.43	4.04
1960	1.25	1.98	3.86	5.61	4.94	4.35
1961	1.31	2.66	3.90	5.71	3.76	3.25
1962	1.46	3.79	4.08	5.87	3.69	3.31
1963	1.60	4.78	4.17	5.85	3.82	3.54
1964	1.53	5.32	4.18	5.93	4.19	4.03
1965	1.47	6.00	4.23	5.91	4.66	4.30
1966	1.16	6.93	4.45	5.97	5.39	5.15
1967	1.29	4.39	4.67	5.97	5.76	5.74
1968	1.51	5.26	4.68	6.17	5.69	5.88
1969	1.47	9.29	4.82	6.31	6.59	6.89
1970	1.43	10.62	5.14	6.56	7.41	7.80

Table 1 (continued)

	Housing Starts[a] (Millions)	FHLBB Advances Outstanding[b] (End of Period, $ billion)	Interest Rates in % (Annual Average) on:			
			SLA Deposits[b]	SLA Mortgages[d]	FHLBB Advances[c]	FHLBB Debt Issued[d]
1971	2.05	7.94	5.30	6.81	7.00	7.54
1972	2.36	7.98	5.37	6.98	6.54	7.00
1973	2.04	15.15	5.51	7.17	7.05	7.22
1974	1.31	21.80	5.86	7.35	8.00	7.89

Sources: a U.S. Bureau of Census; Private Units.

b Journal and Annual Reports of the Federal Home Loan Bank Board

c Data bank of MIT-Federal Reserve (MPS) Econometric Model through 1966; Journal of the Federal Home Loan Bank Board thereafter.

d Grebler (1972, Appendix B) through 1969; Journal of the Federal Home Loan Bank Board thereafter. SLA deposit and mortgage interest rates in 1974 are through June.

167

When a trade-off occurs, FHLBB policy seems to reflect a clear ordering of priorities: savings flows first; then, mortgage market activity; finally, housing investment. Since the FHLBB is closely associated with the SLA industry, and less with the housing market, this appears to be a reasonable bureaucratic response. Also, the effectiveness of System policy on these three objectives is of the same order as the ordering of their objectives (see discussion below). It is reasonable to do first what one does best. Still there is some inconsistency with national goals which put housing first, and a dilemma along these lines could develop.[9]

Efficiency, Safety, and Service Functions of the SLA Industry

Having stressed the macroeconomic objectives of the System, it is important to note a strongly held objective toward the microeconomic aspect of SLA behavior. Given FSLIC insurance, the FHLBB has a strong incentive to maintain standards in the operational and portfolio quality of the member institutions. For example, in the early 1960s, the Board indicated concern with the quality of mortgage debt, and acted to correct the situation. More recently, the Board has shown signs of recognizing the welfare of SLA customers, Regulation Q ceilings notwithstanding. More dramatically, the current FHLBB has increased industry efficiency through the removal of needless regulations (see below).

Reaction Functions of the FHLBB

To ascertain in an empirical fashion the objectives of the FHLBB is appealing. Unfortunately, large scale econometric models treat FHLBB policy as exogenous, while simple correlations do an injustice to the variety of objectives pursued, the number of available instruments, and the lags involved. There have been, however, at least two recent attempts to estimate serious FHLBB reaction funds. Silber (1973) finds that housing is an important objective of the System, although minimization of the spread between borrowing costs and advance rates is more important. Kearl and Rosen (1974), on the other hand, define the model differently, and find that stabilization of savings flows is a prime variable, with stabilization of mortgage flows a weak second. In section III, it is suggested that neither study has accurately specified either the objectives or the instruments of the System, and thus the results must be taken as preliminary.[10]

---

[9] Following the argument of Thygerson (1973), the U.S. Savings and Loan League feels that government mortgage support programs achieve their objective at the cost of SLA profitability; ultimately, there is a conflict between SLA deposit flows and government-sponsored mortgage flows. However, see the review by Jaffee (1974b).

[10] It is noteworthy that neither sample extends beyond 1971, and thus misses any recent shifts in FHLBB priorities. Also, neither study finds a statistically significant shift in FHLBB priorities during the mid-1960s.

B. What Can The System Do?

While objectives are fine, feasibility is a constraint. Recent discussions indicate that the impact of FHLBB instruments on housing markets is limited. To be specific, I will focus on the impact on housing market investment of FHLBB advances to SLAs. Rounding off the polar positions, the situation seems as follows. Arcelus and Meltzer (1973a) and Meltzer (1974) argue that funds are fungible, and that pushing advances on SLAs has no long-run impact on housing. Meltzer (1974) does conceive of a mortgage market in short-run disequilibrium - - with credit rationing and availability effects - - and sees the possibility of affecting the short-run timing of housing investment in such a situation; but fundamentally he does not see disequilibrium as empirically important. In contrast, Smith (1970), Swan (1973), and Jaffee (1974a), among others, argue that mortgage market disequilibrium is frequently a key element and that advance policies can be effective. Granting this, advance policies may be only a "second best" policy; eliminating the disequilibrium might be preferable.[11]

To be more concrete, I try now to compare, using a "barebones model," the long-run position of Arcelus and Meltzer and the short-run disequilibrium position. I then turn to the question of the existence of disequilibrium, and what to do about it.

When the Mortgage and Housing Markets are in Long-run Equilibrium

The following model isolates the principal parameters necessary for the Arcelus and Meltzer position. It is not meant, however, either as an econometric specification or as a general equilibrium system. The equations are:

$$(1) \qquad H = a_0 - a_1 (RM + RG);$$

$$(2) \qquad M^d = b_0 + b_1 (RG - RM);$$

$$(3) \qquad M^s = c_0 D - c_1 (RG - RM);$$

$$(4) \qquad M^d = M^s;$$

$$(5) \qquad D = d_0 + A - d_1 RG;$$

$$(6) \qquad RG = e_0 + e_1 A.$$

---

[11] I have avoided the issue of whether anyone disagrees with the long-run position of Arcelus and Meltzer. Arcelus and Meltzer (1973b, pp. 976-977) provide examples of apparent disagreement. I suspect they underestimate the degree to which most writers assume the case of disequilibrium.

All coefficients are positive numbers. Symbols are defined:

H housing stock;

M^d mortgage fund demand (by borrowers);

M^s mortgage fund supply (by lenders);

D deposits of SLAs;

RM mortgage interest rate;

RG government bond interest rate;

A advances from FHLBS to SLAs.

The equations can be described briefly as follows. Equation (1) determines the housing stock as a function of exogenous and fixed variables (combined in the coefficient a_0) and of the cost of capital given by the average of RM and RG (the divisor of 2 is subsumed in the coefficient a_1). Equation (2) gives the mortgage demand of borrowers as the sum of a constant term and of a term depending on the spread, RG - RM. [12] Similarly, equation (3) bases mortgage supply on the level of deposits and the spread, RG - RM. Equation (4) is the equilibrium condition for the mortgage market. Equation (5) allows for disinter-mediation whereby deposits decline as the capital market rate, RG, rises, and treats advances as a simple additive element to deposits for the purposes of mortgage supply. Equation (6) assumes the rate, RG, is determined by exogenous and fixed forces (in e_0), and by the amount of FHLBB debt issues necessary to finance the advances, A.

The reduced form solution of the system for housing, H^*, mortgages, M^*, and the mortgage rate, RM^*, as a function of advances, A^*, is:

(7) $RM^* = a_0 - a_1 A^*$,

where

$$a_0 = \frac{b_0 - c_0 d_0 + e_0 (c_0 d_1 + c_1 + b_1)}{c_1 + b_1} \text{ , and}$$

$$a_1 = \left[\frac{c_0}{c_1 + b_1} \right] - \left[1 + \frac{c_0 d_1}{c_1 + b_1} e_1 \right] \text{ ;}$$

---

[12] Formally, the mortgage demand is derived from the housing demand. In econometric studies this relationship is frequently captured by specifying an H term directly in the mortgage demand equation. This is unnecessary for the barebones model.

(8) $$H^* = [a_0 - a_1 (a_0 + e_0)] + a_1 (a_1 - e_1) A^* \; ;$$

(9) $$M^* = [b_0 + b_1 (e_0 - a_0)] + b_1 (a_1 + e_1) A^* \; .$$

From equation (7), the decline in RM* when A* rises will be less (i.e., a_1 will be less):

(i)   the greater the interest response of M^d and M^s (i.e., the greater b_1 and c_1);[13]

(ii)   the greater the response of D to RG (i.e., the greater d_1);

(iii)   the greater the response of RG to A (i.e., the greater e_1);

(iv)   the less the response of M^s to D (i.e., the less c_0).

These factors can thus account for a small decline in RM* when A* rises.

Similarly, from equations (8) and (9), the effect of advances policy on housing and mortgages can be calculated. In both cases, the factors that decrease a_1, that is, the factors that limit the response of RM*, also limit the response of H* and M*. However, the coefficients, a_1, b_1 and e_1, enter directly into (8) and (9), and thus the conclusions must be slightly modified:

(v)   large values of e_1, the response of RG to A, strongly dampen the impact on H*, but weakly dampen the impact on M*. This arises because RG enters with a negative sign in the H equation, but with a positive sign in the M^s equation;

(vi)   large values of a_1, the interest response of housing, increase the impact on housing (assuming the impact is positive);

(vii)   large values of b_1, the interest response of M^d, increase the impact on mortgages (assuming the impact is positive).

What are the empirical magnitudes of these parameters? Meltzer (1974) and Swan (1974) survey a variety of empirical studies. My reading of these results is that they provide a strong case against the effectiveness of FHLBB advances policy as a long-run stimulus to housing. Two of these studies, Gramlich and Jaffee (1972), Chapter 5, and p. 259 and Arcelus and Meltzer (1973a) demonstrate the possibility of a perverse negative impact on housing.

As an alternative technique of evaluation, the above model provides for a more intuitive - - back-of-the-envelope type - - calculation. Treat the variables in the model as logarithms, so that the coefficients are interpreted as elastic-

---

[13] This assumes that $d_1 e_1$ is less than unity. This is a necessary condition for a_1 to be positive.

ities. [14] From equation (8), the elasticity of H^* with respect to A^* is given by $a_1 (a_1 - e_1)$. Some, if not most, empirical studies indicate the interest elasticity of housing demand, that is, a_1, to be approximately 1, so that the advances elasticity can be reduced to $(a_1 - e_1)$. From the definition of a_1 in equation (7):

$$a_1 - e_1 = \frac{c_0}{c_1 + b_1} - (2 + \frac{c_0 d_1}{c_1 + b_1}) e_1 .$$

At this point, I leave the reader to his own envelope. [15] However, I suggest the following as a reasonable array: $c_0 = .3$; $c_1 + b_1 = 3.0$; $d_1 = 1.0$; and, $e_1 = .05$. This yields an elasticity of H^* with respect to A^* of about zero. The point is that reasonable parameter values can yield very low or even negative housing elasticities.

When the Mortgage Market is in Disequilibrium

Disequilibrium in the mortgage market is characterized by a situation in which the quoted mortgage rate, $\overline{RM}$, is less than the market clearing value, RM^*. The quantity of loans offered is thus determined by the supply, M^S, evaluated at the rate, $\overline{RM}$, and this amount will be less than the demand, M^d, evaluated at the same rate. Consequently, it does not make sense to count the mortgage rate, $\overline{RM}$, as an element of the cost of capital for housing investment, as specified in equation (1), since borrowers could not freely obtain funds at this rate.

Instead, at least one approach is to calculate, and to use in equation (1), the shadow price of mortgage funds, denoted as $\hat{RM}$. $\hat{RM}$ is defined as the level of the mortgage rate such that demand, M^d, would equal the supply forthcoming at $\overline{RM}$. Formally, equations (1) to (4) of the original model would take the following form:

(1') $H = a_0 - a_1 (\hat{RM} + RG);$

---

[14] This involves a slight fudge in that the additive position of A in equation (5) is correct only in the linear specification. This is taken into account in the estimate of c_0 presented below.

[15] Reference should be made here to two controversial papers by Kwon and Thornton (1971), (1972), that indicate exceptionally high values for d_1 and e_1. The papers have been strongly criticized, however, in a series of comments by Grebler (1973), Kaufman (1973), Van Horne (1973), and Fortune (1974).

(2') $\hat{RM} = RG + \dfrac{b_0 - M^S}{b_1}$;

(3') $M^S = c_0 D - c_1 (RG - \overline{RM})$.

With some algebra, the reduced form solution for H* can be written in a form comparable to (8):

$$(8')\qquad H^* = \left[\frac{a_0 b_1 - a_1 b_0 + a_1 c_0 d_0 - e_1 \,(2a_1 b_1 + a_1 c_1 + a_1 c_0 d_1)}{b_1}\right]$$

$$+ \left[\frac{a_1 c_1}{b_1}\ \overline{RM}\right] + a_1 \left[a_1 \left(1 + \frac{c_1}{b_1}\right) - e_1\right] A^* \ .$$

Two implications should be noted. First, increases in the quoted rate, $\overline{RM}$, have a <u>positive</u> impact on housing investment, H*. This results because increases in $\overline{RM}$ induce a greater mortgage supply, and thus reduce the shadow price of mortgage funds, $\hat{RM}$. It is for this reason that binding usury ceilings in mortgage markets are seen as actually reducing housing investment.

Second, the response of H* to A* given in the disequilibrium system is necessarily greater than the response in the equilibrium system. This can be seen by comparing the coefficients of A* in (8) and (8'). Intuitively, this gain occurs because an advances policy in disequilibrium does not change the quoted rate, $\overline{RM}$, and, therefore, there is no offsetting movement along the supply curve, M^S. In terms of empirical magnitudes, this type of effect does not appear to have been measured. Returning to the back of the envelope, however, the elasticity of H* may increase on the order of .1, in going from an equilibrium to a disequilibrium system. This may appear small, but it should be noted that the ratio of the value of housing to advances is currently at least 30. Thus, an elasticity of .1 would imply a total differential, dH/dA, of at least 3.

What to Do About Disequilibrium

Meltzer (1974) raises the issue of why availability effects and disequilibrium are so important in the mortgage market. He finds the explanation that nonprice terms of the mortgage contract clear the market unsatisfactory, and I think he is right.   The argument as developed, for example, by Guttentag (1960) is that while interest rates move slowly in the mortgage market, nonprice terms adjust rapidly.   This seems incomplete, in that if lenders find it inappropriate to change such a visible and competitive device as the price, then why should they adjust the nonprice terms so rapidly.   A precise and clear theory of the interaction between the interest rate and nonprice terms on financial contracts is lacking. [16]

On the other hand, the slow movement of mortgage rates relative to other capital market interest rates has long been observed, from before the Depression even; it must be accepted as a real phenomenon. This suggests that the sluggish movement can be explained as a function of the structure of the market, and, in particular, as the result of the importance of mutual depository intermediaries in mortgage lending. The depository status of the lenders, for example, means that they are operating on the spread between mortgage and deposit rates; thus, if pressure in the general capital markets is transmitted after a lag to deposit markets, then a similar lag may develop in the adjustment of the mortgage rate. The mutual aspect of ownership plays a part, in that lack of information and simple inertia are prevalent. In structure, mortgage markets are characterized by monopolistic competition--pressure between local markets is transmitted only with considerable lag. Also, a large proportion of mortgage lending is arranged on a forward basis, using advance commitments, and this will create a lag in the adjustment speed of the interest rate.   Finally, the mortgage market is one in which search behavior is important in the dynamics of price or interest rate changes. In such a market, there are advantages to both lenders and borrowers of a stable price.

Government regulations have also played a role in slowing the adjustment speed of mortgage interest rates. The ceilings set on FHA-VA mortgages have lagged market rates over considerable periods. Currently, the usury ceilings set by states on mortgage lending are strongly binding. Consequently, mortgage rates are currently below market clearing levels, and government agencies, principally FNMA and the FHLBS, are forced to support the market. As I have indicated, in such a disequilibrium situation, support may be effective in providing a short-run stimulus to housing investment. However, it is unlikely that there is more housing investment under this regime than would develop out of an equilibrium system. It is a classic case in which one form of government intervention - - ceilings - - invites further intervention - - mortgage support - - in a lengthening chain of inefficiency.

In addition to removing government constraints on mortgage rate movements, it is intriguing to consider alternative ways in which the market can be made more responsive. Behavior imbedded in the market structure itself will not

---

[16] The problem of nonprice terms on financial contracts has certain formal similarities to the problem of quality and durability in microeconomic theory. There has been recent work on the durability problem, and this might be usefully applied to nonprice terms on financial contracts.

be easy to change. Warren Smith's paper on this topic (1970, p. 96) detailed a program for a ". . . market clearing arrangement for the mortgage market." The plan is that the newly created Federal Home Loan Mortgage Corporation (FHLMC) should maintain a secondary market in conventional mortgages by offering to buy and sell the contracts at the same yield as the corporation's own borrowing costs. The supply of funds would be fully elastic, so long as borrowers were prepared to pay the going price. FHLMC has proceeded in a limited way along the lines suggested by Smith, although it is hard to evaluate the impact on mortgage rate flexibility due to the binding set of usury ceilings in force.

Smith also supported the notion of pass-through and mortgage-backed bonds. The principle of such bonds is that an originator pools several mortgages, typically guaranteed by GNMA, and then finances the pool through a debt issue offered on terms more attractive in the capital markets than the pool itself. The FHLBB has recently issued regulations under which mortgage-backed bonds (MBBs) can be issued by SLAs; it remains to be seen what impact they will have.

Finally, it should be noted that the mortgage contract has proved imperfect in the recent period of high interest rates and inflation. The issues have been noted by Poole (1972), and have been examined in the recent MIT Mortgage Project. [17] Proposals for variable rate, graduated payment, and indexed mortgages have appeared, including those by the FHLBS for variable rate lending by SLAs. These are evaluated below.

III. OPERATIONAL ASPECTS OF THE MAIN POLICY INSTRUMENTS

Having outlined the primary policy objectives of the system and their feasibility, I turn to the specific instruments for achieving these goals. The instruments available to the FHLBB include the quantity and interest rate terms of advances, liquidity requirements, Regulation Q ceilings, and mortgage market support by FHLMC. Since 1965, the FHLBB has received considerable advice on the efficient use of these instruments. Much of this advice has been implemented, and with some success. I start with a summary of these events.

---

[17] The proceedings of a conference held by the Project are available in Modigliani and Lessard (1975).

175

A. Liquidity Policy

The Liquidity Needs of the System

Bloch (1963), Cootner (1969), and Duesenberry (1969), among others, make proposals for instruments to meet the System's liquidity needs. Cootner provides a stimulating and lengthy discussion of what amounts to a random walk theory of liquidity. Ex ante, SLAs determine their portfolio size and the mortgage intensity mix as a function of current and expected interest rates in the mortgage and deposit markets. Ex post, unexpected developments may force an SLA to reduce the effective size of its portfolio. Thus, even if SLAs were free to compete for deposits, and could sell mortgages in a perfect secondary market, Cootner argues that risk-averse SLAs would have a precautionary demand for liquidity. Moreover, given poor secondary trading facilities for mortgages, and the imperfect nature of deposit markets - - including Regulation Q constraints - - the demand for liquidity becomes even greater. Cootner considers this demand for liquidity natural, and proceeds to a set of proposals for meeting the need most effectively.

A different view, advanced by Friend (1969), is that the maturity imbalance between SLA mortgages and deposits is untenable and that more is needed than an efficient system of liquidity. Friend's position is a polar case of Cootner's random walk model; with a nonzero probability, any set level of liquidity will prove inadequate even if the disturbances are random. Friend's policy proposals are directed at either shortening the effective maturity of the mortgage portfolio, and/or lengthening the effective maturity of the deposit liabilities. A middle-ground policy, of moderating maturity imbalances while improving system liquidity, is also possible, and in fact the FHLBB has proceeded in this way.

Who Should Hold the Liquidity and in What Form

There is a choice whether the liquidity should be held by the member SLAs or by the FHL Banks. Duesenberry, Cootner, and others have concluded that liquidity responsibility should be with the FHL Banks, because they offer economies of scale from the centralization of reserves.[18] Also, the FHL Banks are responsible for the viability of the system and their effectiveness as lender of last resort would be enhanced if they were to serve also as lender of first resort.

If member SLAs are to hold the System liquidity, the main instrument must be the FHLBB power to set liquidity requirements between 4 percent and 10 percent of total deposits, and to set the terms for qualifying assets. The use of liquidity requirements for this purpose would be reflected in higher require-

---

[18] For a contrary view, see Burnham (1972).

ments on average and in greater fluctuations as members' needs rise and fall.[19] The pattern and details of liquidity requirements set by the FHLBB are shown in Table 2. Between 1950 (when authority for the requirements was first received) and 1968, the requirements were changed only once. Since 1968, there have been 11 changes in both the level and in the definition of qualifying assets. On the other hand, there have been no appreciable changes in the average level of requirements; since 1973, they have been below average. System policy appears to rely increasingly on changes in liquidity requirements for stabilizing mortgage markets. This is difficult to distinguish from a liquidity policy, since low rates of savings flows and low rates of mortgage flows are so highly correlated. The April 1, 1975 increase, for example, occurred at a time of continuing low mortgage activity but improving deposit flows, and thus might be identified as a purely liquidity-motivated change.

To enable the FHL Banks to maintain the System's liquidity, the Board has the choice either of borrowing funds ahead of time and maintaining them in a liquid form, or of borrowing in the capital markets as the needs arise. Two considerations apply. First, the Board should achieve its liquidity goal in the least expensive manner. Borrowing ahead of time, presumably with long-term debt, entails the cost of the rate spread between the long-term debt and the short-term securities held for liquidity. Borrowing on a short-term need basis, on the other hand, generally involves issuing debt during tight money periods when interest rates are highest. Although neither alternative dominates, accurate forecasts of future developments would indicate one or the other technique in specific circumstances.

A second factor, however, makes long-term borrowing the better choice. Debt issues of the FHL Banks must be approved by the Treasury, and in several instances it has denied, or significantly changed, the terms of FHL Bank issues. This is peculiar since the Treasury does not regulate System sales of Treasury securities acquired through previous purchase, although net sales of Treasury securities and new issues of FHLBB debt have the same impact on the government security market (see footnote 7). Within this constraint, the FHLBB maximizes its discretionary power by borrowing long-term ahead of time.

The FHLBB has become more sophisicated and flexible in its financing since the mid-1960s. A list of outstanding debt issues is shown in Table 3. There are a number of bonds with original maturity over 10 years, and many of the issues in 1974 were for at least five years. To some extent, the lengthening of debt maturity reflects a similar change in the maturity of advances, and the

---

[19] The Commission of Mortgages Interest Rates (1969) proposed that liquidity requirements should be adjusted automatically for institutions experiencing savings withdrawals. The Commission also proposed that assured lines of credit be available to meet savings withdrawals.

Table 2

Minimum Ratio[1] of Liquid Assets[2] to Liquidity Base[3] Required of Members of the Federal Home Loan Bank System

[Percent]

Effective date	All liquid assets	Short-term liquid assets[4]	Effective date	All liquid assets	Short-term liquid assets[4]	Effective date	All liquid assets	Short-term liquid assets[4]
Dec. 1950	6	(6)	Apr. 1, 1971	6 1/2	(6)	Aug. 1, 1973[7]	5 1/2	1 1/2
Mar. 1, 1961[5]	7	(6)	May 1, 1971	7 1/2	(6)	Sept. 1, 1974[7]	5	1
Aug. 1, 1968	6 1/2	(6)	Aug. 1, 1971	7	(6)	Apr. 1, 1975	5 1/2	1 1/2
June 12, 1969	6	(6)	Jan. 1, 1972	7	3			
Dec. 1, 1969	5 1/2	(6)	May 1, 1973	6 1/2	2 1/2			

1 Before Dec. 22, 1969, the indicated minimum was required on each day a member closed loans. Beginning Dec. 22, 1969, compliance has been monthly, on the basis of an average of daily liquid asset balances to an average of the liquidity base for the preceding month, or, in the case of members with less than $25 million in assets, to the liquidity base in the case of the preceding month. Special provision is made in the case of deficiencies resulting from the withdrawal of savings.

2 Liquid assets consisted of unpledged cash, deposits, and U.S. Government securities through June 10, 1969. Federal agency securities with 5 or less years to maturity were added June 11, 1969. Effective Dec. 22, 1969, and subject to some additional restrictions, the following were made eligible liquid assets: (a) time deposits at commercial banks with a maturity of 1 year or less, or a notice period of 90 days or less; (b) bankers acceptances with a maturity of 6 months or less; (c) general obligations of State and local governments with a maturity of 2 years or less; (d) eligible liquid assets held subject to a repurchase agreement; and (e) accrued interest on liquid assets, or assets which would so qualify except for maturity. Effective Jan. 1, 1972, the amount of U.S. Government securities with a maturity of more than 7 years that could be counted as liquid assets was limited to one-half of 1 percent of the base and mutual savings banks could elect to hold that portion of required liquidity in excess of 5 percent in Federal funds and commercial paper. Beginning Nov. 21, 1973, unsecured Federal funds loans made eligible liquid assets for member associations.

3 Before Nov. 1, 1970, the liquidity base consisted of a member's net withdrawable accounts (or the policy reserve required by State law, in the case of an insurance company). Beginning Nov. 1, 1970, borrowings payable on demand or due in 1 year or less, were added.

4 Short-term liquid assets consist of the liquia assets defined in footnote 2, except: (a) U.S. Government and Federal agency securities with a maturity longer than 18 months; (b) commercial bank time deposits with a maturity longer than 6 months; and (c) State and local government obligations. The requirement is not applicable to member mutual savings banks or insurance companies.

5 During the period June 27 - Nov. 1, 1966, members were permitted to reduce liquid asset holdings below the requirement by an amount not exceeding the smaller of (a) actual net savings withdrawn, or (b) 1 percent of withdrawable savings.

6 No separate requirement.

7 Penalties for liquidity deficiencies caused by net savings withdrawals during August through December 1973 and April through October 1974 were waived.

Source: Journal, Federal Home Loan Bank Board, March, 1975.

three longest debt maturities were issued by FHLMC. Nevertheless, compared to the mid-1960s, when the bulk of debt was very short-term, the current techniques look good.[20]

B. Advances Policy

Advances by the FHLBS to member SLAs are administered by the regional FHL Banks under guidelines set by the FHLBB. The regional Banks finance the advances by obtaining shares in the consolidated debt issues of the FHLBS. Within the guidelines and their fund allocations, the regional FHL Banks have had considerable discretion in setting the nonprice terms of advances such as maturity and renewal. The interest rate on advances, however, has been more closely regulated by the FHLBB. Until 1965, the rate policy was determined by an average cost rule, whereby the advance rate was equal to the average cost of the FHL Bank's share of the consolidated debt plus a small mark up. This led to an advance rate considerably below the mortgage interest rate, and frequently below the average interest rate paid on deposits (see Table 1). Consequently, it may be surmised that nonprice rationing of advances was practiced by both the regional FHL Bank making the loans and the FHLBB allocating funds.

Since 1965, the guidelines of the FHLBB have changed considerably. The base line for advance rates is now a marginal concept, being the average cost of funds for the most recent obligations assigned to the regional FHL Bank. This feature, together with changes in the structure of interest rates, has caused the base line for advance rates to rise relative to mortgage and deposit rates; advance rates now exceed average deposit rates, and, at times, have approached mortgage rates.[21] In response, the FHLBB has taken a more flexible rate policy relative to the base line, and, at times, has reduced advance rates appreciably below the base in order to stimulate demand for advances. In addition, the programs of "specially priced advances" have made explicit reductions in the advance rates for limited times. For example, during the last 8 months of 1974, the FHLBB was providing $500 million of advances at 3/4 percent below the going rate monthly ($4 billion for the year). The FHLBB has also experimented with a variety of new nonprice terms, including fixed-rate, long-term advances, with penalty costs for prepayment, and variable-rate advances. These incentives, as well as industry need for liquidity, caused the quantity of advances outstanding nearly to triple between 1972 and 1974, to a year-end 1974 value of over $21.0 billion (Table 1).

---

[20] See Grebler (1972, p. 200 and Appendix J) for additional data and discussion.

[21] The cost of the System debt obligations has maintained its normal relationship with other capital market rates. The change has been a relative lowering of deposit rates, in part due to the Regulation Q ceilings, and of mortgage rates, due partly to usury ceilings and perhaps partly to government mortgage market support.

Table 3

Maximum Rates of Return Payable on Savings Accounts by Savings
and Loan Associations that Are Members of the Federal Home Loan Bank System

Type of account	Effective date and percentage rates				
	Sept. 26 1966 [1]	Jan. 21 1970	July 6, 1973	Nov. 1, 1973	Dec. 23 1974
Regular	4.75	2 5.00	5.25	5.25	5.25
90-day notice (for withdrawals).......	(3)	4 5.25	5.75	5 5.75	5 5.75
Certificate with fixed or minimum term or qualifying period:					
Balance less than $100,000:					
Owned by governmental units:					
All terms...............	(6)	(6)	(6)	(6)	7.75
Owned by others:					
90 days to 6 months	(7)	5.25	8 5.75	5.75	5.75
6 months to 1 year	9 5.25	4 9 5.25	8 5.75	5.75	5.75
1 year to 2 years.	9 5.25	8 5.75	8 6.50	8 6.50	8 6.50
2 years to 2 1/2 years	9 10 5.25	11 6.00	8 6.50	8 6.50	8 6.50
2 1/2 years to 4 years	9 10 5.25	11 6.00	8 6.75	8 6.75	8 6.75
4 years to 6 years.	9 10 5.25	11 6.00	(12)	9 7.50	9 7.50
6 years or more	9 10 5.25	11 6.00	(12)	9 7.50	9 7.75
Balance $100,000 [13] or more:					
All owners - - all terms	(14)	(15)	(16)	(16)	(16)

1 Associations in certain geographic areas had higher ceilings than those indicated; see this table in the June 1973 Journal for additional information.

2 5.25 percent in Mass.

3 Not permitted before July 22, 1968. Subsequently, the ceiling was 5 percent for associations in areas permitted 5 percent on regular accounts, provided they were not offering 5.25 percent certificates, and 4.75 percent for all other associations through Mar. 30, 1969, and 5 percent for all associations thereafter.

4 5.50 percent in Mass.

5 Beginning Nov. 27, 1974, maximum rate for notice accounts owned by governmental units was the same as for certificate accounts owned by such units.

6 Before Nov. 27, 1974, maximum rate was the same as for other types of owners; from Nov. 27 through Dec. 22, 1974, maximum rate was 7.50 percent.

7 Not permitted.

8 $1,000 minimum balance required, except in areas where mutual savings banks were permitting lower balance

9 $1,000 minimum balance required.

10 $1,000 Dec. 19, 1969, through Jan. 20, 1970. 6.00 percent was permitted for existing accounts of $10,000 or more only.

11 $5,000 minimum balance required, except in areas where mutual savings banks were permitting a lower balance.

12 No maximum rate with $1,000 minimum balance; 6.75 percent maximum with lower minimum balance.

13 $50,000 for Puerto Rico only, beginning Sept. 3, 1970.

14 Some maximum rate as for certificates with smaller balances.

15 From Jan. 21, 1970, through May 16, 1973, maximum rate was 6.50 percent for accounts with term of 60-89 days; 6.75 percent for 90-179 day accounts; 7.00 percent for 180-364 day accounts; and 7.50 percent for longer term accounts; thereafter no maximum rate.

16 No maximum rate.

Source: Journal, Federal Home Loan Bank Board, March, 1975.

These changes in FHLBB advance policy have satisfied a number of complaints about Board policies during the mid-1960s. One complaint was that the pricing technique was too rigid with too much emphasis on nonprice rationing. This has changed, due both to events - - the structural change leading to a relative increase in the cost of funds to the System - - and to explicit policy. A second concern was that the Board was haphazard in distinguishing the maturity of advances, and, in particular, made no attempt to price advances in line with the existing term structure. Distinctions are now made on the basis of maturity, although a more formal schedule of instructions to the regional FHL Banks might still be desirable. Finally, there was concern that the Board's advance policies and its planning of debt obligations were not satisfactorily integrated. As I have indicated, the Board now has more flexible and innovative techniques for debt issue, and the mechanics of funding no longer appear as a binding constraint on advances policy.

Another important trend is the emphasis on advances as a major intermediate, if not long-run, stimulus to mortgage and housing markets. The large increase in advances in 1973 and 1974 has already been described and cannot be accounted for in terms of the liquidity needs of the System. As I noted in section II, the question concerns the equilibrium or disequilibrium state of the mortgage market. Given the current set of binding usury ceilings, it is clear that the mortgage market is in disequilibrium; thus, the recent growth of advances may be creating a useful stimulus as a "second best" solution. On the other hand, were the market to return to an equilibrium position, either because market rates fell or because other innovations were implemented (see below), then by the previous analysis, advances would no longer be required, and the FHLBB could retire from the market.

C. Regulation Q and FHLMC

Evaluations of the role of Regulation Q ceilings on time deposits are available elsewhere.[22] The status of current FHLBB proposals for deposit rate ceilings is discussed in the following section. One point though should be stressed here. Deposit rate ceilings, like usury ceilings in mortgage markets, create disequilibrium, and thus provide grounds for government support of the affected market. But, the conclusion on usury ceilings above holds equally for deposit rate ceilings - - government support of deposit markets is a "second best" solution compared simply to removing the ceilings.

---

[22] For a brief review and some empirical results on the effects of Regulation Q ceilings on SLA s, see Jaffee (1973).

I turn now, briefly, to the Federal Home Loan Mortgage Corporation (FHLMC). Its mortgage purchasing activities have been stimulated recently in much the same manner as System advances, although by a smaller amount. Specifically, the mortgage holdings of FHLMC have grown from a base of zero, from its start in 1970, to over $4.5 billion at year-end 1974; in addition, FHLMC had mortgage commitments outstanding at year-end 1974 of almost $2.4 billion. I agree with Smith (1970) that the FHLBB would better achieve its target of mortgage market stabilization with aggressive market support carried out by FHLMC, than it will with its current emphasis on advances. A disturbing and continuing theme in U.S. housing and mortgage policy is that policy is always _indirectly_ aimed at the target, while perfectly efficient _direct_ measures are left unutilized. For example, attempts to stimulate housing investment by various measures in the mortgage market have left a variety of tools with direct impacts on housing unused. This has led to an impressive growth in mortgages, but much less housing investment than would otherwise have been achieved.[23]

By the same token, an advances policy will lead to impressive growth, but, due to slippage, the result will necessarily be less than would be achieved by direct mortgage market support.

D. A Digression on Reaction Functions [24]

I have already said that empirically estimated reaction functions are a tool for understanding and evaluating FHLBB policies. The papers by Silber (1973) and Kearl and Rosen (1974) provide a provocative and path-breaking start on the subject, but are weak in the structural specification of the Board's objectives and its operational constraints. In particular, neither paper squarely faces the problem that the FHLBB has sometimes used price rationing and sometimes used quantity rationing in controlling the volume of advances outstanding.[25] In this section, therefore, I will outline a model producing an FHLBB reaction function, and introduce another interesting institutional aspect of the FHLBS.

Consider the following (again barebones) model:

$$(10) \qquad H = a_0 + a_1 A \; ;$$

---

[23] This is one aspect of the problem of the effectiveness of FHLBB policies to support housing. For specific references see Grebler (1972, Appendix I), Gelb (1972), and Jaffee (1974a).

[24] The material in this section is based on joint work with Stephen Goldfeld and Richard Quandt. We hope shortly to carry out empirical estimates of the type of model proposed here.

[25] Kearl and Rosen assume that the FHLBB always rations advances and, therefore, that the advance rate is set below the equilibrium level. Silber considers two cases, the first of which is the same as the Kearl and Rosen case. The second of Silber's cases assumes that the FHLBB never rations, but instead uses the advance rate as the instrument to achieve the desired quantity of advances. The generality of our model is that it allows for both forms of behavior.

(11) $A^d = b_0 - b_1 R$;

(12) $A = \min(A^d, A^s)$.

(13)   Maximize $W = -(H - H^*)^2 - w_1 (R - I)^2 - w_2 (A^d - A^s)^2.$

All coefficients are positive. Symbols are defined:

H   housing stock;
A^d demand by SLAs of advances;
A^s supply by FHLBB of advances;
A   quantity of advances outstanding;
R   interest rate charged by FHLBB on advances;
I   cost of funds (System debt) to FHLBB;
H*   housing goal of FHLBB;
W   gain function (negative of loss function) of FHLBB.

Equation (10) is a reduced form equation showing housing as a function of exogenous factors, (a_0), and of the quantity of advances. [26] Equation (11) gives the SLA demand for advances as a function of exogenous factors, (b_0), and of the negative impact of the advance rate. Equation (12) is the market clearing condition indicating that the quantity of advances outstanding is the minimum of demand and supply. Equation (13) is the objective function of the FHLBB. The objectives as specified here are that the Board try to minimize jointly the difference between (i) housing produced and its housing goal, (ii) the advance rate and the cost of funds, (iii) the demand and supply of advances (i.e., the amount of rationing). The objective function is maximized by choosing optimal values for the quantity of advances and for the rate on advances, denoted as A* and R*. The quadratic form of the objective function is chosen primarily for its mathematical convenience.

The motivation for the objective function (13) should be made clear. The first term represents the FHLBB's housing objective. It assumes the Board has some goal, H*, and attempts to steer actual housing production, H, as close as possible to that end, subject to the constraints and other factors in the objective function. Symmetry is assumed, in that under-producing and over-producing housing are equally bad; this appears consistent with the Board's objectives as defined in section II. I have not, however, specified separate mortgage and savings goals for the FHLBB, although as I suggest above, these should be dis-

---

[26] Section II suggested that advances may affect housing only when the mortgage market is in disequilibrium, so disequilibrium in the mortgage market is one assumption to motivate equation (10). Alternatively, as shown below, equation (10) denotes how the FHLBB perceives advances to affect housing, and, in this sense, the model may also hold for states of equilibrium.

tinguished. This simplification is made so that the structure of FHLBB decision-making is clear; a complete empirical model would have separate terms for mortgage and savings flow discrepancies as well.

The second term of the objective function (13) is the spread between the Board's advance rate and its cost of funds. This is motivated by two considerations. First, the Board wants to be neither a profiteer nor a loss leader. [27] Profiteers are under pressure both from the constituent SLAs and from Congress; [28] loss leaders go out of business in the long run. Second, within the FHLBS, there are mixed incentives toward low and high advance rates. SLAs that tend to be heavy borrowers desire low advance rates. SLAs, that tend to be non-borrowers prefer high advance rates, at least to the extent that the FHL Bank maximizes its income and therefore its dividend to SLA shareholders. [29] As a collusive monopoly, the FHLBS should provide advances such that the marginal borrowing rate the SLAs are willing to pay equals the marginal cost (assumed here equal to the average cost) of borrowing the funds in the capital markets; side payments would then equalize the distribution of income within the System. Without side payments, however, the level of the advance rate determines the distribution of income, and it is reasonable then that the borrowing costs should provide at least the base line for the advance rate.

The third term of the objective function, the difference between the demand and supply of advances, indicates that the FHLBB attempts to minimize the amount of nonprice rationing it must enforce. Two factors also motivate this objective. First, neither borrowing nor non-borrowing member-SLAs want rationing when the advance rate is above the System's cost of funds. Both sets of SLAs will do better when demand is met. Moreover, even when the advance rate is below the cost of funds, it is only the non-borrowing SLAs that want the quantity limited by rationing to minimize their loss; they would still see the rationing as less preferable than raising the advance rate and letting the market clear. Second, nonprice rationing is necessarily a costly mechanism for the Board to enforce, and the costs no doubt rise with the amount of rationing. For example, standards for nonprice allocations must be evolved, and a

---

[27] Formally, the rate criterion in equation (13) should be written as $(R - bI)^2$, where b is a factor (greater than unity) that reflects the cost of administering debt issues and advance lending. This is omitted only to simplify the exposition, and we interpret R - I as the zero profit point. Similarly, we abstract from the maturity of both debt and advances. In principle, the criterion with a variety of maturities would be to equate the advance rate and the cost of funds for each maturity.

[28] The FHL Banks distribute dividends to the stockholding member - SLA s, and, to this extent, high advance rates should not hurt the SLA s. However, the FHLBB tightly regulates the dividend rate of the regional FHL Banks - - currently to the level of the average deposit rate in the region. Thus, once this dividend ceiling is earned, higher rates hurt borrowing SLA s and are of no value to non-borrowing SLA s. See, however, the text following.

[29] The constraints on the FHL Bank dividend rates, as explained in the previous footnote, limit this effect once the dividend ceiling is reached. In other words, neither group of SLA s would have incentive for the FHL Bank to accumulate profits it cannot pay out.

185

staff for sorting out the cases must be employed. Also, as I have indicated, non-price rationing has been criticized from outside the System, and it is clear that the Board has tried to respond to this criticism.

I want to consider the solution to the problem of maximizing W in equation (13), subject to the constraints of equations (10) to (12). For this purpose, it is useful to eliminate A^S as an explicit variable of the system, and to restate the equations in a Kuhn-Tucker format. The restated problem follows.

(14)   Maximize $W = -(H - H^*)^2 - w_1 (R - I)^2 - w_2 (A^d - A)^2$,

subject to the definitions of A^d and H in equations (10) and (11) and

$$A \leq A^d,$$
$$A \geq 0,$$
$$R \geq 0.$$

I have exchanged A for A^S in the criterion. This does not change the value of W, however, since from the minimum condition (12) either $A^d = A^S$ implying $A = A^S$, or $A^S < A^d$ implying $A = A^S$, or $A^S > A^d$ which cannot be a maximum solution to (13). The case, $A^S > A^d$, is ruled out because the Board cannot push the actual advances, A, above the demand, A^d (and therefore cannot affect H beyond its effect on A^d), while it sustains a definite utility loss by setting A^S different from A^d. The advantage of the formulation of (14) is that the constraint, $A \leq A^d$, can be handled in a Kuhn-Tucker format while the minimum condition (12) could not. Taking into account the constraints, the Kuhn-Tucker problem can now be stated:

(15) $Max V = -(H - H^*)^2 - w_1 (R - I)^2 - w_2 (A^d - A)^2 + \lambda(A^d - A)$

with H and A^d defined by (10) and (11).

The necessary conditions for a maximum are:

(16) $\dfrac{\partial V}{\partial A} = -2a_1 (a_0 + a_1 A - H^*) - 2w_2 (A - b_0 + b_1 R) - \lambda \leq 0; \quad A\left(\dfrac{\partial A}{\partial V}\right) = 0;$

(17) $\dfrac{\partial V}{\partial R} = -2w_1 (R - I) - 2w_2 a_1 (A - b_0 + b_1 R) - a_1 \lambda \leq 0; \quad R\left(\dfrac{\partial V}{\partial R}\right) = 0;$

(18) $\dfrac{\partial V}{\partial \lambda} = A^d - A \geq 0; \quad \lambda(b_0 - b_1 R - A) = 0.$

186

The necessary conditions (16), (17), and (18) can be written in a more instructive form; in particular, the solution is either a rationing solution or a price-clearing solution depending on the exogenous parameter values. [30] The two cases are:

Rationing Case

(19a) $a_0 + a_1 (b_0 - b_1 I) > H^*;$

(19b) $R^* = \dfrac{w_1 (a_1^2 + w_2) I + w_2 b_1 a_1 (a_0 + b_0 a_1 - H^*)}{w_1 (a_1^2 + w_2) + w_2 a_1^2 b_1^2} > I ;$

(19c) $A^* = \dfrac{w_2 (b_0 - b_1 R^*) - a_1 (a_0 - H^*)}{a_1^2 + w_2} < A^d \ (= b_0 - b_1 R^*);$

(19d) $\lambda^* = 0;$

Price-clearing Case

(20a) $a_0 + a_1 (b_0 - b_1 I) \leq H^*;$

(20b) $R^* = \dfrac{w_1 I + a_1 b_1 (a_0 + b_0 a_1 - H^*)}{w_1 + a_1^2 b_1^2} \leq I ;$

(20c) $A^* = b_0 - b_1 R^* = A^d;$

(20d) $\lambda^* \geq 0 .$

It is relatively straightforward to derive (19) and (20) from (16) to (18). First, note from (18) that the solution does have two modes: either $\lambda^* = 0$ (the rationing case) or $A^* = b_0 - b_1 R^*$ (the price-clearing case). Given these conditions, the solutions for R^* and A^* can be derived by solving (16) and (17). The key step is to find the parameter value condition, that is (19a) or (20a), that separates

---

[30] We ignore the constraint that A^* and R^* must be positive. This would complicate the exposition of the solution, and it is not empirically relevant.

the regimes. To derive this condition, a proof by contradiction is used. Assume the rationing case:

(21) $\quad\quad \lambda^* = 0;$

(22) $\quad\quad A^* - b_0 + b_1 R^* < 0.$

But suppose the opposite of (19a), namely:

(23) $\quad\quad a_0 + a_1 (b_0 - b_1 I) \le H^*.$

From (16) we know, with the assumed conditions, that: [31]

(24) $\quad\quad a_0 + a_1 A^* > H^*.$

From (17), we know, with the assumed conditions, that:

(25) $\quad\quad R^* > I.$

Substituting (22) into (24) yields:

(26) $\quad\quad a_0 + a_1 (b_0 - b_1 R^*) > H^*.$

Substituting (25) into (26) yields:

(27) $\quad\quad a_0 + a_1 (b_0 - b_1 I) > H^*,$

which contradicts the supposition of (23). The same procedure proves the price-clearing case.

      The implications of the solution given by (19) and (20) are interesting. The regime conditions, (19a) and (20a), can be interpreted as follows. All things being equal, the FHLBB would prefer to set $R^* = I$. So, first, it compares the production of housing, H, when $R^* = I$ with the goal for housing, H^*. If the resulting housing, H, exceeds H^*, it goes to the rationing regime, and both raises R^* above I and rations advances; as either policy creates disutility, the quadratic objective function indicates that the best is to do a little of both. On the other hand, if the production of housing with $R^* = I$ is less than H^*, then the FHLBB can only reduce R^* below I; it would like also "negative rationing," to force advances on the SLAs by edict, but this is not allowed. Finally, if the

---

[31] Following footnote (30), I deal only with the case of equality in equations (16) and (17).

188

resulting housing when $R^* = I$ equals the goal, H^*, then R^* is set at I, the housing goal is met, and there is no rationing.

The above model is non-stochastic, and, therefore, can not be estimated. I will sketch the main points of making the model stochastic, in particular, distinguishing the stochastic elements and uncertainty as seen by the decision-makers at the FHLBB, and as seen by the econometrician-model builder. There are two cases.

Case 1

Assume there are stochastic elements in the equations for housing (10) and for the demand for advances (11), but neither the FHLBB nor the econometrician knows the realized values. Formally, one can think of the constant terms, a_0 and b_0, in these equations as consisting of a fixed and known mean value plus an unknown stochastic term. Also, assume the FHLBB proceeds on a "certainty equivalence" approach, and sets R^* and $(A^S)^*$ in accord with its knowledge of the mean values of a_0 and b_0.[32] So, for the FHLBB, R^* and $(A^S)^*$ are set as non-stochastic decisions. Now consider the econometrician who knows both how the FHLBB behaves and that he himself does not observe the stochastic movements. R^* is determined in a non-stochastic manner, following equations (19b) and (20b), evaluated at the means of a_0 and b_0; thus, in this model, there is still no estimation problem for R^*. Which of the R^* equations, (19b) or (20b), is in force at any specific time is also not a stochastic problem for the econometrician since the FHLBB makes this choice using (19a) or (20a) evaluated at the mean values for a_0 and b_0. The decision on the quantity of advances is more complicated. The FHLBB decision is still non-stochastic, but the observed quantity of advances is determined by the minimum of $(A^S)^*$ and $(A^d)^*$, and since the realized A^d is now stochastic, the observed A^* is stochastic. I will not proceed into the econometric methods for handling this type of situation but to say they are interesting.[33]

Case 2

Consider the same situation as Case 1, but now assume that the FHLBB gets full information on the stochastic element of equations (10) and (11), whereas the econometrician does not have this information. Equations (19) and

---

[32] As noted above, the decision of the Board on the quantity of advances can be thought of as either a supply decision determining A^S or as the net market result determining A; the solution values for the two variables are always the same in the non-stochastic model. In the stochastic model, however, they may be different, and that is why I am careful to use A^S. Also note that the true, expected-utility solution, to this problem is difficult to handle. One could conjecture that a risk-averse FHLBB would set R^* closer to I, and $(A^S)^*$ closer to A^d than the non-stochastic or certainty equivalence solutions indicate.

[33] The techniques involve a cross-breeding of disequilibrium system methods and switching equation methods. There is a growing literature on these topics. For an introduction, see Fair and Jaffee (1972b), Goldfeld and Quandt (1972), and Maddala and Nelson (1974).

(20) now describe the non-stochastic decision of the FHLBB, where a_0 and b_0 take on the ex post values known to the Board. For the econometrician, however, the solution for $R*$ now appears as stochastic since only the mean of a_0 and b_0 can be estimated; moreover, which of the two $R*$ equations is in force is also stochastic since, in making the choice, the Board knew the values for a_0 and b_0 as they entered (19a) or (20a), while the econometrician again knows only the mean.[34] Similarly, for the econometrician, the decision on $(A^s)*$ and the SLA decision on $(A^d)*$ appear stochastic, and therefore the minimum of these, that is, $A*$, will appear stochastic.

Finally, note that these two cases can be combined, and even more complicated patterns can be developed by introducing stochastic elements or asymmetries of information in different ways.

IV. CURRENT PROPOSALS OF THE FHLBB

Since 1965, and particularly under the Board chairmanship of Bomar, the FHLBB has proved energetic and resourceful in proposing and frequently implementing a wide range of innovations. To give the order of magnitude, the first 90 days of Bomar's chairmanship saw no less than 32 regulatory changes; better yet, most of the changes were and continue to be the removal of unneeded constraints from the System. This should be stressed since, in my role as critic, I am bound to discuss at greater length the one policy proposal with which I have strong misgivings - - the new variable rate mortgage proposals. To give the discussion some structure, I divide it into two parts. First, I note some current proposals and actions over wide areas of FHLBB responsibility. Second, I turn to a more extended discussion of the proposals in "A Financial Institution for the Future" by the FHLBB (1975).

---

[34] The alert econometrician, however, will observe that the criterion $R* \gtreqless I$ still serves to distinguish the regimes. Thus, the appropriate $R*$ equation would be known, at least in this simple model (see footnote 27), from a direct comparison of the R and I time series.

A. Some Proposals and Actions Since 1965

Conversions of Mutual SLAs to Stock SLAs

The FHLBB has had a long-standing policy of supporting SLAs wishing to transfer from a mutual to a stock form of ownership. The main argument in favor of allowing such transfers is that the Board sees the stock form as a convenient way to increase quickly the capitalization of SLAs in cases where this is desirable. It also provides a more diverse structure to the System and a better potential for mergers.

Regarding the conditions under which transfers should be allowed, the Board's position has been to rule out the "windfall" or "free distribution" conversion. The issue is that most mutual SLAs have a positive market value. This results not so much from accumulated reserves and retained earnings, as today these are offset by capital losses on mortgage portfolios making technical bankruptcy a problem; but from the charter, the "good will," and the future profit potential for which an investor would be willing to pay a premium. Hence, there is incentive for the owners of a mutual institution to convert it to a stock institution and gain the net market value for themselves. This raises a question of equity, however, as it is not clear to whom this new value belongs; for example, depositors have, in the past, contributed to the net worth and by rights are entitled to some of the gain. Even worse, in some conversions, possibilities for deceptive practices were revealed. For example, a group - - sometimes the management - - took a large position in deposit shares shortly before the net value was distributed on the basis of deposit share proportions. This sort of problem led to a FHLBB and, later, a Congressional moratorium on conversions, and then to a new set of Board guidelines.

The new Board guidelines are complicated, but reduce to this. A fair market price for the SLA would be set - - in some way - - and current depositors would be given first option, or options, to purchase the shares. Otherwise, the shares would be publicly sold in a variety of ways. The funds from the sale of the shares become part of the net worth of the SLA, and are segregated into a liquidation account in the event of subsequent liquidation of the SLA. In addition, there are constraints on the dividend policy of the new stock-SLA, regulations to prevent take-overs, and similar matters.

The guidelines were debated on a number of grounds. One concern was that a windfall would still accrue to the shareholders. For example, consider an SLA with a market value of $4 million that sells the stock and immediately obtains net worth of an additional $4 million, thus doubling its market value. It would appear that the stockholders could sell the shares for an immediate windfall. The FHLBB argues that this could not occur under the guidelines, but

I do not see their point. Neither did Senator Proxmire, who proposed that the funds be placed in a public trust fund and used to stimulate housing. Another view is that these difficulties are grounds for disallowing conversions. I see merit in both of the latter ideas. Recent Congressional action on this matter was a "standby" moratorium whereby 51 selected conversions will be allowed under the Board's guidelines. [35]

Electronic Funds Transfer

Less controversial, but a potentially greater problem, is the FHLBS's entry into electronic funds transfer. So far, the Board has been willing to allow, on a trial basis, designs for automated branches. It also consolidated its regulations in one place, which might have considerable impact. In a different direction, the Board has stimulated greater use of wire transfers of funds within the System, and SLAs can now participate in the Federal funds market. Controversy concerns the role of SLAs in a fully electronic transfer system of the future. The SLAs argue, with some validity, that to be excluded from the future electronic system would put them at a greater disadvantage than they are currently under the bank-only, paper-check clearing system. This is the reason so-called "third party transfer" powers are considered important in the Board's new set of proposals for thrift institutions. [36]

Increased Lending and Service Authority

The new FHLBB has moved quickly and meaningfully to enlarge the lending activities and related services that SLAs can perform. For example, on mortgage lending, "local area" definitions have been broadened; maximum loan to value ratios have been raised to 90 percent and even 95 percent depending on certain insurance and related conditions; and 25 year maturities are now available. Similarly, SLAs can now lend on condominiums, and have extended powers on construction loans. The service corporation divisions of SLA holding companies now have authority to provide various services for depositors and borrowers, including income tax consultation and trust fund functions.

FSLIC Insurance

There have been several changes, as well as a gradual but positive move toward efficiency, in the FSLIC operation. A major change occurred in 1973

---

[35] See the _Journal_ of the Federal Home Loan Bank Board, May 1974, for Chairman Bomar's Congressional statement on the Board conversion policy, and the Depository Institutions Act of 1974 for the final Congressional action on a partial lifting of the moratorium.

[36] While NOWs, POWs, and WOWs are of considerable current interest, the big battle is still to be fought. See Flannery and Jaffee (1973) for a discussion of the impact of electronic transfer on financial institutions.

with the elimination of insurance prepayments and FSLIC's secondary reserve. This had been introduced earlier when FSLIC's reserve/liability ratio had started to decline, and has been eliminated now that the ratio has significantly improved. The release of these funds came at a strategic time for SLA liquidity. On another front, in 1974, FSLIC depositor insurance was raised to $40,000 in a well-publicized change. In terms of gradual but positive progress, supervision and examination is being carried out with increasing efficiency, although it is still shocking that the average SLA requires 25 man-days for its annual check-up. On a related matter, there has been no significant shift since 1965 in the number of defaults, which is notable in view of the technical bankruptcy of so many SLAs. And, one of my favorites, the Old Reliable Savings and Loan is dependably in the state of receivership it has occupied since 1968.

New Liability Powers

The Board has attempted to provide SLAs with extended powers to obtain non-depository capitalization. In 1973, SLAs were allowed to issue subordinated debentures. The idea was to provide SLAs with the power to tap different parts of the capital markets, and, at the same time, improve their net worth position, a continuing concern of the Board. So far, however, there have been few privately placed issues, partly because they have not been risk-rated, and partly because they have not satisfied the Board's net worth regulations.

Another device is the new mortgage-backed bond. Under this scheme, SLAs put together a pool of mortgages and then sell bonds to finance the pool. The bonds would have the characteristics of traditional long-term debt, with fixed-rate coupons and amortization through sinking funds. It is intended that the bonds would find a market among pension funds and similar investors (see Kaplan, 1975).

I am not enthusiastic about either of these developments. The current Board's willingness to allow such powers is a positive feature, and there is no apparent reason to rule out such debt. However, a more innovative and attractive idea would be to allow SLAs to issue price-index linked liabilities. Ultimately, deposits should be available in this form, but some sort of bond would be a useful first step. It is sometimes argued that one of the drawbacks of SLA issue of indexed mortgages is that they would have no hedging base of indexed liabilities. Sometimes the argument against indexed liabilities is that SLAs have no corresponding indexed asset. I think it is time the chicken and the egg chain were broken. Interestingly, a plan for indexed time deposits was introduced recently in England.

B. Financial Institution for the Future

The FHLBB's recent proposals are ". . .designed to stabilize and ensure an adequate flow of housing credit and to better serve the financial needs of consumers." (FHLBB, 1975, p. 1). An occasional split infinitive aside, the discussion is generally accurate, concise, and useful. It is the Board's response to the Report of the Hunt Commission (1971), the Friend Study (1969), and the legislative crawl of the Financial Institutions Act (around since 1973). The theme of the report is that both public interest and self-interest will be served by having SLAs become consumer finance specialists in as many ways as they can devise. The Board sees this as an alternative to the conversion of thrift institutions into commercial banks which they do not like. The chapter headings give the tone: third party powers; consumer credit; other family services; asset maturity and variable rate mortgages; liability maturity and mortgage-backed bonds.

Conspicuous by its absence is the topic of Regulation Q ceilings. More disturbing is the view that the ceilings may have helped the flow of housing credit. It may be true that the ceilings have served as a buffer for an SLA industry in need of innovative change, but I know of no evidence that ceilings have been a net aid to housing (Fair and Jaffee, 1972a). Finally, and worst of all, nowhere in the report is it stated, or even hinted, that the new powers would be in exchange for removal of deposit rate ceiling protection.[37] I feel, or hope, that this is intended as a bargaining position. While such an approach may be fair SLA tactics, it does not seem appropriate for a governmental agency.

On the other side of the coin, the Board is concerned that the policies have a net stimulative effect on housing. The issue is whether consumer loan powers would change portfolio allocation to such a degree as to reduce the flow of funds to housing. As I have argued, the increased ability of SLAs to compete for deposits and thus expand their portfolio size, plus favorable shifts in the demand for SLA deposits due to their increased service functions, would override such a tendency. This has been confirmed in computer simulations of the MPS model by Fair and Jaffee (1972a), and, in an appendix to the report, in computer simulations of the Bosworth-Duesenberry model by Cassidy and Edwards (1975).

---

[37] The strongest statement I could find is (FHLBB, 1975, p. 22), ". . .rate control cannot be counted upon as an effective shelter for thrift institutions over a prolonged period of time. In any case, the ability of the small saver to earn an adequate rate of return on his funds is something that public policy cannot ignore." It is also noteworthy that a technical appendix of simulation results presented in Cassidy and Edwards (1975) makes no reference to Regulation Q ceilings. I find this peculiar since the results are compared to those of Fair and Jaffee (1972a), in which the removal of Regulation Q ceilings was a key item.

I have already commented on the specific powers, such as third party transfer, additional service functions, and extended liability; these have been studied as well in reviews of the Hunt Commission report.[38] In my view, they are clearly desirable in a program to move SLAs into a more competitive and consumer-oriented environment, and without the aid of Regulation Q ceilings. Instead I would like to focus on the variable rate mortgage proposal of the report. These proposals have been the subject of important hearings before Congress; they are clearly controversial, and the issues should be made clear.

C. Variable Rate Mortgages (VRMs)

The Board's proposals consist of four points.

(i) The variable rate feature would be achieved by tying the effective rate on the mortgage over its life to some intermediate-length pegging rate. The Board has considered, for example, the 3-5 year government bond rate and the new issue rate on <u>conventional</u> mortgages. The latter possibility is sometimes confused with a scheme for pegging the effective rate on a VRM to the new issue rate on VRMs themselves. This is also feasible and means that the VRM would be a short-term instrument such that each period, perhaps each year, all VRM contracts would be renegotiated and carried at the new issue rate of that period. This short-term VRM has been considered by the MIT Mortgage project,[39] and a comparison with the Board's proposal is made below.

(ii) The Board has proposed that the number of changes in the rate per year should be regulated, and also the number over the life of the contract. Similarly, the size of an individual change might be subject to some limit, possibly leaving increases to the discretion of the lender, while making decreases mandatory under the contract. These are technical features of the contract that might be examined, but they are not of prime analytic interest.

(iii) The Board proposes that the borrower is to have the right to refinance without prepayment costs. This is a key element, but it is not clear whether to take the Board seriously or not. Presumably, borrowers would want to refinance whenever they find a speculative or arbitrage opportunity requiring a shift between either newly issued and outstanding VRMs or between VRMs and conventional mortgage contracts. Lenders, on the other hand, would, or certainly should, be contractually tied into the contract. One response to this

---

[38] See, for example, the four review articles in the November 1972 issue of the <u>Journal of Money, Credit and Banking</u>, pp. 985-1009.

[39] The proceedings of a conference sponsored by the project are available in Modigliani and Lessard (1975).

195

problem has been the observation that, while there would be no prepayment costs, there would be front-end loads when taking out the new mortgage. I consider this something of a cheat.

(iv) Finally, the Board has been concerned about consumer protection and truth-in-lending. These are valid concerns and must be met, but again have no analytic thrust. The Board seems not to have faced the more important question of usury ceilings. VRMs confront the problem of meeting the requirements at the time of issue, and also if the pegging mechanism calls for a rate above the ceiling in the future.

Arbitrage Opportunities Between VRMs and Conventional Mortgages[40]

Consider a situation in which the short-term Treasury bill rate is 10 percent, the medium-term government bond rate is 7 percent, and both rates are expected to converge within several years to a lower 5 percent value. Now consider the new issue rate on a FHLBB VRM that is pegged to the intermediate-term government bond rate, and think in terms of risk-adjusted rates. The new issue rate must be between the initial long-term and medium-term rates. If the new issue rate were below the medium-term rate, then lenders would have no incentive to issue VRMs. Similarly, if the new issue rate were above the short-term rate, then borrowers would prefer pure short-term borrowing to the VRM. Suppose the new issue rate is 8.5 percent, to split the difference.[41] Then, over time, the effective rate would decline by the same 2 percent as the pegging rate, ending up at 6.5 percent. Note that the borrower would then confront the choice of holding a 6.5 percent mortgage without any expectation of rate change, or of shifting to a new issue VRM costing 5 percent. Presumably, he would shift.

There are only two solutions to this problem. One is some sort of prepayment cost, or at least arbitrage cost, to prevent the transaction. However, this would also prevent speculative shifts that might generally be counted on to stabilize the two markets. Also, there will be cases in which real conditions change, and a transfer to a new contract is useful; transfer costs would then appear a needless friction. The second solution is to make the VRM a short-term instrument in which the rate is renegotiated each year. An efficient institutional arrangement could be designed to handle this, and then all VRMs would have the same interest rate, regardless of initial maturity, and the spread against conventional mortgages would be fully adjusted to reflect current interest rate expectations.

---

[40] For a more extended discussion, see Jaffee (1975).

[41] Actually the pricing of VRMs of this sort is very complicated.

The Cost of VRMs to Borrowers

The FHLBB seems to have sold itself short in exaggerating the cost of VRMs to borrowers. Its concern (1975, p. 50) is that, ". . . the borrower normally would prefer a fixed-rate mortgage, even when the VRM is expected to have the same lifetime interest as a fixed rate mortgage, [because of] the greater uncertainty of a VRM. Even though the lifetime interest cost is expected to be the same, there is always the risk of an increase in the interest cost. . . ." This takes too narrow a view of the borrower's portfolio. Presumably, the borrower also owns a house, and to the extent that movements in interest rates reflect similar movements in inflation rates, that is, to the extent that real rates of interest are constant, any loss on the mortgage due to a higher interest rate will be made up by a capital gain on the house. There is also a residual cash-flow problem in that the interest is due now, while the gain is realized only upon sale. But, here too, the Board seems to have cut its options short. A variety of ideas have been proposed for smoothing the cash flow aspects of VRMs, and simulations done for the MIT Mortgage project show them to work well.

The Gain to Lenders From VRMs

By the same token, the FHLBB appears to have overstated the likely gain to SLA lenders from VRMs. The citation in the previous paragraph suggests that a norm would be for VRMs and conventional mortgage contracts to yield a similar lifetime return. However, as I have indicated, VRMs will have to be priced in line with the existing term structure. Moreover, in the U.S., ascending yield curves, with short rates below long-term rates, and therefore with VRM rates below conventional rates, have been the norm, and there is no reason to expect this to change. Thus, on average, an SLA must expect a lower return from VRMs than from conventional mortgages. The gain is in the timing of the return, and in the elimination of the risk due to the maturity spread between assets and liabilities.

V. CONCLUDING COMMENT

In this paper, I have reviewed the wide range of activities of the FHLBB since 1965. To give a summary appraisal - - a grade, so to speak - - is both difficult and unnecessary. In the last section, however, I have touched on several areas where, I think, the FHLBB is moving in the wrong direction, or is not moving quickly enough in the right direction. What I said earlier should, therefore, be repeated here. On the whole, the FHLBB is operating in a progressive, well-informed, and occasionally innovative capacity. It is not clear what else could be asked for - - except the elimination of Regulation Q ceilings.

REFERENCES

1. Arcelus, F., and Meltzer, A.H., "The Markets for Housing and Housing Services," Journal of Money, Credit and Banking, 5, No. 1, (February 1973a), 78-99.

2. _____, "A Reply to Craig Swan," Journal of Money, Credit and Banking, 5, No. 4, (November 1973b), 973-978.

3. Bloch, E., "The Federal Home Loan Bank System," Federal Credit Agencies, U.S. Commission on Money and Credit, 1963.

4. Burnham, J.B., "Private Financial Institutions and the Residential Mortgage Cycle, With Particular Reference to the Savings and Loan Industry," Federal Reserve System, 1972.

5. Cassidy, H.J., and Edwards,D.G., "Technical Report on Simulated Results of Permitting S&L's to Offer Consumer Credit and Checking Account Services," Working Paper No. 51, Office of Economic Research, Federal Home Loan Bank Board, 1975.

6. U.S. Commission on Mortgage Interest Rates. Report of the Commission to the President, Washington, D.C.: U.S. Government Printing Office, 1969.

7. Cootner, P.H., "The Liquidity of the Savings and Loan Industry," in Savings and Loan Industry, (directed by I. Friend), 1969, 283-344.

8. Duesenberry, J.S., "Appraisal of Selected Policy Instruments Affecting Savings and Loan Associations," in Savings and Loan Industry, (directed by I. Friend), 1969, 1591-1618.

9. Ewalt, J.H. A Business Report: The Savings and Loan Story. Chicago, Ill.: American Savings and Loan Institute Press, 1962.

10. Fair, R.C., and Jaffee, D.M., "An Empirical Study of the Hunt Commission Report Proposals for the Mortgage and Housing Markets," in Policies for a More Competitive Financial System, Conference Series No. 8, Federal Reserve Bank of Boston, 1972a.

11. _____, "Methods of Estimation for Markets in Disequilibrium," Econometrica, 40, No. 3, (May 1972b), 497-514.

12. U.S. Federal Home Loan Bank Board. Annual Report, [Washington], 1967.

13. _____. Annual Report, [Washington], 1969.

14. _____. The Federal Home Loan Bank System ,(ed. C.M. Gerloff), [Washington],1971.

15. _____. Journal, Washington, D.C.: U.S. Government Printing Office, July 1973.

16. _____. Journal, Washington, D.C.: U.S. Government Printing Office, May 1974.

17. _____. The Impact of "Free Distribution" Conversion Windfalls on the Savings and Loan Industry, A Study by the Staff of the Office of Economic Research, 1974.

18. _____. A Financial Institution for the Future: Savings, Housing Finance, Consumer Services; An Examination of the Restructuring of the Savings and Loan Industry. [Washington], 1975.

19. Federal Reserve System. Ways to Moderate Fluctuations in Housing Construction. Publications Services, 1972.

20. Flannery, M., and Jaffee, D.M.The Economic Implications of An Electronic Monetary Transfer System. Lexington, Mass.: Lexington Books, 1973.

21. Fortune, P., "The Effect of FHLB Bond Operations on Savings Inflows at Savings and Loan Associations: Comment," mimeo, 1974.

22. Friend, I., "Summary and Recommendations," in A Study of the Savings and Loan Industry, (directed by I. Friend), 1969, pp. vii-65.

23. Gelb, B.A. Mortgage Debt for Non-Real-Estate Purposes. The Conference Board, 1972.

24. Goldfeld, S.M., and Quandt, R.E. Nonlinear Methods in Econometrics. Amsterdam: North-Holland, 1972.

25. Gramlich, E., and Jaffee, D.M. (eds.). Savings Deposits, Mortgages, and Housing: Studies for the Federal Reserve - M.I.T. - Penn Economic Model. Lexington, Mass.: Lexington Books, 1972.

26. Grebler, L. Housing Issues in Economic Stabilization Policy. Occasional Paper 72, National Bureau of Economic Research, 1960.

27. _____, "Broadening the Sources of Funds for Residential Mortgages," in Ways to Moderate Fluctuations in Housing Construction, Federal Reserve System (1972).

28. _____, "The Effect of FHLB Bond Operations on Savings Flows at SLAs: Comment," Journal of Finance, XXVII, No. 1, (March 1973), 198-202.

29. Grebler, L., and Doyle, T., "Effect of Industry Structure and Government Policies on Housing Demand and Cyclical Stability: Study of 1966 Experience," in Savings and Loan Industry, (directed by I. Friend), 1969, 1241-1354.

30. Guttentag, J., "Credit Availability, Interest Rates, and Monetary Policy," Southern Economic Journal, XXVI, No. 3, (January 1960), 219-228.

31. Hunt Commission. The Report of the President's Commission on Financial Structure and Regulation, Washington, D.C.: U.S. Government Printing Office, 1971.

32. _____, "Eliminating Deposit Rate Ceilings: A Study of the Effect of S&L's," Journal of the Federal Home Loan Bank Board, 6, No. 8, (August 1973), 4-12.

33. Jaffee, D.M., Testimony before Subcommittee on Financial Institutions of the Committee on Banking, Housing and Urban Affairs, Reform of Financial Institutions, September 11, 1974a.

34. Jaffee, D.M., "What to do About Savings and Loan Associations?," _Journal of Money, Credit and Banking_, VI, No. 4, (November 1974b), 537-550.

35. _____, "Innovations in the Mortgage Market," in _Financial Innovation_, (ed. W.L. Silber), Lexington, Mass.: Lexington Books, 1975.

36. Kaplan, D.M., "Mortgage-Backed Bonds: A New Source of Funds for the Savings and Loan Industry," 8, No. 3, _Journal of the Federal Home Loan Bank Board_, (March 1975).

37. Kaufman, H.M., "An Examination of the Financing of FHLB Advances; A Comment," _Review of Economics and Statistics_, LV, No. 2, (May 1973), 257.

38. Kearl, J.R., and Rosen, K.T., "A Simultaneous Equation Model of Housing Starts, Mortgage Flows, Federal Home Loan Bank Board and Federal National Mortgage Association Behavior," mimeo, February 1974.

39. Kendall, L.T. _The Savings and Loan Business: Its Purposes, Functions, and Economic Justification_. Trade Association Monograph, for the Commission on Money and Credit, 1963.

40. Kwon, J.K., and Thornton, R.M., "An Evaluation of the Competitive Effect of FHLB Open Market Operations on Savings Inflows at Savings and Loan Associations," _Journal of Finance_, XXVI, No. 3, (June 1971), 699-712.

41. _____, "Federal Home Loan Bank and Savings and Loan Associations: An Examination of the Financing of Federal Home Loan Bank Advances," _Review of Economics and Statistics_, LIV, No. 1, (February 1972), 97-99.

42. Maddala, G.S., and Nelson, F.D., "Limited Dependent Variable Methods for the Estimation of Markets in Disequilibrium," _Econometrica_, 42, No. 6, (November 1974), 1013-1030.

43. Marvell, T.B. _The Federal Home Loan Bank Board_. New York: Praeger, 1969.

44. McKinley, G.W., "The Federal Home Loan Bank System and the Control of Credit," _Journal of Finance_, XII, No. 4, (September 1957), 319-371.

45.   Meltzer, A.H., "Credit Availability and Economic Decisions: Some Evidence from the Mortgage and Housing Markets," Journal of Finance, XXIX, No. 3, (June 1974), 763-778.

46.   Modigliani, F., and Lessard, D., "New Mortgage Designs for Stable Housing in an Inflationary Environment," Conference Series No. 14, Federal Reserve Bank of Boston, 1975.

47.   Morrissey, T.F., "The Demand for Mortgage Loans and the Concomitant Demand for Home Loan Bank Advances by Savings and Loan Associations," Journal of Finance, XXVI, No. 3, (June 1971), 687-698.

48.   Penner, R.G., and Silber, W.L., "The Interaction Between Federal Credit Programs and the Impact on the Allocation of Credit," American Economic Review, LXIII, No. 5, (December 1973), 838-852.

49.   Pierce, J.L., and Graves, M.A., "Insulating Housing: Effects Upon Economic Stabilization Policy," in Ways to Moderate Fluctuations in Housing Construction, Federal Reserve System, 1972.

50.   Poole, W., "Housing Finance Under Inflationary Conditions," in Ways to Moderate Fluctuations in Housing Construction, Federal Reserve System, 1972.

51.   Schwartz, H.S., "The Role of Government-Sponsored Intermediaries in the Mortgage Market," in Housing and Monetary Policy, Conference Series No. 4, Federal Reserve Bank of Boston, 1970.

52.   Silber, W.L., "A Model of Federal Home Loan Bank System and Federal National Mortgage Association Behavior," Review of Economics and Statistics, LV, No. 3, (August 1973), 308-320.

53.   Smith, Warren L., "The Role of Government-Sponsored Intermediaries," in Housing and Monetary Policy, Conference Series No. 4, Federal Reserve Bank of Boston, 1970.

54.   Swan, C., "The Markets for Housing and Housing Services," Journal of Money, Credit and Banking, V, No. 4, (November 1973), 960-972.

55.   _____, "A Model of Financial Intermediation by the Government," mimeo, 1974.

56. Thygerson, K.J., "The Effect of Government Housing and Mortgage Credit Programs on Savings and Loan Associations," Occasional Paper No. 6, United States Savings and Loan League, 1973.

57. Van Horne, J.C., "The Effect of FHLB Bond Operations on Savings Flows at Savings and Loan Associations: Comment," Journal of Finance, XXVII, No. 1, (March 1973), 194-197.

THE IMPACT ON RESIDENTIAL CONSTRUCTION OF FEDERAL HOME LOAN BANK BOARD POLICY

Craig Swan*

University of Minnesota

I. INTRODUCTION

The purpose of this paper is to assess the impact on residential construction of policy actions by the Federal Home Loan Bank Board (FHLBB). The first section provides a brief discussion of the Federal Home Loan Bank System (FHLBS) and its three major policy variables: advances; liquidity requirements; and Regulation Q authority. The second section discusses some of the issues involved in evaluating the impact of FHLBB actions. In particular, a distinction is made between short-run and long-run impacts; and some of the evidence concerning the existence of credit rationing as an important phenomenon in housing and mortgage markets is reviewed. The third section reviews simulation exercises of three large econometric models. The fourth section offers some conclusions based on the preceding discussion and simulation results.

II. THE FEDERAL HOME LOAN BANK SYSTEM

The FHLBS was established in 1932 as the major federal regulatory agency for savings and loan associations (SLAs). Today the FHLBS consists of the Federal Home Loan Bank Board and twelve regional Federal Home Loan banks. The FHLBB consists of a three-member board, appointed by the President, and associated staff support. Closely related to the FHLBB are the Federal Savings and Loan Insurance Corporation (FSLIC) and the Federal Home Loan Mortgage Corporation (FHLMC). The FSLIC insures deposits at SLAs. The FHLMC holds conventional mortgages which it finances by issuing its own securities and selling participations. The three-member board makes policy decisions for all three organizations.

The FHLBB regulates savings and loan associations through several types of authorities. The FHLBB has broad regulatory powers over federally chartered, FSLIC-insured SLAs, starting with the power to grant charters. The FHLBB

---

* Associate Professor of Economics at the University of Minnesota. I would like to thank Allan Meltzer for his comments on an earlier draft of this paper.

has less broad regulatory power over state-chartered, FSLIC-insured SLAs. Finally, the FHLBB has some regulatory power over state-chartered, non-FSLIC-insured but FHLBS member institutions.[1]

Potentially any and all regulatory decisions by the FHLBB may influence mortgage and housing markets by affecting the ability of SLAs to compete for savings deposits and/or by affecting SLA portfolio decisions. Specialization of labor and diminishing returns dictate that any one researcher narrow the scope of his inquiry. This paper focuses on FHLBB advances to member institutions, liquidity requirements, and the control of deposit interest rates. These three areas are the current major policy levers the FHLBB exerts for influencing home-building.[2]

Advances

Advances are loans from the FHLBS to member institutions. From a member's viewpoint, advances are similar to discounts from the Federal Reserve to member banks. In both cases, there is an increase in the liabilities of the private financial institution. However, there is an important macroeconomic difference. The Federal Reserve can lend reserves to member banks by simple bookkeeping entries, adding to the monetary base in the process. The FHLBS must raise funds for advances in general credit markets.

The necessity of raising funds and the associated impacts on credit markets in general have raised questions about the usefulness of advances as a countercyclical policy variable. Raising the funds to make advances works to raise market interest rates. There is some question as to whether this rise in market interest rates induces shifts in the portfolio decisions of households and other financial institutions of sufficient magnitude to mean no net change in mortgage lending. The answer to this question depends on the magnitude of the effect on interest rates of FHLBS security offerings and on the interest rate responsiveness of various asset demand functions. The simulations reviewed below are meant to shed some light on this question.

Since 1965, FHLBS advances have tended to move inversely to deposit inflows as seen in Figure 1. In periods of declines in savings flows, the FHLBS has used its ability to raise funds in general credit markets to partially offset the effects of the decline in savings flows and to help maintain mortgage lending.

---

[1] As of February 28, 1975, 4,334 financial institutions were members of the FHLBS. Of these, 4,271 were SLAs; 61 were savings banks; and two were life insurance companies. 2,064 member SLAs, or 48.3 percent were federally chartered; 2,068, or 48.4 percent, were state-chartered, FSLIC-insured; and 139, or 3.3 percent, were state-chartered, non-insured. Over the period 1972 to 1974, FSLIC-insured SLAs received 97.9 percent of net savings inflows and made 97.5 percent of mortgage loans closed by SLAs.

[2] A number of the issues surrounding the question of financial reorganization have to do with the implications for housing of reorganized thrift institutions that are less closely tied to the mortgage market. For a discussion of some of these issues, see Fair-Jaffee (1972a).

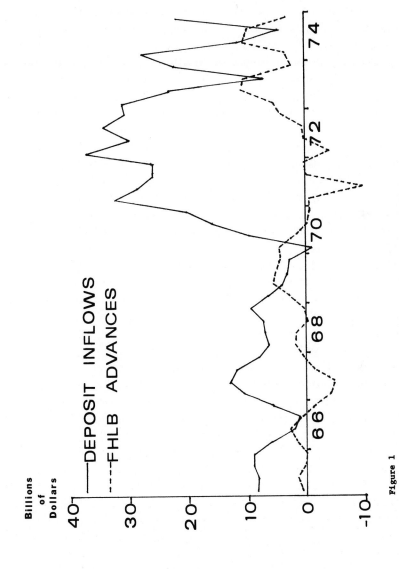

Billions
of
Dollars

——— DEPOSIT INFLOWS
----- FHLB ADVANCES

Figure 1
Deposit Inflows at SLA's and FHLB Advances, 1965:1 - 1974:4 (SAAR)

Source: Federal Reserve, Flow of Funds.

207

What impacts have FHLBS advances had as a countercyclical aid to home-building? Some large model simulation results will be reviewed in an attempt to provide a partial answer to this question. There is another question that is not directly addressed in this paper: what should be the role of FHLBS advances - - or any other FHLBB policy variables - - as a countercyclical aid to housing? To answer this question, one needs information on what, if any, impact FHLBB policy has, as well as an evaluation of the desirability of stabilizing homebuild-ing. This paper addresses the impact of FHLBB policy only. For a discussion of some aspects of the second issue, see Guttentag (1967), Gibson (1973), and Pierce and Graves (1972).

There is a technical question as to whether FHLBB advances policy is made in terms of the quantity of advances or the rate charged on those advances.[3] There is casual evidence to suggest that the FHLBB usually supplies the quantity of advances demanded by SLAs at the going rate.[4] However, there have been times when the FHLBB did consciously limit the quantity of advances, most notably in 1966, when the FHLBS was under some pressure to limit its borrowing. This pressure arose partly because FHLBS borrowings were included in the Federal budget. While FHLBS borrowings have been removed from the Federal budget, the Treasury still retains some influence over the size of FHLBS borrowings and hence their ability to lend. This influence is most likely to be exercised at times of large government deficits and high nominal interest rates, precisely the times when FHLBS borrowings are likely to be large.

Liquidity Requirements

The FHLBB has the power to set liquidity requirements that institutions must meet by holding cash, deposits at commercial banks, and/or specified government securities. At present, liquidity requirements can be varied from 4 to 10 percent of net withdrawable accounts and borrowings payable on demand or due within one year. Table 1 indicates past changes in liquidity requirements.

---

[3] If SLA s had a stable demand function for advances, then one could achieve the same objective by con-trolling either the quantity or the rate. Such a view implies that the rate on advances is manipulated to hit a quantity target. It is not clear that the FHLBB sets the rate on advances in this way. For the most part, the FHLBB appears to price its advances at cost - - average cost in the early 1960s, marginal cost more recently. There have been several cases where the FHLBB deliberately did manipulate the rate on advances to influence the quantity, for example, late 1966, 1970, and, most recently, 1974.

[4] Silber (1973) estimated FHLBB policy reaction functions using both the quantity of advances and the rate on advances as dependent variables. He prefers the rate-determining view of policy determination part-ly because the quantity equation fails an F test for structural stability. However, if there was a change in behavior following the elimination of FHLBS borrowing from the Federal budget, then it would not be surprising if the quantity equation failed the test for structural stability.

Table 1

Liquidity Requirements for SLAs

Date	Ratio of Liquid Assets to Withdrawable Deposits and Short Term Borrowings	
12/50	6	percent
3/1/61	7	"
8/1/68	6.5	"
6/12/69	6	"
12/1/69	5.5	"
4/1/71	6.5	"
5/1/71	7.5	"
8/1/71	7	"
5/1/73	6.5	"
8/1/73	5.5	"
9/1/74	5	"
4/1/75	5.5	"

source: Journal, Federal Home Loan Bank Board, February 1975.

As the table suggests, changes in liquidity requirements were infrequent until 1968. Also liquidity requirements have not varied very much.[5]   Except for a three-month period in 1971, liquidity requirements have been within a range of five to seven percent.

It should be clear that the FHLBB liquidity requirement, per se, does not help SLAs meet their liquidity needs in any substantial manner. At current liquidity requirements, the withdrawal of a dollar of savings reduces required liquidity holdings by only five and one-half cents. Thus, contrary to their name, required liquidity holdings as a class are actually very illiquid assets. Required liquidity holdings for all SLAs together are even more illiquid than the holdings of individual SLAs. This is because total deposits, the largest element determining the size of required liquidity, seldom decline.[6]

If these assets are as illiquid as the above discussion suggests, why not hold them in the most illiquid form available to SLAs - - mortgages?

There are numerous ways to accomplish this. One is simply to eliminate or drastically reduce required liquidity holdings. Such a move would presumably allow for a once-and-for-all increase in mortgage holdings by SLAs. An alternative procedure would be more vigorous countercyclical variation of required liquidity holdings. Indeed, this procedure could serve as an alternative or supplement to advances. For example, during 1974, the FHLBB lent $6.7 billion in advances. At the end of 1974, the required liquidity ratio was 5 percent on a base of about $243 billion. Imagine required liquidity holdings had been reduced to 2 percent. Such a reduction would nave released $7.3 billion in funds from required liquidity holdings.

Would such a reduction have had similar impacts on the behavior of SLAs as the actual increase in advances? If one takes the view that advances are exogenously determined by the FHLBB, or the rate is varied to hit a quantity target, then the presumption is that changes in advances and required liquidity would have similar equilibrium impacts. An increase in advances increases total liabilities of SLAs that must be held in some form, basically excess liquidity holdings or mortgages. A reduction in required liquidity also makes assets available to be held as either excess liquidity or mortgages. One would generally expect similar equilibrium response by individual SLAs to these two changes.

---

[5]   There have been three periods when liquidity requirements were in fact more flexible than Table 1 implies. For five months in 1966, SLA s could reduce their liquidity holdings below required levels but not to exceed the smaller of actual net savings withdrawn, or one percent of withdrawable savings. In late 1973, and again in 1974, the FHLBB waived penalties for liquidity deficiencies caused by net savings withdrawals.

[6]   In the period January 1965 to December 1974, there were 20 months when total savings deposits declined. All but three of these declines occurred in January, April, July, or October- months immediately following the traditional quarterly posting of interest. The largest decline occurred in July 1966 and was $1.5 billion.

Differential responses would be expected only if the liquidity ratio or the volume of advances entered directly into the demand for excess liquidity holdings.[7]

There may be differential adjustment responses to a change in advances or liquidity requirements. In particular, a substantial proportion of SLA liquidity holdings are in the form of longer-term government securities. If liquidity requirements were reduced at times when nominal interest rates rose, SLAs might be reluctant to sell longer-term securities due to capital losses, but instead prefer to accomplish any portfolio adjustments as their government securities matured.[8]

Looking at broader market impacts, changes in advances and required liquidity would be expected to have similar portfolio impacts. Consider first an increase in advances financed by selling FHLBS securities to the general public. The general public will have to absorb the increased issue of FHLBS securities. To a first approximation, these securities are likely to be very good substitutes for traditional government securities, perhaps at a slight rate differential.[9] Consider now a reduction in liquidity requirements of the same magnitude. If nothing has happened to the demand for excess liquidity, SLAs will be induced to reduce their holdings of liquid assets by the reduction in required liquidity. In view of the substitutability between agency securities and government securities, the shift out of liquid assets by SLAs, primarily out of government and agency securities, forces the same kind of portfolio adjustment on the general public as does the issuance of new FHLBS securities.[10]

The thrust of the above discussion is that the use of advances or changes in required liquidity would achieve essentially the same objectives. What sorts of additional arguments might be advanced in favor of one over the other? Traditional arguments for the use of advances might emphasize that advances are more flexible, in that they can be directed at institutions with special needs,

---

[7] I am not familiar with any empirical work that bears directly on this issue - - the determinants of excess liquidity holdings at SLAs. Most empirical work on SLA portfolios has concentrated on mortgage holdings and/or advances. The Fromm-Sinai paper (1975) has a term representing excess liquidity in its mortgage equation, but no explicit equation for liquidity holdings. Empirical work that does deal with the entire balance sheet - - Bisignano (1971), Swan (1970) - - does not incorporate measures of liquidity requirements.

[8] Kane is right when he suggests that a more flexible policy about liquidity requirements might induce SLA s to hold liquid assets of shorter maturity. In fact, since January 1972, the FHLBB has required that a portion of required liquid asset holdings be in the form of shorter-term securities. All the variation in liquid requirements since January 1972 has been in the shorter-term requirements.

[9] See Silber (1972) for an attempt to explain the new issue yield on FHLBS and Federal National Mortgage Association securities as a function of the yield on Treasury securities and the size of the agency issue. See Peskin (1967) for a more general discussion of the market for agency securities.

[10] Allowing for changes in excess liquidity holdings by SLA s in response to changing interest rates would not change the essentials of this story. The basic point is that one would expect similar impacts on interest rates, and hence the demand for excess liquidity following either policy action. It also does not matter if SLA s buy FHLBS securities, as their excess liquidity holdings change to satisfy their basic required liquidity holdings. In fact, having SLA s meet legal liquidity requirements by holding FHLBS securities which are used to make advances is an indirect way of holding legal liquidity requirements as mortgages.

while changes in required liquidity would be experienced by all institutions. However, the development of Federal funds-type markets and further use of loan participations could help to make the resources of all SLAs available to those with special needs.

Frequent changes in required liquidity, especially increases, may make membership in the FHLBS undesirable to individual SLAs.[11] Potentially more important is the possibility that frequent changes in liquidity requirements by themselves would work to undermine their own intended effects, as SLAs refused to make the intended portfolio switch into mortgages on the not irrational expectation that liquidity requirements would soon be raised. However, for SLAs as a group, and surely for most individual associations, the cash flow to meet any possible future increase is more than provided for by the magnitude of mortgage repayments and new savings inflows.

Discussions of advances often talk of restrictions on borrowings by the FHLBB. The traditional example is the 1966 experience when the Treasury effectively denied the FHLBB access to credit markets, and the FHLBB was forced to reduce its advances substantially. Some of the political effects of FHLBS borrowings were eliminated by the 1968 Federal budget reorganization which eliminated sponsored credit agencies from the budget. However, the Treasury still worries about the magnitude of credit agency borrowings and still has influence over the size of offerings. Some of this concern is directed towards the announcement effects of specific offerings. The use of changes in liquidity requirements instead of advances might not have quite the same announcement effects. While I argued above that liquidity requirement changes might well have the same portfolio, and hence interest-rate impacts, they would not be tied to as specific an event as a multimillion dollar security offering.

Regulation Q

Regulation Q, or the power to regulate interest rates on savings deposits, is the third major instrument of FHLBB control. Technically, Reguation Q refers to Federal Reserve control over interest paid on deposits at commercial banks. FHLBB authority to regulate interest payments derives from the Interest Rate Control Act of 1966 and its periodic extensions since then. Since 1966, control of deposit rates has been coordinated by the FHLBB, the Federal Deposit Insurance Corporation, and the Federal Reserve Board. The term Regulation Q has come to be associated with the general policy of deposit rate control.

---

[11] While this possibility might explain some reluctance on the part of the FHLBB to act, I am not sure what broader implications, if any, a reduction in FHLBS membership would have.

Pressures for deposit rate control developed when, as interest rates were rising, commercial banks were also becoming more competitive as regards savings deposits.[12] Another important influence was a group of newer SLAs, without a legacy of old, low-yielding mortgages, which was also aggressively competing for savings deposits. Most SLAs saw their ability to compete for deposits severely limited by their substantial holdings of older, lower-yielding mortgages. Deposit rate control was a way of restricting competition.[13]

Given the existence of Regulation Q ceilings, the FHLBB has been reluctant to raise the ceilings. This reluctance has followed from a belief that a simultaneous raising of ceilings, and an expected simultaneous increase in deposit rates, would have only minor impacts on savings flows and major impacts on SLA earnings, as associations would find themselves paying higher rates on an essentially unchanged stock of deposits. The FHLBB has preferred to help SLAs in times of high interest rates and low deposit inflows by stepping up advances. Such a policy has obvious attractions to SLAs, as they pay higher interest rates on only the advances instead of on the whole stock of deposits. The differentiation of savings accounts by interest rates and maturities is another attempt to discriminate more completely among depositors with different interest rate elasticities.

Has Regulation Q been good or bad for housing? To those who see Regulation Q as vital to the viability of SLAs and, in turn, see a strong savings and loan industry as vital to mortgage and housing markets, the answer is obvious. To others, who see a good deal of substitution between deposits in thrift institutions and general market securities, the issue is less clear cut. At times when general market interest rates have risen, Regulation Q ceilings have prevented deposit rates from rising and guaranteed that deposit inflows to thrift institutions would decline. Whether, in the absence of Regulation Q, SLAs would have been effectively constrained in their ability to raise deposit rates by their existing stock of low-yielding mortgages is not clear. Tobin (1970), for one, has argued that SLAs could have and should have reached into past earnings to pay higher deposit rates.

---

[12] See Jaffee (1973) for an excellent and more extended discussion of the history and issues surrounding Regulation Q control.

[13] The problem of a large stock of low-yielding mortgages has been an important factor in the FHLBB's efforts to promote variable-rate mortgages.

III. THE IMPACT OF FHLBB POLICY ACTIONS

Before looking at specific simulation exercises of FHLBB policy actions, there are a few general considerations that should be mentioned. These simulation results tell one little about the desirability of FHLBB actions. But, if FHLBB actions have no effects at all, then there is a strong presumption that the FHLBB should not worry about attempting to aid housing in a counter-cyclical manner. However, imagine the simulations suggest that FHLBB actions can have important impacts on housing activity. One has still not demonstrated the desirability of counter-cyclical (homebuilding cycle) actions by the FHLBB. To answer the question about the desirability of FHLBB actions, assuming effectiveness, involves issues concerning the role of housing in overall stabilization policy, a topic beyond the scope of this paper. My objective is more limited- what sorts of impacts do FHLBB actions have on housing activity?

It is not entirely clear how one measures whether FHLBB actions have had an important impact on housing and mortgage markets. In particular, the magnitude of the impact following a policy action may differ in the short and long run.[14] A finding of little long-run impact would not be sufficient to dismiss FHLBB actions as of no importance. It may well be that FHLBB actions have little impact in the long run and yet still have substantial short-run impacts. Substantial short-run impacts would suggest that FHLBB actions could have important implications as regards the timing of housing activity.

There are theoretical reasons to suggest that FHLBB actions may not have much long-run impact. Theory suggests that the long-run impact of any actions that affect housing activity is constrained by the determinants of the demand for housing, alternative rates of return to wealth holders, and supply conditions for new houses. The traditional story about consumer durables, such as houses, is that the demand for the flow of services, which is assumed to derive from income and relative prices, implies a demand for the relevant stock. This stock demand, together with the size of the existing stock, determines an explicit or implicit rental price.

Expectations about this rental price, adjusted for taxes and depreciation, together with alternative rates of return, imply an asset price for units of the stock. The comparison of this capital asset price with the cost of new units leads to decisions to add to or subtract from the stock. In equilibrium, consumers are happy with the quantity of the flow of services they are consuming; wealth holders are happy with the returns they are getting from holding the stock; and suppliers are indifferent about supplying additional units.

---

[14] The effectiveness of policy may be measured by more than the magnitude of a particular response. Work on optimal policy shows that, in a world of uncertainty, quadratic loss-minimizing policy makers will also be interested in the effect of policy actions on the variance of outcomes. See, for example, Brainard (1967).

In this sort of world, the only way to change the size of the long-run equilibrium stock is to shift the demand for services, alter alternative rates of return, or affect the supply cost of new units. Do FHLBB policy actions affect any of these three variables? For FHLBB actions to affect the equilibrium size of the housing stock by affecting the demand for housing services, they must work to shift the demand curve. The major determinants of the demand for housing services are population and household formation, income and relative prices. The impact of FHLBB actions on the size of the population and household formation must be quite small. A basic commitment to full employment, independent of the composition of output, means that FHLBB actions could have only transitory effects on income. Similarly, FHLBB actions would not be expected to have much, if any, impact on prices in general. Thus, it appears that one cannot make a strong case that FHLBB policy actions shift the demand for housing services.

It has been argued that fluctuations in homebuilding lead to inefficiencies and higher costs in the construction of new units. If this argument is correct, and if FHLBB countercyclical policy actions could smooth out some fluctuations, then such countercyclical actions might help to increase efficiency and lower costs in the homebuilding industry. The empirical evidence on this point is not well developed. See Gibson (1973), Guttentag (1967), and Manski and Rosen for a more detailed discussion of some of these issues.

The issuance of FHLBS securities, changes in Regulation Q ceilings, and changes in liquidity requirements do require adjustments of portfolios that may alter the structure of interest rates and make wealth holders more or less willing to hold houses. See Tobin (1970) for a discussion of the effect of changes in Regulation Q ceilings, which suggests that these changes have potentially ambiguous effects. See Swan (1974) for a discussion of advances that suggests that an increase in advances is likely to lower the required rate of return on houses. This argument could easily be extended to changes in liquidity requirements, and suggests that FHLBB actions might have permanent effects on the size of the housing stock. Both Tobin and Swan make theoretical arguments. Neither offers strong empirical evidence.

Even if one denies the possibility of FHLBB actions having any long-run impact on the size of the housing stock, the FHLBB could still have important short-run or timing impacts on homebuilding. Such effects could arise because of short-run impacts on interest rates and/or credit availability. As is detailed below, there is good evidence to suggest that while the housing stock is adjusting to a position of long-run equilibrium, the amount of investment in housing units may - - at times - - be constrained by credit rationing. If credit rationing is at times a real short-run constraint, then FHLBB actions, by increasing the availability of mortgage credit, may have important short-run impacts on the amount of homebuilding.

The Case for Credit Rationing

A substantial number of researchers who have examined housing and mortgage markets in the post-World War II period, and especially in the sixties, have concluded that credit rationing is an important phenomenon in these markets.[15] These conclusions have sometimes been stated explicitly, as in Guttentag (1961), and sometimes only implicitly in the structure of particular regression equations. A brief review of some of this evidence will illustrate the point.

The Friend Study

Dhrymes and Taubman (1969) estimated a series of equations to explain SLA behavior as part of the Friend study of the savings and loan industry. Dhrymes and Taubman estimate equations for household demand for mortgage credit with cross sectional data from 1964 through 1966 - - a year when savings flows fell off sharply, mortgage rates rose, and housing starts fell. Dhrymes and Taubman note:

> . . . whenever observations from 1966 are included in our equations, the interest rate and loan to value elasticities are sharply altered - - becoming much greater (in absolute terms) and much more statistically significant; therefore we conclude that the 1966 observations do not lie on the demand [by households] for mortgage curve but are affected by the (non-price) rationing by S & L associations. (p. 111).

When summarizing their results, they again repeat their finding:

> Rationing of mortgages occurred in 1966; thus it is inappropriate to use data from that year to establish the demand for mortgages functions. (p. 71).

---

[15] Much of the confusion about the importance of credit availability and credit rationing as an important influence on housing activity in the short run appears to be related to a failure to distinguish between short- and long-run impacts. Proponents of the credit rationing view have tended to work with recent quarterly data. Opponents of the credit rationing view have tended to use long time series of annual data, or data at decade intervals. For example, see Meltzer (1974). Elsewhere I and others have argued that in periods of excess demand for new units, the volume of mortgage lending is a factor in determining the amount of homebuilding. See Fair (1971) and Swan (1972). I do not see that such a proposition has any necessary implication about the ratio of the stock of mortgages to the stock of houses in the long run.

Huang (1969), in another paper for the Friend study, estimated a housing-mortgage model with time series data from the second quarter of 1953 through the fourth quarter of 1965. After estimating and then forecasting with this model for 1966, Huang concludes:

> In other words our equation estimates based on the pre-1966 behavior probably have made overprediction of the supply of mortgage credit in 1966 by giving relatively less weight to the effect of net savings, since during 1966 the mortgage yield effect on the supply of mortgage credit might not be as important as the credit availability or rationing effect. (p. 1233).

The FMP (or MPS) Model

Both the housing and mortgage sectors of the FMP model allow for credit rationing. The equation for the demand for mortgages is first normalized on the mortgage rate and then estimated in a way that allows for disequilibrium in the mortgage market. "The allowance of a disequilibrium mortgage rate also implies the existence of credit rationing in the market." (Jaffee, 1972, p. 163). The variable measuring the effect of credit rationing, the lagged mortgage rate, has a statistically significant coefficient.

The housing starts relationships are derived from a capital asset pricing model where the demand for housing services together with the cost of capital imply an equilibrium asset price of housing units. The housing starts equations represent the reaction of builders who compare the asset price of housing units to construction costs. In addition, variables are included to measure elements of credit availability. For single-family starts, the variables are a measure of the change in mortgage commitments at SLAs, plus the change in mortgage purchases by the Federal National Mortgage Association (FNMA), and a measure of household wealth available for down payments. For multi-family starts, the credit-availability proxy variables are measures of mortgage commitments at Mutual Savings Banks and life insurance companies.

Disequilibrium Models

Fair (1971) has estimated a monthly model of housing starts allowing for disequilibrium along the lines suggested by Fair and Jaffee (1972b). Fair uses the change in the mortgage rate as an indicator of periods of excess demand or excess supply. This model allows for the possibility of less than complete adjustment of the mortgage rate and rationing in the period of disequilibrium. Fair concludes that "the significance of the estimate indicates that the housing market is not always in equilibrium and that rationing does occur." (p. 81).

217

Fair's model allows for housing starts to be constrained by either the availability of mortgage credit, which is seen as a financial supply of starts, or by the demand for starts. FHLBB actions to increase the supply of mortgage credit would have strong initial effects only when starts were constrained by the availability of mortgage credit.

Swan (1972) has estimated a model similar to Fair's, but using quarterly data, and arrives at a similar conclusion-- there is less than complete adjustment of the mortgage rate each quarter, and hence credit rationing does occur when mortgage rates are rising. Another piece of work in a similar tradition is a paper by Cassidy and Valentini (1972). They estimate a housing, mortgage, savings-deposit model that uses positive changes in the mortgage rate as a measure of disequilibrium in both housing and mortgage markets. They find evidence of credit rationing in periods of excess demand.

Other Models

Numerous investigators have implicitly allowed for the existence of rationing by the inclusion of various "credit availability" variables in equations for housing starts. The sorts of variables used typically include some measure of savings flows, mortgage commitments, or actual mortgage lending; a measure of FHLBB and/or FNMA activity; and some measure of other mortgage terms, primarily loan-to-value ratios or amortization periods. Investigators who have used such variables, primarily in single equation models of housing starts or residential construction, include Maisel (1968), Sparks (1967), Swan (1970), Brady (1973), Kearl and Rosen (1974), Bosworth and Duesenberry (1973), and Fromm and Sinai (1975).

IV. A SURVEY OF SIMULATION RESULTS

This section of the paper surveys the simulation results of three econometric models involving changes in FHLBB policy variables. The models surveyed include the Bosworth-Duesenberry (1973) flow of funds model; the Hendershott-Villani (1974) flow of funds model; and simulations of the DRI model, with an expanded and detailed mortgage sector by Fromm and Sinai (1975).[16]

---

[16] Jaffee has done a series of simulations with the MPS model, for example, (1972),(1973),and Fair-Jaffee (1972a). However, a number of these simulations involve only the mortgage sector, or the mortgage-deposit sector, of the MPS model.

All of these models would be classified as large econometric models. In fact, some minimal size of a model would be necessary before the model would enable one to do simulations with FHLBB policy variables. All of these models include specifications for both real and financial variables. All of the simulations are reported as full model simulations.

It is instructive to review this empirical evidence because many questions about the magnitude and timing of the impact of FHLBB actions hinge on the empirical magnitude of a few key relationships: the interest-rate sensitivity of portfolio allocation decisions by financial institutions ; the interest-rate sensitivity of portfolio allocation decisions by households; and the impact of mortgage market conditions on housing activity. There are numerous studies of each separate relationship, but only these larger modeling efforts attempt to treat all of the relationships at the same time. These models are designed to provide some sort of bracket on the magnitude and timing of responses. However, the simulations, as reported, do have an important limitation as regards the question of timing. The discussion in the previous section makes an important distinction between short- and long-run impacts. The policy simulations reviewed below are reported for only three to six years. Although it is unlikely that three years is a sufficiently long time period to get a handle on long-run equilibrium responses, one can hope to see, however, whether variables are moving in an appropriate direction.

Advances

All three models include advances; however, the models differ in their treatment of advances in two major ways. Fromm-Sinai (F-S) treat the quantity of advances as an exogenous policy variable. Advances enter the mortgage acquisition equation for SLAs. The model does not have any explicit description of how these advances are financed. The Bosworth-Duesenberry (B-D) and the Hendershott-Villani (H-V) models have similar conceptual treatments of advances, a treatment that differs from that of F-S. B-D and H-V view advances as endogenously determined by SLAs, and have equations representing SLA demand for advances. Both models also account for the financing of advances. F-S report the results of a simulated $1 billion increase in advances. D-B and H-V do not report corresponding simulations, as they view advances as determined by SLAs, and not as a simple policy variable to be manipulated by the FHLBB.

H-V do report a simulation result that holds advances at their 1965:IV level. The simulation runs until the end of 1971, at which time advances were in fact about $1 billion above their 1965:IV level. By the end of 1971, the H-V no increase in advances simulation shows a slight increase in the stock of 1-4

219

family homes. However, this increase is most likely a transitory result of the lags in the model. In the H-V model, investment in houses is negatively related to the mortgage rate with a distributed lag. No increase in advances results in a higher mortgage rate on average. Thus, one expects investment in houses eventually to show a cumulative decline. When discussing their results, H-V comment, "Given the lagged response of housing to the mortgage rate, the timing of increases in advances has been optimal for stabilization of housing expenditures." (p. 23).

F-S report the results of a simulation involving an increase in FHLBB advances of $1 billion in the first quarter of 1962. In their simulation, the mortgage rate falls by 3 basis points in the first quarter. It then rises, and after eight quarters has returned to its original level where it remains unchanged. The total stock of mortgages starts to rise and stabilizes after five quarters at an increased level of $700 million. Housing starts increase during the first five quarters following the increase in advances. The cumulative increase in starts during the first five quarters is 22.5 thousand units. Construction lags starts. Through the first six quarters, residential construction shows a cumulative increase of $350 million. In succeeding quarters, housing starts are slightly lower than they otherwise would have been. This slight decline is not surprising if advances have little long-run impact on the housing stock.

The Rate on Advances

F-S also view the rate on advances as an exogenous policy variable and report the results of increasing the rate on advances by 100 basis points in the first quarter of 1962.[17] Initially, the increase reduces mortgage acquisitions by SLAs, increases the mortgage rate and reduces housing starts. After four quarters, starts have been reduced by 42.75 thousand units. After twelve quarters, the mortgage rate is 1 basis point higher. Housing starts still show a cumulative deficit when compared with what would have happened with no policy change; however, current starts have increased.

H-V do not report simulations involving a change in the rate on advances. They view the FHLBS as passing through its own costs of borrowing and exercising no control of its own when setting the rate. Further, their empirical work assumes that SLAs are insensitive to the rate on advances, as the equation to explain borrowing by SLAs does not include the rate on advances. H-V view borrowings as arising mainly in response to fluctuations in deposit inflows.

B-D do not report simulations involving the rate on advances, although in their model the rate is an exogenous variable, presumably capable of control,

---

[17] It is not immediately clear how the FHLBB is able to control both the quantity of advances and the rate on advances, unless the FHLBB is assumed to operate to the left of the SLA demand curve for advances.

and the quantity of advances are negatively related to this rate.

Required Liquidity

F-S are the only investigators who have an explicit treatment of liquidity requirements in their model. They simulate the effect of increasing the ratio of required liquidity by 100 basis points in the first quarter of 1962. As indicated above, one might expect that, to a first approximation, a reduction of liquidity requirements should have an impact similar to an increase in advances of similar magnitude. In both cases, the FHLBS and SLAs together are forcing other sectors of the economy to hold either more government securities or more securities that are very close substitutes. The F-S simulation results are roughly consistent with the view expressed here. (They simulate an increase in required liquidity so one has to make a sign adjustment.)

The F-S simulation involves an increase of 100 basis points in required liquidity. The simulation is run from 1962:I to 1964:IV when SLA deposits increased from $72 billion to $102 billion. Thus, the magnitude of the change involved in the 100 basis point change in the required liquidity ratio is comparable to a $1 billion change in advances. The F-S simulations show an initial increase in the mortgage rate, reduction in the stock of mortgages, and reduction in housing starts. After four quarters, housing starts show a cumulative deficit of 30 thousand units. After twelve quarters, the mortgage rate is still 1 basis point higher; the stock of mortgages is lower - - the absolute size of the difference in mortgage stocks continues to grow as the effect of the liquidity ratio is scaled by the quantity of deposits at SLAs; and housing starts, while still showing a cumulative deficit of 17,000 units, have increased.

Regulation Q

F-S report the result of a 100 basis point increase in Regulation Q ceilings for commercial banks, mutual savings banks (MSB), and SLAs. The simulation starts in the fourth quarter of 1970, a time when ceilings were effective on all institutions. In the F-S model, MSBs and SLAs respond immediately and raise their deposit rates by an average of 98 basis points. Commercial banks do not respond as dramatically, raising their deposit rates by about 40 basis points.[18]

---

[18] The structure of the model that gives this differential response is a bit difficult to understand. Deposit rate equations for all three institutions involve the rate on Treasury bills with a very small coefficient, and lagged own deposit rates with a very large coefficient. In the F-S model, when setting deposit rates, these institutions do not look at the rates paid by other institutions or at the yields on any assets except Treasury bills. Once deposit rates bump into the ceilings, the rates switch over to the ceilings. For MSB s and SLA s, this means that their deposit rates are pulled up immediately with the increase in the ceilings. For commercial banks, however, the response to bumping into the ceiling is lagged one period in a way that, when the ceiling is raised in this simulation, it gets far enough above the basic rate-setting mechanism that it is no longer an effective ceiling. If the switch over to the ceiling was of the same form for commercial banks as it is for MSB s and SLA s, then the commercial bank deposit rate would rise just like that of MSB s and SLA s. At no point, before or after ceilings are effective, is there any consideration of whether an institution is still making profits when paying the F-S deposit rate. See Jaffee (1973) for a discussion of this point as it relates to SLA s and the controversy over Regulation Q.

Deposit flows to thrift institutions, especially SLAs, respond to this rate differential. After 12 quarters, deposits at SLAs are $32 billion higher. This shift of funds to thrift institutions increases mortgage lending substantially.

A special feature of the model increases the mortgage rate along with the increased quantity of mortgages. The equation for the mortgage rate includes a weighted average of deposit rates at SLAs and MSBs. [19] The authors view this variable as reflecting a markup on costs. When deposit rates at MSBs and SLAs rise, this in turn induces an increase in the mortgage rate, that in turn induces more mortgage lending by other mortgage lenders, commercial banks, and life insurance companies. After nine quarters, the mortgage rate is 27 basis points higher, and commercial bank mortgage holdings are $5.9 billion higher, in spite of the $7.2 billion reduction in time and savings deposits other than large certificates of deposit.

The increase in the mortgage rate works to reduce housing starts, but the increased mortgage lending is a much stronger influence that increases starts. Over four quarters, the cumulative increase in starts is 320 thousand units. After nine quarters, starts show a cumulative increase of over 860 thousand units, and residential construction shows a cumulative increase of over $15 billion.

H-V report the results of a 50 basis point increase in deposit rates. There is no question about differential responses to increases in ceilings. In the H-V model, all deposit rates are exogenous. H-V show a shift of funds to nonbank thrift institutions, although of substantially less magnitude than F-S. For H-V, the increase in deposits is only about one-fourth of the F-S estimate. The increased mortgage lending leads to a reduction in the mortgage rate and increased homebuilding. After twelve quarters, the stock of 1-4 family houses is $1.78 billion higher. It is not possible to determine the total effect on homebuilding, as H-V deal explicitly only with 1-4 family construction.

B-D report the results of an increase in deposit ceilings of 50 basis points. All three institutions, commercial banks, MSBs, and SLAs, respond promptly to the increase in the ceiling. Deposit accounts respond quickly. The magnitude of the deposit responses appears to be larger than those of F-S. Mortgage lending also increases, as does residential construction. After three years, residential construction shows a cumulative increase of $12.6 billion.

Federal National Mortgage Association Purchases

The Federal National Mortgage Association (FNMA) is another federally sponsored credit agency that deals with mortgages. FNMA issues its own secur-

---

[19] The model does not include an explicit expression for the supply of mortgage liabilities by the non-financial public. Such behavior is implicit in the equation for the mortgage rate, which includes a measure of residential construction and capital gains on the existing stock, as well as the cost of deposits variable.

ities to buy and hold mortgages. As of December 31, 1974, FNMA held a mortgage portfolio of almost $30 billion. It is instructive to look at simulations of FNMA purchases for they should have impacts on mortgage and housing markets that are similar to FHLBB advances. [20] The effects of FNMA mortgage purchases should also be indicative of the impact of mortgage purchases by the Federal Home Loan Mortgage Corporation, the newest government sponsored mortgage market agency.

F-S report the results of increasing FNMA mortgage purchases by $1 billion in the first quarter of 1962. The initial effect is to lower the mortgage rate and increase housing starts. After four quarters, starts show a cumulative increase of 16.5 thousand units, and the mortgage rate is 1 basis point higher than initially. After 12 quarters, the mortgage rate is unchanged, and housing starts still show a small cumulative increase that is being eliminated.

B-D report the results of the same simulation, a $1 billion increase in FNMA purchases. The initial effect is a drop in the mortgage rate, an increase in residential construction, and a rise in general market rates. After one year, the mortgage rate has risen by 5 basis points. Residential construction shows a cumulative increase of $500 million. The stock of mortgages is $600 million higher, and deposits at MSBs and SLAs have declined by $400 million.

After six years, the mortgage rate shows a decline of 3 basis points; the mortgage stock is $900 million lower; market interest rates are generally 2 basis points higher; and residential construction still shows a cumulative increase of $300 million. [21]

H-V report the results of a slightly different simulation. H-V view FNMA purchases of mortgages as responding to developments in mortgage markets, instead of being an exogenously determined policy variable. H-V thus estimate an equation explaining FNMA purchases. This equation explains FNMA purchases as a function of a constant, a shift parameter that takes effect in 1969, and the change in the mortgage rate. To simulate an increase in FNMA purchases, H-V shift FNMA holdings up by $1 billion but retain the endogenous, rate-sensitive nature of FNMA activity.

---

[20] It is true that FNMA purchases mortgages directly, while the FHLBS lends to SLA s who in turn make mortgages. For a more complete discussion of this point, see Swan (1974). It is also true that FNMA purchases primarily FHA-insured and VA-guaranteed mortgages, while SLA s hold primarily conventional mortgages. Most models of the mortgage market assume there is sufficient substitution among these different forms of mortgages to aggregate all mortgages.

[21] These results are a little puzzling, especially the drop in the stock of mortgages. The cumulative surplus of residential construction, the increase in market interest rates, and the reduction in the mortgage rate would all be expected to increase the supply of mortgage liabilities; yet the stock of mortgages has fallen. This result undoubtedly reflects the form of the equation B-D use to estimate the mortgage rate. The equation does not have an easy interpretation, as regards the supply of mortgage liabilities, by the non-financial public.

The initial effect of this $1 billion shift is to lower the mortgage rate, which in turn reduces FNMA purchases. On net, initial FNMA purchases are only $630 million. Maximum effects occur after six quarters when the mortgage rate has fallen by 5 basis points; the commercial paper rate is 5 basis points higher; FNMA mortgage holdings are $900 million higher; the total mortgage stock is $500 million higher; and the 1-4 family housing stock is $520 million higher.

After 12 quarters, the mortgage rate appears to have stabilized 5 basis points lower; the commercial paper rate is 4 basis points higher; the stock of mortgages is unchanged; and the housing stock is $240 million higher.

V. CONCLUSIONS

There may be reason to doubt whether FHLBB actions will have any permanent impact on the size of the housing stock. To have a permanent impact, FHLBB actions would have to have a permanent impact on either the demand for housing services, the supply price of new units, or the structure of interest rates. As suggested above, there is little reason to expect that FHLBB actions would have a permanent effect on the demand for housing services. There are arguments, but little empirical evidence, to suggest that FHLBB actions could work to lower the supply price of new units. It is most likely that any long-run effects would come from effects on the structure of interest rates. Work using Tobin's portfolio balance approach suggests that FHLBB actions may have permanent effects on the structure of interest rates, although the direction of some of these impacts may be ambiguous.

Even if one denies the possibility of any permanent or long-run impact, it may still be that FHLBB actions have important short-run or timing impacts on the flow of new housing units over time. These short-run impacts are likely to be more important if, as a substantial body of research suggests, housing and mortgage markets are at times affected by credit rationing.

The empirical simulations examined in this paper tend to support the position described above. The simulations report substantial short-run impacts in the appropriate direction. The evidence about long-run impacts is less clear cut as none of the simulations are carried out for a long enough period of time to determine long-run equilibrium impacts. In virtually all cases, the initial impacts are reversed and the models appear to be heading toward a position of little long-run impact. The results of only one policy action, changes in Regulation Q, are at variance with this conclusion. Simulations by both Fromm-Sinai and Bosworth-Duesenberry show large continuing increases in homebuilding in response to an increase in Regulation Q ceilings.

Whether a particular impact is substantial or not is to some extent a matter of judgment. The most optimistic observer could only expect that an increase of $1 billion in advances would lead to about $1 billion in more construction. Loan-to-value ratios less than unity might suggest a larger impact, but mortgages usually cover both structures and land.

From this roughly dollar-for-dollar impact there are several slippages that tend to reduce the impact on residential construction. One slippage is that not all mortgages are used to finance new units. Thus, an increase in mortgage lending may facilitate transfers between existing units with little impact on new construction. [Easing transfers between existing units during periods of tight mortgage markets may be a positive aspect of FHLBB (and FNMA) actions that is not measured by concentrating on new units.]

The other slippages have to do with the effects of changes in interest rates. If expansionary FHLBB action lowers mortgage rates and increases general market rates, then: (1) debt/equity or loan-to-value ratios may increase; (2) financial institutions with portfolio flexibility may reallocate funds out of mortgages; and (3) individuals may reallocate their wealth away from thrift institutions towards general market securities. All of these factors would work to diminish the impact of any expansionary FHLBB action. The simulation results discussed above suggest that a one-time $1 billion expansionary FHLBB action will increase residential construction in the first four to six quarters by $300 to $600 million.

REFERENCES

1. Bisignano, J., "Adjustment and Disequilibrium Costs and the Estimated Brainard-Tobin Model," mimeo, presented to SSRC Subcommittee on Monetary Research, April 30, 1971.

2. Bosworth, B., and Duesenberry, J., "A Flow of Funds Model and Its Implications," in Issues in Federal Debt Management, Boston Federal Reserve Bank Conference Series 10, June 1973.

3. Brady, E.A., "An Econometric Analysis of the U.S. Residential Housing Market," in National Housing Models, (ed. B. Ricks),Lexington, Mass.: Lexington Books, 1973.

4. Brainard, W., "Uncertainty and the Effectiveness of Policy," American Economic Review, LVII, No. 2, (May 1967), 411-425.

5. Cassidy, H., and Valentini, J., "A Quarterly Econometric Model of the U.S. Housing, Mortgage and Deposit Markets," mimeo, presented at the winter meeting of the American Real Estate and Urban Economics Association, December 28, 1972.

6. Dhrymes, P., and Taubman, P., "An Empirical Analysis of the Savings and Loan Industry," in Study of the Savings and Loan Industry, (ed. I. Friend), Washington, D.C.: U.S. Government Printing Office, 1969.

7. Duesenberry, J., and Bosworth, B., "Policy Implications of a Flow-of-Funds Model," Journal of Finance, XXIX, No. 2, (May 1974), 331-348.

8. Fair, R. A Short-Run Forecasting Model of the United States Economy. Lexington, Mass.: Heath Lexington Books; 1971.

9. Fair, R., and Jaffee, D., "An Empirical Study of the Hunt Commission Report Proposals for the Mortgage and Housing Markets," in Policies for a More Competitive Financial System, Boston Federal Reserve Bank Conference Series 8, 1972 (a).

10. _____, "Methods of Estimation for Markets in Disequilibrium," Econometrica, 40, No. 3, (May 1972), 497-514 (b).

11. Federal Home Loan Bank Board. A Financial Institution for the Future, [Washington], 1975.

12. Fromm, G., and Sinai, A., "A Policy Simulation Model of Deposit Flows, Mortgage Sector Activity, and Housing," mimeo, February 1975.

13. Gibson, W., "Protecting Homebuilding from Restrictive Credit Conditions," Brookings Papers on Economic Activity, Washington, D.C.: The Brookings Institution, (1973:3), 647-691.

14. Guttentag, J., "The Short Cycle in Residential Construction, 1946-59," American Economic Review, LI, No. 3, (June 1961), 275-298.

15. _____, "The Federal Reserve and the Mortgage Market: Some Perspective on the 'Crisis' of 1966," in A Study of Mortgage Credit, Subcommittee on Housing and Urban Affairs, Committee on Banking and Currency, United States Senate, May 22, 1967.

16. Hendershott, P., and Villani, K., "The Impact of Government Policies on Financial Markets and Housing Expenditures," mimeo, December 1974.

17. Huang, D., "Effect of Different Credit Policies on Housing Demand," in Study of the Savings and Loan Industry, (ed. I. Friend), Washington, D.C.: U.S. Government Printing Office, 1969.

18. Jaffee, D., "An Econometric Model of the Mortgage Market," in Savings Deposits, Mortgages and Housing, (eds. E. Gramlich and D. Jaffee) Lexington, Mass.: Lexington Books, 1972.

19. _____, "The Impact of the Elimination of Deposit-Rate Ceilings on Savings and Loan Associations," mimeo, presented at Quarterly Bank Economists' Meeting, Federal Home Loan Bank Board, May 16, 1973.

20. Kalchbrenner, J., "A Model of the Housing Sector," in Savings Deposits, Mortgages and Housing, (eds. E. Gramlich and D. Jaffee), Lexington, Mass.: Lexington Books, 1972.

21. Kearl, J.,and Rosen, K., "A Model of Housing Starts, Mortgage Flows, and the Behavior of the Federal Home Loan Bank Board and the Federal National Mortgage Association," M.I.T.-Harvard Joint Center for Urban Studies, Working Paper No. 27, (May 1974).

22. Maisel, S., "The Effects of Monetary Policy on Expenditures in Specific Sectors of the Economy," Journal of Political Economy, 76, No. 4, Part II, (July/August 1968), 796-814.

23. Manski, C., and Rosen, K., "The Implementation of Demand Instability for the Behavioral of Firms: The Case of Residential Construction," M.I.T.-Harvard Joint Center for Urban Studies,Working Paper No. 17,(1972).

24. Meltzer, A., "Credit Availability and Economic Decisions: Some Evidence from the Mortgage and Housing Markets," Journal of Finance, XXIX, No. 3, (June 1974), 763-778.

25. Peskin, J., "Federal Agency Debt and Its Secondary Market," Staff Study 10, Treasury-Federal Reserve Study of the U.S. Government Securities Market, November 14, 1967.

26. Pierce, J., and Graves, M., "Insulating Housing: Effects upon Economic Stabilization Policy," in Ways to Moderate Fluctuations in Housing Construction, Federal Reserve Staff Study, Washington, D.C.: 1972.

27. Silber, W., "The Market for Federal Agency Securities: Is There an Optimum Size of Issue?" Working Paper 72-72, New York University Graduate School of Business Administration, 1972.

28. _____, "A Model of FHLBS and FNMA Behavior," The Review of Economics and Statistics, LV, No. 3, (August 1973), 308-320.

29 Sparks, G., "An Econometric Analysis of the Role of Financial Intermediaries in Postwar Residential Building Cycles," in Determinants of Investment Behavior, (ed. R. Ferber), NBER, Washington, D.C.: 1967.

30. Swan, C., "Homebuilding: A Review of Experience," Brookings Papers on Economic Activity, Washington, D.C.: The Brookings Institution, (1970:1), 48-70.

31. Swan, C., "The Behavior of Financial Institutions: An Econometric Analysis with Special Attention to Mortgage Markets and Residential Construction," unpublished Ph.D. thesis, Yale University, 1970.

32. _____, "A Quarterly Model of Housing Starts: A Disequilibrium Approach," Working Paper 39, Office of Economic Research, Federal Home Loan Bank Board, November 1972.

33. _____, "A Model of Financial Intermediation by the Government," mimeo, January 1974.

34. Tobin, J., "Deposit Interest Controls as a Monetary Control," Journal of Money, Credit and Banking, II, No. 1, (February 1970), 4-14.

A VIEW FROM THE FEDERAL HOME LOAN BANK BOARD:
A COMMENT ON THE JAFFEE AND SWAN PAPERS

Harris C. Friedman*
Senior Vice President
American Savings and Loan Association of Florida

I would like first to congratulate Jaffee and Swan on 'their perceptive comments on the Federal Home Loan Bank System. In Jaffee's own words, we are not generally very talkative about FHLBS policies; both authors were able, at least in general terms, to discern most of these policies and comment on them. Second, I found it intriguing that we are considered lax in our public statements, since our public affairs office takes great pride in the fact that they are getting Thomas Bomar's and the Federal Home Loan Bank Board's name in 3,000 newspapers at least two or three times a week. In any event, our talkativeness follows the lead of our sister financial regulatory agency, located on Constitution Avenue. I will comment first on Jaffee's paper, then on Swan's, though their subject matter is intertwined and my comments will often refer to both papers.

While I do not set out to defend the actions of the FHLBB, I am sure that in this discussion I will end up doing exactly that. I feel that Jaffee made some valid criticisms, but I would like to clarify some factual statements that may prove troublesome, and that may have resulted from our lack of policy statements. Incidentally, our Associate General Counsel was crushed to learn, in a footnote, that there is no compendium of regulations, statutes, etc. The lawyers take great pains in preparing an annotated manual that is readily available, at a very high price.

On more substantive issues, Jaffee indicates that there is a dilemma which finds the Board caught between the national policy of aggregate stabilization, on the one hand, and national housing priorities, on the other. The current and previous Boards, at least since 1969, have not discerned this as a problem. The legislation creating the FHLBS goes a little further than Jaffee indicates - - there is, in fact, a mandate to promote "thrift and homeownership." As a result, the Board has taken the position that its obligation is to stabilize the flow of funds into the housing sector, irrespective of overall economic stabilization. Whether or not Board policies over this time period have performed this function, as Swan indicates, is open to debate. Unfortunately, the policy tools are limited, as Jaffee notes. The Board's position is that, until it can be shown that its use of these

*At the time of the Conference, Dr. Friedman was Director, Office of Economic Research and Chief Economist, Federal Home Loan Bank Board.

policies has _perverse_ effects, it will continue to use them. In the literature review-ed by both Jaffee and Swan, there is very little evidence that the policies of the FHLBB and the FHLBS have a negative impact on housing. Admittedly, most of the results show a smaller impact than we would like, but they are not negative.

With regard to FHLBS borrowing policies, I would like to clarify one erroneous statement concerning the net debt position of the System. Early in the paper, Jaffee defines the FHLBS as consisting of the Board, the 12 regional Banks, and the member Savings and Loan Associations. If this is his definition of the System, then it has always been a net supplier of funds to the government secu-rity market. Even in recent times, it has not become an unequivocable debtor, as Jaffee claims. It is a fact that SLAs are required to hold a substantial portion of their funds in liquid assets, which are primarily government securities. If the Sys-tem is defined more narrowly as the Federal Home Loan Banks, then I would agree that they are unequivocably debtors, but that would have been the case at almost any point in time when advances outstanding to SLAs were greater than zero. In any event, the participation of the System in the government securities is substantial - - gross holdings of government securities are currently about $25 billion.

In the same vein, Jaffee notes that debt issues of the System must be approved by the Treasury. This is true and is not as peculiar as indicated since, while we do have an emergency line of credit with Treasury, they also can say "no," at any point in time, to our borrowing or using that line.

Jaffee perceptively points out a very intriguing ordering of priorities of the System, that is, savings flows, mortgage market activity, and housing invest-ment. I have to agree with him that, in the past, this has been the priority list. I believe that today this ordering can be questioned. In any event, it would be inter-esting to hear this discussed. I make this point because the Board believes strongly that, under their current charter, SLAs exist solely to provide mortgage money. Given that emphasis, it is not at all obvious that savings flows should be the first order of priority.

I found Jaffee's model of the principal parameters of the System quite intriguing, though I do not believe it would be profitable to comment on the model here. He might be surprised to learn that I agree with his conclusion, that one form of government intervention, namely, interest rate ceilings, leads to a second intervention, namely, mortgage market support - - which is inefficient with respect to the market and to the public.

I want now to turn to specific policy tools and objectives of the FHLBS. Jaffee begins with liquidity policy. The ability to set liquidity requirements could conceivably be the most potent tool available to the FHLBS in impacting the mortgage market. Unfortunately, its impact may be more psychological than real.

Once again, Jaffee uses the broad definition of the System in his discussion of liquidity; as Swan has also suggested, it is probably most appropriate to look at total System liquidity, rather than at the liquidity of the FHLBS only, or at the liquidity of SLAs only. It is important to keep in mind that the Board has the authority to set liquidity minimums for the Savings and Loan industry, but it does not have the ability to set maximums. So this tool is somewhat muted in that it is one directional only, not symmetrical. With respect to the liquidity of the FHLBS, the situation is such that, not only the FHLBB, but the U.S. Treasury, has an input into the volume. This is a tool, or set of tools, that gives the Board questionable powers. Finally, Jaffee will be glad to know that the Board is currently taking his advice and trying to borrow as much money long-term as it possibly can. Again, the outcome will in large part be a function of the Treasury's willingness for this to happen.

The second major policy, and one that receives more attention in the academic literature, as well as in the financial press, is the advances policy of the FHLBB and the FHLBS. Again, Jaffee's theoretical model proves very helpful, and points up the problem of the Board that, no matter how progressive or aggressive the advances policy is, the System still plays a passive role in the transaction; it is up to member SLAs either to borrow or not to borrow. Pricing of advances has been an extremely volatile issue throughout the life of the FHLBS, and, as Jaffee points out, it has traditionally been conducted on an average cost basis. As a result, advance rates were extremely low, and it was argued that the System was subsidizing the SLA industry. If one assumes that once the funds are borrowed from the public by the System, the stockholders have a right to them at this borrowing cost, and then there is no subsidy involved. The subsidy in this case is one of timing. This can be argued for days on end, and the answer will depend on your definition of subsidies.

The current board believes that "market" pricing is the only viable approach. As a result, in mid-1974, various maturities of advances were being priced at approximately the same price that commercial bank certificates of deposit were going for in respective maturity ranges. As a footnote, I would like to point out that the Board agrees with Jaffee that binding usury ceilings puts the market into disequilibrium, and, as a result, it has a second-best solution. If he can give us a clever way to eliminate usury ceilings, the Board would be very appreciative. In this case, I doubt if fancy footwork with econometrics will help much.

I agree with Jaffee's comment that the Board would better achieve its apparent target of mortgage market stabilization through Freddie Mac than through advances. Freddie Mac is a relatively new entity, and, I believe, the current policy is designed to do just what Jaffee has in mind. Again, there is a problem of funding, and also one of tradition. It took three years to convince more than a small number of SLAs that they should even sell mortgages to Freddie Mac. This is a time-consuming effort but one that is well underway.

I want to comment on Jaffee's digression into reaction functions. The System includes a group called the Credit and Investment Committee, made up of the three Board members and the 12 regional bank presidents. This group meets quarterly to establish broad guidelines for FHLBB liquidity and for advances policy for the coming quarter. These policies may, of course, be changed between regularly scheduled CIC meetings, but broad guidelines are generally honored.As an aside, at the group's next meeting, I plan to present them with equation (19b) and explain to them that their decision making is really based on a mixed-disequilibrium, switching equation reaction-function. I plan to propose that they begin publishing the equation coefficients they use 60 days after each CIC meeting.

On more current proposals, I should note again that our press office has done its job, and Jaffee was "taken in" by the fact that 32 regulatory changes were made in the first 90 days of Bomar's chairmanship. While these were all liberalizing regulations, they added about 700 pages to our annotated manual.

In a more serious vein, I want to discuss the subject of conversions of mutual SLAs into stock chartered institutions. I cannot believe that, as a free market disciple, Jaffee really sees considerable merit in not allowing further conversions of mutual SLAs. This seems to me to go against all the principles of freedom of choice. As for the question of windfalls, the Board believes that the stock can be priced to eliminate potential windfalls, though there is some disagreement on this point. To the extent that any windfalls did occur, we feel the long-run benefits to the mortgage market of this added flexibility far outweigh the small windfall equity investors may receive.

The second area of policy concern mentioned by Jaffee is that of the financial institution for the future. I think no one believes that SLAs should, or can, continue in their present form indefinitely. If the only problem we have in getting some sort of reform accomplished is the use of an occasional split infinitive, we would be quite pleased. I do think that Jaffee misread our intentions. We did not say that ceilings have helped the flow of housing credit. It is true that we did not call for the elimination of ceilings in this paper; this was strictly a policy/political judgment. Unfortunately, a regulatory agency has to bargain as much as any other group, and this document is being used, not only to support our case in Congress, but also to convince the SLA industry of the wisdom of restructuring. Had the abolition of Regulation Q been proposed in the study, we would not have gotten them to read past page 2. The Board has taken a strong position that Regulation Q must go, but we do not believe that complete elimination immediately would be beneficial to anyone. It is doubtful that the Federal Savings and Loan Insurance Corporation would like this prospect. I will explain that comment in my discussion of Swan's paper.

On the subject of variable rate mortgages, I think that Jaffee again slightly misread our proposed regulations. He made the point that free prepayment would create arbitrage situations for the borrower. That is true, but our proposed regulations require free prepayment only in the event that the mortgage rate is above the initial contract rate of the loan. Arbitrage situations arise when the mortgage rate falls and, at that point, lenders can charge penalties. Thus, the arbitrage opportunities will likely be eliminated.

Concluding my comments on this paper, I would once again like to congratulate Jaffee on his perceptive account of the FHLBS, which I hope will generate further policy recommendations.

Turning to Swan's paper, my first reaction to it, and to Jaffee's as well, is that the titles are somewhat misleading. While they indicate that the purpose of the papers is to assess the impact of policy actions by the FHLBB, what they actually do is assess the impact of FHLBB advances and liquidity requirements on the residential housing market. While this is more a fault of prior research and model builders, I guess it is indicative of the lack of attention the FHLBS has received in both academic literature and research in general.

Unfortunately, other policies have not been discussed by either Swan or Jaffee. Omitted completely are the questions of chartering, branching, and insuring of SLAs. I would assume that all of these have some impact on the competitive balance within the universe of financial intermediaries. In fact, decisions in this area could have an even more dramatic impact on competition and housing finance than either a change in liquidity requirements, or a change in the interest rate charged on FHLBB advances. I do not want to dwell on these points because I do not have any answers.

I think it would be helpful to clear up an historical point raised in Swan's paper. Swan indicates that in 1966 there was some pressure to limit the FHL Banks' borrowings. I think that is a gross understatement. The pressure was a definite "no" by the Treasury, and, since they have the final word, the FHL Banks did not borrow.

I found Swan's discussion of liquidity requirements very well presented; he makes an extremely valid point that required liquidity holdings are actually very illiquid and, as a result, possibly should be held in whatever is going to provide the highest yield to SLAs. The Board recently changed the definition of liquidity, and this point was discussed in some comment letters on the regulations. The Board was not prepared to take such a "radical" position, and required liquidity will remain in a highly liquid form.

Swan made a good point in comparing liquidity policy to advances policy when he indicated that advances are more flexible, in that associations that need the funds and will use them in the mortgage market tend to be the borrowers. This is especially true when the cost of borrowing is substantial, as it was in 1974. Liquidity requirements are a shotgun approach, and advances, while not a rifle, are somewhere in between.

I want now to discuss rate control, or Regulation Q. Swan questions the premise that SLAs would have been effectively constrained to raise deposit rates had there been no Regulation Q. He then cites Tobin, who has argued that SLAs should reach into past earnings to pay higher deposit rates. While I am not a defender of Regulation Q, I think the ability to reach into past earnings is overstated. Let me give an example of the problem. SLAs currently have a residential loan portfolio of approximately $250 billion, with an average yield of 7.5 percent. They have total assets of about $290 billion, savings of $236 billion, and net worth of $17.8 billion. This adds up to a net worth-to-assets ratio of slightly over 6 percent. The current average cost of savings is slightly above 6 percent. If the competitive market forced an increase in the cost of savings of 2 percentage points, for the moment ignoring the impact of certificates, it would effectively cost the industry $4.7 billion. Industry earnings in 1974 were $1.5 billion. This increase in costs of $4.7 billion would thus eliminate current earnings and require a reduction in net worth of $3.2 billion, which would decrease net worth to under $15 billion. This would leave a net worth-to-assets ratio of less than 5 percent. Any increases greater or less than this would have a direct linear relationship. I do not pretend to know an adequate net worth ratio for the industry; I think this is a fascinating research project for the future. If, however, the aggregate industry net worth declined to below 5 percent, I can almost guarantee that the net worth of many SLAs would be eliminated. The prospect of this would create some very unhappy times for my friends in the FSLIC. I know that one can argue about the necessity of paying ceiling rates, but the empirical evidence shows that this is exactly what happens.

As a final point, Swan's evaluation of published results from various econometric models was interesting and informative. Each of these models has its own vagaries and differences, and the results are not directly comparable. As both Swan and Jaffee well know, the various policy and planning objectives of the Board are not easily simulated. As a result, different models with different technical adjustments have been used to answer the many questions we raise. At some point in time, it would be desirable to have one model capable of answering our many questions, but I think this is improbable for the present time.

FEDERAL HOME LOAN BANK BOARD POLICY AND
THE PLIGHT OF SAVINGS AND LOAN ASSOCIATIONS:
A COMMENT ON THE JAFFEE AND SWAN PAPERS*

Edward J. Kane**
The Ohio State University

I want to begin by remarking on the thorough-going professionalism of these papers. The general excellence of the authors' research testifies to the dramatically higher quality of analysis being devoted to Savings and Loan and Federal Home Loan Bank Board problems over the last ten years. This determined purchase of more and better economic advice is, in fact, a policy instrument that Harris Friedman and the authors were perhaps too modest to include in their lists of stabilization weapons currently wielded by the "Bank Board." Since the role of economic research in an agency's stabilization effort is a favorite theme of our genial host, and since the Board has on occasion had me on its payroll too, I will not dwell on this point. But it is worth thinking about. SLA economics is now a respectable sub-field of economic analysis and very much a growth industry. During my 15 years as a professional economist, it has developed from an ugly duckling into a veritable swan. Although lacking in elegance, this metaphor seems especially apt in view of the profession's widespread (but usually unspoken) fear that Savings and Loan Associations may yet take a spectacular swan dive.

Some Complaints

I would like to complain quickly about these papers' neglect of the unpleasant distribution effects of FHLBB policies and of mortgage subsidization, in general. But the principal theme I wish to develop is the need for all of us to take a more skeptical perspective on the "targeting" of FHLBB instruments. I continue to be amazed at how much weight our profession attributes to housing goals in FHLBB decision making. This is the picture that FHLBB spokesmen paint, but I think we would all agree that individuals' statements about their motivations are typically very poor guides to their real goals. Common sense, backed up by careful review of the empirical evidence,[1] suggests that subsidizing SLA mortgage activity has virtually no long-run, and perhaps only a small short-run, effect

---

*The author wishes to thank the National Science Foundation for research support.

**Everett D. Reese Professor of Banking and Monetary Economics.

[1] See Meltzer (1974) and Fair and Jaffee (1972).

(Swan's simulation experiments notwithstanding) on the housing stock. In my view, FHLBB policy is keyed primarily to SLA savings inflows and profit rates and that, except as a matter of public (and especially Congressional) relations, the Board cares about families' housing needs and the welfare of the construction industry only insofar as they impinge on these SLA variables.

Although the link between housing demand and SLA profits is very real, I submit that as model builders we would be better off to concentrate on a deliberately exaggerated counter-model that assumes that the FHLBB is essentially a captive of its SLA clientele, constrained only: (1) by the general supervision of Congress and (in its decisions re rates charged on advances to SLAs) by the Treasury; and (2) to a much smaller extent, by the professionalism of its staff. Except for such matters as payrolls and social accounting, I view the FHLBB as a part of the SLA industry much more than as a part of the government.

Jaffee's Reaction-Function Model

Though I accept most of the policy implications that flow from his analysis, Jaffee's reaction-function model provides a convenient foil against which to contrast my views. In his model, the FHLBB looks at the objective function, W, and seeks to solve the following problem:

$$\text{Max } W = -(H-H^*)^2 - w_1(R-I)^2 - w_2(A^d-A)^2 \; ;$$

subject to:
(1) reduced-form equations for A^d and H;
(2) three inequality constraints:

$$(A^d-A) \geqslant 0;$$

$$A \geqslant 0 \, ;$$

$$R \geqslant 0.$$

The various symbols are defined as follows:

H	housing stock;
H*	housing goal of the FHLBB;
A^d	SLAs demand for advances;
A	quantity of advances outstanding;
R	interest rate charged by the FHLBB on advances;

I   interest cost of funds to the FHLBB.

What do I dislike about Jaffee's objective function? Superficially at least, the answer is <u>everything</u>. In my opinionated way, I would throw out every single argument. By way of explanation, let me simply offer three assertions.

1.   FHLBB talk about a housing goal is for Congressional consumption. H is important only for its effects on SLA deposit flows and profit rates.

2.   The net subsidy or tax inherent in R-I is not a matter of continuous trade-off, but a source of political pressures generated when its magnitude becomes too large in either direction. The two points ($a_{1,t}$ and $a_{2,t}$) where pressure begins can be treated as threshold values that may well shift with political forces over the typical business cycle and with proximity to the next Federal election:

$R > I + a_{1,t}$ bothers the Congress somewhat and the Treasury a lot;

$I > R + a_{2,t}$ bothers SLAs and Congress.

3.   Increasingly since 1966, the total amount of advances has not served as an objective, but is viewed merely as a <u>result</u> of changes in the instrument, I, designed to influence SLA savings flows and profit rates.

My "Barebones Counter-model"

My version of the FHLBB objective function, W', would be linear in the percentage growth of savings deposits, $\frac{\Delta S}{S}$, and quadratic in industry profits, Π. I would formulate the FHLBB decision problem as

$$\text{Max W}' = \left[\frac{\Delta S}{S} - \left(\frac{\Delta S}{S} \right)^* \right] - W'_1 \, (\Pi - \Pi^*)^2,$$

subject to the following constraints:

(1) reduced-form equations for Π and $\dfrac{\Delta S}{S}$, where $\Pi = \Pi_0 + R_M M - R_S S$, and $\dfrac{\Delta S}{S} = f(R, R_S, I), f_1, f_3 < 0$ and $f_2 > 0$;

(2) at least three inequality constraints (one could add a constraint on A):

$$R - I \leqslant a_{1,t} \ ;$$

$$I - R \leqslant a_{2,t} \ ;$$

$$R_M - I \geqslant 0 \ ;$$

where

M	the amount of mortgages held by SLAs;
R_M	the competitively determined mortgage rate;
R_S	the ceiling rate on savings deposits.

I would treat R, R_M, and R_S as exogenous, letting R_S be set in negotiations with Congress, and R_M be determined nationally by the interaction of the public's demand for mortgage credits (which are, of course, not necessarily used to finance housing) and the shifting commitments of marginal suppliers who move funds in and out of mortgages in response to the ebb and flow of SLA mortgage demand.

This "clientele model" has Kuhn-Tucker conditions that have much in common with Jaffee's. In particular, the sign of (R-I) continues to act as a switching variable, but a few testable differences do emerge.

What I most want to challenge is not Jaffee's policy analysis (with which I largely agree) but Swan's view that one _has_ to use a "large" model to assess FHLBB policy. In fact, I suspect that large models that generate substantial short-run effects of FHLBB policy on housing do so primarily because of the difficulty of specifying many relationships accurately. Appealing to Occam's Razor, I hope that Jaffee and Swan will view my counter-model as a null hypothesis against which to test their more complicated structures. I further hope that the results of such tests will make it harder for public officials to sing hypocritical arias on the possibility and social desirability of building more and better low-income housing without doing anything to redistribute income.

Some Comments on Swan's Paper

Let me offer a few opinionated quibbles about several foci of Swan's presentation. First, I do not believe that it is helpful to pretend that the FHLBB controls the SLA deposit rate. Its client SLAs - - acting through their agent, the Congress - - control this rate and will continue to do so as long as the SLA construction lobby retains its cohesiveness. On this issue, FHLBB and other agency bureaucrats (most of whom are embarrassed by the problems deposit-rate controls have visited on them) are more or less under their thumb. This will be all the more so once the higher "differential" ceiling on thrift-institution savings-deposit rates becomes a matter of law rather than custom.

Second, I believe that Swan's discussion of the advisability of eliminating liquidity requirements (e.g., by replacing them with mortgage reserve requirements) leaves out an absolutely essential element. In my view (a view long associated with William Dewald), liquidity requirements are essentially taxes. Such requirements collect 100 percent of the incremental income that would have been earned had SLAs been free to undertake an unconstrained portfolio allocation. Proposing to eliminate these requirements raises the same kind of efficiency issues and equity problems vis-à-vis competitors as the current proposal to replace generous tax deductions for bad-debt reserves with a tax credit on residential-mortgage income. (Curiously, this probably doomed but energetically resubmitted administration proposal is not discussed in either paper.[2])

Third, Swan's discussion of counter-cyclical variation of liquidity requirements would benefit if he were to sharpen his concept of differential "announcement effects." If the cyclical pattern of FHLBB portfolio restraints were openly changed, optimal SLA portfolio policies would change, too. Whether or not this is regarded as an "announcement effect," it is not to be taken lightly. I would guess that one could build a plausible model that would predict that, given full knowledge by client SLAs of a less oppressive FHLBB strategy, SLAs would shorten the maturities of the marketable securities held in their portfolios. More generally, the most important effect of openly relaxing an onerous restraint should be to raise immediately the capitalized value of ongoing SLA firms. If chartering, branching, and deposit-rate policies were not also changed in the process, this increased after-tax profitability should be competed away only very slowly. As an example of substantial SLA response to a relaxed regulatory restraint, let me cite the decline in the proportion of SLA assets in mortgages that has taken place since the Tax Reform Act of 1969 eased the correspondence between percentage mortgage holdings and the percentage of income that could be treated as a deductible transfer to bad-debt reserves. [3] This response makes me suspicious of simulations that assume that SLAs' marginal propensity to invest savings inflows in mortgages is constant in and out of the period over which a

_____

[2] A caustic evaluation of this proposal is contained in Kane (1974).

[3] See Kane and Valentini (1975).

given model was estimated. Consider also SLAs' recent interest in selling term Federal funds. I believe it is a mistake to omit variation in the applicable tax structure from models of SLA behavior. I am equally disdainful of structures that incorporate a rigid link between the amount of new mortgage credit and the flow of housing expenditure. As Meltzer (1974) shows, much switching goes on among alternative forms of household debt in response to variation in relative interest rates.

How Should We Cope with SLAs' Current Financial Weakness?

1. Could variable-rate mortgages be the answer?

I am surprised that many observers seem to think that the power to offer variable-rate mortgages (VRMs) would greatly strengthen the long-run viability of SLAs. My skepticism traces to my understanding of the intermediation that these firms perform. I have always supposed that "term premiums" in the term structure of interest rates explained the genesis of savings banks and SLAs. To be plausible, this explanation requires only that savings institutions be less risk-averse than their typical household customer. I find this a reasonable enough assumption. Households seem willing to pay a two-way premium to savings institutions:

    a.   to obtain fixed-interest mortgage loan contracts of long duration;

    b.   to have their accumulated savings fully insured against fluctuations in nominal value.

This presumption, that the preponderance of households are more risk-averse than SLAs explains the failure of VRMs to burgeon in states (such as Ohio) where state-chartered institutions are already empowered to offer them. In Ohio, state-chartered SLAs have offered discouragingly low rate differentials vis-à-vis fixed-rate mortgage options, seldom more than 25 basis points even at the bottom of the 1970-1974 interest-rate cycle. Ohio SLAs have not been willing to pay the price necessary to persuade a large percentage of household customers to accept the risks inherent in a VRM.

In California, experiments are taking place with respect to the effect of relaxing non-price terms of VRM contracts. In such an unusually mobile society, increasing the ease of prepaying and/or reassigning a VRM contract may offset the increased inflation risk accepted by the borrower. On the other hand, providing a line of credit against the appreciated value of owner equity may hedge an owner's inflation risk by guaranteeing him greater access to low-interest loans to finance his durable purchases when inflation increases.

Even if SLAs can be convinced to design differential contract terms on VRMs sufficiently attractive to overcome market resistance, we must also face up to the issue of political resistance. Homeowners have become used to the idea of having the inflation risk of mortgage loans borne by mortgage lenders, backed up by Congressional willingness to rescue these lenders if and when the gamble goes too badly. With the middle class overtaxed in most other respects, they are not apt to surrender this privilege easily. This combination of political and market resistance suggests that VRMs will have no more than a minor place in U.S. financial markets as long as a residential-housing investment financed by a fixed-rate mortgage represents the only real hedge against inflation open to representative low-income and middle-income households.

2. How can deposit-rate controls be jettisoned?

If I were to conduct a survey of conference participants, I am confident that a vast majority would express a desire to eliminate ceilings on interest rates on savings deposits by 1980 at least. Nevertheless, prospects that Congress will vote such an "early" phase-out seem miniscule. The labor, building, and SLA lobbies have convinced legislators that removing deposit-rate controls would precipitate a collapse of the housing industry, and possibly also a financial disaster.

It is not enough for economists to point out how inefficiently and unfairly these interest ceilings operate in practice. It is time for our profession to start researching the issue of how to manage an orderly transition from deposit-rate ceilings back to competitively determined savings rates. I can sketch only some scattered elements of a solution here.

It is important to realize that SLAs' deposit markets have been "protected" in various ways for over forty years: initially, by placing Federal ceilings only on savings rates that commercial-bank competitors could offer; then, since 1966, by a system of differential ceilings that allows SLAs to pay slightly higher savings rates than banks.

Currently, subsidies for SLAs (shared through "shifting" with mortgage borrowers, builders, and construction workers) are collected implicitly from small savers. If this redistribution of income were monitored and the pattern of costs and benefits convincingly made public, I think that the electorate would demand action. As a minimum, it would surely question whether the protection of this retarded "infant industry" should be continued indefinitely. Publicizing the economic realities of the current situation is, to my mind, the first step in any solution.

For SLAs, the transition problem is twofold. First, they must swallow the bitter medicine of capital losses that currently lie unrealized on their books, and then (assisted by explicit government subsidies)[4] they must deal honestly with the consequences of these losses. The tough legislative questions concern designing both a specific timetable for removing the ceilings, and a politically acceptable system of taxes and subsidies, by which to minimize resulting adjustment costs and spread them fairly across society.

One attractive way to manage the transition would be to legislate the irrevocable demise of deposit-rate ceilings by a date certain. This date should be set three-to-five years into the future: (1) to let the magic of discounting reduce substantially the present value of the costs to be borne during adjustment; and (2) to let bank and thrift institution managements design their own plans for coping with the new environment. Under these circumstances, recriminations and the need for further subsidies and ongoing government intervention would be greatly reduced. It is remarkable how easily the professional sports industry has coped with a spate of failing franchises and leagues. Still, for a number of reasons, I think it would be wise to set up a government receivership agency empowered both to wind up the financial affairs of any banks and SLAs that go bankrupt, and to operate failed institutions until the local need for their future services can be firmly established. Where such a need is established, it should prove possible to put the reorganized firm back in private hands, and to recover some of the agency's expenses in the process.

---

[4] One administratively attractive form of subsidy would be for the Federal government to insure at bargain prices the flow of SLA income from existing low-interest mortgages against further increases in market interest rates.

REFERENCES

1. Fair, R., and Jaffee, D., "An Empirical Study of the Hunt Commission Report Proposals for the Mortgage and Housing Markets," in Policies for a More Competitive Financial System, Boston Federal Reserve Bank Conference Series No. 8, (1972), 99-148.

2. Kane, E.J., "Costs and Benefits of the Proposed Tax Credit on Residential Mortgage Income," Boston Federal Reserve Bank Special Study, (August 1974), and Journal of Bank Research, 6,(1975), 88-99.

3. Kane, E.J., and Valentini, J.J., "Tax Avoidance by Savings and Loan Associations Before and After the Tax Reform Act of 1969," Journal of Monetary Economics, 1 (1975), 41-63.

4. Meltzer, A.H., "Credit Availability and Economic Decisions: Some Evidence from the Mortgage and Housing Markets," Journal of Finance, XXIX, No. 3, (June 1974), 763-778.

REGULATION Q AND THE CURRENT PROBLEMS
OF SAVINGS AND LOAN ASSOCIATIONS: A COMMENT

Robert H. Rasche
Michigan State University

Removal of Regulation Q ceilings seems hung up on the problem of what to do about the Savings and Loan Associations which are technically insolvent; that is, the value of their asset holdings at current market interest rates is less than the value of their liabilities.

A number of participants at the Carnegie-Rochester Conference of April 1975 argued that the associations were entitled to subsidization of some sort if the government were to remove the ceilings on the rates payable on liabilities of various financial institutions. The reasons for the subsidy were never made explicit, nor was it clear who should be the recipient of the subsidy: the creditors of the associations, or the incumbent management.

If the only argument for the subsidy is that it is socially desirable, or that there is a moral obligation to maintain a fixed exchange rate between thrift institution liabilities and government money (given that notice requirements are met), then it is not clear why the problem cannot be met by the existing deposit insurance provided by the FSLIC. Under present rules, creditors of insured SLAs are insured up to $40,000. I have been unable to obtain information on the size distribution of such accounts, but the Savings and Loan Fact Book indicates that the average size of accounts in insured SLAs in 1972 was $3,785.[1] This suggests that all but a few accounts at insured associations are fully covered. As long as the government maintains its insurance commitment, regardless of the size of the reserves of the FSLIC, it would appear that almost all the creditors would be reimbursed in the event of bankruptcies associated with the removal of the ceilings. It is not clear to me, therefore, why the subsidization cannot be handled implicitly under the existing institutions. (Note that the only subsidy involved would be the payments above and beyond the accumulated reserves of the FSLIC.)

Alternatively, the argument may be that it is desirable or necessary to subsidize the management of the existing institutions to maintain their existence in the financial structure of our economy. I can see only one rationale for such an argument, that the managers of these institutions were led into their present portfolios by some government commitment to maintain the existing interest rate ceilings indefinitely; therefore, if the government were to change the rules of the game ex post, any institution which gets into trouble is entitled to a sub-

---

[1] United States League of Savings Associations, 1974, p. 67.

sidy to assure its continuation. The problem with such a blanket sudsidy is that it rewards both the stupid and the naive among SLA managers. It should be added that allowing SLAs to fight it out on their own, after removing the Regulation Q ceilings, would not lead to the certain liquidation of the mortgage market and the collapse of the housing industry. If all creditors of the SLAs are reimbursed by the FSLIC, then initially they are going to have increased amounts of cash or bank deposits. Conceivably the demand for currency could be temporarily increased by the occurrence of SLA bankruptcies, but the Federal Reserve Board is supposed to be capable of handling just such problems. Much, if not all, of the funds from the redeemed accounts should flow back into the financing of investment activity, including home mortgages.

It is clearly desirable to achieve the transition from the current Regulation Q regime to an unconstrained one with a minimum of disruption. One way of doing this is to announce that, as of some future date, there will no longer be any constraints on the interest rates payable on liabilities.

This offers at least two ways out of the present situation. First, implausible as it may sound, market interest rates, at the future date specified, could be so low that technical insolvency is no longer a problem; Regulation Q type ceilings might not be effective constraints and could be eliminated without causing any difficulties. Second, given a sufficiently long transition period during which the ceilings were maintained, SLAs could adjust their portfolios, for example, by increasing the spread between the constrained rates paid on their deposits and those charged on their assets. How long a transition period would be necessary to allow the SLAs to anticipate the new regime and adjust to it? This depends on the speed with which asset portfolios turn over. Information on this point is relatively scarce, but two items are available. First, the FHA has collected data on the termination experience of Section 203-insured mortgages from 1935 through 1970.[2] From these, they have computed survivorship tables and life expectancies of mortgages. For all maturities, their sample indicates a life expectancy of approximately 11 and a half years. There is some suggestion in these data that the life expectancy increases with original maturity, but the interpretation of these data may be clouded by the tendency for increasing initial maturities over time. Inflows of funds from mortgage portfolios of insured savings and loan associations are a second source of data. During 1971-73, such inflows as a percentage of average portfolio value fluctuated between 14.1 and 15.8 percent.[3] This suggests an average life expectancy of mortgages, measured as the reciprocal of this rate of inflow, of about seven years. These numbers are probably more representative of the rate of portfolio turnover, nor

[2] **1972 HUD Statistical Yearbook**, Tables 264 and 265.

[3] United States League of Savings Associations, 1974, p. 88.

does it surprise me that FHA mortgages might turn over more slowly than the average portfolio of all SLAs. If the entire portfolio can be expected to turn over on average in seven years, then it would seem that a five-year announcement period would provide considerable flexibility for SLAs to prepare for the new world.

If direct subsidization of SLAs, as contrasted with subsidization of their creditors, is still regarded as desirable, then it would be appropriate to ask that the SLAs report all mortgages remaining on their books as of the date of repeal of Regulation Q, which were held over from prior to the announcement date. The market value of these assets could be computed using the interest rates prevailing at the time of the repeal, and to the extent that the market value is less than the face value, the associations might be considered eligible for a one-shot subsidy. I can see no reason why they should be allowed to collect a subsidy on the basis of the market value of mortgages which they have assumed during the transition period, as they were forewarned of the impending change in the rules at the time they made those portfolio decisions. Assume that approximately 70 percent of mortgages currently on the books of SLAs turn over during a five-year transition period. The numbers which were casually cited at the Carnegie-Rochester Conference suggest that the magnitude of the technical insolvency problem is of the order of $25 billion. If mortgages turn over at the assumed rate, we could expect this to be reduced to $7.5 billion in five years, assuming no change in market interest rates from recent levels over that five-year horizon. Three- to five-year government security rates have been averaging 7 percent; discounting the $7.5 billion to the present using this rate gives a present value of the required subsidy of $5.35 billion.

An alternative to subsidizing associations directly would be to reimburse the creditors of any associations which went bankrupt under the new regime from the existing insurance programs. FSLIC reserves in 1973 amounted to $3.45 billion.[4] The present value of a subsidy to creditors would be at most of the order of $2 billion.

Either $2 billion or $5.5 billion seem small potential losses in order to rid ourselves once and for all of the interest rate ceiling problem.

---

[4] United States League of Savings Associations, 1974, p. 121. The 1975 value of these reserves, accumulated with 7 percent interest, is $3.95 billion.

REFERENCES

1. U.S. League of Savings Associations. Savings and Loan Fact Book. Chicago, Ill.: USLSA, 1974.

2. U.S. Department of Housing and Urban Development. Statistical Yearbook. Washington, D.C.: U.S. Government Printing Office, 1972.

INFLATION - - ALTERNATIVE EXPLANATIONS AND POLICIES: TESTS ON DATA DRAWN FROM SIX COUNTRIES

David Laidler*

University of Western Ontario

I. INTRODUCTION

Inflation has been the most widely discussed economic problem of the last decade, a problem for all western countries to a greater or lesser extent. There has been a diversity of opinion on its causes and its cures. Different views on causation inevitably lead to different policy prescriptions and, particularly in the last three years, policies toward inflation have taken divergent paths. Divergent policies have not been in force long enough for it to be possible to draw any firm conclusions about their relative long-run effectiveness, though increasingly it appears that countries which have adopted the traditional policies of monetary stringency are having the most success in dealing with inflation. Those countries whose policy makers have relied on new tools specially devised for what they saw as a new type of inflation, and perhaps a type unique to their own countries, seem to have had less success.

The purpose of this paper is to investigate the opposing views on inflation underlying these policies to see whether empirical evidence can distinguish among them. I begin with an account of these views, here called sociological, monetarist, and eclectic, and derive from them certain verifiable predictions which I then subject to tests against data from a number of countries. Though the results are not definitive, they strongly support a monetarist interpretation of inflation, particularly when it is confronted with a sociological approach. The eclectic who maintains that different factors are, nevertheless, of different significance in different economies will find some limited support for his views in the results presented below; but, he will also find that, for each economy studied, his eclecticism will have to be built on a solid foundation of monetarist theory.

The evidence in favor of a basically monetarist interpretation of the data for the countries studied is strong, and there exists evidence from other work that points in the same direction. [1] The final section of this paper discusses the implications of monetarist analysis for policy, both as it has been conducted in the past

* I am grateful to Michele Fratianni, Pieter Korteweg, Allan Meltzer, and George Zis for helpful comments on an earlier version of this paper, and to Geoffrey Hilliard and Zannis Res for research assistance.

[1] See, for example, papers by Brunner (1974); Brunner, et. al. (1973); Laidler (1973), (1974); Korteweg (1974); Spinelli (forthcoming); Parkin, Sumner and Ward (1976).

and as it might be conducted in the future. In it, I examine, first, the likely out-come of recent policy actions; and second, the problems that must arise in the longer run if monetarist analysis of the problem of inflation is indeed broadly accurate.

II. ALTERNATIVE EXPLANATIONS OF INFLATION

Any classification of views on the causes of inflation is, to some extent, arbitrary; but, if empirical evidence is to be used in a systematic fashion to dis-tinguish between those views that are compatible with experience and those that are not, some such taxonomy must be attempted. I divide explanations of infla-tion into three broad groupings: sociological; monetarist; and eclectic. All three schools of thought attempt to provide an explanation of the time path of the general price level in recent years.[2]   As almost every Western country has exper-ienced an acceleration of its inflation rate since about 1966, two questions arise. Why have prices begun to rise more rapidly? Why has this occurred more or less simultaneously in a number of countries? The sociological view of the infla-tionary process ascribes these events to rising and, as between different groups, inconsistent expectations about real living standards. Such expectations generate social unrest and, in particular, increasingly "militant" attitudes on the part of labor. Hence, they produce upward pressure on money wages. Employers, both in the private and public sector, have become increasingly unable, or unwilling, to resist this pressure. This reluctance to resist wage demands is, in turn, attribut-ed to the growing concentration and integration of industry, leading to a marked increase in the power of the strike weapon; this power is further compounded by the commitment of governments to full employment policies. The international character of inflation is explained by "demonstration effects," modern communi-cations having made the international transmission of ideas and news increasingly efficient. Upward pressure on money wages leads to upward pressure on prices.

---

[2]   Brunner's paper (1974), available in England only after this one was underway, provides a similar, but not identical, taxonomy. He talks of Price Theoretic, Institutionalist, and Eclectic approaches to the problem of inflation. His use of the term "institutionalist" corresponds quite closely to my use of "sociological." Within his price theoretic classification, Brunner distinguishes between those economists who regard the first impulse to rising prices arising from an exogenous increase in the quantity of money - - monetarists - - and those who, following the Keynes-Wicksell tradition, see the first impulse coming from an autonomous increase in real expenditure, brought about by fiscal expansion or by a rise in the Wicksellian natural rate of interest. The Wicksellian mechanism still needs an expanding money supply to support continuing inflation, and, if the in-crease in autonomous expenditure originates with the government, then monetary expansion may be how the government's budget constraint is met. Thus, I am content to class both groups under the "monetarist" label. The differences between them seem to me to reflect no fundamental differences of opinion about the way in which the economic system works. As Brunner says, both explanations are well grounded in price theory, in sharp contrast to the institutionalist and certain eclectic explanations of inflation. The differences in emphasis between Brunner and myself implicit here largely reflect differences in emphasis in the debate about inflation in the United States and in Britain. American economists, classifying themselves as "Keynesians," base their analysis on orthodox price theory, while most British "Keynesians" in denying any importance to the quantity of money, either as an active cause of inflation or as an important permissive factor in the process, align themselves with adherents of a sociological view of inflation. In the context of the British debate, price theoretic explanations of inflation are usually classed as monetarist.

Variations in the aggregate demand for goods, services, and hence for labor are seen as having no effect on the rate of inflation (at least within the ranges of those variables that it is politically possible to maintain). In short, inflation is determined outside the market mechanism. Wages and prices are to be viewed as exogenous variables in any economic analysis of the aggregate economy. Thus, inflation is best combatted by resort to one form or another of direct controls on wages and prices. [3]

The monetarist view stands in sharp contrast to the sociological explanation. It begins with the elementary, but often overlooked, fact that the general price level is the inverse of the price of money relative to goods; thus, the basis of the monetarist explanation of inflation is supply and demand analysis. This explanation of inflation has a long history, but modern monetarist analysis has advanced beyond the simple partial equilibrium approach to price level determination implicit in, for example, Pigou's classic (1917) paper. The behavior of the supply and demand for money is a vital part but, nevertheless, only a part of the analysis, for the following reasons.

It is now recognized that the behavior of arguments in the demand for money function other than the price level, for example real income or wealth and nominal interest rates, is unlikely to be always and completely independent of the supply of money's time path; that money is most unlikely to be neutral in the long run, let alone the short run. [4] Although the monetarist theory looks to variations in the rate of monetary expansion to explain variations in the inflation rate, it nevertheless postulates an indirect and potentially extended transmission mechanism as an integral part of the inflationary process. This mechanism has two steps, the first between monetary changes and aggregate demand, and the second between aggregate demand and the inflation rate. It is, moreover, recognized that variations in the inflation rate feed back and influence aggregate demand so that the linkages between the two stages in the transmission process are complicated and by no means unidirectional. The upshot is that the monetarist approach leads to the conclusion that monetary expansion rates and inflation rates will be only loosely correlated (except in long-run averages of data), even though monetary expansion is the prime, or even the sole, cause of inflation.

---

[3] I base this account of the sociological view of inflation on a number of sources. The clearest account of this view, that the behavior of wages as a sociological matter is not involved with market forces but with the working out of competing views on the fairness of the wage structure, is to be found in Hicks (1974, Ch. 3), in which he refers to ideas first propounded in his Theory of Wages (1932). A leading proponent of the view that the strike weapon has become increasingly more powerful is Phelps-Brown, for example (1971). Hicks looks to commodity price behavior to explain international aspects of inflation, but Phelps-Brown and several contributors, for example Marris, to the 1971 Dauphine conference (Claassen and Salin, 1973), advance the demonstration-effect hypothesis to explain the international transmission of inflation. Note also that certain commentators, notably Harrod (1972) and Wiles (1973), view inflation as only one of several symptoms of social breakdown appearing on a worldwide scale.

[4] The need to develop a monetary explanation of inflation in terms of a general, as opposed to partial, equilibrium or disequilibrium model is discussed at length in Laidler and Parkin (1975).

That the quantity of money influences aggregate demand is by now widely recognized, but the nature of the link between aggregate demand and inflation is more open to dispute. [5] The monetarist, in common with many economists who would resist the label, postulates the existence of an "expectations augmented Phillips curve" which makes the current rate of price inflation dependent on the expected rate of price inflation - - usually but not necessarily with a unit coefficient - - and on some measure of excess demand. Thus, in sharp contrast to the sociologist, the monetarist views inflation in terms of traditional economic forces.

The monetarist approach to the international character of inflation is firmly grounded in traditional economics and is differentiated from other economic explanations of inflation in a way that adherence to the expectations augmented Phillips curve is not. It notes that, until 1971, the major countries of the world were linked to one another by fixed exchange rates between more or less convertible currencies; thus, the "economy" in which the supply and demand for money might be expected to interact to determine the price level is the world economy, and not that of any individual nation state. The problem in the monetarist explanation of international inflation is not why inflation rates in different countries have moved roughly in harmony with one another, but why the harmony has been only imperfect. [6] It is the differences among national inflation rates that a monetarist must explain, while the sociologist must explain the similarities.

Just as the sociological approach implies particular policies, so does the monetarist view. If inflation is to be controlled in one national economy, then a policy of monetary stringency must be adopted in combination with one of exchange rate flexibility.

Though this account of the monetarist position leaves some loose ends I will now turn to the so-called "eclectic" explanation of inflation. This approach is based on the plausible proposition that anything as complex as inflation must have complex causes; that there is no reason to suppose that, as a particular inflationary episode progresses, each cause will be of equal importance in explaining the behavior of prices at any moment. Thus, the principal impulse to inflation in one country in a particular year may be monetary expansion, while in the next year it may be the militancy of trade unions, and so on.

---

[5] Whether monetary expansion causes increases in nominal aggregate demand, or is merely necessary for increases coming from other sources to have persistent effects thereon is the point at issue between what Brunner calls the monetarist and the Keynes-Wicksellian views. Since Brunner wrote, the focus of the debate over money and inflation seems to have shifted to questions about the aggregate demand-inflation rate linkage. Hicks (1974, 1975), for example, seems to agree that exogenous monetary contraction would contract the money value of aggregate demand. However, unlike the monetarists, he would expect the contraction to fall heavily on income and employment and have little effect on the inflation rate. Monetarists would expect unemployment increases to lead to a slowdown in the inflation rate.

[6] Thus, an ingredient essential to the monetarist's explanation of inflation in the international economy is the so-called monetary theory of the balance of payments. The most accessible account of the application of this doctrine to the problem of inflation is to be found in Harry Johnson's 1971 De Vries lectures (1972).

Nor, according to an eclectic, is there any reason to suppose that the causes of inflation at any time should exert equal pressure in different countries. In short, the very nature of the eclectic theory precludes the possibility of providing any brief and accurate summary of its salient characteristics. The same may be said of the policy approach implicit in this view. Sole reliance on any one policy tool is unlikely to be successful. What is required is a mixture of policies to deal with the complex mixture of causes underlying the inflationary process.

How are these different views of the causes of the recent inflation to be evaluated? It should be said first that the evidence of the inflation since 1966 can be only of the most limited use in testing these theories. The reason for this is straightforward. If an explanation of any set of facts is made in knowledge of those facts, then its degree of compatibility with those facts is a test of the logical capacity of those who constructed the explanation but not of the explanation's validity. I will illustrate from another area--to be taken seriously, any theory of the consumption function must explain the well-known discrepancy between time series and cross section data on the marginal propensity to consume, but its merits as a theory of the consumption function must be judged by its ability to explain other phenomena that were not taken into account in its construction. In the same way, if an explanation of inflation is constructed explicitly on recent evidence, then that same evidence cannot be used to test it.

This methodological point leads into difficulties with some aspects of both the "sociological" and "eclectic" approaches. There is a tendency among their proponents to claim that since the late 1960s there has been a "new inflation" unlike any experienced in the past. But, this means that data drawn from earlier periods cannot be used to test these views. If there has been a "new inflation," for example since 1966, then incompatibility of evidence drawn from before that year with a theory advanced to explain the data generated since may even be used as evidence in favor of the "newness" of recent experience. [7] The same may be said of using data from different countries to confront an hypothesis about inflation. If a theory asserts that the recent experience of any country is unique to that country, then explanations of that experience cannot be tested with data from other countries.

In short, there is among the proponents of the sociological view of inflation a proclivity towards a non-scientific approach to social questions. Hence, it is difficult to submit their views to scientific processes of assessment, or at least to do so in a way that they are likely to find acceptable. When two explanations of events are offered, and it is impossible to discriminate between them on the basis of observing those events, then the explanation that is more capable of dealing

---

[7] Jones' (1972) The New Inflation is an example of that body of literature proclaiming the uniqueness of recent experience. Hicks (1974), (1975) also seems to be a proponent of this view.

with other observations is usually judged superior on the grounds of greater generality. The "new inflation" theories may be assessed by this criterion. They are not supposed to be capable of treating data from earlier periods - - for example, the 1950s and early 1960s; however, monetarists claim to provide a general theory of the behavior of the price level. If a monetarist explanation deals as well with more recent observations as with earlier ones, then it is a better explanation of recent events. The principle that one should abandon a theory and adopt a special explanation of a set of observations only if the theory cannot deal with them underlies my treatment of "new inflation" theories in this paper. However, I recognize that some of their proponents will find this unacceptable.

A related methodological problem arises with regard to certain aspects of the "eclectic" hypothesis. Its proponents argue that the price level is influenced by several exogenous variables, but that the amount of influence accorded any particular exogenous variable differs at various times and places. There could be two reasons for this: first, because the structure of the relationships between the exogenous variables and the price level is unstable; or because, though the structure remains stable, the amount of variation in the relevant exogenous variables differs from time to time and from place to place. If the second is true, then there is no problem in testing an "eclectic" view of inflation - - though it might be difficult to distinguish it from some forms of monetarist theory; I argue that a monetarist view by no means requires that the quantity of money be the sole variable in an equation determining the behavior of the price level. [8] However, if there is no stable structure determining the behavior of the price level, then its behavior cannot be predicted, but merely described ex post. There is no way of submitting such a view to test, unless evidence that there exists a stable structure explaining the behavior of the inflation rate is regarded as refuting that view.

This discussion has necessarily been rather general; there follows a more specific account of the hypotheses at issue in the empirical work described in this paper. This work has been confined to explaining national price inflation rates. The choice of this dependent variable might seem so obvious as hardly to need discussion, but there are two alternatives which might have been chosen. First, much of the empirical work on inflation conducted in the postwar years has treated the rate of money wage inflation on the (usually implicit) assumption that, if wage inflation is explained, then so is price inflation. This view stems from orthodox post-Keynesian macroeconomics, in which the price level is determined by the behavior of an exogenously given money wage rate; it presupposes a particular view of the inflationary process that ought to be tested. Moreover, concern about inflation as a policy problem arises because of its

---

[8] Once again, the 1971 Dauphine conference provides a useful source of opinion. Lindbeck's contribution seems to me to place him in the category of "scientific eclectic" (see Claassen and Salin, 1972).

disruptive social effects. These hinge upon the income and wealth redistribution and the damage to the market economy as a form of social organization that result from fluctuations in the value of money. This is not to say that the behavior of money wages is an uninteresting problem, or that their behavior is unrelated to price level behavior, but it is to argue that it is the price level whose behavior ought to be the focus of inflation theory.

The second alternative to a national price level variable is some measure of the price level prevailing in the world economy. The monetarist view of inflation leads to the conclusion that the behavior of such a variable is worth explaining for its own sake. However, I am involved in comparing different views of inflation. Sociologists and eclectics, concerned with the behavior of national price levels, would probably regard a world price level as no more than an average of price levels in individual national economies, and not, as would a monetarist, a variable interesting in its own right. Thus, the comparison of the monetarist view with these alternatives must be made in terms of its capacity to explain the behavior of national price levels. Moreover, to the extent that inflation is a political problem for national governments, the ability to explain national inflation rates is of considerable practical importance.

The behavior of the national price level is then the variable to be explained. What factors do the competing approaches suggest ought to be associated with variations in it? And what other associations between variables do they suggest ought also to be observed? Equally important, what variables do they say ought not to be associated with one another? Let me consider the sociological approach first. It views inflation as the outcome of social unrest stemming from competition over shares in real income. It frequently focuses on the power of the strike to generate increases in money wages, which in turn contribute to price increases. Moreover, real income aspirations are transmitted across national boundaries by demonstration effects, as are the militant attitudes underlying the use of the strike weapon. Within politically possible ranges, variations in the level of excess demand, and hence in the unemployment rate, have no effect on inflation.

What should the researcher expect to observe? If the strike weapon has become more powerful, should it be expected to be used more and to produce more rapid inflation, or to be used less? It takes two sides to make a labor dispute. If strike activity has become more damaging, then, though unions may be more willing to threaten a strike, employers may be more willing to concede wage claims before a strike materializes. Several writers have postulated that strike activity should be positively associated with inflation; none has predicted that an inverse relationship ought to hold.[9] Thus, I regard a positive relationship be-

---

[9] The usefulness of strike activity as a measure of trade union "militancy" is discussed at length by Purdy and Zis (1974). They conclude that, in the absence of a properly articulated theory of the behavior of trade unions, which clarifies what it is unions are attempting to maximize, and subject to what constraints, it will be impossible to assess the significance of strike activity for the wage bargaining process. Nevertheless, both Taylor (1975) and Godfrey (1971) have used strike activity as a positive measure of union militancy.

tween inflation and strike activity as consistent with the sociological view of inflation. Increasing strike activity is evidence of increasing social conflict, and a positive relationship between inflation and strike activity can also be rationalized in these broader terms. [10]

As to demonstration effects across national boundaries, there is also some difficulty in anticipating what to observe, particularly if such activity is evidence of social unrest. I suggest that if demonstration effects are important, then there should be a positive correlation between strike activity in different countries. Such an association ought to be closer for countries between which communications are easy, by virtue of free labor mobility or perhaps even a common language, than between more widely separated countries. One thing that ought not to be observed, if the sociological view provides a complete explanation of inflation, is any association between an excess demand measure and the rate of inflation, particularly since the mid-1960s when the "new inflation" was supposed to have begun. [11]

The monetarist hypothesis has been widely studied from an empirical point of view. It is increasingly accepted that the inability to find a "stable" demand for money function would constitute a refutation of this position. However, the existence of such a relationship for a wide variety of countries and time periods is one of the best documented facts in the literature. Moreover, as I noted earlier, the monetarist view, when applied to open economies, suggests that the inflation rate is determined worldwide, rather than country by country. A necessary condition for the monetarist position to be true on this point is the existence of a stable demand for money function at the level of the worldwide aggregate economy. This is another proposition that has been confronted with data and survived the test. [12] I conclude that, though relevant to the monetarist position, it is hardly worthwhile to test again the demand for money function in this paper.

It is my view that, when the inflation rate in a particular economy is the variable to be explained, the monetarist position necessitates testing hypotheses about the transmission of inflation from the world economy to the particular economy, as well as testing hypotheses about the causation of inflation worldwide. It also implies the formulation and testing of explanations of the deviation of national inflation rates from the worldwide trend. It is on the transmission process that I shall concentrate, and on the causes of deviations of the national

---

[10] I am indebted to Zis for drawing my attention to this alternative interpretation of the significance of strike activity for the sociological explanation of inflation.

[11] I advance these hypotheses somewhat tentatively. I am open to the criticism that, as a monetarist, I am likely to propose particularly difficult and perhaps unfair tests of an opposing point of view. The only defence against such criticism is to say that, if proponents of the sociological view of inflation would tell us what evidence might undermine their theories, it would not be necessary for their opponents to do so.

[12] See Gray, Ward and Zis (1976).

from the world inflation rate. [13] Others are working on the generation of the inflation rate in terms of world aggregate data, [14] a problem I regard as vital to the testing of the monetarist position.

Within a monetarist framework, there are at least two alternative theories of the transmission of inflationary impulses between economies. [15] The first of these is the traditional price specie flow mechanism whereby domestically generated monetary expansion in one country, at a rate faster than necessary to maintain its inflation rate consistent with those obtaining abroad, leads to a balance of payments deficit; a corresponding surplus elsewhere; and hence faster monetary expansion elsewhere. In other economies, the acceleration in monetary expansion through the balance of payments leads to excess demand and, ultimately, to a higher inflation rate. In the end, each country winds up with a higher inflation rate, and the country that initially experienced an increase in its rate of monetary expansion from domestic sources finds itself with a balance of payments deficit persisting as long as the higher domestic credit expansion rate persists. This view specifies monetary flows between countries as an active force in transmitting inflationary impulses. It treats the proximate cause of changes in the inflation rate in one country as changes in domestic excess demand brought about by changes in the rate of monetary expansion, regardless of whether the source of the variations in monetary expansion is domestic or foreign.

An alternative view may be described as the "price transfer mechanism." The distinguishing characteristic of this view is that it specifies flows of reserves between countries as playing an accommodating, rather than a causative, role in the transmission of inflationary impulses. This theory is grounded, loosely (as is any macro hypothesis in the current state of knowledge), in the "new microeconomic" theories of price setting behavior. It starts from the proposition that an important determinant of the price setting behavior of an individual firm is its expectations of the pricing behavior of like firms. A firm in an open economy whose output can be arbitraged across national boundaries sets prices for markets that are not only domestic but are potentially worldwide. Moreover, there is

---

[13] There is a potential overlap between monetarist and eclectic theories on this point. An economist seeking to explain the behavior of the inflation rate in one economy might take the inflation rate of the world economy as a given and try to explain, with a variety of special domestic factors, the behavior of domestic prices relative to that trend. The so-called Nordic model of inflation does this, and, as Brunner (1974) notes, is not a theory of the behavior of the general price level, but rather a theory of the behavior of relative prices. Brunner assigns this approach to inflation theory to the eclectic camp. I prefer to regard it as potentially one component of a monetarist theory of inflation concerning the transmission of inflation to one part of the world economy, rather than its generation.

[14] In work in progress, Gray and Parkin attempt to combine a world aggregate demand for money function, a world aggregate supply of money function, and world aggregate price and wage equations into a macro model of the world economy. This will be a more elaborate version of the framework I have constructed and used in analyzing the United States economy (see Laidler, 1973, 1974). Their world consists of ten countries.

[15] These two transmission mechanisms are discussed in more detail in Laidler and Nobay (1975).

no reason to suppose that all firms producing closely related products for sale on a worldwide basis will be located in the same country. Thus, expectations about other firms' pricing behavior feeding into the pricing decision of the individual firm are thought of as being based on observations made at the level of the world market and not of the domestic market.

In aggregate, the behavior of the overall price level in an open economy will be heavily influenced by expectations formed in this way. This influence may be captured by making the domestic inflation rate depend proximately on an "expected inflation rate," which is to be considered an average of expected rates of change of the money prices of all those individual goods and services that make up domestic income. Many of these individual expectations are in turn to be considered as being based on observations of world markets. Excess demand for goods also influences the domestic inflation rate according to this theory, but it is a variable that produces deviations from a trend dominated by expectations of the behavior of a worldwide price level. [16]

In terms of this price-transfer mechanism for inflationary impulses, a domestically generated increase in the rate of monetary expansion in one economy might indeed produce excess demand there, an acceleration in the domestic inflation rate, to say nothing of an increase in the balance of payments deficit. There is nothing here to distinguish the price-transfer and price-specie flow mechanisms. However, the way in which the rest of the world imports the inflation differs between the two approaches. The price-transfer approach has firms in other countries revising upwards their pricing plans because they observe that inflation is accelerating elsewhere, independently of the current state of domestic excess demand for their output. The balance of payments surplus of those countries importing inflation generates an increase in their rate of monetary expansion, but this merely validates the behavior of their price level, and in no sense causes it to occur. [17] As I shall demonstrate, potentially important policy issues hinge on this point. Moreover, there already exists a study which seeks to distinguish between these two views of the transmission process. The evidence of that study is overwhelmingly in favor of the "price-transfer mechanism," showing the inflation rate in the rest of the world playing an important role as a

---

[16] Note that this expected inflation rate is conceptually different from the expected inflation rate that figures prominently as an argument in the aggregate demand for money function in inflationary situations. The latter is, in principle, an average of the expectations formed by individual agents about the behavior of the general price level. The expected inflation rate that is relevant for wage and price setting is, I argue, an average of individual agents' expectations about the behavior of the individual money prices of particular goods and services. Note also that I am referring to domestic excess demand as a determinant of domestic inflation. As Fratianni and Korteweg comment (this volume), there is no logical reason why worldwide excess demand cannot play a role here as well.

[17] In a small, open, fixed-exchange rate economy, a permissive role for the money supply is potentially an integral part of monetarist analysis. Thus, the distinction between the monetarist and the Keynes-Wicksell approach disappears. It is still possible, however, to draw a distinction between the two approaches at the level of the world economy.

proximate determinant of the domestic inflation rate in 19 countries. [18]

The price-transfer mechanism is an adaptation of the "expectations augmented Phillips curve" to the explanation of pricing behavior in an open economy. The key modification to the usual analysis is the hypothesis that inflationary expectations are influenced by both domestic and worldwide inflationary experience. Though the expectations augmented Phillips curve has nothing to say about the role of money in influencing aggregate demand, and though there are many who would subscribe to it without wishing thereby to classify themselves as "monetarists," it has, nevertheless, come to acquire a central position in the monetarist approach to the theory of inflation. The evidence cited here is thus consistent with a monetarist explanation of inflation. However, long before the term "monetarist" was used in the context of the theory of inflation, much empirical work on the problem stressed the influence of import prices on domestic prices in an open economy. In the context of the old "demand-pull/cost-push" dichotomy, import price inflation was looked upon as a "cost-push" factor in the generation of inflation. [19] It is inconceivable that, in a period of worldwide inflation, there should not be a reasonably close correlation between a measure of the "world price level," on the one hand, and a price index of a particular country's imports on the other. This consideration immediately raises the possibility that the results reported above merely reflect the influence of import prices on domestic inflation. Since the work which generated them also found that domestic excess demand usually has a significant influence on the inflation rate, it could be interpreted as showing that both demand-pull and cost-push factors are important in determining inflation, and that import prices are a significant cost-push variable. This suggests that it is worthwhile to try to distinguish between world prices in general, and import prices in particular, as determinants of the domestic inflation rate. Though it would be possible to construct a model (which some might term "monetarist") in which import prices played a special role in the international transmission of inflation, such a model would be further from the spirit of contemporary monetarist analysis than one which emphasizes the importance of inflationary expectations. The discovery that im-

---

[18] See Cross and Laidler (1976).

[19] See Dicks-Mireaux (1961) for an example of an empirical study that stresses the effect of import prices in generating "cost-push" inflation in Britain. Note that Brunner (1974) treats import prices, along with the level of world trade, as one of the principal routes whereby inflation is transmitted between economies. Interestingly, he concludes that import price rises do not seem to account for large domestic price level rises, and suggests that one look to the role of expectations to sustain the view that the behavior of world prices dominates the behavior of domestic prices.

port prices had a special role to play would tend to tip the debate in favor of an "eclectic" view of inflation, albeit one still grounded in economics as opposed to sociology. Hence, this question is investigated in the empirical work which follows as a means of distinguishing between the monetarist and eclectic positions.

It has already been pointed out that the very nature of the eclectic viewpoint can prevent any sharply defined test of its truth or falsity, particularly when it is grounded on the proposition that the structure of the economy is inherently unstable and changeable. However, it has been noted that one aspect of eclecticism simply says that the determinants of inflation are multiple, and that, stable though the structure of the economic system may be, different causes are of different importance at different times and places. This is a proposition that can be investigated; certain of the following exercises investigate the relative importance of different variables as proximate determinants of the inflation rate.

One matter remains before I turn to reporting substantive results and that is the choice of countries to be studied. They are Britain, Italy, the Federal Republic of Germany, Japan, Switzerland, and the United States. The reasons for choosing this group of countries follow. The first five are relatively open, medium-sized economies for which, if the monetarist view of inflation is correct, there ought to be a common model of the generation of price-level changes. On the other hand, an eclectic view of inflation stresses the possibility that different variables have different degrees of importance at different times and places. If there is justification for this view, then there ought to be important differences, at least quantitative, and perhaps qualitative, among the models explaining the inflationary experiences of these countries. The five countries have been selected to enhance the chances of this occurring, for there are many differences among them.

To begin with, Germany and Switzerland have recently experienced inflation rates somewhat lower than the other three. Italy has long been regarded as having one of the more militant labor forces in the industrialized world; more recently, the British labor force has acquired a similar reputation.[20] Germany, Switzerland, and Japan, on the other hand, would usually be considered to have much more disciplined labor forces. As founder members of the EEC, Germany and Italy have in recent years shared many economic institutions, and in particular participate in a common labor market. If demonstration effects are important in the international transmission of inflation, one would expect them to be particularly strong between these two countries. The geographic and linguistic proximity of Switzerland to both of them should also lead to strong demonstra-

---

[20] This consideration suggested that France ought also to be analyzed. However, the absence of strike activity data for 1968, the year when "militancy" was at its peak in France, precluded its inclusion.

tion effects among them. Though geographically close to continental Europe, Britain remained outside the EEC during the period of this study, while Japan is relatively separated from these four countries by culture, language, and geography. If there are sociological demonstration effects between countries, one would, therefore, expect them to be relatively weak as between Japan and the others.

The United States is not a small- or even medium-sized economy, nor is it very open. It is included in this study for three reasons. First, it has had relatively close ties with both Japan and Europe since World War II, and hence might conceivably have influenced both by way of demonstration effects. Second, a monetary explanation of inflation would suggest that internal and external factors ought to have different weights in determining the U.S. inflation rate as compared with that of the other four countries. The U.S. data hence provide an additional test of the monetarist explanation. Finally, the United States' economy has been more closely studied than any other; if the techniques used in this study generate results for the United States markedly out of line with those from other studies, then the validity of the results achieved for the other countries in the study should be questioned. Hence, the United States provides some check on the overall validity of the results to be generated for the other countries.

III. EMPIRICAL EVIDENCE

I will now discuss some tests of the alternative views of inflation outlined above. First, I will try the sociological and monetarist views separately to see how far they go in explaining the data from the countries selected. With respect to the monetarist position, I will also attempt to discriminate between import prices and expected world prices as determinants of the domestic inflation rate, and thus to produce results relevant to an "eclectic" view of inflation. Last, I will discuss the relative performances of the first two views, and consider the extent to which they might contribute to an "eclectic" explanation of inflation.

I consider first the "sociological" approach. As I have formulated it, it would appear to make three basic predictions. First, there should be observable systematic relationships between some measure of strike activity, on the one hand, and the domestic price inflation rate, on the other. Second, there should be no systematic relationship between an excess demand measure and inflation, once the influence of strike activity is allowed for. Third, if the inter-country transmission mechanism of inflation involves a demonstration effect, there should be a correlation between countries in the level of strike activity, particularly between those countries that are close to each other, either geographically or culturally.

A measure of strike activity is needed in order to test these hypotheses. Three such measures are available: the number of strikes in any year; the number of workers involved in strikes in any year; and the number of man-days lost in strikes in any year. As Ward and Zis (1974) have shown, these three measures are correlated, but not too closely. I eliminate one of them, namely the number of disputes, because data on it are not available for Germany, narrowing the choice to the number of workers involved in disputes and the number of man-days lost. As it is reasonable to suggest that the intensity of any particular dispute, and its social importance, will be reflected both in the number of people involved and in its duration, I have decided to use the latter measure in the work that follows. The weight that the reader may attribute to the results will depend on how appropriate he considers this choice.

The second variable required is an excess demand proxy. As in earlier work, I have used the log of the ratio of actual real income to trend real income as the variable here. It is, as the reader will recognize, a ratio measure of what is often referred to as the "GNP gap." This variable has performed well in other studies, and there is no reason to suppose a priori that it will not do the same in this one. Data for these two variables, and for national inflation rates, are available on an annual basis for the period 1954-73. [21] There are relatively few observations here for any one country; but, since one test it might be appropriate to conduct on any fitted relationship is to see how well it forecasts ahead of the sample of data to which it is fitted, I have used the years 1954-70 in estimating the equations below.

Where ΔP is the price inflation rate, y is the excess demand proxy, and S is the number of man days lost in disputes, the first equation fitted to data from the six countries is of the form:

(1) $$\Delta P = a_0 + a_1 y_{-1} + a_2 S_{-1} .$$

I have permitted an intercept to appear in this relationship. Because I have suppressed the intercept in other studies, and will do so below in other equations, it is worth explaining why this is not done here. The decision stems from the belief that, even if social conflict were the sole source of inflation, and even if variations in strike activity were a perfect proxy for variations in the intensity of conflict, a zero inflation rate would, nevertheless, be associated with some positive level of strike activity. Thus, if anything, one would expect the intercept of the above relationship to be negative.

---

[21] Quarterly data are also available for the series used here. However, in this paper my ultimate concern is to compare hypotheses, and the type of data used overall must be governed by what may be termed the "least available" series. The world inflation rate variable used below is readily available only on an annual basis; that is the overriding reason for using annual data in this study.

Finally, note that this equation posits a one-year time lag between excess demand and strike activity, on the one hand, and the inflation rate, on the other. As far as excess demand is concerned, this time lag was imposed on the basis of evidence from earlier studies, and its appropriateness was not subjected to any test. However, experiments with contemporaneous strike activity were also carried out - - though their results are not reported here to economize on space - - to ensure that nothing crucial in the results depends upon the particular time pattern of response imposed upon the equation fitted; in fact nothing does. [22]

The salient characteristics of the results presented in Table 1 are easily summarized. The coefficient of the excess demand proxy variable is significantly positive for every country, as is the intercept of the relationship for every country except the United States. The strike variable is significantly positive only for Italy, though marginally so for the U.S. and the U.K. For Germany, Switzerland, and Japan the variable would appear to play no role. In short, this set of results says that deviations of the inflation rate from an unexplained constant positive value are systematically related to excess demand for every country studied, and to strike activity for, at most, three of them. An eclectic might take some comfort from these results, but not a sociologist. The importance of excess demand is strong evidence against the proposition that market forces have not been important in determining the time path of the inflation rate over the period covered. However, it would appear that "militancy" and "social conflict" have been potentially important contributors to inflation in, at best, three countries.

This last conclusion can be tested further. Militancy is supposed to work through its effect, first, on wages, and through wages, on prices. Thus, for the three countries where the strike variable bears a systematic relationship to price inflation, it ought to be even more closely related to the wage inflation rate. Further work shows this to be the case. Results for a simple wage inflation equation, using unemployment as a proxy for the excess demand for labor, and the same measure of strike activity as that already utilized, are presented in Table 2; except for Switzerland, where the absence of an unemployment variable prevented this test being carried out. In this case, the time pattern imposed in the equation is important. Except for Italy, the results in Table 2 are for an unlagged relationship of the form:

$$(2) \qquad \Delta W = b_0 + b_1 U + b_2 S .$$

For Italy, both independent variables are lagged one period.

---

[22] There is an element of data-mining here, but perhaps the reader will agree that the practice is less reprehensible when used - - in the interests of fairness - - to improve the performance of a model in which one has little faith than when used to bolster one's own hypothesis.

Table 1*

Regression of ΔP on y_{-1} and S_{-1} 1954-1970

	Intercept	y_{-1}	S_{-1}	R^2	RSS	D.W.
U.S.A.	.008	.3808	4.071	.559	.00215	1.14
	(.007)	(.1006)	(2.270)			
Italy	.021	.7500	.0068	.827	.00092	2.50
	(.003)	(.1270)	(.003)			
Japan	.048	.4571	-.012	.376	.00626	1.27
	(.017)	(.1592)	(.038)			
U.K.	.020	.9884	.030	.539	.00173	1.35
	(.007)	(.2442)	(.016)			
Germany	.023	.07923	-.034	.398	.00081	1.10
	(.003)	(.03566)	(.031)			
Switzerland	.026	.369	-2.554	.613	.00124	1.11
	(.003)	(.081)	(1.112)			

*Note: S is measured in units of 10,000 man-days lost in strikes per annum in this and the next three tables.

Table 2

Regression of ΔW on u and S   1954-1970

	Intercept	u	S	R^2	RSS	D.W.
U.S.A.	.074	-.009	2.479	.711	.00064	1.16
	(.009)	(.002)	(1.039)			
Italy	.035	-.002	.036	.671	.00875	1.59
	(.024)	(.003)	(.009)			
Japan	.210	-.064	.124	.518	.00967	0.95
	(.034)	(.024)	(.048)			
U.K.	.064	-.013	.046	.252	.00363	2.08
	(.017)	(.009)	(.017)			
Germany	.091	-.009	.084	.276	.00946	1.12
	(.0010)	(.004)	(.132)			
Switzerland	Not available: no consistent series for u.					

Germany and Japan produce results that show no positive effect of strike activity on the inflation rate, but for the other three countries the coefficient relating wage inflation to strike activity is better determined than that linking strike activity to price inflation. That is what one would expect if militancy or social conflict affected price inflation through wage inflation. One other characteristic of the results reported in Table 2 should be noted, namely, the lack of significance of unemployment - - the excess demand for labor proxy - - as far as the U.K., Germany, and Italy are concerned. As Table 3 shows, with the results for Italy again lagged, the excess demand for goods as measured by y is more closely related to the rate of wage inflation than is unemployment; for Switzerland, the variable is only marginally significant. Thus, Tables 2 and 3 give reason to suppose that wage inflation is, in fact, influenced by excess demand. [23]

What about the international transmission of inflation? Table 4 speaks for itself. In five of six cases, rates of price inflation among the countries are positively correlated with one another, (strongly so in most cases), as are rates of wage inflation; the high correlations among Italy, Germany, and Switzerland are particularly noteworthy in light of their closely linked labor markets noted above. However, the correlations among strike activity in the five countries are more frequently negative than positive. Nor does it make any difference to the overall impression of these results if one permits lags to appear between countries, or if the data period is altered, as results not reported here show.

To sum up, the sociological explanation of inflation emerges rather badly from these simple tests. Excess demand turns out to be systematically related to wage and price inflation rates in all six countries studied. [24] There is a significant positive trend in each country's price level that is not explained by excess demand or by strike activity. Moreover, the correlations among strike activity measures in various countries are systematically lower than those among wage inflation or price inflation rates. On the basis of such results, it would be easier to argue that inflation was the means whereby militancy was transmitted between countries rather than vice versa. Nevertheless, strike activity appears to have had a systematic influence on inflation for Italy, the U.K., and the U.S. I cannot, at this point, rule out the possibility that the sociological approach has an element of truth to it; that certainly would be an eclectic's interpretation of these results. I examine this issue again below; first, I turn to testing the monetarist appraoch.

As I have remarked, there are two components to a monetarist view of inflation in a world of fixed exchange rates: the determination of the "world" infla-

[23] Note that Ward and Zis (1974) found that unemployment entered linearly tended to be a poor proxy for excess demand. They replaced it with the inverse of the unemployment rate in their study, and considerably improved their results. However, they found less role for strike activity than I report here, and it warrants further work to find out why this is so.

[24] This result echoes one of the principal conclusions reached by Brunner, et. al., (1973).

Table 3

Regression of ΔW on y and S   1954-1970

	Intercept	y	S	R^2	RSS	D.W.
U.S.A.	.029	.248	2.943	.557	.00097	1.12
	(.005)	(.067)	(1.289)			
Italy	.026	1.150	.029	.861	.00368	2.15
	(.007)	(.254)	(.005)			
Japan	.137	.473	-.129	.490	.01020	.98
	(.022)	(.199)	(.049)			
U.K.	.034	.691	.041	.350	.00315	2.17
	(.008)	(.326)	(.016)			
Germany	.070	.325	-.020	.383	.00806	.84
	(.009)	(.117)	(.098)			
Switzerland	.040	.235	-.478	.170	.00374	.49
	(.004)	(.141)	(2.446)			

268

Table 4

Correlations between countries 1954-1970 of

A. Price Inflation

	U.S.	Italy	Japan	U.K.	Germany	Switzerland
U.S.	1	-.06	+.36	+.50	+.40	+.38
Italy		1	+.51	+.20	+.52	+.63
Japan			1	+.18	+.41	+.61
U.K.				1	+.63	+.42
Germany					1	+.75
Switzerland						1

B. Wage Inflation

	U.S.	Italy	Japan	U.K.	Germany	Switzerland
U.S.	1	-.03	.33	.52	.09	.05
Italy		1	.61	.41	.61	.63
Japan			1	.44	.28	.71
U.K.				1	.55	.31
Germany					1	.53
Switzerland						1

C. Strike Activity

	U.S.	Italy	Japan	U.K.	Germany	Switzerland
U.S.	1	.26	-.04	.44	-.40	-.31
Italy		1	-.19	.46	-.32	-.07
Japan			1	.20	-.09	-.31
U.K.				1	-.24	-.30
Germany					1	.65
Switzerland						1

tion rate; and, the transmission of that world inflation rate to a particular national economy. In this paper, for reasons already discussed, I treat the second of these issues. Cross and Laidler (1976) presented empirical evidence for a particular hypothesis of the mechanism whereby the world inflation rate influences national inflation rates; in this section, I start from those results, and attempt to carry the argument further.

The key postulate is that the inflation rate in any one country is determined proximately by an expectations augmented Phillips-type relationship of the form:

(3) $\qquad \Delta P = gy_{-1} + X_{-1}$,

where X is the "expected inflation rate." For a closed economy it might be reasonable to think of this expected inflation rate as solely a function of past values of the domestic inflation rate. However, Cross and Laidler argued that, for a fixed exchange rate, open economy, it was more reasonable to suppose that the inflation rate in the rest of the world also affected expectations. Specifically, the following hypothesis about the determination of expectations was formulated and tested, where $\Delta\Pi$ is the world inflation rate measured as a national income-weighted average of consumer price inflation in 19 other countries.

(4) $\qquad X - X_{-1} = d[v(\Delta P - X_{-1}) + (1-v)(\Delta\Pi - X_{-1})]$.

As can be seen, this is a form of error-learning whereby expectations of inflation are corrected by a weighted average of the deviation of the domestic and world inflation rates from the overall expected inflation rate. When combined, the two foregoing equations yield:

(5) $\qquad \Delta P = gy_{-1} - g(1-d)y_{-2} + [1-d(1-v)]\Delta P_{-1} + d(1-v)\Delta\Pi_{-1}$;

or equivalently,

(6) $\qquad \Delta^2 P = gy_{-1} - g(1-d)y_{-2} + d(1-v)[\Delta\Pi_{-1} - \Delta P_{-1}]$,

where the a priori expectations about parameter values are that

$\qquad g > 0 \qquad 0 < d \leqslant 1 \qquad 0 \leqslant v \leqslant 1$.

270

This reduced form was estimated by Cross and Laidler, with all the constraints on its parameter values implied above imposed, for 19 countries, and proved overwhelmingly superior to an alternative hypothesis that treated domestic inflation as having solely domestic determinants. Moreover, for many countries - - including three of those included in this study - - world inflation seemed totally to dominate domestic inflation as far as the formation of expectations was concerned.

In Table 5, results of recomputing the Cross-Laidler regressions for the six countries with marginally different data are presented. [25] These do not differ qualitatively from those generated by the earlier work. [26] In this section, I report the consequences of subjecting this model to further tests along two lines of enquiry. First, a number of constraints are imposed in generating the results presented in Table 5. It is worth asking whether the data satisfy those constraints. Second, it is worth asking if the influence of world prices, which is so strong here, has an alternative and simpler explanation to that advanced, namely, that the variable, $\Delta\Pi$, stands as a proxy for import price inflation with the latter having what used to be called a "cost-push" influence on domestic prices. I will deal with these issues in turn.

Three constraints, or groups of constraints, were imposed in generating the results under discussion. First, restrictions as to sign and magnitude were imposed on the parameters, g, d, and v. Second, the coefficient of the expected rate of inflation, X_{-1}, in equation (3) was assumed and constrained to be equal to unity. Finally, the intercept of the regression equation was constrained to zero because expectations and excess demand are, between them, considered to provide a complete explanation of inflation, and not simply an explanation of variations in the inflation rate about some unexplained trend value. The reader will see that if equation (6) is estimated by unconstrained least squares, it will produce identical parameter estimates to those presented in Table 5, if the first group of constraints is satisfied. In Table 6, the reduced form parameters of equation (6), implied by the structural parameter estimates given in Table 5, are compared with estimates obtained by actually fitting equation (6). The results speak for themselves. For three of the six cases, the estimates are identical, implying that the constraints are completely satisfied; while for Italy, Germany, and Switzerland, the results are slightly weaker so that I am unable to reject the hypothesis that the

[25] The main difference lies in the computation of y. In the earlier study, this was measured as a deviation of national income from a trend measured over the slightly longer period, 1952-72. Note that for the U.K., the measure of $\Delta\Pi$ for 1968 is dominated by the effects of the devaluation in 1967, and that the 1962 observation for Germany is similarly dominated by the small revaluation of the mark. Since one would not expect jumps in the values of fixed exchange rate currencies to have an effect on expectations captured by a simple error learning mechanism, observations using these years' data are deleted from the equations estimated here. Cross and Laidler (1976) discuss this issue more fully.

[26] It is noteworthy that it is the large United States economy, normally regarded as "closed," that produces the heaviest weight on domestic inflation as a source of expectations about inflation. However, the results reported here show U.S. inflation expectations responding more rapidly to experience than those reported by Cross and Laidler (1976).

271

Table 5

$$\Delta^2 P = gy_{-1} - (1-d)gy_{-2} + d(1-v)(\Delta\Pi_{-1} - \Delta P_{-1})$$ 1954-1970

	g	d	v	RSS
U.S.A.	.270	.832	.670	.00112
	(.092)	(.336)	(159)	
Italy	.940	.436	0*	.00262
	(.242)	(.218)	(0)	
Japan	.335	.353	.257	.00621
	(.165)	(.525)	(1.027)	
U.K.+	.894	.470	.575	.00192
	(.272)	(.270)	(.391)	
Germany+	.147	.206	0*	.00109
	(.070)	(.262)	(0)	
Switzerland	.432	.368	0*	.00099
	(.101)	(.203)	(0)	

*Parameter estimate hit constraint

+Note that the observations for 1969 for Britain and 1962
for Germany were deleted from the sample before these
estimates were obtained. The same is true of Tables 6-10.

Table 6

Regression of $\Delta^2 P$ on y_{-1}, y_{-2}, and $(\Delta\Pi_{-1} - \Delta P_{-1})$ 1954-1970

	y_{-1}	y_{-2}	$(\Delta\Pi_{-1} - \Delta P_{-1})$	RSS	Reduced form parameters implicit in Table 5		
					y_{-1}	y_{-2}	$(\Delta\Pi_{-1} - \Delta P_{-1})$
U.S.A.	.270 (.092)	-.045 (.100)	.274 (.126)	.00112	.270	-.045	.274
Italy	.946 (.242)	-.575 (.260)	.455 (.226)	.00260	.940	-.530	.436
Japan	.335 (.164)	-.217 (.172)	.262 (.170)	.00621	.335	-.217	.262
U.K.	.894 (.272)	-.473 (.268)	.200 (.169)	.00192	.894	-.473	.200
Germany	.138 (.061)	-.160 (.053)	.351 (.241)	.00084	.147	-.117	.206
Switzerland	.461 (.093)	-.328 (.615)	.615 (.233)	.00082	.432	-.273	.368

constraints are satisfied. In computing the results given in Table 6, the intercept of the regression fitted was constrained to zero - - implying no unexplained trend rate of acceleration in the inflation rate. It is worth noting that when this equation was reestimated freely, the intercept did not differ significantly from zero in any case, thus confirming that this procedure was appropriate .

The second constraint imposed in generating Tables 5 and 6 is that the coefficient of X in equation(3)is unity; this is important because its imposition amounts to assuming that the "natural unemployment rate" hypothesis is true. However, this constraint implies that if equation(5)is freely estimated, the coefficients on ΔP_{-1} and $\Delta \Pi_{-1}$ will sum to unity. Table 7 presents freely estimated results, and as the reader will see, the constraint is never violated though, in the case of Japan, the sum in question takes a value that might be considered a little too high.

The final constraint was that there be no unexplained trend in prices, that the intercept in equation (5)actually be zero. Table 8 presents the results of relaxing this constraint. Here, the intercept is significantly positive for Germany and Italy, the same countries that supplied minor problems above, and also for Switzerland, though for Germany and Switzerland this intercept is numerically quite small, much smaller than that in Table 1. The intercept is not significantly different from zero in the other three cases, but its presence reduces the size and significance of the coefficients on the lagged domestic and lagged world inflation terms. This characteristic of the results presented in Table 8 is to be expected if there were a strong trend in the price level for all the countries studied (as there is), a trend potentially explicable in terms of the effect of expectations of inflation on the current inflation rate. To this extent, the results support the expectations/excess demand explanation of inflation, but not definitely so. The constraint that there should be no unexplained trend in prices, that the intercept in Table 8 should not differ from zero, is violated in three cases. The monetarist model performs better than the sociological one in terms of minimizing the size of the unexplained trend in prices, but its performance could stand improvement.

One ought not, however, to be too surprised at these results. Cross and Laidler (1976) conclude that the results they generate with the model I am investigating suggest that the behavior of world prices was an important proximate determinant of the behavior of domestic prices; they also conclude, however, that the same results suggest that this model had not been altogether successful in specifying the precise means whereby this influence transmitted itself. The results presented here are quite consistent with that conclusion, and may be interpreted to mean that our understanding of the processes whereby expectations of inflation are formed in open economies is as yet somewhat defective.

Further evidence consistent with this view is presented below, but I want

Table 7

Regression of ΔP on y_{-1}, y_{-2}, ΔP_{-1}, $\Delta \Pi_{-1}$ 1954-1970

	y_{-1}	y_{-2}	ΔP_{-1}	$\Delta \Pi_{-1}$	RSS
U.S.A.	.270	.044	.723	.274	.00112
	(.096)	(.112)	(.170)	(.131)	
Italy	.938	-.578	.540	.502	.00259
	(.252)	(.269)	(.234)	(.285)	
Japan	.320	-.163	.608	.727	.00548
	(.161)	(.172)	(.193)	(.389)	
U.K.	.872	-.552	.766	.344	.00184
	(.278)	(.294)	(.178)	(.262)	
Germany	.132	-.166	.704	.342	.00083
	(.064)	(.056)	(.282)	(.250)	
Switzerland	.472	-.357	.416	.661	.00076
	(.094)	(.108)	(.236)	(.239)	

Table 8

Regression of ΔP on y_{-1}, y_{-2}, ΔP_{-1}, $\Delta \Pi_{-1}$ 1954-1970

	Intercept	y_{-1}	y_{-2}	ΔP_{-1}	$\Delta \Pi_{-1}$	R^2	RSS	D.W.
U.S.A.	.004	.267	-.007	.630	.203	.780	.00107	2.13
	(.005)	(.097)	(.124)	(.212)	(.164)			
Italy	.034	.963	.200	-.354	.191	.785	.00114	1.86
	(.009)	(.175)	(.274)	(.282)	(.213)			
Japan	.018	.368	-.055	.369	.410	.524	.00477	2.15
	(.014)	(.160)	(.186)	(.259)	(.446)			
U.K.	.017	.710	-.054	.362	.149	.524	.00163	1.46
	(.014)	(.306)	(.509)	(.382)	(.305)			
Germany	.010	.110	-.095	.443	.124	.562	.00057	1.83
	(.005)	(.057)	(.058)	(.270)	(.237)			
Switzerland	.007	.445	-.284	.320	.467	.820	.00058	2.12
	(.004)	(.086)	(.104)	(.219)	(.238)			

first to investigate whether the world inflation rate variable in the foregoing regressions is not simply reflecting the simpler influence of import price inflation on domestic inflation. To do this, an import price inflation variable, ΔQ, was substituted for a world inflation variable in equations (5) and (6). The results (some are omitted in order to save space) were strongly, though not universally, in favor of the expectations hypothesis. Only for the United Kingdom did the import price inflation variable consistently show more explanatory power than the world inflation variable, but the superiority here was marginal. For Germany, Switzerland, and Japan, import price inflation appeared to be of no significance in explaining domestic price inflation; the parameter, v, went to unity in these cases when a fully constrained version of equation (5) was fitted. Only when all constraints were removed and an intercept permitted to appear did the substitution of import price inflation for world inflation provide an equation of superior explanatory power in cases other than the United Kingdom. A comparison of Table 9 with Table 8 shows that this occurs in two instances. However, the substitution of ΔQ for $\Delta \Pi$ generates a significantly positive intercept in five of six cases, and a marginally significant one in the sixth - - the U.S. Insisting that import price inflation is the route whereby worldwide influences impinge upon domestic inflation requires accepting that its role is to explain deviations from an otherwise unexplained trend, and not to explain that trend. In any event, the evidence of Tables 5-9, and that above strongly suggests that it is through expectations, rather than through import prices, that world inflation influences the inflation rate in an open economy. Not only does the world inflation variable come closer to explaining the trend in inflation than do import prices, but it also seems to enhance the explanatory power of the type of equation under test here. [27] Thus, the proposition that import price inflation is an important "cost-push" element in an eclectic account of the generation of inflation in an open economy gets scant support from these results.

So far I have tested sociological and monetarist explanations of national inflation rates against what might be termed "absolute" criteria. I have found that an extreme sociological explanation of inflation is refuted by the appearance of a well-determined and systematic influence of excess demand on the inflation rate. It is also notable that, even where strike activity might seem to contribute to the explanation of inflation, it is with deviations of the inflation rate from an unexplained trend that it deals. Moreover, I had no success in tracking down a cross-country demonstration effect. The tests of the monetarist theory give, on balance, a more satisfactory outcome. The constraints on coefficients implied by theory have usually, though not always, been satisfied by the data, while the

---

[27] These results present a striking confirmation of Brunner's conjecture that, if worldwide influences are to be credited with a significant effect on domestic inflation rates, this effect would be found to be working through expectations rather than through import prices.

Table 9

Regression of ΔP on y_{-1}, y_{-2}, ΔQ_{-1}, ΔP_{-1}　　　　1954-1970

	Intercept	y_{-1}	y_{-2}	ΔQ_{-1}	ΔP_{-1}	R^2	RSS	D.W.
U.S.A.	.008	.265	-.018	.062	.660	.758	.00118	2.25
	(.005)	(.106)	(.130)	(.119)	(.221)			
Italy	.038	.924	.160	.072	-.334	.801	.00106	1.78
	(.008)	(.168)	(.266)	(.054)	(.268)			
Japan	.023	.450	-.127	-.071	.437	.513	.00488	1.89
	(.012)	(.175)	(.205)	(.096)	(.264)			
U.K.	.024	.498	.071	.245	.156	.642	.00123	1.42
	(.011)	(.278)	(.377)	(.331)	(.079)			
Germany	.018	.065	-.044	.247	.094	.633	.00047	1.50
	(.006)	(.053)	(.061)	(.268)	(.060)			
Switzerland	.012	.375	-.281	.092	.549	.774	.000725	1.80
	(.004)	(.106)	(.123)	(.114)	(.200)			

superiority of an inflationary-expectations hypothesis of the influence of world inflation on domestic inflation over an import-price hypothesis is reasonably clear-cut.

These tests do not end matters, however. A theory may need improvement but still be acceptable if it is the best available. It is worthwhile to ask which of two imperfect hypotheses is the better, to compare the results presented in Table 1 with those in Table 5. This comparison is more straightforward than might seem at first, as each table presents regression results that involve estimating three parameters.

The residual sum squares generated by the two equations give no real basis for choice between them. On this criterion, equation (1) is marginally superior to equation (5) in every case, except for the U.S., but the U.S. is one of the three instances for which strike activity looked important. For the U.K., the margin is extremely thin, resting on a fourth decimal place. Only for Italy and Switzerland does equation (1) look clearly better on this criterion. On the other hand, the overall trend of prices for each economy, except the U.S., is explained by equation (5) in terms of the influence of world inflation on domestic inflation expectations, while it is left unexplained by equation (1). I would regard this point of comparison as somewhat more important than the error sum squares criterion, not to mention the poor performance of the strike activity variable in three cases. Hence, on the basis of this evidence, I regard the monetarist explanation as the more satisfactory of the two. However, it would not be surprising if advocates of the sociological approach disagreed. Potential disagreement aside, the predictive power of the two equations over data drawn from beyond the original sample period may be used as a basis for further comparison; here, the monetarist approach is clearly superior.

Before discussing the substance of these results, it is worth digressing to examine the appropriateness of extrapolating either of these relationships beyond the sample period. I have noted the body of opinion suggesting that the power of the strike weapon has increased recently. If that is so, one might not expect the relationship between inflation and strike activity extant in the 1950s and 1960s to illuminate that of the early 1970s. My views on what is and is not a testable explanation of inflation are set out above. Suffice it to say that, in the absence of a clearly specified postulate about how this relationship might be expected to change in the 1970s, I would expect no objection to my procedure along these lines.

What about the monetarist equation? I omitted observations for years when exchange rates changed from its estimation over the period 1954-70 because it seemed a priori implausible that a rise in world prices expressed in domestic currency, arising from a once-and-for-all devaluation under a regime of fixed exchange rates, would affect expectations of inflation in the same way as would an increase in world prices, measured in foreign currency with the exchange rate constant. [28] In 1971, there was a major realignment of currencies; this was merely the prelude to the adoption of a system of more-or-less floating exchange rates, under which there have been frequent and indeed sometimes continuing changes in parities. Is it reasonable to expect the fixed exchange rate results to extrapolate to a regime of more flexible rates? I think they might, though there is no logical necessity that they should.

It is one thing to say that, once a devaluation occurs under a fixed exchange rate regime, it is unlikely to generate an expectation that it will be repeated immediately; and quite another to say that, once an exchange rate begins to fall under a regime of flexible rates, it will not generate expectations that the fall will continue - - particularly among those who are not specialized foreign exchange dealers. It is possible, therefore, that results obtained for a period of fixed exchange rates will extrapolate to a period of flexible rates. Indeed, if economic agents form their expectations about the behavior of the exchange rate under such a regime with the same adaptive-expectations mechanism that they apply to forming expectations about the inflation rate in the rest of the world, extrapolation ought to be possible. Thus, in using the parameter estimates presented in Table 5 to forecast for the years 1971-73, I am testing two propositions: first, that the relationship originally estimated is robust; and second that, under a flexible exchange rate regime, expectations about the inflation rate in world markets, in terms of domestic currency, are influenced by current observations of that rate of inflation in the same terms, whether those observations result from inflation of foreign currency prices, on the one hand, or a falling exchange rate, on the other.

Charts 1-12 compare the actual with the predicted time path of the inflation rate for each country studied. The predictions in the first six charts are based on the strike hypothesis embodied in the parameter estimates reported in Table 1; those in the second six follow from the parameter estimates in Table 5. These charts speak for themselves. The first six show a marked deterioration in predictive power as soon as the sample period is passed; this is as true for those countries in which strike activity appeared to have some predictive power over the inflation rate in the years before 1970, as for those in which it did not. Either there is agreement that the years since 1970 have seen a "new inflation," or the sociological explanation of inflation must be regarded as further undermined by these results.

The results for the monetarist equation set out in Charts 7-12 are somewhat better. Strike activity took a positive coefficient for three countries, the

---

[28] This matter is more fully discussed in Cross and Laidler (1976). Also, see footnote 25.

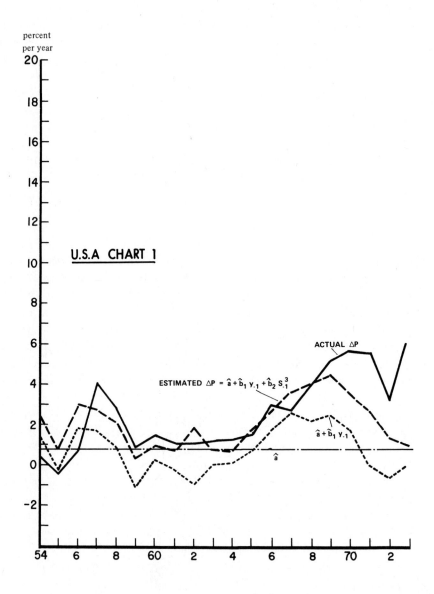

U.S.A CHART 1

ACTUAL ΔP

ESTIMATED ΔP = $\hat{a} + \hat{b}_1\, y_{-1} + \hat{b}_2\, S_{-1}^3$

$\hat{a} + \hat{b}_1\, y_{-1}$

$\hat{a}$

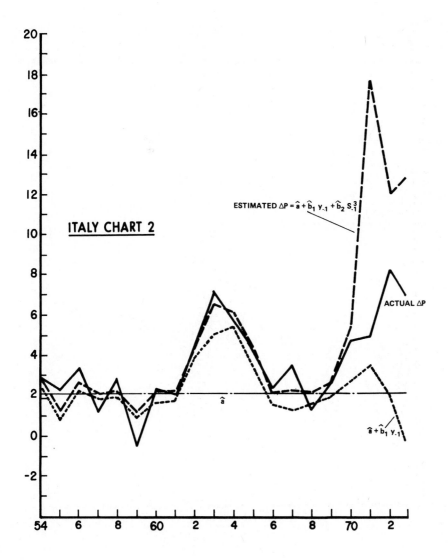

ITALY CHART 2

ESTIMATED $\Delta P = \widehat{a} + \widehat{b}_1 \, y_{-1} + \widehat{b}_2 \, S_{-1}^3$

ACTUAL ΔP

$\widehat{a}$

$\widehat{a} + \widehat{b}_1 \, y_{-1}$

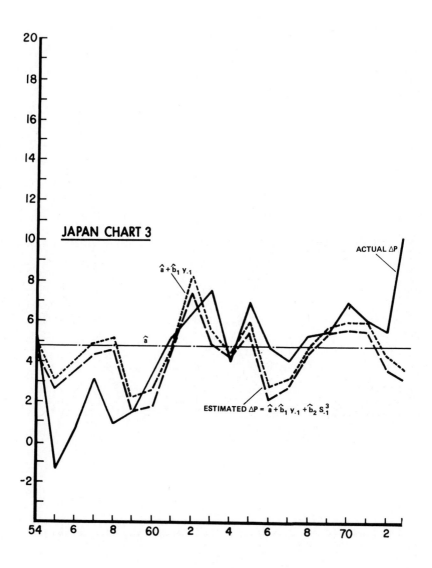

JAPAN CHART 3

ACTUAL ΔP

$\hat{a} + \hat{b}_1 y_{-1}$

$\hat{a}$

ESTIMATED $\Delta P = \hat{a} + \hat{b}_1 y_{-1} + \hat{b}_2 S_{-1}^3$

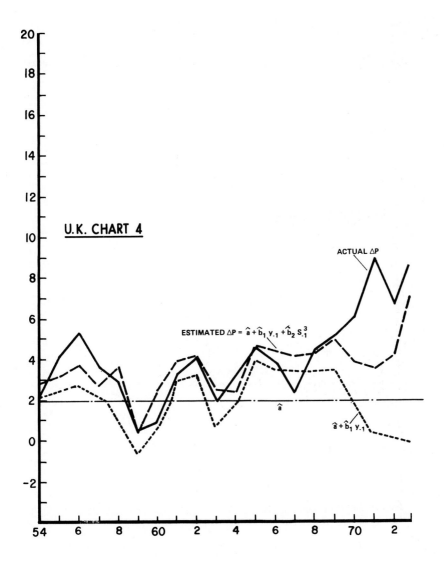

U.K. CHART 4

ACTUAL ΔP

ESTIMATED $\Delta P = \hat{a} + \hat{b}_1 y_{-1} + \hat{b}_2 S_{-1}^3$

$\hat{a}$

$\hat{a} + \hat{b}_1 y_{-1}$

283

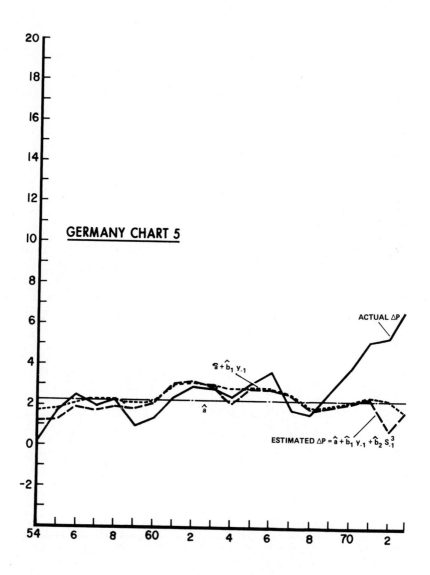

GERMANY CHART 5

ACTUAL ΔP

$\hat{a} + \hat{b}_1\, y_{-1}$

$\hat{a}$

ESTIMATED $\Delta P = \hat{a} + \hat{b}_1\, y_{-1} + \hat{b}_2\, S^3_{-1}$

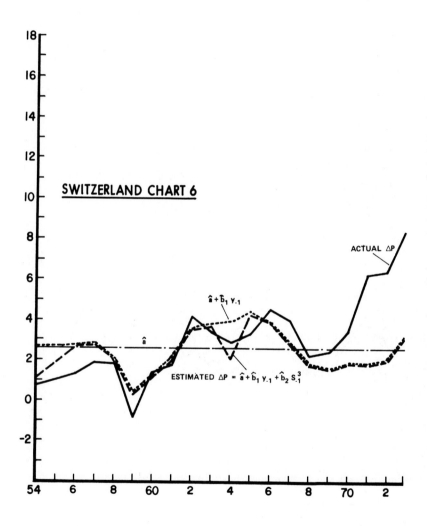

SWITZERLAND CHART 6

ACTUAL ΔP

$\hat{a}+\hat{b}_1 \, y_{-1}$

$\hat{a}$

ESTIMATED ΔP $= \hat{a}+\hat{b}_1 \, y_{-1} +\hat{b}_2 \, S_{-1}^3$

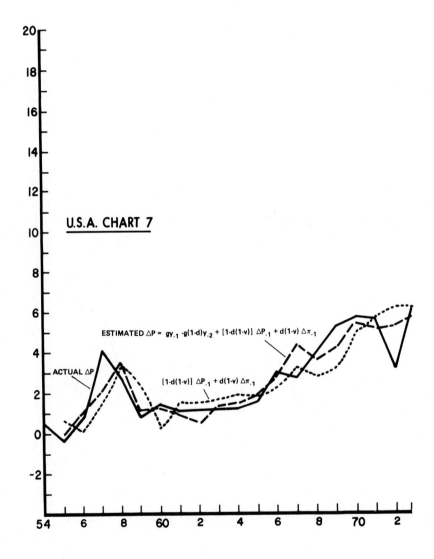

U.S.A. CHART 7

ESTIMATED $\Delta P = gy_{-1} - g(1-d)y_{-2} + [1-d(1-v)] \Delta P_{-1} + d(1-v) \Delta \pi_{-1}$

ACTUAL ΔP

$[1-d(1-v)] \Delta P_{-1} + d(1-v) \Delta \pi_{-1}$

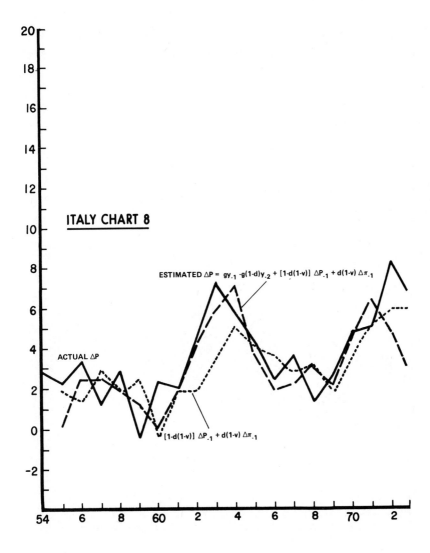

ITALY CHART 8

ESTIMATED $\Delta P = gy_{-1} - g(1-d)y_{-2} + [1-d(1-v)] \Delta P_{-1} + d(1-v) \Delta \pi_{-1}$

ACTUAL ΔP

$[1-d(1-v)] \Delta P_{-1} + d(1-v) \Delta \pi_{-1}$

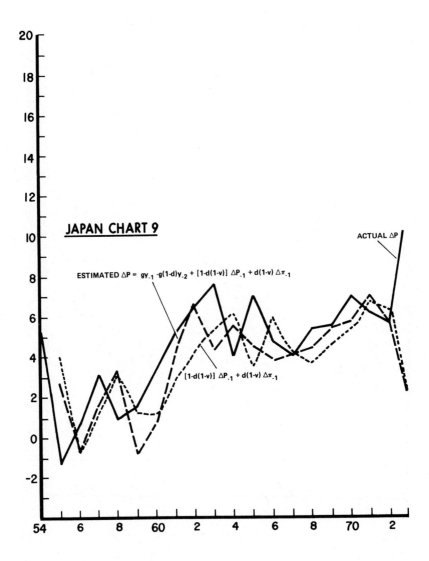

JAPAN CHART 9

ESTIMATED $\Delta P = gy_{-1} - g(1-d)y_{-2} + [1-d(1-v)] \Delta P_{-1} + d(1-v) \Delta\pi_{-1}$

$[1-d(1-v)] \Delta P_{-1} + d(1-v) \Delta\pi_{-1}$

ACTUAL ΔP

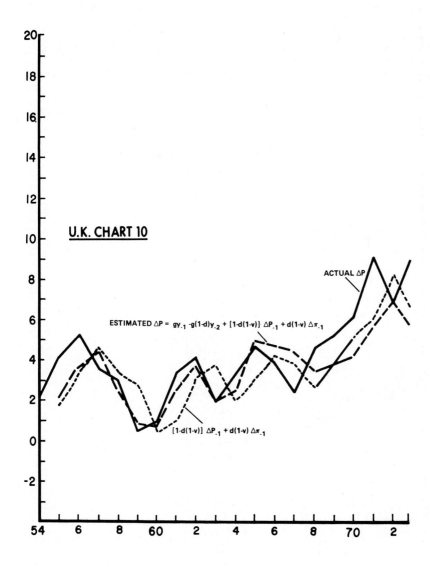

U.K. CHART 10

ACTUAL ΔP

ESTIMATED $\Delta P = gy_{-1} - g(1-d)y_{-2} + [1-d(1-v)] \Delta P_{-1} + d(1-v) \Delta \pi_{-1}$

$[1-d(1-v)] \Delta P_{-1} + d(1-v) \Delta \pi_{-1}$

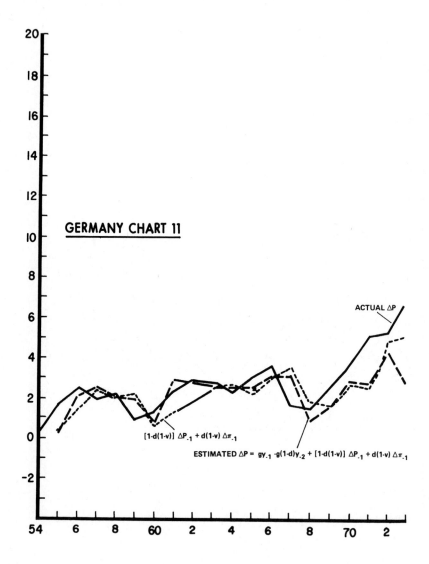

GERMANY CHART 11

ACTUAL ΔP

[1-d(1-v)] ΔP$_{-1}$ + d(1-v) Δπ$_{-1}$

ESTIMATED ΔP = gy$_{-1}$ -g(1-d)y$_{-2}$ + [1-d(1-v)] ΔP$_{-1}$ + d(1-v) Δπ$_{-1}$

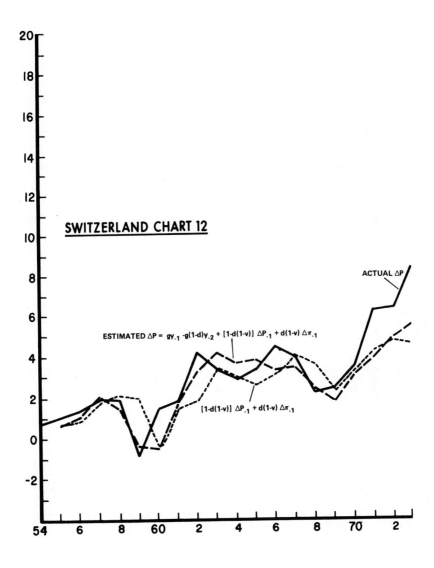

SWITZERLAND CHART 12

ESTIMATED $\Delta P = gy_{-1} - g(1-d)y_{-2} + [1-d(1-v)] \Delta P_{-1} + d(1-v) \Delta \pi_{-1}$

$[1-d(1-v)] \Delta P_{-1} + d(1-v) \Delta \pi_{-1}$

ACTUAL ΔP

U.S., the U.K., and Italy; it is noteworthy that for each of these the strike activity equation fails to forecast ahead of the sample as well as does the monetarist equation. It fails in the other three instances as well, but this is not surprising. [29] However, though the monetarist equation performs better, it is still far from satisfactory. While predicting well for the United States, it shows a systematic tendency to underpredict inflation for other countries after 1970, and particularly for 1973; the exception is the forecast for Germany. [30]

One point about the results presented in Charts 7-12, particularly for the period until 1970, is worth noting. When the predicted value of the inflation rate is broken down to show the contribution of inflationary expectations, captured in the terms, $(1\text{-}d)(1\text{-}v)\Delta P_{-1} + d(1\text{-}v)\Delta\Pi$, as distinct from domestic excess demand, captured in the terms, $gy_{-1} - g(1\text{-}d)y_{-2}$, it is clear that the overall trend in the inflation rate is dominated by expectations, with excess demand largely accounting for deviations from this trend. Since for every country except the United States, expectations are dominated by worldwide trends (completely so for Italy, Germany, and Switzerland), these results strongly confirm the monetarist view that, under a system of fixed exchange rates, it is sensible to regard the overall trend value of inflation as determined at the level of the world economy, with domestic variables accounting for the deviation of national inflation rates from this worldwide trend. With respect to a more flexible rate regime, the results are ambiguous. The hypothesis would have suggested that exchange rate variations could either cancel out these worldwide influences, or magnify them, depending on the direction of change of the exchange rate; flexible exchange rates, therefore, confer on domestic policy makers a power over domestic inflation that they do not possess under a fixed exchange rate regime. However, the poor extrapolative performance of the equations, particularly for the relatively "open" economies, prevents any firm conclusion on this issue. I will return to this point in my discussion of the policy implications of these results.

I want to present, first, one more set of empirical results. I have been comparing one equation with another, asking which is the better of the two; to an eclectic, there is no reason to suppose that either the sociologist or the monetarist has a monopoly on the truth about inflation. In the terms of this work, he might suggest that strike activity, expectations, and excess demand were complementary in the explanation of inflation. If I modify equation (5) so that it includes a strike activity variable, lagged one year to be consistent with equation (1), then:

---

[29] Note, however, that for Japan the two equations perform equally badly. The superiority of the monetarist equation is only marginal.

[30] The temporary overprediction for 1972 for the United States probably reflects the short-term effects of the Nixon administration's price control legislation during 1971-72. I have discussed this in some detail in Laidler (1974) where, however, only domestic inflation was allowed to influence U.S. inflationary expectations.

(7) $\Delta P = gy_{-1} + X_{-1} + bS_{-1}$;

with X defined as above, this expression implies:

(8) $\Delta P = gy_{-1} - g(1-d)y_{-2} + [1-d(1-v)]\Delta P_{-1} + d(1-v)\Delta\Pi_{-1} + bS_{-1} - b(1-d)S_{-2}$.

The results of fitting, with all constraints imposed, are presented in Table 10; these are of some interest. First, as compared with Table 5, the introduction of a strike variable does not reduce the importance of excess demand as an explanatory variable. Moreover, it makes little difference to the estimate of v, and hence to the extent to which a particular economy is considered to be open to outside influence through an inflationary expectations mechanism.

The inclusion of strikes influences the estimates of d to some extent, increasing and improving the apparent precision of the estimate of this parameter for Japan, but lowering and reducing the apparent precision of the estimate for Italy. Nevertheless, if strike activity is important as a proximate determinant of the inflation rate, it would appear to be effective mainly in addition to, rather than instead of, those variables regarded as important by a monetarist. Comparison of Table 10 with Table 1, on the other hand, shows that monetarist variables, particularly those associated with expectations of inflation, affect the assessment of the importance of strike variables. For Germany and Switzerland, strike activity remains of no importance, while for the United States the introduction of inflationary expectations pushes it out of the picture entirely. With respect to Italy and the United Kingdom, the significance of strike activity as an influence on inflation is placed in some doubt by Table 10. The coefficient of the variable is still positive but its statistical significance is reduced, as compared with Table 1. Japan provides an exception to this general tendency for the apparent importance of strike activity to be reduced by considering its role at the same time as that of inflationary expectations. The variable takes a positive coefficient and is marginally significant in Table 10, whereas it was slightly negative in Table 1. However, work not reported here shows that inclusion of this variable reduces the ability to forecast for 1971-73 in the case of Japan; therefore, too much should not be read into this.

All in all, there is support for the monetarist view in the results set out in Table 10. They show that, when excess demand, inflationary expectations, and strike activity appear together in a regression equation, the influence of excess demand on inflation is strong; that the influence of inflationary expectations is just as discernible as it is in the absence of strike activity; but that the influence of strike activity gets downgraded in four cases out of five. A monetarist might

Table 10

$$\Delta^2 P = gy_{-1} - (1-d)gy_{-2} + bS_{-1} - (1-d)bS_{-2} + d(1-v)(\Delta\Pi_{-1} - \Delta P_{-1}) \quad 1954\text{-}1970$$

	g	d	b	v	RSS
U.S.A.	.277	.755	.572	.665	.00109
	(.096)	(.349)	(.974)	(.178)	
Italy	.741	.235	.007	0*	.00217
	(.253)	(.281)	(.004)	(0)	
Japan	.342	.945	.030	.387	.00504
	(.152)	(.396)	(.016)	(.208)	
U.K.	.942	.480	.016	.319	.00168
	(.266)	(.244)	(.012)	(.467)	
Germany	.149	.210	.007	0*	.00109
	(.072)	(.277)	(.030)	(0)	
Switzerland	.433	.366	.080	0*	.00993
	(.105)	(.212)	(.893)	(0)	

*Coefficient hit constraint

suggest, on the basis of these results, that strike activity is to some extent correlated with inflationary expectations, and perhaps partly to be explained by them. An eclectic could argue, on the basis of these same results, that strike activity cannot be discounted as a possible autonomous influence on inflation in some countries; but he would have to concede that the variable could be accorded only a minor role. Only for the U.K. does the inclusion of this variable improve the forecast beyond the sample period, and then only marginally so.

In summarizing to this point, I note, first, that the role of excess demand as a proximate determinant of inflation is strongly supported by all the results presented - - regardless of the other variables in the regression, and of the country under consideration. This is strong evidence opposing the view that market forces have no part in explaining inflation. The proxy variable for non-market influences on inflation was strike activity, even though I noted that there are potentially serious objections to this interpretation of such a variable. Its contribution was dependent on the other variables included in a particular equation, and on the particular country studied. Moreover, though strike activity seemed to have been potentially important for three countries until 1970, it was not possible satisfactorily to forecast beyond this date on the basis of pre-existing relationships. This means either that sociological forces were more important in influencing inflation in the 1950s and 1960s than since, a view that most advocates of the sociological approach would not accept; or that the nature of their influence has changed in the last few years; or that the correlations observed for earlier periods should not be interpreted as evidence of causation. I prefer the third of these explanations, particularly in the absence of any inter-country correlation of strike activity, and particularly in view of the fact that, even at the best of times, excess demand and strike activity appeared to leave a strongly determined trend in prices to be explained, or rather not to be explained, by an intercept.

While excess demand figures large in a monetarist explanation of inflation, another variable of importance is inflationary expectations formed, as they are, partly on observations of inflation rates in the rest of the world. The expectations variable did not perform as consistently well as excess demand, but it proved decisively superior to strike activity. For one thing, unexplained trends in prices are much less prone to turn up in the presence of this variable; for another, it seems to be important for all the countries studied and not just for a sub-set of them. The worldwide inflation rate variable also performed better than import price inflation, adding further confidence to the belief in the importance of expectations. Thus, the monetarist hypothesis performs better than the sociological one, while an attempt to add strike activity to a monetarist equation contributes only marginally to the explanation. In short, these results suggest that eclecticism has little to add to a monetarist explanation of inflation. [31]

This being said, however, the monetarist equation I have tested nevertheless leaves room for improvement. As Cross and Laidler(1976) have noted, the way in which expectations are incorporated into this equation leaves something to be desired. The difficulties encountered in forecasting for a period of flexible exchange rates only serve to confirm this conclusion. I conjecture that further work will show that expectations of the behavior of the exchange rate must be treated separately from expectations of world price inflation in trying to identify the influence of worldwide factors on domestic inflation.

IV. IMPLICATIONS FOR ANTI-INFLATION POLICY

The empirical results generated in the previous section are hardly definitive, but they point to an economic, as opposed to a sociological, view of the inflationary process. Moreover, expectations variables seem to dominate excess demand variables as proximate determinants of the inflation rate even though the latter are consistently statistically significant. At the beginning of this paper, I argued that a sociological view of inflation, or an eclectic view with strong sociological content, was usually associated with advocacy of wage-price controls as a major ingredient of anti-inflation policy. Thus, one might regard the case for such policies as having been undermined by my empirical results. However, it has also been argued, notably by Phelps (1972), that if expectations play an important role in the inflationary process, there is a case to be made for wage and price controls, namely, that such controls can reduce inflationary expectations, and in so doing, can lower the inflation rate independently of the level of aggregate demand. There is nothing unique about wage and price controls in this respect. The widely publicized adoption of any anti-inflationary policy measure that the public believes will be successful will influence expectations in the same way. However, the question remains whether or not wage and price controls do in fact have such an effect. Of the six countries studied, two, the United States and the United Kingdom, resorted to such measures during the period under in-

---

[31] Unless, of course, it is regarded as an "eclectic" characteristic to lay strong emphasis on the world inflation rate when discussing domestic inflation.

vestigation while the other four did not. [32] I can perhaps determine whether such measures were effective by comparing the actual time path of inflation during the time when controls were in force with that predicted by the expectations/excess-demand equation, the estimation for which ignored any possibility of such extraneous influences on expectations.

Consider the United Kingdom results first. Inspection of Chart 10 shows that the equation in question performs well until 1966, but then begins to falter. It seriously overpredicts the inflation rate between 1966 and 1967, and thereafter systematically underpredicts it. It is significant that a statutory wage- and price-freeze was introduced in the United Kingdom in July 1966; was only slightly relaxed in the succeeding twelve months; and was rapidly and progressively relaxed for the following two years, being finally abandoned in 1969. The data in Chart 10 strongly suggest that introduction of this freeze had an initial effect of lowering the inflation rate below the level that might otherwise have prevailed. However, whatever gains were achieved initially were lost in subsequent years as the inflation rate "caught up" with its underlying trend, this "catch up" tendency being compounded, perhaps, by the once-and-for-all effects on the price level of the November 1967, devaluation of sterling. Since the end of this episode of wage and price controls saw the inflation rate considerably higher than at its inception, and further accelerating, these controls can hardly be termed successful. Britain experimented further with statutory controls, beginning in November 1972, with another complete freeze. The adoption of such policies coincided with a rapid acceleration in the inflation rate, one which has continued ever since; it is difficult to claim even initial short-term success for this second experiment.

The second British experiment was closely modeled on the wage-price control program begun in the United States in August 1971. The latter policies were widely regarded in Britain as successful, and, indeed, as in the case of Britain in 1966-67, Chart 7 shows a sharp fall in the U.S. inflation rate below its predicted value between 1971 and 1972, but rapid reversal of this movement the following year. Again, initial success was followed by failure in the longer term just as

---

[32] This is not to say that other countries did not have policies towards the behavior of prices and wages. I refer here to the statutory control of these variables. Note that, as the United States had "wage-price guidelines" in the early 1960s, Britain also had a series of so-called "voluntary incomes policies" during earlier periods. A survey of the literature on the effectiveness of British policies is to be found in Parkin, Sumner and Jones (1972), where it is also pointed out that Cripps' voluntary wage freeze of 1948-49, which had trade union cooperation, worked for a short time but was followed by a "wage explosion," in 1950. This was the only period in which such policies could be discerned to have had any effects. Note that, in 1973, Switzerland set up an official body for the surveillance of wages, prices, and profits, thus implementing what amounts to a voluntary wage-price control policy. Given Switzerland's very strong anti-inflationary monetary policy from 1973 onwards, it is going to be impossible to judge its contribution to reducing inflation.

for Britain in the late 1960s. [33] This is what one would expect if wage and price controls indeed affected inflationary expectations. For a given time path of nominal aggregate demand, a policy that, through its effects on expectations lowers the inflation rate below what it otherwise would have been, must also ensure that the level of excess demand in the economy will be greater than it otherwise would have been. It thus sows the seeds of an eventual increase in the inflation rate. Only if aggregate demand is managed in such a way as to prevent excess demand developing when the inflation rate is brought down by wage and price controls can the resulting benefits be anything more than temporary. [34] Moreover, the experience of Britain since 1972 suggests that even temporary benefits are unattainable when a policy of wage and price controls is tried a second time. These controls were seen to fail over the 1966-69 period, and it is plausible to argue that as a result the introduction of a new set of regulations in 1972 did not lead to any downward revision of inflationary expectations and, hence, did not have any effect on the actual inflation rate either.

If the analysis of inflation consistent with the evidence presented in this paper gives little support to wage and price controls as effective tools of anti-inflation policy, it also casts considerable doubt upon the extent to which any individual country can use domestic demand-management policies to regulate its inflation rate independently of that prevailing in the rest of the world; at least for so long as it also attempts to maintain a fixed exchange rate. This follows immediately from the way in which (as Charts 7-12 confirm) inflationary expectations dominate the long-run trend of the inflation rate in all the countries studied, and from the way in which, in all countries except the United States, the formation of expectations is dominated by the inflationary experience of the rest of the world. This domination is total in the cases of Germany, Italy, and Switzerland, if the results presented in Tables 5 and 10 are taken at face value. Except for the United States, which these results, plausibly enough, suggest is a rather "closed" economy with respect to the influence of world prices on domestic inflation, variations in domestic aggregate demand can have only a relatively minor impact on domestic inflation in both the short and the long term.

---

[33] For a more detailed account of this short-lived success, see Laidler (1974) where a somewhat different model, which explicitly incorporates the effects of monetary expansion rates, but ignores overseas influences, also fails to predict the fall in the inflation rate between 1971 and 1972. Thus, the conclusion offered here about a short-term success for this particular policy is rather robust. Note also that both Parkin (1973) and Laidler (1974) point to a sharp but short-lived fall in the level of short-term nominal interest rates immediately after August 1971. This is entirely consistent with wage-price controls having an effect on inflationary expectations.

[34] There is an awkward problem of timing here. Policies that influence aggregate demand, and particularly monetary policies, operate with a long lag, one that is widely regarded as variable. Thus, there are grave practical difficulties in implementing a coordinated policy of demand management and wage-price controls in such a way that each policy tool is effective at a time appropriate for the success of the overall package. See Laidler (1974).

It is a well-known implication of monetarist analysis of the <u>long-run</u> properties of open economies operating fixed exchange rates that their inflation rates cannot perpetually differ from that prevailing in the rest of the world. If a country's inflation rate differs from the prevailing rate, the cumulative effect of payments imbalances on foreign exchange reserves must eventually force either a change of the exchange rate or the adoption of policies compatible with those being pursued elsewhere. However, it was widely believed in the 1950s and 1960s that central banks' powers of stabilization enabled them to render the behavior of the domestic money supply independent of the state of the balance of payments for significant periods of time, to be measured in years rather than in months. Thus, it was believed that a country that did not wish to import a bout of inflation from the rest of the world could keep it out for a worthwhile period by permitting exchange reserves to accumulate while pursuing a relatively tight monetary policy.

No one ever believed that such a policy could have permanent effects; it was as well widely recognized that international capital mobility placed severe limits on the time period over which it could be pursued. The implementation of a relatively tight monetary policy in one country inevitably produces an interest rate differential in its favor that, in turn, leads to a capital inflow. This in turn places further upward pressure on reserves. There is no question that international mobility of capital increased greatly in the 1960s and made it much more difficult for particular countries to pursue independent monetary policies. Therefore, it is perhaps not surprising that the two important surplus countries of the six, Germany, first, and then Switzerland, both resorted to a variety of measures to control inflows of foreign capital. [35]

The data in Table 11 show no clear-cut or long-term effects of these controls on the rate of monetary expansion - - though the short-lived fall in the German monetary expansion rate during 1971-72 might owe something to controls. However, the results reported in this paper strongly imply that such measures, even had they been successful in controlling monetary expansion, would have had relatively little effect on the inflation rates of those two countries. The ability to insulate its money supply from the balance of payments would only give a fixed exchange rate economy the power to choose its own inflation rate if the proximate determinants of domestic inflation were themselves domestic; if, in short, what I have termed above the price-specie flow mechanism were the means whereby inflationary impulses are transmitted between countries. If,

---

[35] Both Switzerland and Germany operated some restrictions on capital inflows throughout the 1960s. These involved limits - - or prohibitions - - on interest payments on overseas holdings of deposits; special reserve requirements against non-resident owned deposits; and, in the case of Switzerland, limits on non-resident ownership of securities and real estate. Ironically, the end of the 1960s saw a considerable relaxation of the controls by both countries; controls were rapidly re-imposed, however, beginning in mid-1970 in Germany, and toward the end of 1971 in Switzerland.

Table 11

Annual Percentage Rates of Change of "Narrow Money" from Preceding Year

Year	U.S.	Italy	Japan	U.K.	Germany	Switzerland
1954	1.6	9.3	NA	3.8	9.6	3.9
1955	3.1	10.1	NA	-1.1	11.2	2.3
1956	1.2	9.2	14.1	0.5	9.0	5.1
1957	0.6	6.5	12.8	-1.6	10.3	4.7
1958	1.2	8.6	5.5	2.5	12.8	6.2
1959	3.8	13.4	16.4	8.3	13.8	9.1
1960	-0.1	13.0	19.9	0.4	8.3	6.4
1961	2.1	14.1	25.1	2.0	9.6	13.4
1962	2.2	17.8	15.9	4.8	10.6	12.1
1963	2.9	16.9	26.4	3.4	7.0	8.9
1964	4.0	6.2	16.8	3.2	8.5	7.6
1965	4.2	13.4	16.8	3.9	9.6	5.1
1966	4.5	15.8	16.3	-0.1	4.5	3.2
1967	3.9	12.9	13.4	7.6	3.3	6.0
1968	7.0	13.1	14.6	4.1	7.7	10.8
1969	6.3	13.2	18.4	0.3	10.1	9.7
1970	4.5	22.4	18.3	9.3	6.1	10.0
1971	7.1	21.0	25.5	15.3	12.1	18.5
1972* 1	6.8	16.2	26.4	14.0	13.5	20.3
2	6.3	18.3	22.2	17.2	12.7	15.7
3	6.7	19.5	17.0	15.2	14.0	12.4
4	8.4	22.4	23.1	14.4	14.4	5.9
1973* 1	8.5	21.7	26.0	9.9	12.8	0.1
2	8.0	23.8	30.5	11.9	8.5	-0.1
3	7.2	22.9	29.3	6.4	1.7	-1.9
4	6.2	19.6	19.8	6.5	0.9	0.5
1974 1	5.9	20.0	16.4	3.2	0.9	-1.4
2	5.7	17.9	13.6	-0.1	3.5	-1.0
3	5.3	14.5	11.9	7.9	9.0	-1.8

*Annual rates of change over the preceding year
source: Federal Reserve Bank of St. Louis

instead, as these results strongly indicate, a more direct price transfer mechanism is at work, in which foreign inflation rates dominate domestic expectations, then the domestic inflation can be maintained below that prevailing in the rest of the world only for as long as the domestic economy is run at less-than-capacity output.[36]

I would conjecture that this matter contributed as much to the failure of German and Swiss attempts to insulate themselves from an accelerating world inflation after 1968, as did the more often attributed cause - - increased capital mobility. (This point is worth further investigation.) If this conjecture is correct, then controls on capital movements, or even separate, and perhaps flexible, exchange rates for capital account transactions, are no substitute for exchange rate flexibility on the trade account when striving to insulate an open economy from inflationary impulses originating abroad.

I have specified inflation originating abroad as a dominant factor in the inflation rates of every economy except that of the United States. Given the exchange rate regime in force in the 1950s and 1960s, there was considerable asymmetry in the relationships between the United States and the rest of the world with respect to the generation of inflation. This asymmetry arose both from the dominant position of the United States as the source of the world's major reserve currency and from the size of the United States' economy relative to those of other countries.[37] Domestically generated variations in the inflation rate in one overseas economy could have only a trivial effect on the U.S. inflation rate, but variations in the U.S. inflation rate would seem to have had a strong effect on the inflation rate in other countries.

Given that the government of the United States pursued the fiscal and monetary policies that it did in the 1950s and 1960s, and given a commitment to maintain a fixed exchange rate, the long-run behavior of the inflation rate in other countries was dictated to them. This was acceptable as long as the United States itself maintained reasonable price stability. Even in Britain, a continual pursuit of extremely high employment targets with fiscal policies coupled with a policy of interest rate stabilization - - inevitably producing a close correlation between domestic credit expansion and the government borrowing requirement - - resulted not in an inflation rate deviating far from that prevailing elsewhere, but in a secularly growing balance of payments problem; this problem culminated in the forced devaluation of November 1967. This diagnosis of the problem leads to the conclusion that the acceleration of inflation that took place throughout

---

[36] This conclusion gets strong support from the evidence presented in Cross and Laidler (1976).

[37] The influence of United States policy on the "world" money supply is analyzed by Parkin, et. al., (1975) while the stability of a "world" demand for money function is demonstrated by Gray, et. al., (1976). Thus, it makes sense to think of United States monetary policy playing a dominant role in the behavior of prices worldwide.

the world in the late 1960s was a direct result of the U.S. fiscal and monetary policies accompanying the intensification of the Vietnam War; and that it was, in the case of Britain, exacerbated by the 1967 devaluation.

Until 1971, the rest of the world was unable to avoid importing inflation from the United States; further, it is not clear that certain countries - - notably Britain, whose reliance on wage and price controls after 1966 was premised on the belief that inflation was being generated domestically by "cost-push" forces - - knew that they were importing inflation. Germany and Switzerland, on the other hand, with their imposition of restrictions on capital inflows showed signs of having known what was happening. However, the strain as different countries tried to combat inflation by different means caused the system of fixed exchange rates to begin to disintegrate in 1971, resulting in the so-called "dirty float" system. In monetarist terms, the adoption of exchange rate flexibility can be seen as giving to the domestic authorities control over the extent to which worldwide inflation influences domestic expectations. This is so because it is the rate of inflation measured in terms of domestic currency that influences domestic price setting; a flexible rate permits the effects of inflation in the rest of the world to be offset by an appreciating currency, and vice versa. This is the case in theory, but the forecasting ability of the monetarist equation for the years 1971-73 suggests that this hypothesis needs much more investigation and refinement.

From the foregoing argument follow certain implications for which there are as yet insufficient data to provide a test. The abandonment of a commitment to fixed exchange rates has allowed national governments greater freedom in the choice of policies towards inflation, but given widely accepted assessments of the length of the time lags inherent in the use of demand management policies - - two years or more in the case of monetary policy - - 1974 is the first year in which one would expect to observe divergent policies producing divergences in national inflation rates that can be expected to persist. Whether these differences do in fact persist is something that can only be observed in the future. As Table 10 shows, Switzerland began to reduce her rate of monetary expansion in 1972 and Germany soon after. The United Kingdom slowed down a little in 1972, while Japan let its rate of monetary expansion accelerate until mid-1973. After mid-1973, both countries began to reduce their monetary expansion rates drastically. The United States began its contraction early in 1973, rather gently at first. Italy let its rate of monetary expansion accelerate in 1972, and made only a small reduction in 1973. If monetarist analysis is correct, if exchange rate flexibility is maintained, and if the policies described here are adhered to through

1974-75, 1974 will prove to have seen the peak of Germany's and Switzerland's inflation rates, while 1975 will see the peak for the others.[38]

All of this has implications for the behavior of exchange rates. A view of money that stresses its information-producing role (e.g., Brunner and Meltzer, 1971) implies that _stable_ exchange rates are desirable and that the debate over fixed vs. flexible rates should concern which system most promotes exchange rate stability. The abandonment of fixed rates after 1971 produced a strong divergence in national inflation rates as different domestic policies were pursued. This has resulted in considerable movements in exchange rates which might be expected to continue for the next year or so. But in this fact lies one of the most important policy implications of those aspects of the monetarist theory tested in this paper. I have shown that, under fixed exchange rates, relatively small open economies can have only a marginal influence over their own inflation rates. It is also true that, if they take the option that exchange rate flexibility offers of pursuing their own domestic goals, and if their domestic policies diverge markedly, then exchange rate instability results. To achieve exchange rate stability, therefore, whether under a scheme of formally fixed or formally flexible rates, requires that individual countries, perhaps with the exception of the United States, accept that they cannot have any but marginal control over their own inflation rates.[39] Policies towards inflation must be coordinated across countries if exchange rate stability is to be achieved. It is the pursuit of _stable_ exchange rates rather than the maintenance of institutionally fixed exchange rates that makes inflation an international monetary phenomenon; it follows that there is a vital political problem inherent in devising the institutional framework within which national policies can be so coordinated that inflation is tackled at the international level.

---

[38] This was written in early 1975. In fact, U.S., Italian, and Japanese inflation peaked in the final quarter of 1974 according to FRB of St. Louis data.

[39] This is an important argument in the case for a monetary union among Common Market countries. Though a single country can have little control over its own price level in a stable exchange rate regime, acting collectively, a monetary union could have considerable influence.

REFERENCES

1. Brunner, K., "Monetary Management, Domestic Inflation, and Imported Inflation," in National Monetary Policies and the International Financial System, (ed. R.Z. Aliber), Chicago and London: University of Chicago Press, 1974.

2. Brunner, K., Fratianni, M., Jordan, J.L., Meltzer, A.H., and Neumann, M.J.M., "Fiscal and Monetary Policies in Moderate Inflation," Journal of Money, Credit and Banking, 5, No. 1, Part 2, (February 1973), 313-353.

3. Brunner, K., and Meltzer, A.H., "The Uses of Money: Money in the Theory of an Exchange Economy," American Economic Review, 61, No. 5, (December 1971), 784-805.

4. Claassen, E., and Salin, P. (eds.) Stabilization Policies in Interdependent Economies. Amsterdam: North Holland, 1972.

5. Cross, R.B., and Laidler, D.E.W., "Inflation, Excess Demand and Expectations in Fixed Exchange Rate Open Economies: Some Preliminary Empirical Results," in Inflation in the World Economy, (eds. J.M. Parkin and G. Zis), Manchester: Manchester University Press, 1976.

6. Dicks-Mireaux, L.A., "The Inter-Relationship Between Cost and Price Changes, 1945-1959: A Study of Inflation in Postwar Britain," Oxford Economic Papers (NS) 13, No. 3, (October 1961), 267-292.

7. Godfrey, L., "The Phillips Curve: Incomes Policy and Trade Union Effects," in The Current Inflation, (eds. Harry G. Johnson and A.R. Nobay), London: MacMillan, 1971.

8. Gray, M.R., Ward, R., and Zis, G., "World Demand for Money," in Inflation in the World Economy, (eds. J.M. Parkin and G. Zis), Manchester: Manchester University Press, 1976.

9. Harrod, R.F., "The Issues: Five Views," in Inflation as a Global Problem, (ed. R. Hinshaw), London: Johns Hopkins Press, 1972.

10. Hicks, J.R. The Theory of Wages. London: MacMillan, 1932.

11. Hicks, J.R. The Crisis in Keynesian Economics. Oxford: Blackwell, 1974.

12. _____, "The Permissive Economy," in IEA Occasional Paper Special No. 43, Crisis '75, London: Institute of Economic Affairs, 1975.

13. Johnson, Harry G. Inflation and the Monetarist Controversy. Amsterdam: North Holland, 1972.

14. Jones, A. The New Inflation: The Politics of Prices and Incomes. London: Penguin Books and Andre Deutsch, 1972.

15. Korteweg, P., "The Inflation Problem, A Multi Country Study of Inflation-- The Dutch Cash 1952-1972," Carnegie-Mellon University, mimeo, 1974.

16. Laidler, D.E.W., "The Influence of Money on Real Income and Inflation: A Simple Model with Some Empirical Tests for the United States, 1953- 1972," Manchester School, 41, No. 4, (December 1973), 367-395.

17. _____, "Two Issues in the Economic Report of the President: The Control of Inflation and the Future of the International Monetary System," American Economic Review, 64, No. 4, (September 1974), 535-543.

18. Laidler, D.E.W., and Nobay, A.R., "Some Current Issues Concerning the International Aspects of Inflation," in Essays on Money and Inflation, (ed. D.E.W. Laidler), Manchester: Manchester University Press, 1975.

19. Laidler, D.E.W., and Parkin, J.M., "Inflation: A Survey," Economic Journal, 85, No. 340, (December 1975), 741-809.

20. Parkin, J.M., "The 1973 Report of the President's Council of Economic Advisers: A Critique," American Economic Review, 63, No. 4, (September 1973), 535-545.

21. Parkin, J.M., Richards, I., Zis, G., "The Determinants and Control of the World Money Supply Under Fixed Exchange Rates 1961-1971," Manchester School of Economics and Social Studies, 43, (September 1975), 293-316.

22. Parkin, J.M., Sumner, M.T., and Jones, R.A., "A Survey of the Econometric Evidence on the Effects of Incomes Policies on the Rate of Inflation," in Incomes Policy and Inflation, (eds. J.M. Parkin and M.T. Sumner), Manchester: Manchester University Press, 1972.

23. Parkin, J.M., Sumner, M.T., and Ward, R., "The Effects of Excess Demand, Generalized Expectations and Wage Price Controls on Wage Inflation in the U.K.," The Economics of Price and Wage Controls, Carnegie-Rochester Conference Series, 2, (eds. K. Brunner and A.H. Meltzer), Amsterdam: North Holland, (1976), 193-222.

24. Phelps, E.S. Inflation Policy and Unemployment Theory: The Cost-Benefit Approach to Monetary Planning. New York: Norton, 1972.

25. Phelps-Brown, E.H., "The Analysis of Wage Movements Under Full Employment," Scottish Journal of Political Economy, 18, No. 3, (November 1971), 233-243.

26. Pigou, A.C., "The Value of Money," Quarterly Journal of Economics, 32, No. 1, (November 1917), 38-65.

27. Purdy, D.L., and Zis, G., "On the Concept and Measurement of Union Militancy," in Inflation and Labour Markets, (eds. D.E.W. Laidler and D.L. Purdy), Manchester: Manchester University Press, 1974.

28. Spinelli, F., "Determinants of Price and Wage Inflation in Italy," in Inflation in Open Economies, (eds. J.M. Parkin and G. Zis), Manchester: Manchester University Press (forthcoming).

29. Taylor, J., "Wage Inflation, Unemployment and the Organized Pressure for Higher Wages in the U.K. 1961-1971," in Current Economic Problems, (eds. J.M. Parkin and A.R. Nobay), Cambridge: Cambridge University Press, 1975.

30. Ward, R., and Zis, G., "Trade Union Militancy as an Explanation of Inflation: an International Comparison," Manchester School, 42, No. 1, (March 1974), 46-65.

31. Wiles, P., "Cost Inflation and the State of Economic Theory," Economic Journal, 83, No. 3, (June 1973), 377-398.

INFLATION - - ALTERNATIVE EXPLANATIONS AND POLICIES:
TESTS ON DATA DRAWN FROM SIX COUNTRIES: A COMMENT

Robert H. Rasche

Michigan State University

Laidler's lengthy paper presents a menu of problems and confusions, several of which I feel warrant comments.

First, Laidler states, ". . .modern monetarist analysis has advanced beyond the simple partial equilibrium approach to price level determination implicit in, for example, Pigou's classic (1917) paper." After reading this introduction, one expects Laidler to provide some sort of "monetarist" general equilibrium analysis of the inflation problem. It is disappointing to discover that Laidler's analysis is another partial equilibrium approach to the inflation problem. His emphasis is on estimating the equation,

$$\Delta P = gy_{-1} + X_{-1} \ .$$

As is seen from the recent work by Turnovsky (1974), this is only one equation in a system of equations. It is surprising to see it as a so-called "monetarist" hypothesis. To get from the usual "expectations augmented Phillips curve" specification, which is developed in the literature with the rate of change of the nominal wage rate as the dependent variable, to the form that Laidler uses, with the rate of change of commodity prices as the dependent variable, requires an assumption that the ratio of prices to money wages is constant. My impression is that this assumption is regarded by many monetarists as the ultimate "Keynesian heresy"- -that prices are not determined by wages (presumably in the partial equilibrium sense), but rather by the money stock.

Nowhere in Laidler's partial equilibrium analysis does the stock of money appear. We are told that we are monetarists if we believe that excess commodity demand and inflation expectations are capable of explaining, to within some stochastic element, the observed rate of inflation. If this is true, then I do not understand what macroeconomists, particularly those in North America, have been arguing about for the last ten to fifteen years.

Laidler's stochastic specification raises a number of econometric issues which were swept under the rug in the paper, and which make it impossible to interpret any of his results. The "monetarist model," equation (3), with the addition of a stochastic term, is:

(1) $\Delta P = gy_{-1} + X_{-1} + u, \; u \sim N\,(0, \sigma^2)$ and independently,

where X_{-1} is "expected inflation rate" defined as

$$X\text{-}X_{-1} = d\,[v(\Delta P - X_{-1}) + (1 - v)\,(\Delta\Pi - X_{-1})].$$

Solve this for

(2) $X = dv\Delta P + (1 - v)d\Delta\Pi + [1 - dv - (1 - v)d]\,X_{-1}.$

Substitute (2) into (1) lagging it one period:

(3) $\Delta P = gy_{-1} + dv\Delta P_{-1} + (1 - v)d\Delta\Pi_{-1} + (1 - d)X_{-2} + u.$

Add and subtract $(1 - d)\Delta P_{-1}$:

(4) $\Delta P = gy_{-1} + [1 - d(1 - v)]\;\Delta P_{-1} + (1 - v)d\Delta\Pi_{-1}$

$$+ (1 - d)\,(X_{-2} - \Delta P_{-1}) + u \; ,$$

but note from (1) lagged $(X_{-2} - \Delta P_{-1}) = (\text{-}gy_{-2} - u_{-1}),$ so

(5) $\Delta P = gy_{-1} + [1 - d(1 - v)]\;\Delta P_{-1} + (1 - v)d\Delta\Pi_{-1}$

$$- (1 - d)\,gy_{-2} + u - (1 - d)\,u_{-1}.$$

Note that Laidler specifies $0 < d \leqslant 1,$

so we can rewrite (5) as

(5a) $\Delta P = gy_{-1} - (1 - d)\,gy_{-2} + [1 - d(1 - v)]\,\Delta P_{-1} + (1 - v)d\Delta\Pi_{-1}$

$$+ u - \lambda u_{-1}$$

$$0 < \lambda < 1 \; ; \; \text{define } v_t = u_t - \lambda u_{t\text{-}1} \; .$$

This is the kind of error structure that is generated by the usual adaptive expectations model, which has disturbance covariance matrix,

$$E(vv') = \begin{bmatrix} 1 + \lambda^2 & -\lambda & 0 \ldots & & 0 \\ -\lambda & 1 + \lambda^2 & -\lambda & 0 \ldots & 0 \\ 0 & -\lambda & 1 + \lambda^2 & & \\ \cdot & 0 & & & \\ \cdot & \cdot & & & \\ \cdot & \cdot & & & \\ 0 & 0 & 0 & 0 & 1 + \lambda^2 \end{bmatrix}$$

(See Johnston, p. 313.) Thus, the error structure has <u>negative</u> first order serial correlation. Note that the presence of the serial correlation and the value of the autoregressive coefficient are part of Laidler's maintained hypothesis.

As is known, the coefficient on the lagged dependent variable under this condition is biased asymptotically toward zero. Also, the standard Durbin-Watson statistic is inappropriate for testing for serial correlation in these circumstances. An alternative test for serial correlation is Durbin's h statistic, but this seems inappropriate given Laidler's limited sample size ($n = 17$). Laidler's work is complicated, therefore, by three econometric problems which he ignores: (1) serial correlated residuals; (2) the presence of a lagged dependent variable; (3) a non-linear constraint on the autoregressive coefficient in terms of the other parameters of the system. It is impossible to interpret Laidler's tests of the "monetarist" model without some attention to these problems.

REFERENCES

1. Johnston, J. <u>Econometric Methods</u>, 2nd edition. New York: McGraw-Hill, 1972.

2. Turnovsky, S.J., "On the Role of Inflationary Expectations in a Short-Run Macro-Economic Model," <u>Economic Journal</u>, 84, No. 334, (June 1974), 317-337.

INFLATION, UNEMPLOYMENT AND MACROECONOMIC POLICY IN OPEN ECONOMIES: AN EMPIRICAL ANALYSIS

Michael J. Hamburger and Rutbert D. Reisch*
Federal Reserve Bank of New York

During 1974, there was a sharp and unanticipated upward surge in the United States' price level. The most common reaction to this development among popular commentators and, to some extent, professional economists was that something was seriously wrong with traditional economic analysis, in general, and its explanation of inflation, in particular. Although the force of this argument was substantially weakened by the economy's apparently rapid response to the restrictive monetary policy pursued during the second half of 1974 and the early part of 1975, it seems reasonable to consider this a temporary phenomenon. Future spurts of inflation or other unexpected events are likely to renew the call for alternative approaches to analysis and policy which promise greater control over the economy.

This study has two principal objectives. First, we seek to determine the extent to which existing theory can explain fluctuations in prices and output (employment). Within the limits of this knowledge, we then attempt to evaluate the role that traditional economic policy can play in moderating these fluctuations. Consequently, the analysis is not restricted to the American experience in 1974. Instead, we examine the explanatory power of a set of relatively standard macroeconomic models across a number of countries and time intervals. The work drawn upon is that of Lucas (1973), Stein (1976) and Korteweg (1975). Lucas' model treats aggregate demand as an exogenous variable and seeks to explain the trade-off between real output and inflation, under the assumption that suppliers possess rational price expectations. The model is tested using data for nearly twenty open economies, but no allowance is made for any special effects which the international sector may have on the domestic economy.

The Stein model, which was developed to help resolve some outstanding issues in the monetarist controversy as it pertains to the U.S. economy, is more traditional. Aggregate demand is taken to depend on domestic policy variables and little attention is devoted either to the foreign sector or to supply behavior. Reduced-form equations are explicitly derived to explain the rate of price change and the unemployment rate. Korteweg's work, which is specifically

---

* We are grateful to M. Arak and K. Brunner for helpful comments and suggestions, and are indebted to H. Ferster and N. Marks for excellent research assistance. The views expressed are ours alone and should not be attributed to the Federal Reserve Bank.

oriented to the Dutch economy, relies heavily on the Brunner-Meltzer (1974), (1976) analyses of open and closed economies. The reduced-form equations he develops for aggregate production and the inflation rate are similar in spirit to Stein's. One important difference is that Korteweg includes two variables to measure the influence of the foreign sector.

In the analysis which follows, we first update the Lucas equations for the United States, the United Kingdom, Germany, France, and the Netherlands. Second, we modify the Stein model in the manner suggested by Korteweg and estimate the resulting equations for the U.S., the U.K., Germany, and the Netherlands. Finally, we assess these alternative approaches to the inflation/real output trade-off and draw implications for the efficacy of macroeconomic stabilization policy.

I. INFLATION, OUTPUT AND AGGREGATE SUPPLY

In the final analysis, real output and inflation should result from a two-equation system describing aggregate demand and aggregate supply. We concentrate first on the supply side only and treat aggregate demand as an exogenous variable. To describe suppliers' behavior and to explain real output, we adopt Lucas' (1973) approach. Lucas assumes that aggregate supply depends on the discrepancy between actual and expected prices, and on the cyclical component of last period's real output. Aggregate demand - - determined exogenously and hence a proxy for all policy variables - - is assumed to be of unit-price elasticity, which implies that the breakdown of nominal aggregate demand into prices and real output is entirely supply-determined.

More specifically, Lucas assumes rational suppliers distributed over a large number of competitive markets with unevenly distributed demand in which suppliers know the price $P_t(z)$ in market z at time t and the history of the system, but not the current general price level, P_t. In each market z, supply consists of a long-run trend component y_{nt} common to all markets, and a cyclical component y_{ct}:

(1) $\qquad y_t(z) = y_{nt} + y_{ct}(z) \qquad$ (log of real output in z at t),

with

(2) $\qquad y_{nt} = a + \beta t \qquad$ (log of trend component of real output);

312

and the cyclical component determined by $P_t(z)$ relative to the general price level P_t expected on the basis of information $I_t(z)$ available in z at time t, and by its own lagged value:

(3) $\qquad y_{ct} = \gamma[P_t(z) - E(P_t/I_t(z)] + \lambda y_{c,\,t-1}(z),$

where all symbols denote the logarithms of the variables.

Assuming the unknown general price level P_t is normally distributed with mean $\overline{P}_t$ and variance σ^2, and that $P_t(z) = P_t + z$ where z is distributed normally with mean 0 and variance τ^2 and independently of P_t, the joint density function is:

$$f(P_t, P_t(z)) = \frac{1}{2\pi\sigma\tau} e^{-1/2[\frac{(P_t - \overline{P}_t)^2}{\sigma^2} + \frac{(P_t(z) - P_t)^2}{\tau^2}]}$$

$$= \frac{1}{2\pi\sigma\tau} e^{-1/2[\frac{(\overline{P}_t - P_t)^2}{\sigma^2} + \frac{(P_t - P_t(z))^2}{\tau^2}]}$$

$$= f(\overline{P}_t, P_t) = f(P_t|\overline{P}_t) \cdot h(\overline{P}_t),$$

with $h(\overline{P}_t) = \int\limits_{-\infty}^{\infty} f(\overline{P}_t, P_t)\, dP_t.$

Collecting terms in P_t, substituting

$$\sqrt{\frac{1}{\sigma^2} + \frac{1}{\tau^2}} \left[P_t - \frac{\dfrac{\overline{P}_t}{\sigma^2} + \dfrac{P_t(z)}{\tau^2}}{\dfrac{1}{\sigma^2} + \dfrac{1}{\tau^2}} \right] = \rho,$$

and using $\int\limits_{-\infty}^{\infty} e^{-\rho^2/2}\, d\rho = \sqrt{2\pi}$,

the marginal density function can be written as:

$$h(\overline{P}_t) = \frac{1}{\sqrt{2\pi}\sqrt{\sigma^2 + \tau^2}} e^{-1/2\frac{(\overline{P}_t - P_t(z))^2}{\sigma^2 + \tau^2}}$$

313

Dividing this into $f(\overline{P}_t, P_t)$:

$$(4) \qquad f(P_t | \overline{P}_t) = \frac{\sqrt{\sigma^2 + \tau^2}}{\sqrt{2\pi}\ \sigma\ \tau}\ e^{\ -1/2\ \frac{\sigma^2 + \tau^2}{\sigma^2\tau^2}\left[P_t - \frac{\tau^2\overline{P}_t + \sigma^2 P_t(z)}{\sigma^2 + \tau^2} \right]^2}$$

Hence, $E(P_t | \overline{P}_t, P_t(z)) = \dfrac{\tau^2\overline{P}_t + \sigma^2 P_t(z)}{\sigma^2 + \tau^2}$,

and $V(P_t | \overline{P}_t, P_t(z)) = \dfrac{\sigma^2\tau^2}{\sigma^2 + \tau^2}$.

Introducing $\theta = \dfrac{\tau^2}{\sigma^2 + \tau^2}$, the mean and the variance can be expressed:

$$E(P_t | \overline{P}_t, P_t(z)) = (1 - \theta)\ P_t(z) + \theta\ \overline{P}_t,$$

and

$$V(P_t | \overline{P}_t, P_t(z)) = \theta\sigma^2 .$$

Combining $E(P_t | \overline{P}_t, P_t(z))$, (1), and (3), and averaging over all markets z yields the aggregate supply function:

$$(5) \qquad y_t = y_{nt} + k[P_t - \overline{P}_t] + \lambda[y_{t-1} - y_{n, t-1}],$$

with $k = \gamma\theta$.

Lucas' aggregate supply function, which we will use for our empirical analysis, is only one form to describe suppliers' behavior. For instance, the aggregate supply function could depend only on the discrepancy between actual and expected prices (Sargent, 1973):

$$(6) \qquad y_t = y_{nt} + k(P_t - E(P_t));$$

or include several lagged values of the cyclical component:

(7)
$$y_t = y_{nt} + k(P_t - E(P_t)) + \sum_{i=1}^{T} \lambda_i (y_{t-i} - y_{n, t-i});$$

or incorporate adjustments in expected future price movements:

(8)
$$y_t = y_{nt} + k[P_t - E(P_t) - (\frac{1}{n} \sum_{i=1}^{n} E_t P_{t+i} - \frac{1}{n} \sum_{i=1}^{n} E_{t-1} P_{t+i})]$$

$$+ \sum_{i=1}^{T} \lambda_i (y_{t-i} - y_{n, t-i}),$$

which could be further modified by introducing a more sophisticated weighting pattern instead of $\frac{1}{n}$. Finally, $E(P_t)$ has to be specified. A simple formulation is the well-known adaptive expectations model:

(9)
$$E(P_t) = \sum_{i=1}^{\infty} w_i P_{t-i},$$

which will not be pursued further here. Rather, following Lucas, we assume rational price expectations:

(10)
$$E(P_t) = E(P_t | \text{history of the system, policy variables, other exogenous variables}).$$

In this framework, suppliers know past movements of nominal aggregate demand, past shifts of real output, the trend component of real output; and assess current nominal aggregate demand x_t on the basis of:

(11)
$$x_t = x_{t-1} + \Delta x_t,$$

where Δx_t is the proxy for a current policy shift which by assumption follows

(12)
$$[\Delta x_t] \sim dn (\delta, \sigma_x^2).$$

Postulating the solution,

$$(13) \qquad P_t = \pi_0 + \pi_1 x_t + \pi_2 x_{t-1} + \ldots + \eta_1 y_{t-1} + \eta_2 y_{t-2}$$

$$+ \ldots + \xi_0 y_{nt},$$

we obtain:

$$(14) \qquad E(P_t) = \pi_0 + \pi_1(x_{t-1} + \delta) + \pi_2 x_{t-1} + \ldots + \eta_1 y_{t-1}$$

$$+ \eta_2 y_{t-2} + \ldots + \xi_0 y_{nt}.$$

To complete his model, Lucas assumes an exogenously determined demand function with unit-price elasticity:

$$(15) \qquad x_t = y_t + P_t,$$

where x_t = log of nominal aggregate demand.

Questions may be raised regarding the applicability of this function to an open economy. At the very least, it seems appropriate to distinguish between domestic and foreign prices, both of which are included in P_t. Moreover, with foreign sources of supply available, we would expect the price elasticity of the demand for domestic output to rise and, at least with respect to domestic prices, it could exceed unity. [1]

Returning to the standard Lucas model, we solve the system (5), (15) for fluctuations in real output and the inflation rate to obtain:

$$(16) \qquad y_{ct} = -\pi\delta + \pi\Delta x_t + \lambda y_{ct-1}, \text{ with } \pi = \frac{k}{1 + k};$$

$$(17) \qquad \Delta P_t = -\beta + (1 - \pi)\,\Delta x_t + \pi\Delta x_{t-1} - \lambda\Delta y_{ct-1},$$

$$\text{with } \Delta P_t = P_t - P_{t-1}.$$

Lucas fitted these two equations to annual observations for 18 countries for the period 1953-1967, to test the natural unemployment rate hypothesis by comparing the results for countries with different time patterns of nominal income.

---

[1] Some support for the latter contention is provided by Arak (1975), who reestimated the Lucas model for the U.S., and found the elasticity of aggregate demand with respect to P_t (the general price level) to be greater than one.

This was not our objective. Instead, we sought to determine whether the model would continue to adequately explain the real output/inflation trade-off when high and fluctuating inflation rates became more the rule than the exception, as they were during Lucas' time period. In particular, we were interested in comparing the performance of the model with the more traditional analyses which focus on the explanation of aggregate demand. Moreover, there are the questions of what effects, if any, the general increase in inflationary tendencies had on the real output/inflation trade-off in different countries, and the extent to which the 1974 experience can be explained from the supply side.

The regressions performed for the period 1953-1973 (Table 1) indicate that the measures of goodness of fit are generally similar to Lucas' except that, whereas his equations explain real output better than prices, we find the same explanatory power to prevail for both output and price equations. (Following Lucas, the unadjusted R^2 is used as the measure of goodness of fit in these equations.) The equations are estimated without constraints. Comparing the coefficients of the output and price equations shows that the model performs reasonably well. While it is interesting to note that the U.S. shows the most favorable trade-off in the concurrent period, no conclusions can be drawn from the price equations as to how the inflationary impact is distributed over time, since the full effect on prices must be transmitted in the concurrent and subsequent periods on the basis of the model's specification.

To test for structural shifts, we also ran our regressions for two sub-periods - - 1953-1962 and 1963-1973 - - in order to investigate whether the trade-off terms have changed significantly during the period 1953-1973. The Chow test reveals that eight of the 10 equations (five for output, five for prices) show no significant shift between the two sub-periods. This suggests that overall the trade-off terms have neither improved nor deteriorated during 1953-1973. The Chow test rejects the hypothesis of no shift only for the output equations of Germany and the Netherlands. Since such a shift in the output equations should be accompanied by a shift in the corresponding price equation - - which is not the case here - - this result is probably of little relevance. However, the deterioration in the trade-off terms observed for Germany and the Netherlands is of some interest. The reason for any given stimulatory policy to be reflected in a significantly smaller increase in real output in the later period may be the changing labor supply conditions between the two periods; until 1961, there was a continuous labor inflow from East Germany as some 3 million people were absorbed by the German economy after 1945. On the other hand, labor migration from other E.E.C. countries into Germany did not take place on any substantial scale until the late sixties. Thus, the highly elastic labor supply in the earlier period may account for the more favorable trade-off terms during that

317

Table 1

Lucas Output Equation

$$y_{ct} = -\pi\delta \quad + \quad \pi \Delta x_t \quad + \quad \lambda y_{ct-1} \qquad R^2$$

		$-\pi\delta$	$\pi \Delta x_t$	λy_{ct-1}	R^2
U.S.	1953-73	- .050 (-7.566)	0.782 (7.993)	0.756 (9.363)	0.8824
U.K.	1953-73	- .012 (-1.311)	0.184 (1.483)	0.550 (2.804)	0.3258
Germany	1953-73	- .052 (-3.521)	0.614 (3.842)	0.862 (8.714)	0.8169
France	1953-73	- .011 (-1.074)	0.103 (1.026)	0.741 (4.520)	0.5351
Netherlands	1953-73	- .037 (-3.415)	0.408 (3.726)	0.655 (4.848)	0.6571

Lucas Price Equation

$$\Delta P_t = -\beta + (1 - \pi)\Delta x_t + \pi \Delta x_{t-1} - \lambda\Delta y_{ct-1} \qquad R^2$$

		$-\beta$	$(1-\pi)\Delta x_t$	$\pi \Delta x_{t-1}$	$-\lambda\Delta y_{ct-1}$	R^2
U.S.	1953-73	- .038 (-4.533)	0.090 (1.460)	0.971 (7.296)	- .746 (-5.798)	0.7894
U.K.	1953-73	- .025 (-2.110)	0.513 (2.823)	0.440 (1.900)	- .046 (- .228)	0.6921
Germany	1953-73	- .061 (-3.282)	0.402 (3.200)	0.662 (4.053)	- .666 (-3.706)	0.6051
France	1953-73	- .054 (-4.152)	0.886 (8.229)	0.132 (1.483)	- .165 (- .799)	0.8236
Netherlands	1953-73	- .037 (-2.359)	0.470 (4.021)	0.403 (2.710)	- .284 (-1.380)	0.6707

period. For the Netherlands (where the Chow test is far less significant), it is conceivable that the results simply reflect the change in Germany's labor market conditions, since the Dutch economy is closely linked to Germany's through its export sector.

Finally, we tested the model's ability to predict. Using the results presented in Table 1 to predict 1974 real GNP and the inflation rates for the U.S. and Germany shows that real GNP is overpredicted and the inflation rate underpredicted for both countries. For the U.S., the predicted GNP was $871.3 billion (1958 prices) versus the actual $821.6 billion; for Germany, it was DM 625.8 billion (1962 prices) versus the actual DM 596.4 billion. The annual inflation rates, on the other hand, are forecast at 6.2 percent for the U.S. versus the actual 9.7 percent, and at 4.0 percent for Germany versus the actual 6.4 percent. The difference between the actual and predicted GNP deflators - - 3.5 percentage points for the U.S. and 2.4 percentage points for Germany - - may be accounted for by the foreign sector, which is not explicitly included in Lucas' model. Specifically, the sharp boost in import prices beginning in late 1973 - - largely because of escalating oil prices - - must have caught suppliers by surprise, and should help to explain the divergence of predicted from actual values. Therefore, it seems more appropriate to test the model's predictive ability for 1973. Running the regressions for the period 1953-1972, and then predicting the 1973 values, reveals that real GNP is overpredicted for the U.S., Germany, and the Netherlands; and underpredicted for the U.K. and France (Table 2). Conversely, inflation rates are underpredicted for the U.S. and the Netherlands, overpredicted for the U.K. and France, and forecast correctly for Germany.

The absence of significant shifts over time suggests that the underlying structure is stable and that the model reflects basic trends. Short-run predictions, however, remain problematic since various exogenous factors not incorporated in the model can exert a sizable impact on output and prices. For the 1974 predictions, the oil crisis is one such factor. For 1973, the forecast errors are smaller for countries with stable import prices (Table 2). Price controls are another exogenous factor not incorporated in the model; they also help to explain the comparatively large 1973 forecast errors in inflation rates for the U.S. and the U.K. Presumably, the reported U.S. inflation rate was "catching up" in 1973 after the 1971 and 1973 price controls, thereby overstating the "true" inflation rate. On the other hand, the U.K. imposed a total price freeze from November 1972 to April 1973, which was followed by somewhat relaxed controls, hence suppressing "true" inflationary pressures. Thus, the forecast errors in the inflation rates are consistent with the impact of price controls on the 1973 inflation rates in both countries.

Table 2

1973 - Forecasts of Real GNP and Inflation Rates on
Basis of Lucas 1953-1972 Regressions

	Real GNP (billions of units)		Inflation Rate (percent)	
	Forecast	Actual	Forecast	Actual
U.S. (1958-$)	854.9	839.2	4.04	5.45
U.K. (1970-£)	56.1	57.0	9.89	7.28
Germany (1962-DM)	611.6	594.0	5.73	5.70
France (1970-FF)	942.9	953.6	7.11	6.95
Netherlands (1963-NG)	91.2	90.1	7.32	7.60

Import Prices   1970 = 100

	1968	1969	1970	1971	1972	1973	1974
U.S.	90.6	93.4	100.0	105.2	113.0	134.3	198.8
U.K.	92.7	95.5	100.0	105.2	109.1	138.1	210.3
Germany	98.1	100.0	100.0	99.0	96.5	102.7	128.7
France	84.8	90.2	100.0	103.5	104.4	112.1	165.5
Netherlands	91.	93.	100.	104.	103.	111.	154.

II. AGGREGATE DEMAND

We turn next to the more traditional approach to macroeconomic analysis, i.e., models that focus on the determination of aggregate demand. Stein's (1976) study is used as the basis for this analysis because of its simplicity, its completeness, and the impressive empirical results that he reports. The purpose here is to evaluate the applicability of such models to countries with different economic structures, and to compare their explanatory power to that of the supply-oriented approach discussed above.

Included in the Stein model are: a labor market characterized by wage and price flexibility and an endogenously determined unemployment rate; asset markets for capital and bonds; an excess demand equation for goods; two price-change equations; and a government budget constraint.

In summary form, the model may be expressed by the following equations:

(18)   real wage change, $\dfrac{\Delta w}{w} = a + \pi^* - \pi + h(U)$,

> where π is the rate of price change, π^* is the currently expected rate of price change, and $h(U)$ is a function of the unemployment rate, $h < 0$;

(19)   unemployment rate, $U = F(\dfrac{w}{A(t)}, G_1)$,

> where $A(t)$ is the level of productivity which grows at rate a and G_1 is the government demand for labor (per unit of capital);

(20)   bond market, $\rho = g(U, \pi^*, m, \theta)$,

> where ρ, the nominal rate of interest depends on m, real money balances (per unit of capital), θ, the ratio of government interest-bearing debt to the money supply, U and π^*;

(21)   government budget constraint, $G - T = [\Delta\theta + (1 + \theta)\mu] m$,

> where $G - T$ denotes real government purchases of goods and services minus real taxes (both per unit of capital), and μ is the rate of monetary expansion;

(22)   Change in real money balances/capital, $\dfrac{\Delta m}{m} = \mu - n - \pi$,

where the only new variable, n, is the growth rate of capital;

(23)   price change, $\pi = P(U, \pi^*, m, G, \theta)$;

(24)   adaptive price expectations, $\pi^* = b(\pi - \pi^*)$.

A key element of the model is the price-change relationship (23), which is assumed to represent the sum of two elements: a demand-pull effect and a cost-push effect. The cost-push effect is $\dfrac{\Delta W}{W} - a$, the growth of the nominal wage in excess of the rate of labor augmenting technical change. The demand-pull effect is a function of real excess demand for goods per unit of capital, E. Letting λp denote a finite speed of response, this hypothesis may be expressed:

(25) $\pi = (\dfrac{\Delta W}{W} - a) + \lambda_p E(\cdot)$,

where the real excess demand for goods per unit of capital is the sum of real planned investment (I) plus real planned consumption (C) plus real government purchases (G) less output (y), all per unit of capital; i.e. :

(26) $E \equiv C + I + G - y$.

Noting that $\Delta W/W = \Delta w/w + \pi$, substituting (18) into (25), and writing E as a function of π^*, m, G, θ, and U yields the price-change equation (23).

Solving this system, Stein obtains estimation equations for the rate of price change (π) and the unemployment rate (U) in terms of three independent control variables: the rate of monetary growth (μ); real government purchases of goods and services per unit of capital (G); and the ratio of government interest-bearing debt to the money supply.

(27) $U(t) = \text{const.} + a_1 U(t - \delta) + a_2 \pi(t - \delta) + a_3 \sum_1^\delta \mu(t - i)$

$+ a_4 \sum_1^\delta G(t - i) + a_5 \sum_1^\delta \theta(t - i) + j_1(t)$.

$$(28) \qquad \pi(t) = \text{const.} + b_1 U(t-\delta) + b_2 \pi(t-\delta) + b_3 \sum_1^\delta \mu(t-i)$$

$$+ b_4 \sum_1^\delta G(t-i) + b_5 \sum_1^\delta \theta(t-i) + j_2(t),$$

where j_1 and j_2 are error terms; δ is an arbitrary constant; and $t-\delta$ represents some earlier time period. Thus, conditions at time t are assumed to depend on the state of the world at $t-\delta$ and on the pattern of control inputs applied from that date to the present.

The Stein model is appealing but contains a number of deficiencies. Among the more important ones, from our point of view, are the treatment of price expectations, and the failure to make any explicit allowance for the influence of the foreign sector on the domestic economy. There is now considerable evidence to suggest that an autoregression on past price movements may not be the most appropriate model of inflationary expectations. [2] A prominent alternative is to assume that economic units form their expectations rationally, i.e., they make some effort to learn the structural model that describes the economy and form their expectations accordingly. Given the current level of abstraction, it is not clear how the model's solution would be altered by the replacement of equation (24) with a rational expectations scheme. Hence, we have assumed that π^* may be treated as an endogenous variable, and that this is why Stein failed to obtain significant coefficients for the variable when it was included in equations (27) and (28). Consequently, like Stein, but for different reasons, we do not include an explicit measure of inflationary expectations in the estimation equations.

On the other hand, it does seem important to modify the model to incorporate the influences on the domestic economy emanating from the foreign sector. Here we follow Korteweg (1975), who identifies two kinds of foreign trade impulses: those relating to variations in the foreign sector's demand for private domestic output; and those relating to changes in the prices the home country has to pay for its imports of goods and services (the effects of international capital flows other than those which occur as a result of changes in the domestic monetary base on the money supply, are not considered).

The foreign sector's demand for domestic output is measured by Korteweg's weighted volume of world trade, e - - a measure of predetermined exports:

$$e = \sum_f w_f i_f,$$

---

[2] See, for example, Fama (1975), Rutledge (1974), Sargent (1973), and Lucas (1973).

where i_f denotes the total import demand of each of the home country's trading partners; and w_f, a weighting factor, is measured as:

$$w_f = \left[\frac{i_{fh}}{i_f}\right]_{-1} ,$$

the share of trading partner f's imports in the preceding period which came from the home country. In other words, e indicates the volume of a country's exports, assuming that the distribution of all its trading partners' imports remain unchanged from the previous period. [3]

As a measure of the influence of foreign prices on the domestic economy, we use the index of home country import prices denominated in the local currency. The effect of changes in import prices, arising either from varia-tions in foreign prices per se or from changes in exchange rates, depends on the degree of substitutability between domestic and foreign goods, and whether the effects are transmitted through the supply or the demand side of the domestic economy. Thus, to the extent that there are no domestic substitutes for im-ported goods, a rise in the price of the latter could be contractive with respect to domestic employment (output) and prices.

To incorporate the above discussion in the Stein model, we rewrite the price-change equation (25):

(25') $\qquad \pi = [(\frac{\Delta W}{W} - a) + \gamma(p_m)] + \lambda p E(U, \pi^*, m, G, \theta, e, p_m),$

where p_m, the percentage change in the index of import prices, is added to both the cost-push and demand-pull components of (25); and e, the measure of pre-determined export demand, is included as an additional determinant of excess demand. As a result of this substitution equation (23) may be replaced by

(23') $\qquad \pi = P(U, \pi^*, m, G, \theta, p_m, e).$

---

[3] An alternative measure of the foreign sector's demand for domestic output is the volume of the home country's exports. The problem with this measure is that, to the extent a country's exports depend on the current value of the domestic price level relative to foreign prices, it will be at least partially endogenous.

Solving this extended version of the model yields the estimation equations relevant for an economy that is open to international trade:

$$(27') \qquad U(t) = \text{const.} + a_1 U(t - \delta) + a_2 \pi(t - \delta) + a_3 \sum_1^\delta \mu(t - i)$$

$$+ a_4 \sum_1^\delta G(t - i) + a_5 \sum_1^\delta \theta(t - i) + a_6 \sum_1^\delta p_m(t - i)$$

$$+ a_7 \sum_1^\delta e(t - i) + j_i(t);$$

$$(28') \qquad \pi(t) = \text{const.} + b_1 U(t - \delta) + b_2 \pi(t - \delta) + b_3 \sum_1^\delta \mu(t - i)$$

$$+ b_4 \sum_1^\delta G(t - i) + b_5 \sum_1^\delta \theta(t - i) + b_6 \sum_1^\delta p_m(t - i)$$

$$+ b_7 \sum_1^\delta e(t - i) + j_2(t).$$

To test the proposition that the extended version of the Stein model provides a general explanation of price and employment movements, our intention was to estimate equations $(27')$ and $(28')$ for the five countries under consideration. Unfortunately, data limitations restricted this portion of the analysis to four countries: Germany; the Netherlands; the United Kingdom; and the United States. Furthermore, the data for Germany and the Netherlands are measured on annual average bases and hence do not permit a reproduction of Stein's lag structure. [4]

One modification that was introduced into the estimation procedure, even for the U.S. where data is plentiful, is to take observations on the dependent variables spaced four quarters apart rather than every quarter. This is done to eliminate any problems that might result from seasonal variation in the data, and to reduce the serial correlation which might be introduced into equation

---

[4] In estimating his equations, Stein assumed that $\delta = 3$. This implies that each dependent variable is a linear function of all the dependent variables three quarters ago and a simple unweighted average of each of the control variables over the three previous quarters. While no justification is provided for this structure and it seems doubtful that it represents a crucial element in the specification, the model did fit the U.S. data more closely when we approximated Stein's lag structure, as opposed to incorporating the restrictions imposed by annual average data.

Table 3

United States Unemployment Rate Equation

(t-statistic in parentheses)

	Stein's Results Quarterly Observations 1960:IV - 1970:IV		Fourth Quarter Observations, 1954:IV - 1970:IV			
			Modified Equation (27)		Open Economy Equation (27')	
constant	3.9	(5.3)	2.4	(1.9)	1.74	(1.7)
$U(t-\delta)$	.41	(3.9)	.59	(2.8)	.75	(4.2)
$\pi(t-\delta)$	.12	(1.3)	.30	(1.9)	.27	(2.3)
$\Delta G(t-\delta)$	-.005	(1.3)	-.002	(1.1)		
$\mu(t-\delta)$	-.33	(8.8)	-.28	(3.0)	-.312	(4.3)
p_m					.145	(2.2)
e					-.022	(3.4)
S.E.	.36		.69		.52	
R^2	.9		.65		.82	
D-W	.5		1.67		2.63	

Table 4

United States Price Change Equation

(t-statistic in parentheses)

	Stein's Results Quarterly Observations 1960:IV - 1970:IV		Fourth Quarter Observations, 1954:IV - 1970:IV			
			Modified Equation (28)		Open Economy Equation (28')	
constant	2.4	(4.0)	4.7	(4.0)	3.6	(3.7)
$U(t - \delta)$	-.37	(-4.4)	-.72	(-3.8)	-.56	(3.7)
$\pi(t - \delta)$	.72	(10.0)	.49	(3.4)	.46	(4.9)
$\Delta G(t - \delta)$	-0.000	(-0.6)	-.001	(-0.6)		
$\mu(t - \delta)$	.097	(3.3)	.105	(1.2)	.19*	(2.5)
P_m						
e					.014	(2.7)
S.E.	.29		.62		.43	
R^2	.96		.86		.93	
D-W	.9		2.30		2.32	

* In equation (28'), $\mu(t - \delta)$ is lagged one year.

327

(28') because of the way π is measured, i.e., as the rate of price change over the past three quarters. [5] Finally, because θ was the least significant policy variable in Stein's tests and because of the well-known conceptual problems associated with measuring the public debt, θ is excluded as a control variable from all tests.

With these modifications, Stein's closed-economy equations, (27) and (28), were fitted to U.S. data for the period 1954:IV to 1970:IV. Our purpose was to determine the combined effects of: (1) the changes in the estimation procedure; and (2) the lengthening of the sample period (the most common period used by Stein was 1960:IV to 1970:IV). The results shown in the center of Tables 3 and 4 are quite similar to Stein's, reproduced in the left-hand columns of the tables. The main differences in the results are a substantial drop in the serial correlations of the residuals and a decline in the significance of money (μ) in the price-change equation. However, given the similarity in the parameter estimates, and the much smaller number of degrees of freedom in our sample as compared to Stein's (12 versus 36), this finding may be neither very surprising nor disturbing. (To facilitate comparison of our results with Stein's, the unadjusted R^2 is used as the measure of goodness of fit in these tables; hereafter, we use $\bar{R}^2$.)

We next test for the influence of exports and import prices on employment and the inflation rate. The right-hand columns of Tables 3 and 4 present the parameter estimates and other results for equations (27') and (28'), when all insignificant variables are eliminated, and the lagged value of μ is substituted for the current value. Assuming that p_m and e are at least approximately exogenous, the evidence provides strong support for the proposition that the U.S. is an open economy. Exports are highly significant with the appropriate sign in both equations. Moreover, during the sample period, 1954-1970, increases in import prices tended to reduce aggregate output (employment), but apparently had little impact on the domestic price level. The latter result is a bit puzzling, but it makes it somewhat difficult to attribute the open economy results for the U.S. to the endogeneity of the index of import prices.

The effects of changes in the domestic policy variables are also interesting. According to the right-hand columns of Tables 3 and 4, a change in the growth rate of the money supply first affects real output and employment, and then, prices. Such a result is consistent with the generally accepted view of how monetary policy influences the economy, and with our earlier findings for the Lucas model. The estimates of the effects of fiscal policy are similar to most

---

[5] Another adjustment incorporated in the estimation procedure - - as much for convenience as any other reason - - was to allow the control variables to begin to influence the state variables in the current period. As a result, the summations associated with each of the control variables in equations (27') and (28') now begin at zero instead of one. With the dependent variables measured in the fourth quarter of the year, this permits the use of annual averages for the control variables, which may be an important simplification for countries other than the U.S.

other analyses of this type. They suggest that such policy operations have no significant effect on either employment or prices.

A final test of the applicability of the Stein model to the U.S. is provided by extrapolating the price and unemployment equations through 1974. The results shown in Tables 5 and 6 are not very impressive, but the patterns of the errors are informative. The open-economy equation (28') does a good, but not outstanding, job of tracking the inflation rate during the post-sample period. Considering the insignificance of the import-price coefficient during the sample period, this may not be very surprising. As far as the unemployment rate is concerned, the closed-economy model, equation (27), provides the superior predictions. There is a sense, though, in which the open-economy results are the more reasonable of the two. Indeed, the major problem with the 10.3 percent unemployment rate prediction for 1974:IV could be that it occurred one quarter too soon.

Let us now turn briefly to the results for other countries. Those for the U.K. do not support the open-economy version of the Stein model. Although the estimates of goodness of fit for the U.K. inflation and unemployment equations are similar to those for other countries, all efforts to obtain statistically significant parameter estimates consistent with standard macroeconomic theory proved unsuccessful. The only variable whose parameter even approached statistical significance was ΔG, and it invariably had the wrong sign, both currently and with a one-year lag, i.e., increases in government expenditures were associated with increases in the unemployment rate and a fall in inflation. Such results cast some doubt on the general applicability of the Stein model. However, in the case of the U.K., the problem may simply be due to multicolinearity among the variables included in equations (27') and (28').

Turning to the Netherlands, we again draw on the work of Korteweg (1975). In explaining Dutch inflation during the 1953-1973 period, he finds the most important determinants to be: the lagged rate of change in the narrow-money supply; the rate of unused industrial capacity lagged one year, $Q(t - \delta)$, which serves the same function as the lagged unemployment rate in our specification; and a summary measure of the effects of changes in government policy variables, such as indirect taxes, subsidies, rents, and E.E.C. and Kennedy-round adjustment measures, $p_{au}(t - \delta)$.

The parameter estimates for Korteweg's price-change equation (fitted to annual averages of the variables) are shown on the left side of Table 7. The results on the right side are those for a similar equation estimated for the period 1953-1971. This shorter time interval was used in an attempt to obtain a consistent series for the unemployment rate. Although such a series is obtainable for this period, it appears less appropriate than the rate of unused industrial capacity

Table 5

U.S. Unemployment Rate Predictions

	Actual Unemployment	Predicted Unemployment	
		Modified Eqn.(27)	Simplified Eqn. (27')
1971:IV	6.0	5.3	5.6
1972:IV	5.3	5.0	6.0
1973:IV	4.8	4.4	4.9
1974:IV	6.6	5.8	10.3

Table 6

U.S. Price Change Predictions

	Actual Inflation Rate	Predicted Inflation	
		Modified Eqn. (28)	Simplified Eqn.(28')
1971:IV	3.5	3.8	4.0
1972:IV	3.7	2.7	3.3
1973:IV	7.4	3.4	4.8
1974:IV	12.0	5.5	7.2

Table 7

Netherlands Price Change Equations
(t-statistics in parentheses)

	Korteweg Results 1953-1973		New Results 1953-1971	
constant	2.79	(3.34)	3.46	(4.96)
$\pi(t - \delta)$			- .30	(2.63)
$Q(t - \delta)$	- .43	(2.80)	- .37	(3.04)
$p_{au}(t - \delta)$	1.29	(3.73)	1.44	(5.75)
$\Delta G(t - \delta)$	.14	(1.14)	.24	(2.82)
$\mu(t - \delta)$			.11	(1.94)
$\mu(t - 1 - \delta)$	.21	(2.81)		
p_m	.10	(0.95)	.25	(3.33)
e	- .02	(0.23)		
S.E.	1.21		.77	
D-W	2.12		2.00	
$\overline{R}^2$	.81		.87	

Table 8

German Price Change Equation, 1953-1973
(t-statistics in parentheses)

constant	4.31	(3.66)
$U(t - \delta)$	-4.03	(5.43)
$\mu(t - \delta)$	.32	(3.45)
$e(t - \delta)$	.21	(4.06)
S.E.	1.08	
$\overline{R}^2$	.70	
D-W	2.18	

as an indicator of the slack in the Dutch economy. Consequently, we follow Korteweg and use $Q(t - \delta)$, rather than $U(t - \delta)$, as a lagged state variable, and do not report the parameter estimates for the unemployment rate equation. [6]

Two aspects of the results warrant particular attention. First, regardless of the sample period, the most important determinant of year-to-year variations in the Dutch price level (as measured by the t-statistics) is p_{au}, a policy variable specific to the Netherlands. Its omission from the 1953-1971 regression causes the coefficients of most other variables to lose statistical significance. Second, when the sample period is extended to include 1972 and 1973, the effects of import prices and fiscal policy (ΔG) become difficult to assess, i.e., the t-statistics drop below 1.20. Since these were years in which the money supply and the price level both rose very rapidly, the problem may be that the parameter estimates are sensitive to the movements in the variables. Even if the apparent instability in the Dutch price-change equation can be explained in this way, the present results, like those for the U.K., raise questions regarding the general usefulness of the Stein model. For example, the sensitivity of the estimates of the parameters in the Dutch price level equation to the inclusion of p_{au} suggest that unless all important policy variables are included in the specification, it may be difficult to measure the effects of those that are.

German data accord the Stein model a more favorable reception. The inflation-rate equation (fitted to annual averages of the variables for the period 1960-1973) is quite similar to its U.S. counterpart (see Table 8). According to both equations, the principal determinants of year-to-year movements in the price level are: the lagged unemployment rate; the growth rate of the money supply; and the foreign sectors' demand for domestic output. Moreover, unlike the Netherlands, the results for Germany and the U.S. reveal no significant instability in the parameters when the sample periods are extended beyond 1971. However, there are two interesting differences in the way the price level responds to changes in its determinants in the latter countries. First, as might be expected, increases in foreign demand appear to be more inflationary in Germany than in the U.S. Second, the insignificance of the lagged price-change term in Table 8 suggests that, regardless of the stimulus, the domestic price level responds more quickly to changes in its determinants in Germany than in the U.S. This may also be a consequence of the greater openness of the German economy. Whatever the reason, the similarity between this result and the corresponding one for the Lucas model would seem to increase our confidence in both formulations.

---

[6] However, these estimates were generally consistent with the implications of the Stein model.

III. ASSESSMENT, INTEGRATION AND POLICY IMPLICATIONS

The empirical evidence presented in the previous sections does no lend itself to an unambiguous interpretation of the ability of existing theory - - as represented by the Lucas and Stein models - - to explain fluctuations in prices and output.   Tests of the Lucas model suggest considerable stability on the supply side of the Dutch, French, German, U.K., and U.S. economies. Moreover, with the exception of the U.K., the constraints the model imposes on the para- meters are generally fulfilled.   On the other hand, the model fails to explain the extent of the 1974 price increases in all the countries included in the sample. Considering the focus of the Lucas model - - the supply side of the domestic economy - - and one of the important causes of the 1974 disturbance - - a sharp, unanticipated increase in the import prices - - it is difficult to assess the serious- ness of this deficiency.

The results for the Stein model, which focuses on the sources of variation in aggregate demand, differ in some respects from those for the Lucas formulation.   Nevertheless, the overall performance of the two approaches is similar.   For Germany, the Netherlands, and the U.S., Stein-type price equations fit the data quite closely, and the specific determinants of the price movements are readily identifiable.   The difficulties with this formulation are: (a) the equations do not fit the U.K. data very well; and (b) for other countries, there is considerable variation in the parameter estimates both over time and across countries.   One noteworthy element of constancy, though, is that the growth rate of the money supply always appears as a significant determinant of the inflation rate.   Finally, the errors involved in explaining the 1974 price move- ments are of the same order of magnitude as those for the Lucas model.

Three properties of the results are of particular interest. First, the overall comparability in the explanatory power of supply- and demand-oriented models suggests that the overriding attention macroeconomics devotes to the latter may be misplaced. The qualitative similarity in results for the various countries examined is also an important finding, implying that the underlying structures of these economies may have more elements in common than not. However, the variability of the parameters in Stein's aggregate demand model is a matter of concern. It suggests that such a model, and the theory upon which it rests, does not provide a general explanation of year-to-year fluctuations in prices and output.

A number of hypotheses could be put forward to account for this deficiency. The one we wish to explore holds that,although simple aggregate demand models of the Stein type can identify longer term economic trends, a year is too short a period in which to observe such movements. Such a view stands in sharp contrast to current econometric practice which seeks to explain not only annual fluctuations in economic data but quarterly movements as well. The specific formulation we use to test our hypothesis posits that, over five-year periods, the growth rate of the money supply is a reliable predictor of the growth of nominal income and, for all practical purposes, this is independent of a country's institutional structure: [7]

$$(29) \qquad \dot{Y}_{it} = a + b\dot{M}_{it} + \epsilon_{it},$$

where $\dot{Y}_i$ is the five-year growth in nominal income of country, i, measured from the average annual level of Y;

$\dot{M}_i$ is the five-year growth in the narrow-money supply of country, i, measured from end-of-year to end-of-year, so that each observation leads the corresponding one for $\dot{Y}$ by approximately one-half year;

a and b are constant both over time and across countries;

ϵ_i is an error term.

Data for four countries (Germany, the Netherlands, the U.K., and the U.S.) are used to estimate a and b, with five non-overlapping observations spanning the sample period, 1951-1974, for each country. [8]

The parameter estimates and other results presented in the left-hand column of Table 9 indicate that equation (29) fits the data rather closely. However, the key results - - the t-statistics for a and b - - do not provide a powerful test of the hypothesis that these coefficients are the same for all countries. The other results in Table 9 address this question directly. Those in the middle column report the estimates for equation

$$(29a) \qquad \dot{Y}_{it} = a + b\dot{M}_{it} + a_{us}D_{us} + b_{us}D_{us}\dot{M}_t.$$

This equation is similar to (29), except that it includes the dummy variable D_{us} which equals 1, when U.S. data are used in the equation, and zero otherwise.

---

[7] The choice of a five-year time period is somewhat arbitrary. For the U.S., though, such a period corresponds roughly to a complete business cycle. One problem in using such a long observation period is that it substantially reduces the sample size and hence restricts the number of independent variables that can be considered. We focus on the money supply because it is the one variable that was consistently found to be significant in the Stein equations.

[8] All observations are five-year growth rates, except those for the last period, 1971-74, which are three-year rates extrapolated to five years. It is important that the observations be non-overlapping because otherwise we run the risk of introducing complicated serial correlation patterns among the residuals. The data are from the International Financial Statistics (IFS)-1972 Supplement. The most recent figures are drawn from later IFS issues and/or national sources.

Table 9

Pooled Nominal Income Equations, 1951-1974
(United States, United Kingdom, Germany, Netherlands)
Observations are Five-Year Growth Rates*
(t-statistics in parentheses)

	All Pooled	United States versus Others Pooled	United States versus Others Individually
constant	27.37	31.03	16.57
	(7.85)	(7.07)	(2.11)
u	.62	.55	1.00
	(7.62)	(6.01)	(2.98)
$c_{U.S.}$		-14.46	
		(1.50)	
$u_{U.S.}$		.44	
		(1.18)	
$c_{U.K.}$			14.17
			(1.54)
$u_{U.K.}$			-.37
			(1.02)
c_G			11.57
			(0.61)
u_G			-.49
			(1.09)
c_N			5.67
			(0.46)
u_N			-.17
			(0.43)
S.E.	7.61	7.53	6.89
D-W	1.96	2.09	2.79
$\bar{R}^2$	.75	.76	.80
F-stat.		1.19	1.65
Crit. Value (5%)		3.63	3.00

*Except for the last periods (1971-74) which are three-year rates extrapolated to five years.

It is easily shown that the estimated values of a_{us} and b_{us} represent the differences in the parameters for the U.S. and the average of the other countries. [9] Since the t-statistics for both of these coefficients are less than 2, we may reject the hypothesis that the U.S. parameters taken individually are significantly different from the average of the others. The F-statistic presented at the bottom of the column is substantially less than its critical value at the 5 percent confidence level. This implies that we may also reject the hypothesis that the two U.S. parameters taken together are different from their counterparts in the other countries.

The numbers in the right-hand column of Table 9 may be used to assess the hypothesis that the parameters for each of the other three countries (the U.K., Germany, and the Netherlands), taken separately, are different from those for the U.S. Once again, both the F- and the t-statistics lead us to reject this view. Numerous other combinations of parameters could be considered and some of them were, in fact, evaluated. In every case, though, we were unable to reject the hypothesis that the data for all countries were drawn from the same population.

Given the difficulties encountered with the Stein model, it is also relevant to test our simple quantity theory model for temporal stability. Here, equation (29) was reestimated, dropping the last observation for each country. The parameter estimates are essentially identical to those shown in Table 9, while the standard error of the equation increases slightly to 8 percent (1.6 percent at an annual rate).

(29') $\qquad \dot{Y} = 27.38 + .61\dot{M}.$
$\qquad\qquad$ (7.17) $\quad$ (6.21)

$\qquad \overline{R}^2 = .72;$ S.E. $= 7.96;$ DW $= 1.44$
$\qquad\qquad$ (sample period, 1951-1970).

When equation (29') is extrapolated through the last observation, 1971-74, the following error statistics are obtained.

---

[9] Put another way, the regression coefficients for the other countries are given by a and b, while those for the U.S. equal $a + a_{us}$ and $b + b_{us}$.

	Predicted Income Growth	Actual Growth	Difference
United States	46.9	54.1	-7.2
United Kingdom	68.0	72.1	-4.1
Germany	62.1	51.1	11.0
Netherlands	67.2	71.9	-4.7

Relative to the standard error of the equation the predictive errors are small and offsetting. Thus, the same stable long-run relationship appears to exist between money and income in all the countries, explaining the events of the early 1970s as well as it does those of the 1950s and 1960s. Considering the differences in the money-supply processes in these economies and their evolution over time, the results are impressive. [10] They suggest that, over five-year periods, variations in the growth of money have a significant and well determined effect on the growth of income, essentially independent of the process that determines the money stock. [11]

Over periods as long as five years, we would expect, and the data tend to confirm, that most of the effects of changes in the money supply are on prices. It would be desirable to go further and make more precise statements regarding the effects of monetary policy and the determinants of inflation. At the moment, we are unable to do so. Although all the economies we considered exhibited considerable structural stability in both the short- and the long-run, in the course of a year (or less), numerous exogenous factors can exert a sizable impact on output and prices, and overshadow the effects of money. Over longer periods, though, it is clear that increases in the money supply, which exceed the growth in real output, will result in a predictable amount of inflation. Thus, we find that, to the extent governments (or their central banks) are able to control the domestic money stock, they will be able, within narrow limits, to determine a country's long-run inflation rate. Whether they choose to exercise such control is, of course, another question.

---

[10] Among the reasons for these differences and the variation over time are: the position of the dollar as a reserve currency; the development of the international payments mechanism; and the emphasis each central bank has given to the control of interest rates and the money supply.

[11] The close fit of our general model, equation (29), to the U.K. data ($\bar{R}^2 = .88$) suggests that, despite the fact that the Bank of England has not sought to actively manage the growth rate of the narrow money supply, variations in this variable have had the same important impact on economic activity in Britain as they have had in other countries. Hence, the present results are in strong opposition to the views expressed by Kaldor (1970).

REFERENCES

1. Arak, M., "The Trade-Off Between Inflation and Output: A Comment on the Lucas Model," Research Paper 7515, Federal Reserve Bank of New York, 1975.

2. _____, "Monetary and Fiscal Policy in Open Interdependent Economies with Fixed Exchange Rates," mimeo, (March 1974).

3. Brunner, K., and Meltzer, A.H., "An Aggregative Theory for a Closed Economy," in Monetarism, (ed. J. Stein), Amsterdam: North Holland, 1976.

4. Fama, E.F., "Short-Term Interest Rates as Predictors of Inflation," American Economic Review, LXV, No. 3, (June 1975), 269-282.

5. Kaldor, N., "The New Monetarism," Lloyds Bank Review, No. 97, (July 1970), 1-18.

6. Korteweg, P., "Inflation, Economic Activity and the Operation of Fiscal, Foreign and Monetary Impulses in the Netherlands - - A Preliminary Analysis, 1953-73," De Economist, 123, No. 4, 1975.

7. Lucas, R.E. Jr., "Some International Evidence on the Output-Inflation Tradeoffs," American Economic Review, LXIII, No. 3, (June 1973), 326-334.

8. Rutledge, J. A Monetarist Model of Inflationary Expectations. Lexington, Mass.: Lexington Books, 1974.

9. Sargent, T.J., "Rational Expectations, the Real Rate of Interest, and the Natural Rate of Unemployment," Brookings Papers on Economic Activity, No. 2, Washington, D.C.: The Brookings Institution, (1973), 429-480.

10. Stein, J.L., "Inside the Monetarist Black Box," in Monetarism, (ed. J.L. Stein), Amsterdam: North Holland, 1976.

11. Statistics Bureau of the International Monetary Fund. International Financial Statistics, Supplement, Washington, D.C., 1972.

INFLATION - - ALTERNATIVE EXPLANATIONS AND POLICIES

and

INFLATION, UNEMPLOYMENT AND MACROECONOMIC POLICY IN OPEN ECONOMIES:

A COMMENT ON THE LAIDLER AND HAMBURGER AND REISCH PAPERS

Michele Fratianni*
European Commission and
Catholic University of Louvain

and

Pieter Korteweg
Erasmus Universiteit, Rotterdam

We should be grateful to Laidler and to Hamburger and Reisch (H-R) for telling us once more that the phenomenon of inflation does not fall within the domain of sociology and crystal-ball gazing, but rather remains an integral part of macroeconomic analysis in general, and monetary theory in particular. There is no collapse of economic theory; demand and supply schedules are alive and apparently cross.

The similarity of the topics treated by both Laidler and H-R has encouraged us to integrate our comments in order to save space, avoid repetition, and emphasize points in common between the two studies. At the outset it must be said that our critical remarks about the papers, an inevitable outcome of the role assigned to discussants, should not be construed as detracting from the overall quality of these studies which we found rich in analytical and empirical content.

Our comments are organized in three sections. In the first, we take up issues of research strategy, methodology, and model building. Empirical findings and test procedures are considered in section II, and policy implications in section III.

---

*The views expressed are personal and need not be attributed to the Commission.

I. RESEARCH STRATEGY

Laidler's central theme is to expose competing views of inflation to empirical testing. Largely influenced by the discussion which has taken place among British economists, he proposes a three-way classification of theories: the sociological view which attributes inflation to social frustration as indicated by greed, aspirations, social conflict over income shares, or to institutional arrangements such as trade unions, monopolies, etc.; the monetarist view which asserts that inflation results from market conditions; and the eclectic position which combines elements of both the sociological and monetarist views of inflation with the proportions differing over time and places.

H-R, by contrast, do not take seriously the sociological and eclectic positions and prefer to concentrate on hypotheses which, while steeped in traditional economic analysis, differ from each other by emphasis on either demand or supply forces. To some extent, H-R extend and deepen the level of analysis carried out by Laidler.

Both papers conclude that inflation can be explained by market forces and, more specifically, by the growth of the money stock.

Both papers suffer from methodological weaknesses. Laidler mistakenly equates the monetarist hypothesis with the excess demand expectations hypothesis. In addition, we find his three-way classification of theories elusive in terms of both theoretical interpretation and empirical testing. H-R consider two models, both of which are not in opposition to each other (by their own admission) but whose link is not spelled out in the paper. The reader is bound to consider the tests on the Lucas and Stein models as two separate exercises, realizing that there is some common but unspecified ground between the two hypotheses.

A. Laidler's Three-way Classification

The sociological, "monetarist" (in Laidler's sense), and eclectic views of inflation are neither mutually exclusive nor altogether representative of major schools of thought about inflation. Consider the use of strike activity as a measure of social frustration to discriminate between the sociological and the monetarist hypotheses.

Regardless of its quality as a sociological variable, the number of working days lost in strikes translates into production (or real income) lost. Since Laidler's excess demand variable (the difference between the logs of actual and trend real income) does not seem to be corrected for the production losses of strikes, an increase in strike activity must be expected to <u>lower</u> his excess demand proxy. At the same time, the production losses accompanying strikes lower production relative to the demand for production. Given the amount of money and a stable money demand function, the production losses resulting from working days lost in strikes induce increases in the amount of money per unit of real income which, in turn, produce an excess supply of money and rising prices. Laidler's strike variable may thus be considered just another excess demand proxy picking up elements not included in his particular excess demand proxy. Working days lost in strikes - - no matter their quality as a sociological indicator - - are accompanied by production losses which have a <u>positive</u> effect on money per unit of output and the price level, and a <u>negative</u> effect on Laidler's proxy of excess demand. Nevertheless, it is likely that Laidler's regressions produce downward biased estimates of the coefficient and significance of this excess demand proxy and upward biased estimates of the coefficient and significance of his strike variable, thereby generating test results unjustifiably favorable to the sociological hypothesis. This may well be why Laidler finds his strike variable to be of either full or marginal significance in explaining inflation in two strike-prone countries, Italy and the U.K., respectively.

In addition, Laidler's classification clouds important issues which still divide the economics profession. For example, does a rising share of national output absorbed by the government imply sustained price increases, independently of how this absorption is financed? Or, more specifically, is a bond-financed deficit inflationary (the single most important theme, according to Stein, in differentiating fiscalists from monetarists)? In our view, resolving such a dispute, easily subsumable under "market-oriented" theories, is more relevant to our understanding of inflation than erecting a debate between sociologists and market economists. We say this because we believe that there is no bridge between the language systems and methodologies of sociologists and market economists. We are confident that those holding the sociological position will not accept Laidler's strike activity as an appropriate measure of their view on the ground that this variable carries too little sociological substance ever to present them with a fair chance to validate their hypothesis. But, how can one possibly find empirical counterparts to concepts such as greed, frustration, aspiration, power, etc.? Having recognized the futility of establishing a dialogue in which the participants agree to debate using a common scientific approach, would it not be more useful to dismiss the sociological view that social frustration produces inflation <u>independent</u> of market supply and demand conditions as economic nonsense? The sociological theory of inflation may be able to predict the direction of price movements, but it cannot predict the rate of inflation. A theory which is unable to do that should not concern us further. Those who remain believers will have to ignore certain implications of their faith, namely, accelerating inflation implies increasing greed, frustration, and dissatisfaction; decelerating inflation implies more charity and happiness; inter-country differences in inflation suggest equivalent differences in greed, frustration, and aspiration, with Germany and Switzerland more avid and unhappy than the U.S. in the 1960s and early 1970s and, more recently, more virtuous and happy than before.

Laidler considers two "scientific" aspects of eclecticism: one originating from a changing socio-economic structure and the other from variable changes in the exogenous variables, with the structure remaining unchanged. The first version of eclecticism is usually stated in such a way as to imply that the potential contributors to inflation have shifting and unpredictable weights. In this case, it is clear that there is no testable hypothesis but only a series of ad hoc ex post propositions whose sole purpose is to salvage the original hypothesis (the use of dummy variables is a good indicator of the practice of this form of eclecticism). Discussion of the second form of eclecticism raises the important question of why the values of the parameter estimates should be invariant to the size of the changes in the exogenous variables. Indeed, Lucas (1976) argues that the econometrician must reestimate the structure of his model whenever the system is shocked in a way that is new to the system.

B. Laidler's Conception of the Monetarist Hypothesis

Laidler calls the excess demand expectations model a monetarist hypothesis. While not intending to quibble over terms, we find this equivalence misleading because the expectations augmented Phillips curve hypothesis is, in principle, consistent with a variety of impulses which can generate excess demand. Indeed, monetarists, fiscalists, and proponents of the Wicksellian natural rate-of-interest argument can all be accommodated under the umbrella of this hypothesis. The monetarist explanation of inflation, on the other hand, provides a further restriction on the data in the sense that the dominant impulse generating excess demand is the money stock.

The same eclecticism with regard to what makes aggregate demand shift is present in the Lucas model used by H-R. In both models, firms readjust their prices relative to a market average in the face of an excess demand for or supply of their products, with shifts in aggregate demand brought about exogenously and in an unspecified manner.[1]

In our view, a monetarist model of inflation consists of the following three building blocks.

---

[1] While Lucas is explicit on this point, Laidler ignores aggregate demand factors.

1) Inflation and output fluctuations are proximately determined by excess demand augmented by inflationary expectations. The transmission of excess demand in price and output fluctuations is governed by a relative-price inter-action and a stock-flow interaction. In sum, inflation is an economic, i.e., price-theoretical, phenomenon, not a sociological phenomenon.

2) Excess demand is determined by systematic impulses and does not result from random disturbances distributed over the system. That is, inflation is a systematic phenomenon and cannot be explained eclectically. The systematic impulses underlying excess demand and inflation are real and financial. The real impulses are fiscal, foreign, and private. They result from governmental policies with respect to expenditures and taxation, from changes in foreign absorption of domestic production, from changes in the price to be paid for domestic absorption of foreign production, and from changing anticipations of the real rate of return on real capital. The financial impulses consist of changes in the stocks of money and debt resulting from monetary policy, the financing of the government budget, and the financing of the balance of payments.

3) The effects of real impulses on excess demand, inflation, and economic activity are dwarfed by the financial impulse effects, especially by the effects of changes in the money stock. This monetarist contention derives from specific, empirically testable behavioral constraints which restrict a fairly eclectic relative-price stock-flow model of the mechanism transmitting the impulses to the demand for and supply of output, output and prices.

What Laidler has tested is the validity of the price-theoretical approach to inflation, which is a valuable thing to do. But, he has added little to our know-ledge of whether the main impulses on the economy are random or systematic, whether they are real or monetary, and whether the monetarist behavioral con-straints hold or not.

C. The Lucas and Stein Models in H-R

The two main parts of the H-R paper remain largely unintegrated because the Lucas and the Stein models do not, on the whole, ask the same questions. The essence of the Lucas model is, ". . .not to 'explain' output and price level movements within a given country, but rather to see whether the terms of the output-inflation 'tradeoff' vary across countries in the way predicted by the natural rate theory" (Lucas, 1973, p. 330). Stein and Brunner and Meltzer provide instead an explanation of the movements of both output and the price level.

There are no new theoretical developments in the H-R rendition of the Lucas model whose main elements are that (1) shifts in aggregate demand are given; (2) the division of nominal income between the price level and output largely depends on the behavior of suppliers of goods and labor; (3) partial rigidities in the system are dominated by (short-run) lack of information on the part of suppliers of labor and goods about some of the prices relevant to their decisions; and (4) inferences on relevant unobserved prices are made "rationally." Of particular importance is the role of the trade-off coefficient π, whose value depends on the variance of individual prices relative to the variance of the general price level and the variance of aggregate demand shifts, σ_x^2. The value of π drops as σ_x^2 rises in accordance with Lincoln's dictum that, "...you may fool all the people some of the time; you can even fool some of the people all the time; but you can't fool all of the people all the time." Regardless of the value of π, aggregate demand shifts cannot affect the permanent level of output. This is true because on the average $\Delta x_t = \delta$, $y_{ct} = 0$, and inflation is equal to $\delta - \beta$ or the average rate of demand expansion minus the long-run rate of output growth.

We have noted that the Lucas model, like Laidler's excess demand cum expectations hypothesis, is eclectic with respect to the stimuli which affect δ. H-R note a second problem in the model, namely, that the unit value elasticity of aggregate demand does not square with the notion that in an open economy the wide range of substitutes for domestic output tends to raise the elasticity potentially to infinity. H-R do nothing to correct these shortcomings. In the section "Aggregate Demand," H-R test the Stein model presented at the Brown Conference and run modified reduced-forms following Korteweg. The impression is given that the models are substitutes for each other, with Korteweg's interpretation of the Brunner-Meltzer model having a distinct advantage over the Stein model for its treatment of the open economy under fixed rates of exchange.

Two separate issues are involved here. First, Korteweg's reduced-form equations are not the reduced-form equations of Brunner and Meltzer, but idealized equations of a class of hypotheses which treats the fiscal impulse, the monetary impulse, a measure of exogenous exports, and import prices in local currency as either policy-determined or exogenous variables. Without additional information, one cannot reconstruct the unique structure underlying Korteweg's tested equations. Having recognized this point, we note secondly that the Stein and Brunner-Meltzer models are different in several respects. For the purpose of this comment, we emphasize only one difference.

Stein's interpretation of monetarism is that P_5, the partial derivative of the price change function given by equation (23) with respect to the fifth argument (θ), is non-positive. In contrast, the monetarist propositions of Brunner and Meltzer do not depend on P_5 being zero or negative. On the contrary, the equivalent of Stein's P_5 must be positive in Brunner and Meltzer if their model is to be stable. At the empirical level, Stein finds that the effect of interest-bearing debt on U.S. inflation is negative and significant in one of his regression results, while Korteweg finds it non-significantly different from zero and drops it from his regressions. H-R do not tackle this crucial issue which still divides fiscalists (see, for example, Blinder and Solow, 1973) and monetarists, "...because θ was the least significant policy variable in Stein's tests and because of the well-known conceptual problems associated with measuring the public debt, θ was excluded as a control variable from all tests." We are not told whether these conceptual problems are any more arduous in the U.K. and the Netherlands than they are in the U.S. Our understanding is that they are not.

II. TEST PROCEDURES AND EMPIRICAL FINDINGS

A. The Lucas Model

In Table 1, we have summarized the value of the trade-off coefficient π reported by Lucas (1973) for the period 1953-1967, and by H-R for the period 1953-1973. It is clear that π declines and becomes less significant, with the exception of France, moving from left to right in the table. The declines are dramatic for Germany and the U.K. These observations do not square with the H-R statement, "...that overall the tradeoff terms have neither improved nor deteriorated during 1953-1973." The Chow test applied to the entire equation is not the relevant procedure to ascertain whether significant changes in π have occurred. The null hypothesis that $\pi_z = \pi_v$, where z and v define two particular sub-sample periods, could be directly checked by rewriting equation (16) as

$$y_{ct} = -\pi\delta + \pi_z \Delta x_t' + \pi_v \Delta x_t'' + \lambda y_{ct-1},$$

where

$$\Delta x_t' \begin{cases} = \text{actual values for the z sub-sample period} \\ = 0 \text{ for the v sub-sample period,} \end{cases}$$

and

$$\Delta x_t'' \begin{cases} = 0 \text{ for the z sub-sample period} \\ = \text{actual values for the v sub-sample period.} \end{cases}$$

Table 1

Values of π Reported by Lucas and H-R

	Lucas 1953-1967	H-R 1953-1973
U.S.	.910	0.782
(t-values)	(10.58)	(7.993)
Germany	.820	.614
	(6.02)	(3.842)
Netherlands	.531	.408
	(4.78)	(3.73)
U.K.	.665	.184
	(2.29)	(1.48)
France	N.A.	.103
		(1.03)

Table 2

Test of the Null-hypothesis that $\pi_v = \pi_z$

	π_z	π_v	t_{17}
U.S.	.98992	.73906	2.21*
(t-values)	(11.273)	(10.268)	
Germany	.8649	.48821	2.77*
	(8.7137)	(5.2584)	
Netherlands	.4622	.39792	0.379
	(3.6136)	(3.5759)	
U.K.	.62109	.36172	1.21
	(3.4786)	(3.0418)	
France	-.017	.0931	
	(.155)	(1.00)	

z - 1953-1967   v - 1968-1973   * significant at the 5 percent level

H-R, at our request, provided us with the regression results bearing on the above equation; the values of π_z and π_v are summarized in Table 2. To judge whether or not π_v is statistically different from π_z, we define the test statistic[2]

$$t_{n-k} = \frac{\hat{\pi}_z - \hat{\pi}_v}{s_{\hat{\pi}_z - \hat{\pi}_v}} \quad ,$$

where $\hat{\pi}_z, \hat{\pi}_v$ are unbiased estimators of π_v and π_z, and $s_{\hat{\pi}_z - \hat{\pi}_v}$ is an unbiased estimator of the standard error $\sigma_{\hat{\pi}_z - \hat{\pi}_v}$, defined as

$$s_{\hat{\pi}_z - \hat{\pi}_v} = \sqrt{s_{\hat{\pi}_z}^2 + s_{\hat{\pi}_v}^2} \quad ,$$

on the assumption that covariance between the efficient estimators of π_v and π_z is absent since they apply to different non-overlapping sub-periods.

[2]   See Kmenta (1971), p. 372, equation 10.46.

It is clear from Table 2 that the trade-offs have significantly deteriorated over the period 1953-1973 for the U.S. and Germany. We were surprised to find no significant deterioration for the U.K. H-R, on their initiative, reran the U.K. equation splitting the Δx_t variable into two components: one covered the entire sample period; a second variable had zero values for 1953 through 1967, and the actual values of Δx_t for 1968 through 1973. Such a procedure implies that π_v is equal to the difference of the two structural coefficients and that the t-statistic of the sub-period coefficient shows directly whether or not any change has occurred. The results indicate that the value of π has fallen significantly also for the U.K. The trade-off coefficients have remained stable for the Netherlands, whereas they have been non-existent for France.

B. Laidler's Test Procedures and Results

Table 3 summarizes the testable implications and the key empirical findings of Laidler's price expectations transfer version of the monetarist hypothesis. Although agreeing with the general conclusion that his monetarist model outperforms the sociological view in explaining domestic inflation and the international transmission of inflation, we have some reservations about the form of the tested equation (5), test procedures, and outcomes.

First, Laidler's equation (5) implies that, to stabilize inflation over the long run, excess demand should decline at a constant rate.[3] Standard price theory would lead us to expect, however, that a falling excess demand lowers the rate of inflation over time. This suggests that the test implication of Laidler's version of monetarism is inconsistent with relative price theory.

---

[3] This point was brought to our attention by Manfred Neumann who correctly identifies $y_{-1}/y_{-2} = 1\text{-}d < 1$ as a possible long-run condition of equation (5). We note that, according to Laidler's equations (5) or (6), the condition $y_{-1} = y_{-2} = 0$ is also consistent with a steady state rate of inflation. However, there is nothing in the paper to indicate that this condition rather than the one we mentioned is operative.

Table 3
Laidler's Implications and Findings

Implications

1. Inflationary expectations explain the trend rate of inflation, and excess demand the variations around this trend. Together, they offer a complete explanation of inflation. Consequently, in regressing these variables on inflation, we should not find a significant constant term.
2. The natural rate hypothesis is true in that a 1 percent increase in the weighted averaged expected rates of domestic and foreign inflation raises the domestic rate of inflation by 1 percent.
3. The signs of the coefficients estimated should be as indicated and not attributable to chance, and the freely estimated coefficients should satisfy the constraints indicated ($0 \leqslant v \leqslant 1, 0 < d \leqslant 1$).
4. For relatively large and closed economies, the role of expectations of foreign inflation should be smaller than for relatively small and open economies. That is, the estimated value of v should be larger for relatively closed economies than for relatively open economies.

Findings

1. The hypothesis that the constraints $0 \leqslant v \leqslant 1, 0 < d \leqslant 1$ are satisfied is never rejected (see Table 6).
2. The coefficients estimated for the once- and twice-lagged excess demand proxy have the expected signs (see Tables 5 and 6).
3. The natural rate hypothesis $\beta = 1$ is never rejected (see Table 7).
4. The estimated value of v is indeed larger for closed than for open economies (see Table 5).
5. The coefficients for the lagged domestic and rest-of-the-world rates of inflation have the expected signs (see Tables 5 and 7).
6. The forecasting ability of the monetarist model of inflation is poor outside the sample period, although it outperforms somewhat the sociological model (see Charts 7-12).
7. Over the sample period, the contribution to inflation of the weighted averaged expected rates of domestic and world inflation indeed parallel and dominate the trend rate of domestic inflation (see Charts 7-12).

Second, Laidler views firms marking up their prices over time at a rate equal to some weighted average of the expected rates of inflation at home and abroad. Firms adjust this rate of mark-up, however, in view of the state of domestic excess demand. The question then arises: why do firms not also adjust their mark-up behavior in view of the state of excess demand abroad? It seems reasonable to assume that domestic firms expect competing foreign firms to demonstrate the same kind of mark-up behavior as their own, namely, that they will discount the home economy's state of excess demand in translating inflationary expectations into price increases.

A third and related question is whether Laidler's use of the world rate of inflation does not simply pick up the effects of import price inflation on domestic inflation. To some extent, the question of how properly to construct a world price level series is involved here. Laidler's world price level is the sum of individual country price levels weighted by each country's real income share in total world real income. From Laidler's description of firms' price setting and mark-up behavior, it would seem that trade, rather than income weights, is the proper weight to use in constructing a world price level and a world rate of inflation. In marking up their prices, firms are led by the rate of inflation they expect will occur in foreign markets - - not each and every foreign market, we presume, but only those in which they buy and sell and trade. There seem to be two reasons why Laidler is opposed to the use of import prices. At the analytical level, Laidler fears that by using import prices he will drift away from the spirit of contemporary monetarism towards the cost-push approach of eclecticism, and thus be unable to test the monetarist hypothesis of inflation. At the empirical level, when using import price inflation instead of his own concept of world price inflation, Laidler encounters outcomes partly falsifying his version of the monetarist hypothesis.

Specifically, what Laidler finds, when the import price version of his monetarist model is estimated unconstrained and with a constant term permitted, is that (see Table 9): (1) the model's explanatory power in terms of R^2 tends to outperform that of the world price version of his model; (2) the constant term is found to be significantly positive in all cases except for the U.S., implying that the import price version of the model does not provide an explanation of the complete inflation phenomenon by leaving (part of) the trend rate of inflation unexplained; (3) the coefficients of the lagged rates of domestic and import price inflation in all cases imply a violation of the natural rate hypothesis ($\beta = 1$); (4) the coefficients of the once-lagged excess demand proxy are not significantly different from zero in the case of the U.K. and Germany, whereas the coefficients of the twice-lagged excess demand proxy and of lagged import price inflation never reach statistical significance, although the coefficients of lagged domestic inflation occasionally do so.

These findings hardly permit us, however, to prefer the Laidler world price version of the monetarist model over the import price version, as Laidler does, in light of the following considerations.

First, when Laidler's version of the model is estimated with no constraints and with the intercept permitted, it is also found (see Table 8) that the intercept is significantly positive, be it only in the case of Germany and Italy; and that the coefficients of the lagged rates of both domestic and world inflation, in most cases, are insignificant, and, in all cases, imply a violation of the natural rate hypothesis.

Moreover, the natural rate hypothesis that expected inflation is fully accounted for in actual inflation is not necessarily an essential building block of the monetarist hypothesis, as least not as a short-run (annual) proposition.

Third, the presence of significant positive intercepts, representing trend rates of inflation, need not imply the defeat of Laidler's monetarist model in either its import price or world price version. The positive trend rates of inflation picked up by the intercept may well be explained by the trend rate of growth of velocity. But this would mean taking into account a proper money demand function, a task Laidler did not undertake in his paper.

Fourth, although the estimated coefficients of Laidler's monetarist model have the expected signs, not all of the coefficients are statistically significant. For instance, the coefficient of the twice-lagged excess demand variable is more often than not insignificant (see Tables 5 and 6). Moreover, the coefficient of the lagged rate of world inflation is either insignificant or only marginally significant when estimated partially unconstrained (see Table 7).

Finally, according to Laidler's partially free estimates, some of the constraints imposed are clearly violated. We would consider the case of Japan (Table 7, in which the coefficients of the lagged rates of domestic and world inflation sum to 1.33), as clearly violating the natural rate constraint. Moreover, the constraints with respect to the values of v and d would imply the inequality, $g > g(1-d)$, to hold when freely estimated. In the case of Germany, however, the opposite holds (see Table 7).

C. The Stein-Korteweg Equations in H-R

We have already noted that a key element of the Stein model, the effect of interest-bearing debt on inflation, is missing in the H-R version of the model.

In addition, the authors run all regressions as if the relevant policy mix consists of controlling government expenditures and the money stock, thus implying that tax revenues (and debt) adjust endogenously in the system. There is no reason to believe that this policy mix has been actually followed by the countries under consideration and, if so, for the entire sample period.

The other striking characteristic of Tables 3, 4, 7, and 8 is the implied steady-state values of the coefficients of the growth of the money stock and import prices. In Stein's closed economy, inflation in the long run is equal to the growth rate of the money stock net of the growth rate of capital. In an open economy operating under fixed rates of exchange, the money stock adjusts so as to enforce (in one extreme case) the law of one price. Discrepancies between domestic and world inflation rates provoke a redistribution of the world money stock which comes to a halt when the domestic and world price levels roughly coincide. It follows that, for a small, fixed exchange rate, open economy, the growth rate of the money stock depends exclusively on the growth of world reserves. Any autonomous change in the domestic component of the money stock is bound to be fully offset by an opposite change in its foreign component. Since the small open economy idealized in the Mundellian analysis is a price taker and cannot control its money stock, we should expect the latter variable to be irrelevant, in the long run, as a regressor, and the world inflation rate to have a unit coefficient. In the world of H-R, however, the economies are not small nor are their money stocks completely beyond the control of the authorities. An expansion of the domestic source components of money in the U.S. and, to a lesser extent, in the U.K., France, and Germany will not be completely offset by opposite reserve flows and will contribute to world inflation. Therefore, both the growth rate of the money stock and world prices should appear on the right side of the regression, each with long-run coefficients between zero and 1 but with their sum equal to unity. In H-R, the sum of the coefficients of μ and P_M for all countries is far from unity: in the U.S., the coefficient of P_M is zero and the long-run value of μ = .40; in the Netherlands, the sum of the impact of μ and P_M in the long run does not exceed .30; in Germany, it is .32.

III. POLICY IMPLICATIONS

Both papers are relatively thin on policy implications, though the subject matter lends itself to an investigation of where policy has failed with respect to the recent world inflation. For example, the Lucas model is well-designed to explore how governmental policies might have contributed to the worsening of the output-inflation trade-off through a growing activism in aggregate demand management. Indeed, we think that one of the most useful exercises would have been to explore what forces were accountable in the period 1968-1973 for the presumably more erratic policies than in the previous sub-period. The insights afforded by this undertaking might serve to alert economic agents as to the unpredictable nature of the game, thereby affecting the very basis of discretion in economic policy.

REFERENCES

1. Blinder, A.S., and Solow, R.M., "Does Fiscal Policy Matter?" Journal of Public Economics, 2, (1973), 319-337.

2. Kmenta, J. Elements of Econometrics. New York: Macmillan, 1971.

3. Lucas, R.E., Jr., "Some International Evidence on Output-Inflation Trade-offs," American Economic Review, LXIII, No. 3, (June 1973), 326-334.

4. _____, "Econometric Policy Evaluation: A Critique," The Phillips Curve and Labor Markets, Carnegie-Rochester Conference Series, 1, (eds. K. Brunner and A.H. Meltzer), Amsterdam: North Holland, (1976), 19-46.